DISCUSSION AND DEBATE

Tools of a Democracy

DISCUSSION and DEBATE

TOOLS of a DEMOCRACY

Henry Lee Ewbank
University of Wisconsin

J. Jeffery Auer
Oberlin College

SECOND EDITION : NEW YORK

APPLETON-CENTURY-CROFTS, Inc.

Editor's Foreword

TEN YEARS have passed since the first edition of this book was published. During this period it has found favor in the eyes of many college and university teachers. In the present revision the authors have made an attempt to improve their work while retaining the essential features which have made it so popular. Some of these distinctive characteristics are:

1. The presentation of discussion and debate as an unbroken continuum rather than as separate entities only adventitiously related to each other.

2. The derivation of guiding principles directly from sound psychology and sociology without any parade of knowledge apart from its actual utilization.

3. The summarizing of available objective evidence gathered in relevant scientific research and its use as a basis for understanding and practice.

4. The realistic description of the reasoning process in harmony with the generally-accepted viewpoint that thinking is the servant of life's driving motivations rather than their master.

5. The simplification of terminology without diminution of its accuracy and adequacy.

6. The functional arrangement of materials, beginning with the recognition and analysis of a problem, taking the student step by step through the process of solving it, and concluding with a consideration of the techniques which must be employed in inducing others to adopt the approved solution.

7. The abundance of fresh and stimulating illustrative material which makes the book fascinating reading.

8. The classroom-tested exercises which are closely integrated with the text itself.

Those who compare the new edition with the original will discover that this is no perfunctory revision consisting merely of minor modifications. It is a painstaking, thorough-going effort to add to the earlier work the full fruits of the decade of studying and teaching which the authors have lived since the book first appeared. It was good then; it is still better now.

ANDREW THOMAS WEAVER

Preface

OUR PUBLISHER's style book says that a preface "deals with the genesis, purpose, limitations, and scope of the work and may include acknowledgments of indebtedness." Most of these matters are stated, over-generously we fear, in the *Editor's Foreword*. Our purpose stems from our belief that discussion and debate are the essential tools of a democratic society and that students should be trained in their ethical and effective use.

We are indebted to those who have written about the subject, and to our own teachers, whose ideas we have borrowed freely; to our students who pointed out sections they thought irrelevant or obscure in the first edition; to our wives for their understanding and encouragement; and to Andrew T. Weaver, the editor of this series, who patiently and expertly read the entire manuscript. We hasten to add that the burden of proof for all statements of fact or opinion rests upon our shoulders alone.

H. L. E.
J. J. A.

Contents

Part IV

DISCUSSION

Part V

DEBATE

Part I

A POINT OF VIEW

CHAPTER 1

What This Book Is About

DISCUSSION AND DEBATE are not simply courses in a college curriculum. They are the essential tools of a democratic society. As the editors of *Time* reported in their "mid-century appraisal": [1]

A significant 20th Century characteristic of U.S. life is the revival of public discussion. There is plenty to talk about. All over the U.S., colleges, newspapers, businessmen's clubs, churches, and women's clubs arrange lectures, forums, panel discussions. Busy and learned men give their time to these gatherings in the American belief that an informed and alert citizenry is the basis of democracy.

To train students in the intelligent and effective use of these basic tools of democracy is the aim of this book.

As the editorial observers of American life indicate, discussion and debate are not newly-discovered techniques, though they may be, in fact, rediscovered. The whole history of democratic processes bears eloquent testimony to the truth of Macaulay's view that "men are never so likely to settle a question rightly as when they discuss it fully." Though we may on occasion relapse into the use of violence in settling our problems with other people and other nations, fundamentally we subscribe to the notion that it is better to talk it out than to shoot it out. The cracker barrel discussion and the ballot box decision are both basic to our way of life. We believe in decision by discussion, in majority rule in a climate of free speech.

Admittedly the working of democracy, in our clubs, associations, family relationships, and in our government, is sometimes slow and we are apt to be impatient. When Charles Lindbergh made his famous non-stop flight from New York to Paris, Charles F. Kettering first heard the news from his wife. "And how wonderful," she concluded,

[1] *Time*, Vol. 53 (April 11, 1949), p. 27.

"that he did it all alone!" "It would have been more wonderful," observed the General Motors executive, "if he had done it with a committee!" This is a fair comment on some of our experiences with discussion and debate; it is not always easy to achieve direct and immediate results. But we have adopted and maintained "cracker barrel democracy" in America not because it is the easiest method of government, but because it is the best method of *self*-government. It is the only way that a people can hammer out their own decisions in the competitive market of ideas. The techniques of discussion and debate are as American as Patrick Henry, as old as the taverns of Boston where we planned the Revolution, and as up-to-date as the Town Meeting of the Air.

In almost any area of group activity, nation-wide or neighborhood-narrow, we can find today an increasing use of discussion and debate. Once, perhaps, we thought of them as belonging only to the sphere of politics and politicians: we easily associate discussion with the Constitutional Convention, or debate with Lincoln and Douglas. But today we recognize that anyone who believes in the values of common counsel can find in these techniques the basic tools for democratic problem-solving, whether that task be undertaken in the realm of public or private affairs. When former president Herbert Hoover, in an address on his seventy-fifth birthday, August 10, 1949, referred to the current proposals to provide "security" for individual citizens, he underscored the necessity of widespread discussion and debate on the issues involved.

And finally, may I say that thinking and debate on these questions must not be limited to legislative halls. We should debate them in every school. We should resort to the old cracker barrel debate in every corner grocery. There phrases and slogans can be dissolved in common sense and integrity.

We use the terms *discussion* and *debate* in our everyday talk to mean many different things. We are as likely to use "discussion" to describe a party-line telephone call as to refer to a labor-management conference. Or we may say that we had a "debate" with a traffic cop, and also use the term to describe what happens on the floor of Congress. Thus we must define the terms as we will use them in this book. We may start by suggesting that "discussion and debate" are synonymous with "investigation and decision." Together the two processes, discussion (investigation) and debate (decision), form a continuum along which is ranged public thinking, from the initial awareness of a problem to a final decision as to the best solution and an effort to persuade others to accept it. When we use the words *discussion* or *debate*, therefore, we refer to the activity of problem-solving through purposeful talk by a group, with or without an audience. The precise aspect of the problem to be discussed or debated, however, must be determined by how far public thinking about it has progressed. For example, the purpose of the discussion or debate may properly be any one or all of these:

1. Locating and defining the problem
2. Exploring the problem
3. Examining suggested solutions
4. Choosing the best solution
5. Securing acceptance of the chosen solution

Together these five stages in the discussion-debate continuum represent the complete act of problem solution, from investigation of an unknown or ambiguous situation to decision on what to do about it. The individual follows this same pattern of investigation and decision when he employs what we call "reflective thinking." When a number of people undertake the process together we often refer to it as "group thinking." And when group thinking occurs in a national election, a labor union meeting, around the family dinner-table, at a public forum, in a classroom, or in a legislative chamber, we describe it as *discussion* if the problem is being investigated, or as *debate* if a solution is being decided upon. A few examples may make clear what happens at various stages along the discussion-debate continuum:

1. Several years ago a handful of citizens in Saginaw, Michigan, met around a table, after a few earlier and casual conversations, to discuss their local government. Members of the group were a grocer, a lawyer, an accountant, a lumber dealer, a car dealer, a wholesaler, the president of a foundry workers' council, a manufacturer, and a retired businessman. None of them was exactly sure what the problem was, but all sensed that something was wrong: taxes were high, tangible civic improvements were few; elections were held regularly, but charges of corruption against public officials were freely made. These men wanted to correct the situation, once they could determine just where the trouble lay. Their immediate purpose, therefore, was *locating and defining the problem*. Out of their discussions, which eventually included a wider circle of voters, they concluded that the city needed, like any business corporation, a man

trained in management, and at the same time free of party control. The result was a spirited campaign to adopt the city-manager form of government, and a consequent house-cleaning which gave Saginaw better government and more public services at less cost.

2. Turtle Creek is a sooty suburb of a big city where, a few years ago, the students in the vocational high school broke out in a rash of pro-Communist activities. Many citizens in this industrial town were disturbed, but the traditional public school approach apparently barred a forthright and realistic appraisal of the doctrines of communism. Eventually, however, a core of citizens who cared persuaded the school board to employ a principal who launched what is now known as "The Turtle Creek Experiment." Instead of concentrating on lectures extolling the virtues of democracy the school faculty undertook a positive teaching program which raised, and frankly considered, the conflicts between communism and democracy. Discussion was the technique employed, and in economics, history, and civics courses the students thrashed out the alleged merits of the two ideologies, digging up the facts that related to the problem and talking about their meaning. In short, they were *exploring the problem*. It is significant, of course, that communism has now lost status in Turtle Creek; but equally important is the training afforded the students in reaching decisions by discussing the facts.

3. In this automotive age, most cities have traffic congestion and parking problems. The National Association of Real Estate Boards undertook, at its 1948 convention, to assemble information on methods of dealing with traffic situations found helpful in various cities. They were concerned with *examining suggested solutions*. This they did in a symposium where spokesmen from Chicago, Philadelphia, Cleveland, Dallas, Indianapolis, and Denver gave short talks, each telling what his city had done to lessen traffic congestion and provide parking facilities. In a forum period audience members asked questions to clarify specific points or to elicit further details. The meeting gave those present information that might be helpful in meeting the situation in their home cities.

4. In a Southern state during the summer of 1949, there was a severe outbreak of night-riding and flogging by groups of men who concealed themselves behind hoods and masks. The people of the state were aroused and demanded official action to prevent further outbreaks. Public meetings were held to discuss what ought to be

done; private organizations like the American Legion appointed special committees to recommend courses of action; and the judiciary committees of the state legislature discussed specific pieces of proposed legislation. In this situation public, private, and legislative discussion centered on *choosing the best solution*. Everyone thought he knew what the problem was; he was ready to make a decision. Ultimately an "anti-mask" bill was submitted to the legislature. It was debated with vigor, alternative solutions were presented, and the machinery of parliamentary procedure was used as the legislature enacted the law.

5. During the 1948 presidential primaries two of the leading contenders for the Republican nomination were Thomas Dewey, governor of New York, and Harold Stassen, former governor of Minnesota. The two men agreed that something should be done to combat the influence of the Communist Party; they disagreed as to the best method. Stassen supported the Mundt-Nixon Bill, then pending in Congress; Dewey opposed it. *Each wanted to secure acceptance for his solution.* During the primary campaign in Oregon, in the best American political tradition, the two men met in a radio debate on a national network. Speaking from the same platform, and for equal amounts of time, each candidate attempted to persuade his listeners to accept his point of view. Those who heard the debate made their own decisions in the voting booths a few days later.

These are, of course, but a handful of the ways in which discussion and debate are being used in the process of investigation and decision. We shall present in a later chapter further examples of the rôle of discussion and debate in various areas of our society. Here we are concerned only with a preview.

The effective use of these basic tools for democratic living is not a simple task. It requires not only an understanding of individual and group behavior, and of the logical aspects of problem-solving, but a familiarity with the specialized techniques of leadership and participation in various types of discussion and debate. Along with the revival of public discussion has come an increasing body of knowledge concerning its uses and effectiveness. From 1920 to 1935, for example, only twenty articles on public discussion were indexed in the *Readers' Guide;* at least as many are now listed each year. Twenty-five years ago relatively few manuals or textbooks on the subject were available; today such publications are numerous, and many national organizations provide their local groups with special

handbooks and discussion guides. Of at least equal importance are
the experimental studies measuring the effects of discussion on listeners and participants. While most of these studies are the work
of individuals, the most extensive were conducted by the Army and
Navy orientation divisions, the National Institute of Social Relations,
and the Research Center for Group Dynamics. The findings are
reported at appropriate places in this book.

The reader should understand, however, that studying a book will
not train him completely for intelligent leadership and participation.
He must learn as well by observing others discuss and debate, and
he will master the skills involved only by practising them. No writing about discussion and debate can do more than shorten the trial-
and-error process.

This book is divided into five parts, each dealing with an important
element in the effective use of discussion and debate.

Part I, "A Point of View," includes a brief history of discussion
and debate in the United States, an explanation of our belief that
they are the basic tools of democracy, and an analysis of what we
hopefully call thinking.

Part II, "The Problem," treats, in logical order, the steps in problem analysis: locating and defining the problem, exploring the
problem, examining suggested solutions, and choosing the best solution. The final step, securing acceptance of the chosen solution, will
be taken up later.

Part III, "The Listener," is concerned with the audience in discussion and debate: it begins with a brief survey of group behavior,
centering on how individuals think in group situations, includes a
review of some special characteristics of audiences, and presents a
method of audience analysis. The concluding chapter in this section
takes up the rôle of persuasion as a means of securing acceptance
of the selected solution of a problem.

Part IV, "Discussion," treats first the nature, purposes, and limitations of the discussion method. Then it presents general principles
for organizing and leading discussions, as well as recent developments
of special discussion techniques. Separate chapters take up specific
types of discussion: informal group discussions, committees and
conferences, panels and public hearings, symposiums and lecture
forums, and so on. A final chapter reports significant experimental
studies of discussion and suggests methods of evaluation.

Part V, "Debate," deals with the nature, purposes, and limitations of that special form of presentation, examines the various types of debate, and such special problems as building the case, developing the debate speech, and handling refutation. It concludes with a chapter on means of evaluation.

At all points we have attempted to interweave common concepts with the evidence of experimental studies that the reader may learn what procedures are most effective, and why. In this way, we believe, he may be better equipped to evaluate the work of others and to incorporate the results of both study and observation when he participates in discussion and debate.

CHAPTER 2

Democracy, Discussion, and Debate

OUR DEMOCRATIC SOCIETY operates through public opinion, the expression of the minds of many people. This fact is basic to an understanding of the rôle of discussion and debate in a democracy, whether we are concerned with the public opinion of the nation in a presidential election, or of lesser publics organized into labor unions, church congregations, service clubs, or farm groups. If our form of government and private association relies upon factoring down individual opinions into a majority judgment, it is essential that means be available for the development of intelligent conclusions.

In our nation we have many channels of communication: speeches, discussions, debates, newspapers, magazines, books, movies, television, and radio. Through the influence of each of them we are constantly reshaping our individual collections of facts, ideas, and attitudes. The resulting mental mosaic, for better or worse, determines our opinions. In this book we are not unaware of other means of communication, but we are primarily concerned with discussion and debate. We believe, as Harold Laski has written, that "the art of public discussion . . . is central to the achievement of the democratic purpose." [1] Democratic government has often been called government by discussion. Those who do not like this concept, who demand "action, not talk," forget that purposeful talk necessarily precedes intelligent action.

This belief in discussion and debate as essential tools of democracy is as old as Pericles: "We decide or debate carefully, in person, all matters of policy, holding that acts are foredoomed to failure when

[1] Harold J. Laski, *The American Presidency, An Interpretation* (New York, Harper & Bros., 1940), p. 256.

undertaken undiscussed." But to sustain public discussion two keystone freedoms are required: freedom of speech and freedom of
assembly. This need was clearly understood by our nation's founders,
and it has since been reënforced in the courts. In a famous Supreme
Court decision, Justice Louis D. Brandeis marked out the meaning
of the First Amendment: [2]

> Those who won our independence ... believed that freedom to think
> as you will and to speak as you think are means indispensable to the dis-
> covery and spread of political truth; that without free speech and as-
> sembly discussion would be futile; that with them, discussion affords
> ordinarily adequate protection against the dissemination of noxious doc-
> trine; that the greatest menace to freedom is an inert people; that public
> discussion is a political duty; that this should be a fundamental principle
> of American Government....
> Believing in the power of reason as applied through public discussion,
> they eschewed silence coerced by law—the argument of force in its worst
> form. Recognizing the occasional tyrannies of governing majorities,
> they amended the Constitution so that free speech and assembly should
> be guaranteed....

Few questions of public policy have been so persistently trouble-
some as that involved in maintaining freedom of speech and discussion. The ideal position on this question was phrased by Supreme
Court Justice Oliver Wendell Holmes: "If there is any principle of
the Constitution that more imperatively calls for attachment than
any other it is the principle of free thought—not free thought for
those who agree with us but freedom for the thought that we
hate." [3] It is easy to fall short of this American ideal. Not long ago
a student group in a leading western university invited a left-wing
union leader to speak on the problems of organized labor. One of
the regents of the university, a prosperous businessman, protested
against holding the meeting: "Of course I believe in free speech,"
he said, "but I do not believe in free speech for people like that." [4]
Thomas Jefferson would not like these sentiments; writing of the
University of Virginia, which he founded, he declared: "This institution will be based on the illimitable freedom of the human mind.
For here we are not afraid to follow truth wherever it may lead,
nor to tolerate any error so long as reason is left free to combat

[2] *Whitney* v. *California*, 274 U.S. 357.
[3] *United States* v. *Schwimmer*, 279 U.S. 644.
[4] *Safeguarding Civil Liberty Today*, in "The Right to Know—and Speak,"
Talk It Over, No. G-121-1947, p. 5.

it. . . ." [5] Nor would John Stuart Mill, author of the classic *Essay on Liberty*, approve current proposals to deprive any minority groups of the right of free speech, or the purge of their spokesmen from college faculties. He believed that there is no time and no place when suppression of free discussion by any authority may be justified.

The fatal weakness of the notion that "speech is free but some people's speech should be curbed," is its assumption that only majorities possess the truth. But "there is something very dangerous about the doctrine that only the truth has a right to be heard." In the realm of public affairs today's truth may become tomorrow's fallacy. "The fatal tendency of mankind to leave off thinking about a thing when it is no longer doubtful," wrote Mill, "is the cause of half their errors."

To combat just such errors as result from hastily formed and inadequately discussed judgments, though they may be supported by a majority, the American tradition has been to determine the ultimate good by encouraging free trade in ideas, believing, as Justice Holmes once said, "that the best test of truth is the power of thought to get itself accepted in the competition of the market." [6] Essentially, this freedom for discussion and debate is the only type of freedom which differentiates a democracy from a dictatorship. There are others, of course, but their maintenance invariably depends upon freedom of discussion. Americans share with the people of other lands comparable forms of physical and intellectual force, but in a democracy alone do we find the very potent force of free and vigorous discussion and debate. Mrs. Franklin D. Roosevelt underscored its value in her reply to Russia's Vishinsky on October 3, 1947, at a United Nations meeting: "Sometimes the government and certain people disagree but we cling to the right of criticism and disagreement. It is the price one pays for freedom and for democracy that the government often has to wait for the enlightenment of the people. Totalitarianism may move faster, for good or ill, but we believe democracy and free people stand on a firmer foundation."

We should point out that while the Bill of Rights protects the citizen against encroachments upon his freedom of speech by Con-

---

[5] Letter to William Roscoe, December 7, 1820, in Adrienne Koch and William Peden, eds., *The Life and Selected Writings of Thomas Jefferson* (New York, Random House, 1944), p. 702.

[6] *Abrams* v. *United States*, 250 U.S. 616.

gress, and the Fourteenth Amendment has been interpreted since the Gitlow decision in 1925 as a similar protection against state and local governments, the precise obligations of the citizen in using his freedom are not always clear. An analogy frequently made is this: "You're free to swing your arm. But your freedom to swing your arm stops where the other fellow's nose begins." It is true that there are limits to free speech but, as someone has said, those limits are not as plain as the nose on the other fellow's face.

The first working principle normally followed by the Supreme Court in deciding cases on free speech today was stated in 1919 by Justice Holmes: "The question in every case is whether the words used are in such circumstances and are of such a nature as to create a clear and present danger that they will bring about the substantive evils that Congress has a right to prevent." [7] The following year Justice Brandeis added a note of advice on applying the "clear and present danger" test: "Like many other rules of human conduct, it can be applied correctly only by the exercise of good judgment, and in the exercise of good judgment, calmness is, in time of deep feeling and on subjects which excite passion, as essential as fearlessness and honesty." [8] Seven years later Brandeis again spoke for the Court: "Fear of serious injury cannot alone justify suppression of free speech and assembly.... There must be reasonable ground to believe that the danger apprehended is imminent.... The wide difference between advocacy and incitement, between preparation and attempt, between assembling and conspiracy, must be borne in mind.... Moreover, even imminent danger cannot justify resort to prohibition of these functions essential to effective democracy, unless the evil apprehended is relatively serious." Perhaps Brandeis did not speak the last word on the problem, but in this statement he offered a touchstone for today: [9]

Those who won our independence by revolution were not cowards. They did not fear political change. They did not exalt order at the cost of liberty. To courageous, self-reliant men, with confidence in the power of free and fearless reasoning applied through the processes of popular government, *no danger flowing from speech can be deemed clear and present, unless the incidence of the evil apprehended is so imminent that it may befall before there is opportunity for full discussion.* If there be time to expose through discussion the falsehood and fallacies, to avert

[7] *Schenck* v. *United States,* 249 U.S. 47.

[8] *Schaeffer* v. *United States,* 251 U.S. 466.

[9] *Whitney* v. *California,* 274 U.S. 357 (Italics ours.)

the evil by the processes of education, *the remedy to be applied is more speech, not enforced silence.* Only an emergency can justify repression. Such must be the rule if authority is to be reconciled with freedom.

These considerations are all pertinent to an understanding of the rôle of discussion and debate in our democratic society. For if we cherish freedom of speech, tolerate the expression even of loathsome ideas, and concede any man's right to be "agin' the government," then we must expect that the ignorant as well as the intelligent citizen will be heard. The charlatan, the self-seeker, and the demagogue will also have access to our councils. This makes it imperative that the intelligent and educated citizen, in government or in private associations, understand the American tradition of free speech, master the techniques of discussion and debate, and make everyday use of these essential tools for democratic living.

I. HISTORICAL BACKGROUNDS

Political theorists and progressive educators have been among those most interested in the development of discussion and debate. The first group believe that these techniques are basic to the democratic process, that they provide essential tools for problem-solving in a period of increasingly complex group relationships. The educators have advocated discussion and debate as a basic educational method, especially in adult education which has grown in importance in an age of extended leisure time. These uses of discussion and debate may be seen in a brief historical survey.

A. Discussion and Debate in the Democratic Process

Part of America's national heritage has been the principle of majority rule by persuasion rather than by force. Ramsey Muir, the English historian, describing England in 1660, wrote that the great civil war had taught the English people "that even the noblest and the most enlightened aims are vitiated and will eventually be frustrated if those who advocate them try to secure their victory by force, and not by discussion and persuasion. These [discussion and persuasion] were to be henceforth the characteristic notes of the growth of free institutions in the British Commonwealth." [10] These

---

[10] Ramsey Muir, *A Short History of the British Commonwealth* (London, Philip & Son, Ltd., 1920, 2 v.), I, p. 487.

essentially democratic methods were carried across the seas: when the Mayflower Compact was drawn up by forty-one adult male Pilgrims as their ship lay in Plymouth Harbor, its articles were adopted "by the most voices." Thus was the simple transference of the democratic process to what are now the forty-eight United States.

One of the first needs of the early colonists was a forum where "the most voices" might find expression, and this was provided in the *Massachusetts Body of Liberties*, Article 12, adopted in 1641:

Everyman whether Inhabitant or Forreiner, free or not free, shall have libertie to come to any publique Court, Council, or Towne meeting, and either by speech or writing to move any lawfull, seasonable, any materiall question, or to present any necessary motion, complaint, petition, or Bill of Information.

As "little democracies" the New England town meetings not only served their day, but in some smaller villages still constitute the chief governing body. In the South men like Thomas Jefferson worked for the adoption of the town meeting system, which he called "the wisest invention ever devised by the wit of man for the perfect exercise of self-government, and its preservation." [11] In the typical town a schedule of proposed legislation was posted well in advance to give time for careful thought, meetings were held weekly and attendance was compulsory, with absentees paying a fine. The meetings were attended by the cantankerous as well as by the coöperative people of the community, and the debates often yielded heat as well as light. As Emerson noted, ". . . their records reflect vindictiveness, petulance and ignorance as faithfully as sympathy, temperance and wisdom. For here was no 'church of saints' or 'metropolis of patriots' but an open democracy where every human feeling found expression." [12]

One of the most famous town meeting moderators, Samuel Adams, made use of these assemblies as forums for protest against British rule, and the Committees of Correspondence became the clearing house for the ideas debated in them. "The town-meeting at Boston is the hot-bed of sedition," wrote one Tory. "It is there that all their

[11] See James K. Hosmer, *Samuel Adams* (Boston, Houghton Mifflin Co., 1885), p. 429.
[12] Ralph Waldo Emerson, "Historical Discourse, at Concord, on the Second Centennial Anniversary of the incorporation of the town," September 12, 1845.

dangerous insurrections are engendered; it is there that the flame of discord and rebellion was first lighted up and disseminated over the provinces...." [13] In truth, it was there that many of the leaders of the American Revolution received their first training in public discussion.

Much has been written about the Constitutional Convention in Philadelphia and copious reports of the debates which took place behind closed doors indicate the character of the meetings where delegates came not to deliver fervid orations or to sway popular galleries, but for "honest negotiation and accommodation." This aim was not easily achieved; even when the venerable Benjamin Franklin proposed that a daily prayer be offered for divine guidance he could not get a unanimous vote. In short, the records disclose humans, at their best and worst: [14]

They do not portray a group of inspired individuals convinced in advance that only one project of government could accomplish the general purposes they had clearly in mind. Instead of a disciplined crew under a stern and bright-eyed captain steering the ship of state by the north star, we see a wrangling body of thoughtful, experienced, and capable men, but harassed men, torn by interests, prejudices, and passions, drifting one day in one direction and the next in another, deciding long debated issues, opening them again, altering their previous views, and adopting novel solutions.

Discussion and debate did not provide for them a key to Utopia where all is sweetness and light; but they were the essential tools for their task. As Thomas Jefferson observed, the example of assembling the wise men of a state to debate a new constitution, instead of assembling armies to enforce one, was significant for the whole world.

When the "bundle of compromises" was finally completed it was submitted to the states for ratification. In the Convention at Philadelphia the process had been one of conference; in the state assemblies it was formal debate, men were either for or against the proposal. This was, in fact, "The Great Debate," and it was carried on in conventions, town meetings, taverns, and plowed fields. By public

---

[13] "Sagittarius," quoted by Richard Frothingham, "The Sam Adams Regiments in the Town of Boston," *Atlantic Monthly*, Vol. 11 (November, 1863), p. 601.

[14] Charles A. and Mary R. Beard, *The Rise of American Civilization* (New York, 1927), I, p. 316. By permission of The Macmillan Company, publishers.

discussion and persuasion the Constitution was adopted; through the same techniques it has been preserved.

It is conceivable that the entire history of American democratic growth could be written in terms of great discussions and debates. Some form of speechmaking is almost always involved when men deliberate and decide issues of the day. Even when we can recognize no carefully phrased proposition, and the procedure is informal, debate goes on as citizens seek solutions for their problems. The great controversies over Manifest Destiny, antislavery and disunion, populism, imperialism, and isolationism, continued for many years. They involved not only such well-known figures as Webster and Hayne, Lincoln and Douglas, Wilson and LaFollette, but the debaters at the country crossroads and around the cracker barrel. Names now long forgotten were prominent in the discussions which led to social reforms such as temperance, woman suffrage, and free public education. And in our own times the problems of American democracy are no less rigorously tested in debate by the Tafts, Reuthers, Stassens, Vandenbergs, and Lilienthals, and by millions of nameless citizens who "talk it over" first and then vote.

Let us look at these nameless citizens. To what extent do they "talk it over"? Some suggestion of the extent of their activity is reflected in a 1947 survey by the Research Division of the National Education Association. Fifteen of thirty-four selected national organizations reported 47,198 state, district, or local discussion groups. Eight of these described local discussion groups as a major activity, and gave these figures:

American Association for Adult Education	80
American Association for the United Nations	70
Coöperative Extension Service, U.S. Dept. of Agriculture	35,000
Federal Council of Churches of Christ in America	635
Kiwanis International	2,527
League of Women Voters of the United States	525
National Institute of Social Relations	6
Town Hall and America's Town Meeting	5,000
Total	43,843

In 1948 a committee representing twelve Ohio colleges and universities, under the chairmanship of William E. Utterback, conducted sampling surveys of local groups in eight counties and among fifteen state organizations with local units. The groups sampled held 22,665 meetings in the preceding year: 85 per cent employed some form of discussion or debate.[15] The range of topics discussed is indicated by these figures based upon 5,196 meetings reported in the Ohio survey:

Local	29%
State	9
National	20
International	19
Mixed	13
Other	10

The kind of discussion and debate that goes on as citizens exchange information and form opinions on matters of public policy is typified by such organizations as Cleveland's Council on World Affairs. During 1948 this non-partisan association augmented its usual program of lectures, study committees, and workshops with a series of 200 neighborhood forums and discussion groups, and provided discussion leadership training for 150 persons. Another notable undertaking was the Veteran-Civilian Discussion Project, sponsored by the New York Adult Education Council in 1946. Thirty community discussion groups were established, ranging in size from fourteen to sixty, divided between veterans and non-veterans. Skilled discussion leaders were provided and standard topic outlines were furnished on eight questions such as full employment, housing, and education. A selected group of documentary films, and other audio-visual aids, was used. Trained observers wrote descriptive reports of each discussion and at the close of the series an evaluation questionnaire and an attitude test were administered. While forces other than the discussion were undoubtedly present, changes in opinion reported on eleven questions ranged from 6 to 46 per cent. On the average nearly one-fourth of those who took part in the discussion shifted their opinions.[16]

In addition to these locally sponsored projects, there have been a number of attempts to organize discussion of public problems on a national basis. All local branches of the League of Women Voters, for example, conduct discussions and debates on the same public problems so that formulation of a national legislative "support" program is developed from the grass roots of local groups. Unlike the

[15] Slightly more than half of these meetings were reported by the 1,400 local units of the Ohio Farm Bureau; the median response by units of all state organizations was 22 per cent, for the Farm Bureau 100 per cent.

[16] See Joseph Cahn, et al., The Story of a Discussion Program (New York, New York Adult Education Council, 1946).

non-partisan League of Women Voters program, the Republican Open Forums, in operation from April, 1946, to July, 1948, were intended not only as an educational but also as a political movement. Although not connected with the Republican National Committee, the project was definitely oriented toward that party and financed by individual Republicans who wanted to provide younger voters with a means of participating in the party program. Approximately 100,000 people took part in the nearly 1,000 discussion groups which made up the movement. Fourteen discussion guides were published on such topics as the Marshall Plan and the Taft-Hartley law. A special feature of this project was the use of a detailed ballot, covering as many as a dozen aspects of each topic, to be filled in by each participant at the close of each meeting. These ballots were then forwarded to the national office where they were distributed to congressmen from the appropriate districts. By this procedure it was hoped that representatives would have a clearer picture of what their constituents were thinking on current issues. The administration of such a large-scale project is costly. The Republican Open Forums spent about $120,000 in maintaining a national headquarters, in preparing, publishing, and distributing about 125,000 discussion guides, and in processing the ballots. In the judgment of its sponsors, the project justified its cost by providing broader understanding of political issues and by the chance it gave to alert and articulate citizens to speak up in meeting and say, "Now the way it looks to me is this. . . ." [17]

These contemporary examples are, we believe, in the best tradition of the old town meeting. Intelligent controversy over public issues is the lifeblood of the democratic process. And when free discussion provides the means for dealing with controversy, it clarifies rather than confuses, unites rather than divides, expedites rather than delays.

B. Discussion and Debate as an Educational Method

It would be difficult to determine just when those interested in education first began to use discussion and debate as a methodology for learning. Among the earliest employers of the method, at any rate, were the Lyceum and the Chautauqua movements in the last century. Josiah Holbrook, an itinerant natural science lecturer, organized the first unit of the American Lyceum system in 1826 at

[17] Data in a letter to the authors from Cynthia S. Zimmerman, Executive Director, Republican Open Forums, August 17, 1948.

Milbury, Massachusetts. Within a few years this movement for "the diffusion of useful information" by "mutual education" had spread to nearly every state. Counties, communities, and professional groups organized their own Lyceums, held weekly lecture-forum meetings, and listened to their own members, or paid lecturers, discuss the topics of the day. At various times Daniel Webster, Ralph Waldo Emerson, Susan B. Anthony, and Frederick A. Douglass were among the most popular Lyceum leaders. In thousands of communities the Lyceum attracted Americans to an enterprise in adult education and instilled in them a desire for mental growth. In the middle of the last century "the American Lyceum was easily the great disseminator of knowledge in the country." [18]

The Chautauqua movement developed from the Sunday School Institutes held during the summer camping season at Lake Chautauqua, New York. It grew out of the conviction that Sunday School teachers should be able to apply their teaching to current problems. Lewis Miller, one of the co-founders, said in 1874: "The statesman, the humanitarian, must be brought to her platform, and there, free from caste and party spirit, discuss questions, solve problems, and inaugurate measures that will mould and inspire for the right." [19] At one time there were about four hundred annual summer assemblies, with camping facilities and meeting rooms. Later Chautauqua circuits were organized to take education to the people. These flourished from 1904 to 1924, and, in the peak year an estimated thirty million Americans sat in tents to hear almost every prominent political leader, social reformer, preacher, and man of science and letters discuss the social, political, and economic issues of the time. As one observer has written, "It is probable that no single wholly American institution, with the possible exception of the Model T, left a greater imprint upon the social and cultural life of the rural communities of the nation than the Chautauqua movement." [20]

The "open-forum" movement was, and is, another significant effort to broaden public understanding of current problems. In general the term is used to describe any meeting to which the public is invited, often at a fee, and where questions and discussion by the

[18] Stewart H. Holbrook, *Lost Men of American History* (New York, The Macmillan Co., 1946), p. 132.

[19] J. H. Vincent, *The Chautauqua Movement* (Boston, Chautauqua Press, 1886), p. vii.

[20] Victoria Case and Robert Ormond Case, *We Called It Culture: The Story of Chautauqua* (Garden City, N. Y., Doubleday & Co., 1948) p. v.

audience follow the formal presentation. Sometimes the opening presentation is a panel or a symposium, although it is more frequently a lecture or a debate. Often, especially in recent years, a documentary film has been used as an introduction. The first open forum was established in 1897 at New York's Cooper Union; the movement has since spread until perhaps two thousand communities have public forums. As Mary Ely concluded, after a national survey: [21]

Forums are meeting in churches and synagogues; in schoolrooms, libraries, museums, and public auditoriums; in settlement houses, club houses, and apartment houses; in the assembly rooms of labor unions and professional associations; in shelters for transient dwellers and in parks for passers-by. They meet in the morning, the afternoon, the evening; at luncheon, at tea, at dinner.

One special development is worthy of mention: the Des Moines Public Forums, established in the early days of the depression with the help of a foundation grant, were held in school buildings. Nearly six hundred meetings were held annually, and in the first two years over 17 per cent of the total population of the city attended. Using discussion and debate techniques, the leaders aimed at these objectives: "(1) exchange of information and points of view; (2) development of tolerance and open-mindedness; and (3) development of critical intelligence." [22] Mr. Studebaker, who had initiated the Des Moines project, was later appointed U.S. Commissioner of Education, and in that post was responsible for establishing the Federal Forum Project. In the first year of operation, under the direction of local educational officers and trained forum leaders, over a million people attended more than ten thousand forum meetings in nineteen demonstration centers. Because of the curtailment of federal funds, the project has been abandoned, but in many cities where it operated independent groups of adults are continuing similar projects. And there are many who still believe that a permanent federally-sponsored forum movement would be worth far more than its cost, in developing a more intelligent citizenry. It should be noted in passing that the wartime forum activities, developed by the Office of War Information and the Office of Civilian Defense, demonstrated anew the

[21] Mary L. Ely, "Talking It Over: The Old Town Meeting Reincarnated," *Survey Graphic,* Vol. 74 (January, 1938), pp. 57-9.
[22] John W. Studebaker, *Plain Talk* (Washington, National Home Library Foundation, 1936), p. 103.

democratic values of discussion and debate. As President Roosevelt said: "Forums for widespread and free discussion of public affairs are very much more than convenient expedients—they are vital necessities in the maintenance of democratic institutions."

While it does not have the status of a formal movement, the increasing use of discussion techniques in the nation's classrooms should be recorded. Progressive educators, led by such men as John Dewey, Harry A. Overstreet, and Lyman Bryson, have been instrumental in demonstrating that for certain types of students and subject areas, the discussion method produces better results than the traditional lecture. "Only in a small group," believes Barzun, "can the student learn to marshal his thoughts, expose his weaknesses, argue out his beliefs, and gain that familiarity with the 'ropes' of a given subject which, if not learned early, will never be learned at all." [23] The values of this method were demonstrated in the educational programs of the armed forces; they are utilized in the widespread Great Books discussion groups; and they were employed in many special wartime industrial training programs. [24] Perhaps one of the most striking testimonials to the values of this method is the announced plan of the New York Adult Education Council to train at least ten thousand discussion leaders who can conduct educational discussion activities through business and industry, labor unions, and similar organizations. [25]

Comparatively new, but important, are the attempts to apply the methods of social research to the analysis of what goes on in discussion. The leaders of such organizations as the Research Center for Group Dynamics, and the National Training Laboratory in Group Development, point out that discussion leadership skills are more than techniques of manipulation and control. They should also involve a general awareness of the group structure, a mutual sensitivity to group tensions and integrations, and an understanding of group behavior. [26] When discussion skills are used with a broad

[23] Jacques Barzun, *Teacher in America* (Boston, Little, Brown & Co., 1945), p. 40.
[24] See Cyril O. Houle, *et al., The Armed Services and Adult Education* (Washington, American Council on Adult Education, 1947), pp. 138-9, 237-45; Milton Mayer. "Great Books," *Life*, Vol. 21 (Oct. 28, 1946), pp. 2+; Milton Dickens, "Discussion Method in War Industry," *Quarterly Journal of Speech*, Vol. 31 (April, 1945), pp. 144-50.
[25] New York *Times*, January 9, 1949.
[26] Leland P. Bradford and John R. P. French, eds., "The Dynamics of the Discussion Group," *Journal of Social Issues*, Vol. 4 (Spring, 1948), pp. 1-75.

understanding of human relations, conflict situations may be resolved constructively, rather than by force.

The history of collective bargaining in labor-management relations is, of course, an outstanding example of the attempt to use discussion instead of force.[27] The conference table technique is not always successful; strikes do occur and they are often settled only after physical or economic exhaustion of one of the parties. But the record of such agencies as the United States Conciliation Service, and mediators like Cyrus Ching, is one of increasing significance in this specialized use of discussion and conference methods.

Another recent development is the use of discussion in group therapy and counseling. First used in private practice as an economy device, group psychotherapy soon demonstrated its unique value in enabling patients to help themselves by helping others: instead of concentrating upon their own mental problems they may be helped through discussing the problems of others and discovering some common denominator in their own experience. The psychiatrist's responsibility is not unlike that of any other discussion leader; but "It's like a party," reports one doctor, "in the beginning the host has to run it, but after everyone has actively participated, it goes along by itself."[28] Since the war the group counseling technique has been widely used in Veteran's Administration mental-hygiene clinics. In addition to gaining special insight into his own difficulties through discussion with fellow sufferers, and losing his sense of uniqueness when he discovers that others also need help, the patient, who is commonly disturbed in his personal relationships, has an opportunity to practise in group therapy sessions improved techniques in human relations.[29] In the expanding field of mental health, group therapy, based essentially upon discussion techniques, is a promising development.

Probably the most widespread use of discussion and debate methods was by the Army and the Navy during the wartime orientation programs. They were designed to provide strong, conscious motivations for men who needed to understand "why we fight," to get a sense of purpose in being in uniform. This involved training

[27] Neil W. Chamberlain, "Group Discussion and Collective Bargaining," *Adult Education Bulletin*, Vol. 13 (February, 1949), pp. 77-84.

[28] See Edith M. Stern, "Ganging Up on Personal Problems," *Reader's Digest*, Vol. 52 (May, 1948), p. 95.

[29] Hillier Kreighbaum, "Rehabilitation by Self-Help," *Survey Graphic*, Vol. 84 (January, 1948), p. 16.

thousands of officers as discussion leaders, providing them with discussion guides, fact sheets, and background materials, and organizing informal discussions and forums at training centers, aboard ships, and at overseas bases. At its peak, for example, *Army Talk*, the discussion guide furnished to Army, Navy, and Marine Corps orientation officers, was published in a weekly edition of 300,000 copies. Fifteen thousand copies of *Now Hear This: Handbook for Discussion Leaders* were distributed in the Navy alone. Topics ranged from those of international significance, like "How Shall Lend-Lease Accounts Be Settled?" through national ones such as "The Army in a Democracy," and to personal postwar problems like "Where Will the Good Jobs Be?" This large-scale attempt to train citizen soldiers and sailors psychologically as well as physically paid off in higher morale wherever it was permitted to function effectively. It exposed millions of men to the experience of talking over their common problems in organized groups and was instrumental in developing their attitudes and opinions on current affairs.[30]

Some form of discussion and debate has always been on the college scene. A century ago the literary societies flourished, providing forums for oratory, debate, and declamation. In the old debating societies, Calhoun was trained at Yale, Webster at Dartmouth, Bryan at Illinois College, and George W. Norris at Valparaiso University. By 1900, however, there was a growing emphasis upon intercollegiate debate, and it continues as an important extracurricular activity. Within recent years forensic programs have been extended to include legislative assemblies, congresses, conferences, and conventions. The former are usually patterned after American legislative bodies: the Delta Sigma Rho and the Pi Kappa Delta National Student Congresses, the Model Senate Association in New England, the Indiana Assembly at Purdue University, and the Ohio State University Conference on Public Affairs. In these assemblies, usually lasting several days, student delegates elect their own officers, prepare legislative bills in committee meetings, and debate them in parliamentary sessions. The conferences and conventions, on the other hand, are usually modeled upon other legislative or political agencies: the Pacific Northwest College Congress and the annual University of

---

[30] See J. Jeffery Auer, "Discussion Programs and Techniques in the Armed Forces," *Quarterly Journal of Speech*, Vol. 32 (October, 1946), pp. 303-10; Julius Schreiber, "Discussion in the Armed Forces," *Adult Education Bulletin*, Vol. 13 (February, 1949), pp. 73-7.

Chicago conventions patterned after the United Nations Assembly, and the Oberlin College Mock Convention which has duplicated quadrennial party conventions since 1860. A third development in colleges has been the establishment of speaker's bureaus and public discussion groups to provide talks, panels, symposiums, and debates before off-campus audiences, such as service clubs, women's organizations, farm and labor groups. These three patterns of discussion and debate activity are also developed on the high school level.

Finally, it should be noted that the advent of radio has increased tremendously the use of discussion and debate as a method of informing and shaping the opinions of American citizens. When millions more homes have radios than have telephones, automobiles, or bathtubs, the potential social force of radio is almost unlimited. Although the medium is used primarily to provide entertainment, the discriminating listener may tune in on numerous weekly local and network discussion programs of high quality, such as the University of Chicago Round Table (NBC), America's Town Meeting of the Air (ABC), The Reviewing Stand (MBS), and People's Platform (CBS). In a typical week, for example, these four programs offered discussions of "World Trade and the British Crisis," "What Should Be Turkey's Rôle Between the East and the West?" "Should the President Be Elected by the Direct Vote of the People?" and "The Supreme Court and Political Appointments." Participants in these broadcasts included congressmen and senators, government officials of two nations, a former presidential candidate, and academic specialists. Some of the programs are presented as panel discussions, others as symposiums, and many as debates. Radio audience surveys estimate that some of these network discussions have had as many as five million listeners, and one program annually sells nearly a million copies of printed transcripts of its discussions. Perhaps the most startling evidence of the impact of radio upon opinion in America is found in a recent survey of the Book Manufacturer's Institute, seeking to discover the source of people's current ideas. Excluding the rural population, this was the finding: radio 49 per cent, newspapers 21 per cent, magazines 11 per cent, movies 11 per cent, and books 8 per cent.[31] Certainly a large part of this influence of radio comes through the regular programs of discussion and debate.

[31] Joseph A. Brandt, "Intellectual Slave Market," *Saturday Review of Literature*, Vol. 31 (June 5, 1948), p. 20.

No one would contend that discussion and debate are the only essentials of the democratic process or of educational methodology but, as this review of historical backgrounds has suggested, in both of these areas deliberation and decision through purposeful talk has long held a central position.

II. NEW DEMANDS FOR PROBLEM-SOLVING TECHNIQUES

Almost half a century ago James Bryce described the ideal democracy where "every citizen is intelligent, patriotic, disinterested. His sole wish is to discover the right side on each contested issue, and to fix upon the best man among competing candidates. His common sense, aided by a knowledge of the constitution of his country, enables him to judge wisely between the arguments submitted to him, while his own zeal is sufficient to carry him to the polling booth." [32] Whether such a democracy ever existed, any candid observer of the American scene would have to deny its existence today. Even assuming the best intentions on the part of the average voter, his "common sense" is an inadequate guide for solving the increasingly complex problems which confront him. The fact that almost half of the eligible voters stayed away from the polling booths at the last presidential election also raises serious doubts about the "zeal" of the American citizen. This problem cannot be charged off entirely to indifference. Many failed to vote because they lacked adequate information about the candidates and the party platforms; others, because they did not know how to analyze the issues.

We are not trying here to sound the traditional cry: "These are perilous times!" All times are hazardous, and especially for the uninformed citizen. Indeed, the times cannot be otherwise, since we live in a world of continuous change, and the alert citizen willingly accepts the challenge of new concepts. What we do suggest here is that today the task is greater, and the need more urgent.

In the past, communication has with difficulty kept pace with the growing demands made upon it by social evolution. The resulting chronic maladjustment has now reached the dimensions of a crisis. Despite the remarkable contribution of science to the rapid transmission of intelligence and the wide dissemination of information and appeal, it is a fair

[32] From his introduction to M. Ostrogorski, *Democracy and the Organization of Political Parties* (New York, The Macmillan Co., 1902), I, p. xliv.

question whether modern man will succeed in understanding his world and his neighbors well enough and quickly enough to escape disaster. His struggle to understand has become a race between communication and catastrophe.[33]

If intelligent men and women today hope to control their own destinies, and the destiny of their democracy, they must first recognize the obstacles to be overcome. We submit brief considerations of five recognizable obstacles.

1. *We are witnessing an ever increasing expansion of the scope of government.* This is particularly true at the national level, somewhat less true among the states. The inevitable result is that as government activity grows and becomes more complex, it functions more and more at points far distant from the local level; thus the citizen feels remote from his government. What we are seeing is the "bigness" in business being paralleled by "bigness" in government. When government was stronger in the local community and the citizen felt better able to grapple with its problems, the town meeting type of pure democracy was unexcelled. Until 1822 in Boston, and 1850 in many other large centers, the town meeting was not replaced by city governments as we know them. A recent investigation of town meetings which still govern two New England communities of 5,000 population each, and one of 30,000, however, indicates that that form of government is outmoded today. So many of the issues which affect our lives—jobs, wages, social security, union organization, prices, hours of work, war and peace—are settled at the state and federal government levels, and by economic forces far beyond the control of the community that the town meeting is powerless to affect their solution.[34] Our problem as citizens has become acute: How, we ask, can I participate effectively in the democratic process when government is so complex and so far away?

2. *Not only has our government become more complex, but we ourselves have become more specialized in our interests and our knowledge.* Thus, even if we would, we find it increasingly difficult to understand public issues and the arguments about them. We also

[33] W. Hayes Yeager and William E. Utterback, eds., "Communication and Social Action," *Annals of the American Academy of Political and Social Science,* Vol. 250 (March, 1947), p. vii.

[34] John W. Alexander and Monroe Berger, "Is the Town Meeting Finished?" *American Mercury,* Vol. 69 (August, 1949), pp. 144-51.

tend to take on the same ideas and to talk in the same language as our fellow-specialists. As this increasing narrowness develops we find ourselves, and those in our specialty group, growing apart from other groups in our society. This development not only makes it more difficult to communicate with others, but may also lead us to suspect their ideas and their motives, so that inter-group tensions and prejudices result. We recall that Charles Lamb once said to a friend: "See that man across the street? Well, I hate him." "But," protested the friend, "you don't even know him." "That's why I hate him," Lamb replied. For all that specialization has done to add to our happiness, it has also created a new obstacle to the effective functioning of democracy. We are less likely to know or to be tolerant of the other man's point of view.

3. *While the age of specialization has made it necessary for congressmen to concentrate in one or two areas of legislation, if they would master any, we are also witnessing a gradual change in the nature of representative government.* This is a trend away from the notion of the framers of the Constitution that representatives should exercise their own best judgment in the management of governmental affairs, and toward a newer concept of the representative as a mere spokesman for the wishes of his constituents. The earlier view resulted in part from the fact that eighteenth-century communication and transportation made virtually impossible any immediate and direct pressure upon legislators. It also conformed to what was then the prevailing concept of representation in England, sharply set forth by Edmund Burke in a 1774 speech to his constituents: [35]

> Your representative owes you not his industry only, but his judgment; and he betrays, instead of serving you, if he sacrifices it to your opinion.... If government were a matter of will upon any side, yours without question ought to be superior. But government and legislation are matters of reason and judgment, not of inclination; and what sort of reason is that, in which the determination precedes the discussion; in which one set of men deliberate and another decide? ... Parliament is not a *congress* of ambassadors from different and hostile interests; which interests must maintain, as an agent and advocate, against other agents and advocates; but parliament is a *deliberative* assembly of one nation, with one interest, that of the whole; where not local purposes, not local prejudices ought to guide, but the general good, resulting from the general reason of the whole.

[35] F. W. Raffety, ed., *The Works of the Right Honourable Edmund Burke* (London, Oxford University Press, 1906), II, pp. 159-66.

In practice since that time most representatives have tended to adopt the position taken by Abraham Lincoln when he ran for the Illinois legislature in 1836: "While acting as ... [my constituents'] representative, I shall be governed by their will on all subjects upon which I have the means of knowing what their will is; and upon all others, I shall do what my own judgment teaches me will best advance their interests." [36] But doubts have frequently been expressed concerning the proper attitude of a member of Congress. Liberal Senator Norris argued that conscience should be his guide: "Otherwise, a member of Congress giving weight to expressed public sentiment becomes only an automatic machine. If that is the line of duty of a member, then Congress requires no patriotism, no education, and no courage." [37] "Uncle Joe" Cannon, longtime Speaker of the House, made the point in saying of William McKinley that "he kept his ear so close to the ground that it frequently got full of grasshoppers." Today the representative who is eager to please his constituents reads the latest Gallup Poll, weighs the pro-and-con mail from his district, and casts his vote. Indeed, a student of congressional debate on the proposed repeal of the Selective Service Act in 1941 concluded that one of the chief results of that debate was to stall off the final vote long enough to give the "folks back home" time to write or wire their wishes.[38] The American Institute of Public Opinion reported, on September 23, 1949, that nearly two out of every ten voters (19 per cent) questioned in a national survey, said that they had written or wired their representatives in Washington on current issues; this figure represented an increase of 5 per cent over a similar poll taken three years earlier. Whether this trend in representative procedure is good or bad, it exists, and it increases the need for citizens who, if they acquiesce in it, will become well-informed on legislative proposals.

4. *The tendency of representatives to become increasingly responsive to the wishes of their constituents is encouraged by the growth of pressure groups.* These tightly organized segments of the total electorate are an additional brake upon the democratic process. They exist apart from political parties, although they frequently

[36] Letter to the *Sangamon Journal*, in Philip Van Doren Stern, ed., *The Life and Writings of Abraham Lincoln* (New York, Random House, 1940), p. 225.

[37] *Fighting Liberal: The Autobiography of George W. Norris* (New York, The Macmillan Co., 1945), p. 198.

[38] Giraud Chester, "Contemporary Senate Debate," *Quarterly Journal of Speech*, Vol. 31 (December, 1945), pp. 407-11.

work within parties. The Americans for Democratic Action and the CIO Political Action Committee, for example, have had their spokesmen in both major parties, as have the National Association of Manufacturers and the U.S. Chamber of Commerce. The *World Almanac* lists nearly nine hundred such groups, each devoted to advocacy of a particular interest or doctrine. But whether they speak for labor or management, farmers, veterans, landlords, or anti-vivisectionists, each group has its own panacea for the nation's ills, and it is seldom weighed in the traditional scales of "the greatest good for the greatest number." Though they function within the democratic framework, pressure groups do not generally make democracy work better.

5. *One of the worst effects of the growth of pressure groups is their tendency to increase social tensions.* Sometimes these tensions are subtle, beneath the surface; at other times they flare into conflict situations resulting in violence. This has often been true in labor disputes and in race relations. In part this tendency results from the fact that while it is very easy to learn autocratic skills, such as suppression, emotionalism, and "scapegoating," it is more difficult to develop democratic skills of problem-solving. The possibility of conflict also results from the fact that few pressure group leaders are interested in seeing "the other point of view." As Supreme Court Justice Harold Burton once said of certain labor leaders, "When I tell them that the job of a man in public life is to try to reconcile all interests, and when I ask them what they would do if we exchanged places at the table, they have replied, 'We're not on that side of the table.' " [39] In theory democracy works because it integrates conflicting interests, but this integration cannot take place unless there is a willingness to use the tools of coöperation.

In sum, we believe that the task of making democracy work, in which all citizens are partners, is made increasingly difficult by a series of obstacles which have developed through the years. To overcome them we must discover effective problem-solving techniques.

[39] New York *Times,* September 22, 1945.

III. ADAPTING THE SCIENTIFIC METHOD
TO SOCIAL PROBLEMS

After the invention of every wartime engine of destruction we are made aware again that our techniques for social control lag far behind our capacities for scientific progress. "Modern man is obsolete," we fear, unless the two can be equalized. A year after the first atomic bomb was dropped John Dewey again reminded us of this need: "There have been more scientific changes in the last fifty years or so than in centuries. But management of human relations still goes by guesswork. It needs to catch up. People ought to use scientific methods in handling human relations." [40]

Some of us may have difficulty in understanding what is meant by applying scientific methods to the problems of human relations. The traditional picture is that of a white-coated specialist in a laboratory, dealing with known chemicals, established formulae, or unchanging laws of nature. What method can he offer for handling ever changing social problems, unpredictable human beings, and variable economic and social conditions? Is it not true, as one atomic scientist put it, that "the scientist's job is to invent bombs, not decide when and if they should be used"? This view does an injustice to the scientist and his method, for he is properly concerned with both discovery and application. Although it is not possible to stabilize and direct human reactions as easily as chain reactions, we may study with profit the method by which atomic behavior is controlled.

Briefly we may describe the method of science as experimentation, a procedure which integrates theory and practice by (a) *inquiry* into the available facts concerning a given problem, followed by the formulation of a (b) *hypothesis*, or theoretical solution, which is used as the basis for (c) *experiment*, or practical application of the theory, from the results of which a (d) *conclusion* is drawn, which may or may not validate the hypothesis.

A detailed analysis of the scientific method would show that in the procedure just outlined most, or all, of the following factors are present:

1. A recognized problem, properly located, defined, and limited.
2. A body of facts concerning the problem derived from observation and investigation.

[40] *Time*, Vol. 47 (June 24, 1946), p. 45.

3. A set of principles or laws, applicable to the problem at hand, which have been established by previous observation or experimentation.
4. A knowledge of the basic laws of logic which may be needed to establish or verify claimed or acknowledged relationships.
5. A hypothesis or predicted solution derived from observation, analysis, and inference.
6. Experimentation in which the hypothesis is applied to the problem to determine its practicability or validity.
7. A conclusion, reached as a result of the experimentation, which states the validity of the original hypothesis or predicted solution, and provides a basis for future action.

If a procedure could be devised, implementing the processes of democracy by an adaptation of the scientific method, we could hope to discard tradition, conjecture, self-interest, and accidental circumstance as bases for solving social problems. The laws we live by might be enacted only after rigorous testing; our human relations could be handled with greater predictability.

In spite, then, of all the records of the past, the great scientific revolution is still to come. It will ensue when men collectively and co-operatively organize their knowledge for application to achieve and make secure social values; when they systematically use scientific procedures for the control of human relationships and the direction of the social effects of our vast technological machinery. Great as have been the social changes of the last century, they are not to be compared with those which will ensue when our faith in scientific method is made manifest in social works.[41]

But how may the elements of the scientific method be adapted into a procedure to implement the democratic process? The answer, we believe, lies in the development of improved methods and greater skills in discussion and debate. For these techniques provide more than a rough approximation of the scientific method; they parallel it. To be sure, when we are concerned with discovering the best national program of social security we cannot test alternative proposals on a handful of citizens in the laboratory before we apply the best method to the nation at large. Yet we may use an experimental approach by testing working principles in action; the result is an experimental production of social change. This has been the case with social security legislation; when first adopted it was definitely experimental, but now it has been expanded by new legislation to

[41] John Dewey, *Philosophy and Civilization*, "Science and Society" (New York, 1931), 329-30. By permission of Minton, Balch & Company, publishers.

include more people and to provide greater benefits. We have, in short, adapted the scientific method to deal legislatively with a social problem.

The adaptation of the scientific method has been made by formalizing the techniques of discussion and debate along a continuum of social inquiry and judgment, using, as we have indicated, five distinct steps: (a) locating and defining the problem, (b) exploring the problem, (c) examining suggested solutions, (d) choosing the best solution, and (e) securing acceptance of the chosen solution. When these steps are taken by groups of citizens thinking together, we are following a psychologically sound procedure: "Man is a *social* animal. He is part of and lives in—for good or bad—a *social* group. ... Since social problems are products of social living, the best approach to the understanding and solving of these problems lies in *social* (group) *consideration* and in *social* (group) *action*." [42]

There will always be, of course, differences between the scientific method and the techniques of discussion and debate. It is well that we recognize them.

1. *On the basis of those who use them we find the first major difference.* The scientific method is usually reserved for those who are experts in their particular fields and skilled in handling the method. The process of discussion and debate, however, may not only take advantage of expert opinion, but it also has the virtue of offering the layman an opportunity to express his opinions and reflect his experiences. He may crystallize his individual conceptions through a coöperative exchange of information and ideas, even though his skill in using the technique may be limited.

2. *According to the fields in which they operate we also find a difference.* Scientific methods of investigation are followed in areas of relatively unchanging phenomena, such as the laws of physics, whereas discussion and debate are used in areas of constantly varying factors. The scientific method is concerned with the static phenomena of nature, whereas discussion and debate are concerned with problems of a dynamic society. Thus a conclusion reached by the method of science is usually characterized by its permanency; a conclusion reached through discussion and debate may be only temporarily applicable. Newton's laws of gravity were premised upon unchangeable phenomena; the political conditions upon which the

[42] Julius Schreiber, ed., *It Pays to Talk It Over* (Washington, National Institute of Social Relations, 1947), p. 7.

United States must base a foreign policy, however, may change every week, in critical periods.

3. *Judged by their end results, another difference is apparent.* Scientific inquiry establishes a *probability* which may be verified by controlled experiment. But discussion and debate are employed in areas of constantly varying factors. The "raw materials" are not constant, precise, or static. Therefore the result of discussion and debate is the establishment of an *opinion.* The point may be illustrated by supposing that a chemist is instructed to create a new plastic compound; he may develop a formula (establish an hypothesis) using various chemicals in combination and establish a high probability that the desired plastic will result. His "raw materials" are sufficiently constant and uniform to warrant prediction. A discussion group attempting to discover a formula for solving racial conflicts in a given community, however, can establish only an opinion that a certain solution (or hypothesis) will work.

4. *The varying degrees of the applicability of their results presents the final difference between the scientific method and the discussion and debate technique.* The scientific method may demonstrate that a particular procedure will function the same way for all people and for all times and places. But a belief or course of action that seems advisable after a debate on its merits may apply only to certain people, times, and places. An experiment performed in London by an English physicist may be reproduced in a Chicago laboratory with identical results; but the bases of a tax policy for London may be quite inappropriate in Chicago.

Despite these differences, however, discussion and debate offer the best method of adapting the scientific method to the processes of democracy. They are the most efficient techniques yet developed to take the guesswork out of social problem-solving.

IV. EVALUATING THE TECHNIQUES OF DISCUSSION AND DEBATE

In this book we are concerned with discussion and debate as tools for use in the democratic process. Before studying specific procedures, however, the reader may ask for the evidence on what we can expect from discussion and debate. It will be found in Chapters 22 and 28, based upon experimental studies. The evidence will show that the participant or listener is apt to find the techniques of discussion and debate useful as effective means of acquiring new information and solving new problems; he is likely to develop improved attitudes and sounder opinions; and he does these things in a coöperative process which is the essence of democracy. As a result both his social and his political behavior should be more intelligent and more effective.

In writing this about discussion and debate we are aware of other ways of acquiring information and forming opinions, but we believe these three factors are distinctive in discussion and debate: (a) the general pattern is apt to be familiar to most people; (b) when conducted with relative informality the method encourages general participation; and (c) when a discussion or debate is carefully planned and conducted by skilled leaders and participants, it gets somewhere, not by propagandizing but by providing evidence and argument upon the basis of which people may reach their own conclusions. Discussion and debate provide the only methods of bringing people face to face for a mutual give and take which tests and challenges their thinking. In the 1949 elections in Western Germany where people voted freely for the first time since 1933, one German said to an American observer: "Under Hitler, the choice was simpler —each ballot had a big *Ja* and small *Nein*." [43] It may be true that dictatorship is easier and simpler, and that democracy is difficult. People in a democracy may make mistakes, and sometimes even repeat the same mistakes, but as long as they have freedom of discussion and debate, and use that freedom, they may correct their errors. The end result is good. "I say discuss all and expose all," sang Walt Whitman. "I am for every topic openly.... There can be no safety for these States ... without free tongues, and ears willing to hear the tongues."

READINGS

CAHN, Joseph, *et al.*, *The Story of a Discussion Program* (New York, New York Adult Education Council, 1946).

COFFEY, Hubert, *et al.*, "Community Service and Social Research—Group Psychotherapy in A Church Program," *Journal of Social Issues*, Vol. VI (July, 1950), pp. 1-65.

COYLE, G. L., *Group Experience and Democratic Values* (New York, Woman's Press, 1947).

CHESTER, Giraud, "Contemporary Senate Debate," *Quarterly Journal of Speech*, Vol. 31 (December, 1945), pp. 407-11.

[43] *Time*, Vol. 55 (August 22, 1949), p. 18.

KAEMPFFERT, Waldemar, "The Atom and the Scientific Mind," New York *Times Magazine* (October 9, 1949), pp. 15+.

LASKER, Bruno, *Democracy Through Discussion* (New York, H. W. Wilson Co., 1949), Chaps. 1, 2, 3.

LIPPMANN, Walter, *Public Opinion* (New York, The Macmillan Co., 1922).

OVERSTREET, H. A., and OVERSTREET, B. W., *Town Meeting Comes to Town* (New York, Harper & Bros., 1939).

SCHREIBER, Julius, ed., *It Pays to Talk It Over* (Washington, National Institute of Social Relations, 1947), pp. 1-7.

STANDEN, Anthony, *Science Is a Sacred Cow*, (New York, E. P. Dutton & Co., 1950), Chap. 1.

UTTERBACK, W. E., *et al.*, "Group Discussion," *Adult Education Bulletin*, Vol. 13 (February, 1949), pp. 67-90.

WECTER, Dixon, "In Defense of Talk," *Saturday Review of Literature*, Vol. 32 (November 5, 1949), pp. 9-11, 36-8.

YEAGER, W. H., and UTTERBACK, W. E., eds., "Communication and Social Action," *Annals of the American Academy of Political and Social Science*, Vol. 250 (March, 1947), pp. 1-11, 32-40, 70-5, 113-20.

EXERCISES

1. Prepare a three-minute talk commenting upon and illustrating the ideas contained in one of the following statements as they relate to this chapter:

   a. "The world is not divided into scientific people and unscientific people, but rather into groups of problems for which our general culture provides us with a scientific or unscientific approach." (Edward S. Robinson, *Law and the Lawyers*, p. 8)

   b. "It is an erroneous impression, fostered by sensational popular biography, that scientific discovery is often made by inspiration—a sort of *coup de foudre*—from on high. This is rarely the case. Even Archimedes' sudden inspiration in the bathtub; Newton's experience in the apple orchard; Descartes' geometrical discoveries in his bed; Darwin's flash of lucidity on reading a passage in Malthus; Kekule's vision of the closed carbon ring which came to him on top of a London bus; and Einstein's brilliant solution of the Michelson puzzle in the patent office in Berne, were not messages out of the blue. They were the final coördinations, by minds of genius, of innumerable accumulated facts and impressions which lesser men could grasp only in their uncorrelated isolation, but which—by them—were seen in entirety and integrated into general principles." (Hans Zinsser, *As I Remember Him*, pp. 331-2)

   c. "The purpose of discussion, then, is to give you and your fellow members of the group an opportunity to find out first of all what you think. After that you have the opportunity to test your thinking—to see whether it is as good as you thought, or perhaps better. "The testing of your thinking comes in allowing persons to examine your ideas, to weigh your reasons and conclusions. You will welcome this testing if you can remember one thing: the other members of the group are not criticizing you but rather your logic. Try to put your ideas out in front of you and to look at them as carefully as you would at someone else's ideas." (*How to Discuss*, Town Hall Advisory Service Publication, p. 5)

d. "If Americans love their liberty, if they hope to make the democratic experiment succeed, if they wish to avoid servitude in the future, it is imperative that the knowledge of the people begin as soon as possible to approximate the knowledge of the leaders; that the people come to know the problems which their leaders are attempting to solve sufficiently well to enable them to distinguish success from failure, to permit them to co-operate with a will rather than to yield blind obedience which must be blind and sullen because it is forced." (William F. Russell, in John W. Studebaker, *Plain Talk*, p. i)

e. "It is always dangerous for a man to have the floor by himself." (Woodrow Wilson, speech to American Federation of Labor convention, Buffalo, N. Y., Nov. 12, 1917)

f. "I tell them [the historians] that everyone writes [or speaks] at some time in space, in some social milieu, from some angle of vision, and according to some scheme of values." (Charles A. Beard, New York *Times*, Sept. 2, 1948)

g. "...I have learned from my many years of experience that it is essential to have all the pertinent facts before venturing an opinion or an argument on a public issue.... I do not believe that representatives in Congress should be only glorified personifications of a Gallup poll. A member of congress must lead and mould public opinion as well as reflect it." (Robert M. LaFollette, Jr., Madison, Wis., *Capital Times*, Aug. 3, 1946)

h. "I hold to the belief that if folks get around a table and talk things through they usually can come to the right and fair answer." Supreme Court Justice Harold H. Burton, New York *Times*, Sept. 22, 1945)

i. "Let us admit the case of the conservative; if we once start thinking, no one can guarantee where we shall come out, except that many objects, ends, and institutions are surely doomed. Every thinker puts some portion of an apparently stable world in peril, and no one can wholly predict what will emerge in its place." (John Dewey, in *Saturday Review of Literature*, Nov. 5, 1949, p. 29)

j. "...It is essential to the effective working of democratic government that the great majority of citizens should be sufficiently easy in their present circumstances and sufficiently secure in their future prospects to afford certain intangible luxuries—the luxury of good will, of tolerance for opinions not shared and of consideration for interests not their own, the luxury of believing in the value of rational discussion and of entertaining the conviction that their common interests can be better served, in the long run, by relying upon the methods of persuasion than by appealing to the methods of force." (Carl L. Becker, *New Liberties for Old*, p. 105)

2. Arrange to visit a series of meetings of a policy-forming discussion group in your community, such as the city council, the library board, the Chamber of Commerce, or the board of education, and write a report of your observations. Was there adequate discussion of each topic? Were all points of view represented? Could you observe any apparent shift of opinion in members during the meeting?

3. Select a current problem on your campus and trace the steps through which it might be developed before action is taken upon it.

4. Organize a series of short speeches by members of the class on the question "What is freedom of speech?" Let each speaker deal with one of these questions:

  a. Do we protect our own freedom to speak when we insist upon that right for those with whom we disagree?
  b. Should the laymen have the same freedom to speak as the expert?
  c. Is critical analysis of accepted ideas compatible with the maintenance of democracy?
  d. Does the scientific method conflict with the principle of majority rule?
  e. Is there a limit beyond which citizens in a democracy should not enjoy freedom of speech?

5. Listen to or read a printed transcript of a public discussion or debate from the list in the Appendix. Evaluate it from the standpoint of its adherence to the principles of the scientific method.

6. Make a short case study of a public issue, its basis, how it came to public notice, the way in which it was discussed and debated, and the action taken, if any. A hospital bond issue, a city ordinance, a problem considered by the student council, or by the faculty, might be appropriate.

CHAPTER 3

How Individuals Think

IN THE LAST CHAPTER we looked at discussion and debate as essential tools in a democracy. Now we take a look at ourselves: how do we think? What, for instance, do we do when confronted with two seemingly irreconcilable points of view, either of which a rational person might accept as valid? We say that we "make up our minds," but that is an unsatisfactory generalization. *How* are our minds made up? How do we form opinions, solve problems, or make decisions? Historically in democracies, it has been assumed that men do these things rationally. As Carl Becker has phrased the eighteenth-century doctrine of liberal democracy, it runs like this: [1]

Major premise: The sole method of arriving at truth is by the application of human reason to the problems presented by the universe and the life of men in it.

Minor premise: Men are rational creatures who can easily grasp and will gladly accept the truth once it is disclosed to them.

Conclusion: By allowing men freedom of speech and press, relevant knowledge will be made accessible, untrammeled discussion will reconcile divergent interests and opinions, and laws acceptable to all will be enacted.

We now believe that the minor premise of that argument is false: men may *want* to be rational creatures; may, indeed, *think* they are; but there is nothing which automatically compels men to act rationally. We do not say that man cannot be rational; we simply note "the danger, for all human activities, but especially for the working of democracy, of the intellectualist assumption that every human action is the result of an intellectual process, by which a man first thinks

[1] Carl Becker, *Everyman His Own Historian* (New York, Appleton-Century-Crofts, Inc., 1935), p. 102.

of some end which he desires and then calculates the means by which that end can be attained." [2]

This is a severe, but not an extreme, view. It does not deny that man is a rational animal but, as Harry Overstreet observes, it is only man's fulfillment of his maximum potentialities that calls for the exercise of his reason: "Reason ... is a *capacity* in man, not necessarily an achievement. In most men it lies largely dormant while something else, which is far from reason, takes over." [3]

To see what that "something else" is, we need to consider how man reacts to situations which confront him, from the moment he stops the irritating ring of the morning alarm clock to the time he turns out the light at night. When we say that we react to situations we mean that as we face problems, familiar or unique, we feel a lack of adjustment and are impelled to action which will restore our sense of adjustment. We act because we want to feel that "all's right with the world."

It is traditional to speak of these reactions as being emotional or intellectual. In fact, of course, our behavior patterns contain something of both; there is probably no such thing as a completely emotional or a purely intellectual state. There are large emotional components, for example, in most of our behavior; the motivation for *wanting* to adjust ourselves to a situation or meet a problem is emotional, though the adjustment itself may come through intellectual processes. Our discussion will be easier to follow, however, if we differentiate emotional and intellectual behavior.

I. EMOTIONAL BEHAVIOR

At birth, humans are endowed with the capacity for certain unlearned reactions, sometimes called primary emotions. This original, native emotional response is the most primitive form of human reaction. Psychologists do not agree on how many types of emotional response may be identified: "such emotions as anger, fear, pity or disgust do not exist in unique independence, but ... the phenomena we find are such things as fighting reactions or fearfulness, the experience of pitying or the withdrawal from obnoxious objects.

[2] Graham Wallas, *Human Nature in Politics* (New York, Appleton-Century-Crofts, Inc., 1921), p. 5.

[3] H. A. Overstreet, *The Mature Mind* (New York, W. W. Norton & Co., Inc., 1949), pp. 104-5.

Neither emotion nor emotions exist as discrete entities." [4] Thus we speak here not of separate emotions but of a single, basic and diffused pattern of response. Emotional behavior, prompted as well as modified by our environment, has these characteristics:

a. It is often disorganized and unspecialized, reflecting a lack of discrimination in perception as well as in reflection. Thus the same stimulus may at different times draw different responses, since emotional behavior lacks the specialized use of muscles and highly localized tensions of intellectual behavior. Again, however, some emotional behavior may appear to be calculated and economical.

b. It is often excessive behavior, involving more activity than is essential for a response to the stimulus calling it forth. At other times emotion may actually inhibit excessive action, or even make momentarily impossible any overt action at all.

c. It is usually accompanied by an aroused physiological and psychological state, resulting in total, all-in-one-piece response. This condition is characterized by pronounced glandular and muscular activity, a sensory awareness of these bodily changes, and a motor set rendering the individual capable of reacting.

d. It is subject to only limited control, usually on a subcortical level, probably centering in the thalamus.

In sum, emotional reactions tend to be impulsive, extreme, intense, excessive, and disorganized.

Even so, they may serve a good purpose by furnishing the dynamic for problem-solving. How does this happen? We must explain, first, by observing that a state of affairs which satisfies or annoys an individual does so not solely because it brings him pleasure or pain, happiness or irritation, joy or depression, but because it either satisfies or thwarts particular desires or wants. These desires or wants give an emotional impulse toward behavior which will help us adjust ourselves to the situations and problems which confront us. There are many classifications of these drives, wants, or desires, which impel us to action. Here is the list suggested by Eisenson:

a. Human beings direct their activities to the satisfaction of physical wants and general physical well-being.

b. Human beings normally behave in ways that will lead them toward success, mastery, or achievement.

c. Human beings tend to behave in ways that will help them to gain recognition, admiration, respect, or approval.

[4] Carney Landis, in E. G. Boring, H. S. Langfeld, and H. P. Weld, *Psychology* (New York, John Wiley & Sons, Inc., 1935), p. 397.

d. Human beings generally act in ways that will lead toward their being loved, and the realization of a feeling of being wanted.

e. Human beings usually act in ways that will bring about peace of mind, security, and a feeling of release from worry and anxiety.

f. Human beings indicate by their behavior that they seek some adventure, new experience, and zestful living.[5]

Some of these wants may be unlearned, but the interests or attitudes which they generate can be, and usually are, learned: they are derived from a mixture of training, tradition, imitation, experience, and general cultural patterns. The net result is that "the amount of organized human behavior that is not determined by an individual's wants, interests, and purposes is so small as to merit attention only because of its rarity."[6]

We cannot measure with precision the importance of these drives in determining our behavior, but psychologists are generally agreed that they provide the dynamic emotional impulse behind what we do. Studies by Malinowski and others demonstrate the extent to which our desires affect what we perceive. As G. T. W. Parker has put it, "We see things not as they are but as we are." In its simplest terms this means that we tend unconsciously to follow this pattern: "If I accept this proposition, I will satisfy my desires and, therefore, I will accept this proposition." We do not assert that individuals consciously and deliberately "reason" in this way; the pervasive influence of our basic drives is seldom discerned by the individual. One's emotional motivations are not open to discrete labeling, for they are inextricably interwoven with experience and integrated with the specific situation.

In many cases, of course, emotional behavior provides action adequate to meet specific problem situations. No deliberate intellectual behavior is called for. In those instances where our emotional behavior patterns are inadequate to solve a problem we have never before encountered, we must go further and try to make an intellectual adjustment to the problem. The limitations of emotion must be compensated for by intellect. Thus even a scientist conducting rigorously controlled experiments in his laboratory may work with zeal and enthusiasm provided by his emotional drives. His task may be

[5] Jon Eisenson, *The Psychology of Speech* (New York, Appleton-Century-Crofts, Inc., 1938), pp. 249-51.

[6] *Ibid.*, p. 248.

an intellectual one, but he undertakes it in an effort to satisfy his emotional desires. This illustrates what is meant when we say "the intellect is a tiny speck afloat on the vast sea of emotion." Purposeful problem-solving, which may take the form of intellectual behavior, is buoyed up by motivations stemming from our emotional natures.

II. INTELLECTUAL BEHAVIOR

In the development of the individual, as in the history of the race, emotional behavior precedes intellectual; and, as we have said, some emotional elements always remain in what is called intellectual. In some individuals the development of intellectual behavior is arrested; as Harry Overstreet makes clear in *The Mature Mind*, such people remain psychologically immature, failing to make satisfactory adjustments to those problems for which emotional behavior is not adequate. They "never grow up."

Many situations in the life of any person may be met by response patterns that are fundamentally emotional. This appears to be particularly true of reactions which have to do with such vital processes as acquiring food or avoiding danger, and with some types of struggle and conflict. Such behavior is quite proper; we tend to move on to intellectual behavior only when our emotions are incapable of developing satisfactory adjustments to the situations we encounter. Indeed, if we were compelled to intellectualize all of our behavior we should accomplish far less each day than most of us are now able to do.

When we speak of intellectual behavior we refer to what is also called thinking. This is the process by which man reflects, incorporating and integrating his habits, experiences, beliefs, and attitudes into an organized whole. When he encounters an indeterminate situation he seeks to transform it into a determinate one. In this process he may analyze the elements in the situation, call upon his accumulated stock of knowledge and belief to provide ways of meeting the problem, speculate about the probable results of each alternative, and finally make a choice. Man undertakes these intellectual processes with varying degrees of rationality. But, generally, man wants to be rational. Indeed, the story of a man's education, maturation, and development might be written in terms of his efforts to develop increasingly intellectual patterns of behavior.

III. HABITUAL BEHAVIOR

When an individual has made a satisfactory adjustment to a situation through an emotional or an intellectual response, or a combination of them, and has repeated the response many times in similar situations, he tends to develop a pattern of habitual behavior. The habitual response is thus acquired, organized, and patterned. Many of our daily acts are "from force of habit," and it is well, for we can thus do routine things without expending emotional or intellectual energy. Habits have been described as being the residues of emotional and intellectual reactions; as they become more set, less of their original emotional or intellectual character is apparent.

Because our habits are in part the result of our culture, they vary from person to person, and we may sometimes label the habits of others as "good" or "bad," depending upon how well they conform to our own habit-responses. For the individual, however, well-established habitual behavior results in satisfying adjustments to familiar situations. Our basic desires, wants, and interests may be served as well by habitual as by emotional or intellectual behavior.

Since our major concern in this book is with the improvement of techniques for problem-solving in discussion and debate, we must explore further what happens when individuals engage in intellectual behavior. We have already suggested that not all intellectual responses are of the same kind or calibre; for our purposes we may use a simple classification: *non-logical thinking* and *logical thinking*. Logical, or reflective, thought we define as "active, persistent and careful consideration of any belief or supposed form of knowledge in the light of the grounds that support it and the further conclusions to which it tends." [7] Thinking which departs from that standard we define as non-logical.

IV. NON-LOGICAL THINKING

It is impossible to set up discrete categories of ways in which individuals think, but it is possible to describe certain common tendencies. Here we are concerned with those tendencies in our behavior which may be called aspects of non-logical thinking.

[7] John Dewey, *How We Think* (New York, D. C. Heath & Co., 1933), p. 9.

A. We Tend to Think in Random Fashion

Traditionally this type of thinking has been represented by day-dreaming, when our thoughts wander idly from topic to topic without any definite pattern, and when only by happy chance we come upon an idea which may solve a problem. Even then the seemingly good idea may dissolve under the sobering attempt to put it into words.

Foreign to the concept of random thinking is any notion of deliberate exploration of a problem, or conscious weighing of pertinent evidence. It is only by habit that we keep a problem "on our minds" as we go about our daily business; from time to time we may recall it, concentrate upon it momentarily, and then pass on to something else. Sometimes, during our mental meanderings, even when thinking of something else, we have a flash of insight, an "inspiration," and stumble upon a solution for our problem. Such, we are told, was the experience of Archimedes who "happened onto" the principle of specific gravity as he lay in his bath, and then dashed naked through the streets of Syracuse shouting "Eureka!" We may characterize our tendency toward random thinking as haphazard intellectual activity, lacking both pattern and persistence.

B. We Tend to Rationalize

This mode of non-logical thinking may be defined as the process of alleging rational motives and arguments to justify our non-rational, or non-logical, beliefs and desires. We attempt to rationalize or "make rational" that which is non-rational. To take a familiar example, consider John Student: he has fifty pages of reading in history to do for tomorrow's class, a speech to deliver the following day, and a term paper due next week. He is settling down for an evening of study when he recalls that a movie he wants to see is playing at the local theatre. Now the process of rationalization begins. As William Jennings Bryan once observed, "it is a poor mind that can't fix up good reasons for doing what it wants to do!" John Student tells himself that he has been studying too hard this semester, he needs the relaxation offered by the movie; his eyes are tired from reading, watching a movie would rest them; he can do some studying after he comes home from the movie; perhaps the instructor won't give a quiz in history tomorrow, and so on, until John finds himself comfortably seated in the Apollo Theatre.

In John's case we have described rationalization *before* the act; it can come as easily *after* the act. If Johnson loses his job, he may rationalize that the boss was prejudiced against Swedes; if a candidate is defeated for office he may reflect that he was just running for the experience, anyway; if a student fails to make an "A" in a course he feels that at least he has proved that he isn't a "grind." Those of us who are as honest as Benjamin Franklin must recognize frequent cases of rationalization in our own behavior. On a sea voyage, Franklin related, in his autobiography, his ship was becalmed; in order to eat, the sailors caught some cod. For a time Franklin's philosophical vegetarianism made him resolute in the face of this "unprovoked murder."

But I had formerly been a great lover of fish, and, when this came hot out of the frying-pan, it smelt admirably well. I balanced some time between principle and inclination, till I recollected that, when the fish were opened, I saw smaller fish taken out of their stomachs; then thought I: "If you eat one another, I don't see why we mayn't eat you." So I dined upon cod very heartily, and continued to eat with other people, returning only now and then to a vegetable diet. So convenient a thing it is to be a reasonable creature, since it enables one to find or make a reason for everything one has a mind to do.

As James Harvey Robinson has pointed out, thousands of volumes have been written "to find or make a reason," no matter how stately their arguments may appear. Dewey, the philosopher, Veblen, the economist, and Pareto, the sociologist, all contended that many of the conclusions reached in their respective fields are rationalizations, founded on traditional beliefs and customs.[8] These men would not contend, however, that rationalization is always bad. As Hollingworth has observed, it is a distinct advance in the civilization of the human race to *want* to be rational. Primitive man, says Brigance, was content to rely chiefly upon *authority* and *experience* as bases for his behavior, while only more alert and intellectually aggressive individuals use *reason* as a behavior determinant.[9] In short, while we prefer the use of reason to rationalization, we must also recognize that rationalization sometimes appears as the only method of resolving emotional and intellectual conflicts. This is apparent in an examination of the reasons why we tend to rationalize.

[8] James Harvey Robinson, *The Mind in the Making* (New York, Harper & Bros., 1921), p. 45.
[9] W. Norwood Brigance, "A Genetic Approach to Persuasion," *Quarterly Journal of Speech*, Vol. 17 (June, 1931), pp. 329-39.

1. In the first place, there is a commendable human desire to "be rational." Indeed, we may become quite emotional if we are accused of not being rational! Rationalization, then, often occurs subconsciously in an effort to maintain our own self-esteem.

2. There is considerable social pressure upon us to justify our actions on rational grounds. In reacting to this pressure we may often rationalize largely as a defense. As Hollingworth points out, "we would, it seems, prefer them [our neighbors] to think that we ourselves believe on the grounds of logical arguments. Social education, indeed, has taught us that there is something childish about an attitude that lacks cogent support." [10]

3. Often, as in the case of John Student, we may rationalize as a technique of self-persuasion. In this sense, White says, "rationalization consists in attempting to maintain self-respect in the midst of discrediting circumstances," and we rationalize in one of these ways: [11]

    a. by making our irrational behavior appear rational
    b. by justifying our improper behavior
    c. by excusing ourselves for our failure
        (1) by declaring the unattainable to be undesirable
        (2) by declaring our present status to be satisfactory
        (3) by attributing our failure to some other person, thing or circumstance

4. Finally, we may use rationalization as a "short circuit" appeal in persuading others to accept conclusions we have reached on a rational basis. This is not a mere combination of logical and emotional (rationalized) motives, but an organization of them in a deliberate pattern "in which the very motives that are emotionally aroused are given explicit foundation through inductive inferences and deductive conclusions." [12] The purpose, of course, is to present via the "short circuit" approach what cannot, for reasons of time, perhaps, be presented in detail. And the persuader may feel himself ethically justified in using a non-rational technique to gain acceptance of a conclusion which he himself has reached on a rational basis. Further explanation of our views on the ethics of persuasion will be found in Chapter 14.

[10] H. L. Hollingworth, *The Psychology of the Audience* (New York, American Book Co., 1935), p. 112.
[11] Wendell White, *The Psychology of Dealing with People* (New York, 1936), p. 183. By permission of The Macmillan Company, publishers.
[12] Hollingworth, *op. cit.*, p. 113.

C. We Tend to Confuse Desire and Conviction

This tendency is closely allied with the one just discussed: we tend to believe what we wish to believe. The pattern is simple: "We like to do right; we do what we like; what we do must be right." William James, in his pragmatic essay on "The Will to Believe," partially justifies this tendency on purely philosophical grounds; our point, however, is that it is a form of non-logical thinking: we tend to accept or reject a proposition not on the basis of relevant evidence, but upon its desirability. If we can satisfy a basic desire by believing that the federal government should help finance our local schools, for example, our desire and our belief may easily become identified.

In this connection we refer to belief not as a judgment made after the collection, observation, and evaluation of the evidence, but as a prejudgment, without benefit of evidence, stemming from instruction, tradition, or imitation. We tend to make these prejudgments because they seem desirable: they are to our own advantage, support other already accepted beliefs, or justify an already determined course of action. This description of belief is not written entirely in condemnation. We recognize that no one can, even in a lifetime, demonstrate for himself the validity of all of the beliefs, assumptions, and truths which he uses in his daily living. It is necessary, if not reasonable, that we take a great many things on faith, and accept more conclusions than we ourselves can demonstrate. Our complaint, if we have one, concerns the degree to which this tendency to adopt beliefs only because they are satisfying interferes with logical thinking about matters of vital concern.

Other studies support the findings of Lund, who examined the ratings of several hundred individuals on propositions where they scored both "belief strength" and "desirability." He found a high correlation between the two factors.[13] As Hollingworth observes, "The most reasonable interpretation [of these studies] is that our beliefs are not dependent upon the available evidence alone, but are definitely warped, even against the evidence, by our desires. In fact, more than half of the determination of our belief in a proposition seems to flow from our desires with respect to its correctness."[14]

[13] F. H. Lund, "The Psychology of Belief," *Journal of Abnormal Psychology*, Vol. 20 (April, 1925), pp. 194-5.
[14] Hollingworth, *op. cit.*, pp. 116-7.

D. We Tend to Be Suggestible

The professor smiles at his class as he says, *"If* we should have a quiz next time, it would surely cover the material in my lecture today." Do his students take more careful notes than usual? Or a political candidate declares that "A vote for Blank is a vote against boss rule!" Do his hearers take the hint? In each of these instances the speaker is employing suggestion, a process in which a social stimulus elicits an uncritical and more or less automatic response. Unless the suggestion encounters a contradictory idea or attitude (i.e., "I don't care about passing the quiz," or "Why worry about boss rule?") it is likely to be accepted; we incorporate it into the body of belief which supports our attitudes and judgments. This process operates constantly; we are familiar with the implications of "guilt by association" charges, where suggestion is often substituted for evidence.

Whenever we are tempted to accept uncritically what we hear we should recall the famous Mr. Dooley's sage observation: "I'll belave anything, if ye only tell it to me often enough." And Bronson Alcott warns us of the dangers of suggestion in print: "Ideas, when vended in a book, carry with them a kind of dignity and certainty which awe many into implicit belief.... Reason, thus hushed into slumber, sleeps in secure repose. To dare to think, to think for oneself, is denominated pride and arrogance. And millions of human minds are in this state of slavery and tyranny." [15]

There are two general explanations for this tendency to accept unvalidated and uninvestigated assertion. First, we seem to prefer to remain in a passive rather than to adopt an active state. Acceptance is the norm, requiring little sense of discrimination or mental activity. Doubt, on the other hand, is often hard work; it requires active questioning and continuing analysis. As Clarke's young woman put it, "I am satisfied with what I have been taught to believe. It is easy for me to believe it. Why should I trouble myself to study out this matter?" [16] In the second place, this susceptibility to suggestion exists in most of us because the weight of authority and experience are initial determinants of belief. Genetically, we might suggest that

[15] Odell Shepard, ed., *The Journals of Bronson Alcott* (Boston, Little, Brown & Co., 1938), pp. 6-7.

[16] Edwin Leavitt Clarke, *The Art of Straight Thinking* (New York, Appleton-Century-Crofts, Inc., 1929), p. 45.

doubt develops in the individual and in the race only as reason comes
to play a larger part in determining beliefs; what Alexander Bain
has called "acquired skepticism" demands an active, not a passive
state of mind.

In a later chapter we consider the use of suggestion in persuasion.
Here we present a series of generalizations about the nature of
suggestion:

1. Suggestion operates most effectively when it is directed toward
   an existent response-pattern.
2. Suggestion operates most effectively when it encounters a receptive attitude; there must be no other suggestions that set
   off stronger or better established response patterns.
3. Suggestion is increased when there is a lack of adequate knowledge concerning the subject at hand.
4. Suggestion is increased when it is related to desire—a fundamental want, drive, or belief.
5. Suggestion is increased by the prestige of the person making it.
6. Suggestion is increased by excitement which is usually accompanied by a relaxation of reason.
7. Suggestion is usually increased by group situations.

We like to think that we are doing our own thinking, and if suggestion is too obvious we may be suspicious of it. The chief danger
to logical thinking, then, comes when the individual who uses suggestion in lieu of sound reasoning is so skillful that we do not recognize it for what it is.

E. We Tend to Succumb to Personal Appeals

Long ago William James observed that "the deepest principle of
human nature is the desire to be appreciated." [17] It is this fact that
guides those who rely upon personal appeals, or implied flattery of
the reader or listener, instead of logic. In books, interviews, group
discussions, or public speeches, the individual who inflates our ego
may blind us to his fallacies.

Overstreet has described this as the "Putting-It-Up-To-You-
Technique. . . . Here is something aimed directly at *you*. *You* are
asked a question. *You* are expected to reply." [18] We remember that

[17] Henry James, ed., *Letters of William James* (Boston, Atlantic Monthly
Press, 1920), Vol. II, pp. 33-4.
[18] H. A. Overstreet, *Influencing Human Behavior* (New York, W. W. Norton
& Co., Inc., 1925), pp. 18-21.

we are reasonable men when the speaker asks "Would any reasonable man support a plan that is pure socialism?" The ad-writer uses the same appeal: "The Thinking Fellow Calls a Yellow." And Shakespeare has Brutus ask his audience, "Who is here so rude that would not be a Roman? If any, speak; for him have I offended. Who is here so vile that will not love his country? If any, speak; for him have I offended. I pause for a reply." There was no overt reply to this combination of suggestion and personal appeal.

Those who use what propagandists call the "together" device, who assure us that they have only our best interests at heart, may be right. The speaker who binds himself to his audience by such phrases as "*we* must all join this crusade," or "*our* children will bear the burden," may be an honest man. The use of the personal appeal is not bad, per se; what is bad is its substitution for logical thought.

F. We Tend to Accept Specious Arguments

We tend to accept arguments which are in themselves inconsistent and illogical, or arguments which are not supported by adequate evidence. This is particularly true, of course, when those arguments happen to support our views, satisfy our needs or desires, or make it easier to believe in things as they are. In the seventeenth century, for example, Galileo's announcement of the discovery of a new planet was attacked by many of his contemporaries. Francesco Sizzi, of Florence, argued this way: "... the satellites are invisible to the naked eye ... and therefore do not exist." Reduced to a syllogism the fallacy is at once apparent:

> What is not visible to the naked eye does not exist.
> Galileo's planet is not visible to the naked eye.
> Therefore, Galileo's planet does not exist.

Though we now recognize Sizzi's argument as specious, it was accepted by many people in his day since it fitted into the scheme of things as they were, whereas Galileo's contention disrupted the status quo.

We need not turn back to the seventeenth century to prove our point; an analysis of most everyday discussions will yield examples of specious argument. In later chapters dealing with the proper use of evidence and argument we will find many such contemporary examples.

Sometimes we accept specious argument because it enables us to

rationalize our non-rational beliefs or attitudes. When a Sizzi claims
to possess all knowledge, the easiest way for him to treat a new fact
is to deny its validity. "You can't tell me anything good about government regulation," says a friend, and thereby keeps the circle
closed, and his own beliefs intact. Or another friend seizes upon a
single instance, no matter how atypical, of business irregularity, to
fortify his predisposition for government controls. Again, we may
accept specious argument because it strengthens an already present
link between desire and conviction. The man who wants to believe
in world government is not likely to be critical of any argument
which helps satisfy that desire.

The Federal Trade Commission may prevent the false advertising
of a "cure-all" drug, but only logical thinking can prevent us from
accepting the alleged panacea of the political demagogue.

G. We Tend to Ignore Intellectual Appeals

If the desire to be rational, which exists with most of us, were
strong enough, we might never ignore intellectual appeals. As man
is, however, his tendency toward non-logical thinking usually takes
precedence; the inevitable result is that he often ignores logical arguments, especially if they encounter his rationalizations or desires. If
he is suggestible, or susceptible to personal appeals, then so much the
poorer chance for reason to prevail.

Even in discussions we often incline to retain our basic orientations and assumptions, refusing to permit analysis of our thinking
even though we may accept additions to it. Thus while an exchange
of ideas may always take place, there is often no real interaction of
ideas.

Woodrow Wilson once observed that "Life is essentially illogical
. . . and we should pray God that the good passions outvote the bad
passions." This may be putting the case rather strongly. But if we
will observe the domination of non-logical thinking in our own
thought processes and in those of our associates we will see the
inhibitions and restrictions which it places upon the process of logical
thinking. And we may conclude with John Dewey that "The essential need . . . is the improvement of the methods and conditions of
debate, discussion and persuasion. That is the problem of the public." [19] The basis of such improvement lies not only in breaking the

[19] John Dewey, *The Public and Its Problems* (New York, Henry Holt &
Co., Inc., 1927), p. 208.

domination of non-logical thinking, but in understanding and applying the techniques of logical thought.

V. LOGICAL THINKING

We are now ready to examine the capstone level of intellectual activity, logical thinking. Since the process of logical or reflective thinking is a major concern of this book, we offer here only a preliminary statement. Reflective thought is "active, persistent and careful consideration of any belief or supposed form of knowledge in the light of the grounds that support it and the further conclusions to which it tends." And the function of reflective thought is "to transform a situation in which there is experienced obscurity, doubt, conflict, disturbance of some sort, into a situation that is clear, coherent, settled, harmonious." [20] Thus we are concerned with the thought process which ordinarily takes place when we are aware of a difficulty, or face a problem, and attempt to work out a satisfactory practical solution. We are not concerned with non-logical processes, but with deliberate and purposeful problem-solving.

Occasionally we may ask a friend what he thinks about a particular problem; he replies that he does not have to think about it, he knows. Much of what commonly passes for thinking is of that order: instead of reflecting we simply pluck out a conclusion from our mental stockpile of ideologies, stereotypes, biases, desires, inhibitions, and notions. Yet the truth is seldom so easily arrived at; as Oscar Wilde has Algernon say in *The Importance of Being Earnest*, "The truth is rarely pure and never simple. Modern life would be very tedious if it were either...."

Man's ability to think out the truth, to find a solution for his problems, instead of having to work them out on a trial-and-error basis, is precious, but it can also be tedious. This fact may be quite as important as our tendencies toward rationalization and other forms of non-logical thinking in explaining our avoidance of reflective thinking. Yet if we are to solve the problems which confront us in our increasingly complex society we must be willing to tackle those problems on a mature reflective basis. We must, in short, take time to think.

[20] Dewey, *op cit.*, pp. 9, 99.

A. Five Phases of Logical Thinking

The first step in establishing a methodology for problem-solving is to analyze the process of logical thought. To do this we shall turn, as many writers before us have turned, to John Dewey. In the complete act of logical or reflective thought, he says, we may ordinarily perceive five fairly distinct phases.[21]

1. The *first* step in logical thinking is to be aware of the existence of a problem. This would seem to be fairly obvious advice, until one observes that many discussions and debates begin at this very point: Susan's mother worries about her daughter's tomboyishness, but her husband says, "There's no real problem there, dear; Susan will grow out of it." Or Senator X urges Congress to enact legislation providing federal aid to local schools, while Senator Y argues that the states can handle the matter, it's not a problem for the federal government. When there is agreement concerning the existence of a problem the most "natural" thing to do is to think of a solution, to take action. If the problem is *exactly* like one previously encountered and successfully resolved, there may be some basis for acting immediately and along familiar lines. When the problem is new, however, several possible courses of action may suggest themselves; then action must be arrested temporarily while further inquiry is made. "Some inhibition of *direct* action is necessary to the condition of hesitation and delay that is essential to thinking. Thought is, as it were, conduct turned in upon itself and examining its purposes and its conditions, its resources, aids, and difficulties and obstacles."[22] Leaping, that is, should come only after looking.

2. The *second* step in logical thought is the location and definition of the problem. "I don't know just what it is, but *something's* wrong..." is a common opening remark. Until that "something" is defined and described, with proper limits established, solution-seeking is interrupted. A good deal of discussion may be necessary before a group can agree upon the precise problem it wants to discuss. The outcome, in a parliamentary situation, is usually a bill opening with the words "An act to..." and then proceeding to a careful and precise definition of its scope. For an individual, or for a group, this step is often referred to by psychologists as "goal-

[21] John Dewey, *How We Think* (Boston, D. C. Heath & Co., 1910), pp. 68-78.
[22] *Ibid.*, p. 108.

setting." This label is a happy one, emphasizing the need for a clear vision of the target before taking aim.

3. The *third* step in logical thinking is the suggestion of possible solutions for the problem. These may be multiple, some readily seen at first examination, and others becoming apparent only after careful investigation. The key to logical thinking is being sure that all possible solutions are considered before making an intelligent choice among them. The rat in the laboratory maze would naturally be expected to try first one path and then another in a trial-and-error process of selection. It is within the range of human capacity, however, to consider the alternatives rationally, utilizing past experience as well as present inquiry, and avoiding the common impulse-frustration-new impulse pattern of simple trial-and-error. Thinking man can, moreover, illuminate his search at this point by prediction, forecasting possible courses of action and anticipating their probable consequences.

4. The *fourth* step is a natural consequence of the last: the rational elaboration of the solutions which have been suggested. It means gathering relevant evidence and argument, examining the problem at first-hand, or calling upon those who have special knowledge. It requires synthesis as well as analysis, an incorporation of all data and separate elements of the problem into a unified whole. The result should be a comprehensive and well-ordered file of information: this is the raw material for reasoning. It makes possible the selection of the most likely hypothesis or problem solution.

5. The *fifth* step in logical thinking is experimentation or testing which will lead to verification or rejection of the solution selected in the preceding phases. This may be done, first, by direct observation of the application of the hypothetical solution to the problem. It may also be done by deliberately arranging conditions "in accord with the requirements of an idea or hypothesis to see whether the results theoretically indicated by the idea actually occur." By either method the proposed solution may be verified or disproved. Even should the hypothesis fail to pass the test, the procedure followed will have been of value: every failure should be instructive and lead to greater efficiency in formulating a new hypothesis or evolving a new solution.

In the area of social problems, of course, the final testing must wait upon the enactment of the solution into a law, or its voluntary acceptance as a guide to conduct. For many of our personal problems as well as social ones, this is an important difference from the testing done in a controlled laboratory experiment. It is difficult to imagine trying out a new federal income tax law for a month, though we might adopt a personal budget on such a trial basis. Thus it is important that we emphasize the value of a final rechecking of the evidence and reasoning which led us to a particular solution, a rigorous examination of our procedures, and a final evaluation of the solution, as a substitute for a direct-action test.

From our discussion of the process of logical thought it may appear that the five phases are discrete and necessarily sequential. This would be a false assumption. Grappling with a problem begins with a confused, incoherent, or conflict situation; it ends with a clear, coherent, and unified one. What happens in between we have categorized for convenience under five separate headings, but these steps in the process may be interrelated, overlapped, or interchanged. How many of them are distinguishable and in what order they appear in any particular problem-solving process depends upon the peculiarities of that problem. Sometimes we must begin at the beginning; at others we come upon a carefully located and defined problem, or even one for which several solutions have already been tested. It is important, therefore, that the reader regard this not as a fixed pattern, but as an *approach* to ideal logical thinking. It indicates both a method and a goal.

In this discussion we have adhered rather closely to John Dewey's analysis of the thought process. The reader may wish to examine other writers on this matter, such as Helmholtz, the great German physicist, Poincaré, the French mathematician, or Graham Wallas, the noted English political psychologist.[23].

B. Logical Thinking in Discussion and Debate

The story is sometimes told of a man whose reputation for intelligence was not too high among his neighbors, who determined to run for selectman in a New England village. In a campaign speech he said: "I hear you don't believe I know enough to hold office. I wish you to understand that I am thinking about something or other most of the time." Most of us do a great deal of thinking "about

[23] See H. V. Helmholtz, *Vortrage und Reden* (Braunschweig, Germany, F. Vieweg, 1884), Vol. I, pp. 3-21; H. Poincaré, *Science et Methode* (London, T. Nelson & Sons, tr. by Francis Maitland, 1914); and Graham Wallas, *The Art of Thought* (New York, Harcourt, Brace & Co., 1926), pp. 79-107.

something or other," and in various ways. Our purpose, in the succeeding chapters, is to disengage logical thinking from non-logical processes and to study it as a method for problem-solving by groups in democratic discussion and debate. To do this we have established the following pattern:

1. locating and defining the problem (Chapter 4)
2. exploring the problem (Chapters 5-9)
3. examining suggested solutions (Chapter 10)
4. choosing the best solution (Chapter 11)
5. securing acceptance of the chosen solution (Chapter 14)

The last step, that of securing acceptance by others of the chosen solution, is included here because we believe that thinking is primarily for the sake of action. As Susan Stebbing has said, to think effectively is to think to some purpose. That purpose is, and ought to be, action, which may include persuading others to think the same way. It is true that there are those who like to think they can see both sides of any question, who enjoy an argument for its own sake. It was for them that someone quipped, "Of course there are two sides to every question, if we really are not interested in either of them."

We hope the reader of this treatment of logical thinking will have an open mind, one that will stay open until all the evidence is in. But we also believe that the purpose of discussion and debate is to solve problems, that when we have reached a solution we should act upon it. George Bernard Shaw, in his preface to *Androcles and the Lion*, phrases this well:

The open mind never acts: when we have done our utmost to arrive at a reasonable conclusion, we still, when we can reason and investigate no more, must close our minds for the moment with a snap, and act dogmatically on our conclusions. The man who waits to make an entirely reasonable will dies intestate.

We should, indeed, do our utmost to arrive at a reasonable conclusion for any problem before we act. In that undertaking the process of logical thinking is indispensable.

READINGS

BLACK, Max, *Critical Thinking* (New York, Prentice-Hall, Inc., 1946), Chap. 14.

Columbia Associates in Philosophy, *Introduction to Reflective Thinking* (Boston, Houghton Mifflin Co., 1923), Chap. 1.

DEWEY, John, *How We Think* (Boston, D. C. Heath & Co., 1910), pp. 68-78; (rev. ed., 1933), pp. 102-18.

DOOB, L. W., *Public Opinion and Propaganda* (New York, Henry Holt & Co., Inc., 1948), Chap. 2.

FOLLETT, Mary, *Creative Experience* (New York, Longmans, Green & Co., 1924), pp. 53-77.

LASKER, Bruno, *Democracy Through Discussion* (New York, H. W. Wilson Co., 1949), Chaps. 10-11.

LEIGH, R. D., *Group Leadership* (New York, W. W. Norton & Co., 1936), Chap. 2.

McBURNEY, J. H., and HANCE, K. G., *Discussion in Human Affairs* (New York, Harper & Bros., 1950), Chaps. 3-4.

OVERSTREET, H. A., *The Mature Mind* (New York, W. W. Norton & Co., Inc., 1949), Chaps. 5-9.

THOULESS, R. H., *How to Think Straight* (New York, Simon & Schuster, Inc., 1941) Chaps. 2, 11.

EXERCISES

1. Arrange a discussion program on the question "How do we think?" Let each student prepare a three-minute speech commenting upon and illustrating the ideas contained in one of the following statements. Follow the speeches with an informal discussion, under the leadership of a member of the class, upon the information thus presented.

   a. "The discreet and effective showing up of revered prejudices, including the sacred dogmas of all the frantic simplifiers of human riddles, should be at least one of the main precautions to be taken in our efforts to make a good man out of a college boy." (James Harvey Robinson, *The Human Comedy*, p. 334)

   b. "From the point of view of social welfare, the rationalization appeal is easily capable of abuse, just as is the purely emotional appeal. But it also has its ethically and socially justifiable occasions. These are under circumstances in which the emotional appeal is required in order to arouse initial interest and adequate appreciation of the importance of the topic. Rationalized support of emotionally established convictions may thus lead to concern and action which could not have been aroused without the initial emotional stimulus." (H. L. Hollingworth, *The Psychology of the Audience*, pp. 113-114)

   c. "The writers of formal logic seem to assume that man is but a logical machine, that he weighs evidence, formulates it in the syllogistic order and then reaches the conclusion on which he bases his actions. The more modern conception of man is that he is a creature who rarely reasons at all. Indeed, one of the greatest students of the human mind assures us that most persons never perform an act of pure reasoning, but that all their actions are results of imitation, habit, suggestion or some related form of thinking which is distinctly below that which could be called reasoning. Our most important actions are performed and our most sacred conceptions are reached by means of the merest suggestion." (Walter Dill Scott, *The Psychology of Public Speaking*, p. 155. By permission of Noble and Noble, publishers.)

d. Reporting on Nazi propaganda *Life* says: "The message to the crowd is a series of simple, basic, memorable words—nation, people, blood, family, comrade, friend, home, soil, bread, work, strength, hope, life, fight, victory, birth, death, honor, beauty." (*Life* Magazine, May 2, 1940, p. 21)

e. "Modern audiences are more homogeneously selected than formerly and their increasing sophistication gives added value to the appearances of logical persuasion, even if the true basis of the appeals is emotional and even if the logic is fallacious." (H. L. Hollingworth, *The Psychology of the Audience*, pp. 137-138)

f. "Thinking government always provokes a maximum resentment against itself, since the first thing upon which men economize is thought." (Harold J. Laski, *The American Presidency*, p. 265)

g. "Any educated man or woman should know what is evidence, should know when a thing is proved and when it is not proved. . . . should know how many interpretations the same rival propositions would fairly bear, and what weight is to be attached to rival authorities." (Viscount Morley, in a speech reported by *The Boston Herald;* see J. M. O'Neill, Craven Laycock, and R. L. Scales, *Argumentation and Debate*, p. vii)

h. "The present world crisis is not due to bad heredity, nor to inexorable nature, nor to the Devil, but to bad education in cultivating habits of fear, intolerance, and hate of alien individuals and races, of foreign religions, nations, and ideologies. The peace and progress of mankind depend on the acquiring of habits that make for peace and progress." (Edwin Grant Conklin, in a speech reported by *Time*, July 3, 1939, p. 42)

i. "Thinking applies to the entire procedure of arriving at a conclusion. It includes the starting-point, the premises, the equipment for the venture, and the completing stage—the inference. Thinking is supported by observation, perception, memory, imagination, association. The logical technique focuses upon the processes of inference with constant reference to the psychological components. Thinking is the vital movement of mental behavior." (Joseph Jastrow, *Effective Thinking*, p. 14)

2. The following tests of reflective thinking, summarized by Columbia

Associates in Philosophy, *An Introduction to Reflective Thinking*, pp. 330-42, are those upon which nearly all logicians agree: clarity, consistency with the facts, consistency with other beliefs, utility and simplicity. From the following list of beliefs select one for careful analysis in terms of the tests suggested above:

a. The Republican party is the party of prosperity.

b. The Democratic party is the party of reform.

c. Where there's a will there's a way.

d. The study of logic is more important than the study of calculus.

e. The function of education is the inculcating of socially useful habits.

f. Nationalization of the munitions industry will prevent possible wars of aggression.

g. A child born under the zodiacal sign of the Lion will be courageous.

h. All men are created equal in capacity for achievement.

i. Long, slender hands indicate an artistic nature.

3. Write a short case history (300-500 words) of a personal experience which illustrates one of the factors in non-logical thinking.

4. Select a current campus problem and prepare a three-minute speech outlining the steps in logical thinking as they might be utilized in its consideration.

5. Select a newspaper editorial which exhibits one of the factors in non-logical thinking; analyze it, and suggest ways in which it might be counteracted.

Part II

THE PROBLEM

CHAPTER 4

Locating and Defining the Problem

No MATTER HOW men *think* they think, they seldom think logically. That was the lesson of our last chapter. We carry innumerable handicaps when we attempt to rise above the level of non-logical thinking and solve our problems by reflective thought. If we are to resolve perplexing situations on a rational basis we must employ a sound method of attack. In this and succeeding chapters we propose a simple sequence of four steps in problem-solving:

1. locating and defining the problem (Chapter 4)
2. exploring the problem (Chapters 5-9)
3. examining suggested solutions (Chapter 10)
4. choosing the best solution (Chapter 11)

This methodology is not infallible; it is unlikely that we shall ever find one that is. Logical thinking, it must be remembered, provides only a method for intelligent problem-solving; it does not guarantee intelligent solutions. Four men might investigate the same problem, each following the steps of reflective thought, yet find different solutions. They might not all discover the same evidence, some particular argument might have meaning for only one of them, and they might give different weights to the same evidence. But while they might differ in their conclusions, each man would have resolved the problem in a way superior to that offered by random or emotionalized thinking. It is conceivable, of course, that occasionally the same conclusion might be reached by non-logical as by logical thought. That would be a rare hit, but we would still commend only the man who solved the problem by examining the available evidence and argument; we expect him to hit more consistently.

I. ISOLATING THE SPECIFIC PROBLEM

"If we could first know where we are, and whither we are tending," said Lincoln in the "House Divided" speech, "we could better
judge what to do, and how to do it." Finding out where we are,
bringing our problem into sharp and clear focus, is the first step in
logical thinking. In proposing a method for isolating a specific problem we phrase the separate steps in question form to emphasize their
exploratory nature.

A. What Is the Present State of the Problem?

1. *The problem for discussion* is not necessarily concerned directly with finding a solution. We may have given little thought to
it other than to become aware of its existence; we may be perplexed,
irritated, or disturbed, yet not recognize the problem as such. The
first step, then, is to orient ourselves toward the problem, and establish a point of departure for further investigation. The "what's
wrong?" problem is of this sort: "What's wrong with radio?" or
"What's wrong with American capitalism?" We are not ready to
debate a solution, but only to discuss a problem, or perhaps to see
if there *is* a real problem. "Is our immigration policy too strict?"
"Do we need to revise our tax laws?" "Is anything seriously wrong
with our educational system?" are other problems for exploratory
discussion.

2. *The problem for debate*, on the other hand, has been located,
defined, and explored; we now seek a solution, or want to determine
the validity of a proposed solution. "Should we do thus-and-so?" is
the approach we take: "Should we build a St. Lawrence waterway?"
or "Resolved, that our club should sponsor an annual carnival to
raise money for charity." It is assumed, in such cases, that exploratory
discussion has led us to the point of wanting to make up our minds
on an issue, so we phrase the most likely solution into form for a
debate; then we argue it, pro and con. If previous discussion has
yielded several possible solutions, each one may be tested separately
in debate; this happens in legislative bodies when alternative solutions
may be introduced as substitute amendments for that proposed in
the main motion. Here are other typical problems for debate:
"Should we strengthen the Sherman Anti-Trust Law?" "Is socialism
the way out for Europe?" "Resolved, that Glenrock adopt the city-
manager form of government."

The pattern of congressional legislation illustrates the differences between problems for discussion and those for debate. The Senate Committee on Foreign Affairs may investigate this question: "What can we do to provide political stability in the Far East?" Here is a problem for discussion; it needs to be located and defined, it requires thorough exploration and careful consideration of alternative solutions. This is usually accomplished through informal committee discussion and public hearings until the committee agrees to report a bill entitled "An act to provide for the establishment of a Pacific Union." On the floor of the Senate we now have a problem for debate; through parliamentary processes the senators will decide whether to adopt this specific solution.

B. What Are We Trying to Decide?

1. *The problem of fact* calls for the ascertainment of certain truths or factual reports of observable phenomena. It is not primarily concerned with belief, probability, or wisdom; no policy or solution is involved. Some problems of fact can be settled by reference to available and authoritative sources. The question may be simple, as "Has Anglo-American trade regained its prewar levels?" and be answered by referring to the *World Almanac*, the *Statesman's Yearbook*, or the annual reports of the Department of Commerce. The problem of fact may also be complex, requiring more extensive research: "What is the cheapest form of life insurance for me to buy?" or "What city would be the best in which to locate a new plastic products plant?" In some cases what appear to be simple questions of fact are very difficult to settle; the facts may be hard to find and hard to interpret. It was not until 1949, ten years after the signing of the famous Hitler-Stalin pact, for example, that enough evidence was accumulated to answer the question, "Who made the first overtures for the Russo-German Pact of 1939?"

2. *The problem of belief* is concerned with the acceptance or rejection of general statements of attitude rather than with the application of these attitudes to specific situations. It may not require ascertainment of facts or even support of a specific policy. Indeed, it may sometimes be impossible to find a factual basis for solving the problem. "Would a world federal government insure peace?" is such a problem. We may believe that world government would bring peace, yet be unable to prove it, and unwilling to initiate the steps necessary to form such a government. Many public

opinion surveys are concerned only with finding out what people believe, not what they know to be the facts, or whether they would be willing to support measures to carry out their beliefs: "Do you think the Un-American Activities Committee is doing a good job?" or "Do you think economic planning by government can avoid another depression?" Other problems of belief might be "How much life insurance should a man carry?" "Are Americans becoming more conscious of their responsibilities as citizens?" or "Resolved, that capitalism will outlive communism."

3. *The problem of policy* is concerned with the validity, feasibility, or desirability of a certain course of action or a specific solution. It is derived, presumably, from an examination of the facts, the formulation of a belief, and now a willingness to implement that belief. In a club meeting it might be "Resolved, that this organization establish a consumer's coöperative," or "Shall we send a delegate to the state convention?" The legislator might debate the question "Should we pass the federal aid to education bill?" or a motion stated as "I move that the City Council appoint a special committee to investigate sewage disposal facilities." The citizen asks "Shall I vote for the reëlection of Senator Brown?" or "Will I support the proposed amendment for a special school tax?" Around the family dinner-table the problem of policy may deal with these questions: "Shall we spend our summer vacation at Twin Lakes?" or "Will we buy a new car or make a down payment on a house?"

In sum, the differences between questions of fact, belief, and policy represent different methods of approaching problems, depending upon the end in view. The problem of fact asks simply "Is this a fact?" The problem of belief inquires "Is this probably true?" And the problem of policy asks "Ought we to do this?" A board of directors of a corporation may discuss this *question of fact*, "Is our production sufficiently diversified to insure a constant market?" This may be answered in the negative and the board moves on to a *question of belief*, "Would we find a more constant market if we develop a greater variety of products?" If this is answered affirmatively, the directors may take up this *question of policy*, "Shall we stabilize our market by adding such-and-such a product?"

C. What Type of Problem Is It?

It is useful to determine the general class of problems in which a particular one falls, as part of the process of isolating it. If, for example, we are concerned with combating juvenile delinquency in our community we should recognize the general type of problem we are dealing with in order to facilitate our search for relevant facts, to indicate what kind of expert advice we need, to determine where responsibility for a solution may lie, and to suggest ways and means of carrying out a solution. We would know that a recreation program would primarily benefit children; that leads us to find out how many children might be interested; it takes us to teachers, juvenile delinquency officers, and playground directors for advice; and it suggests that the city officials, schools, and civic groups might share responsibility in such a program. If we think through the problem in this way we will make fewer false starts in working toward a solution.

If we are planning a public discussion meeting, say a symposium with three speakers, on the future of atomic energy, we should recognize that this is the type of problem with which physicists or industrial engineers may be familiar. We would not usually invite dairymen or traffic experts to serve as symposium speakers or panel members. Or if we are preparing to debate a question relating to the tariff, the mere classification of the problem would be helpful in searching for evidence; it would suggest that we ask for help from the man in the economics department who teaches courses in international trade and finance, not the instructor in money and banking.

D. What Basic Assumptions Are Important?

First let it be said that men's basic assumptions are often more important than their opinions; they may consider their opinions debatable, but seldom their assumptions. Opinions may differ as to what punishment a certain traitor should receive, but it is generally assumed that traitors ought to be punished. Or, most people would not think debatable the question as to whether starving people need help. But they might differ violently on how to provide that help.

Those preparing for discussion or debate will find their understanding of a problem broadened if they look for the basic assumptions early in their investigations. If you are going to discuss civil rights, for example, you may discover that while many people in the North assume that federal legislation is needed, most people in the South assume that it is a problem for individual states. The Southerner may work just as hard as his Northern neighbor does to extend civil rights to all citizens, but each proceeds in terms of his basic assumptions. Though you may accept neither of these assumptions in its entirety, it is important that you recognize them as inherent factors in the situation.

E. What Are Its Relationships to Other Problems?

A common fault of discussion leaders and debaters is to assume that each problem with which they deal is unique and separate from all others. But few problems can be neatly packaged by themselves: the price of steel is related to the size of pensions for retired steel-workers; the repayment of international loans is often tied to national tariff policies; and the purchase of a new family car may be determined only after considering the relative urgency of the need for a washing machine or a new kitchen stove. In studying any problem it is important to discover whether it is single and capable of isolation; if it is not, what its relationships are with other problems. In an era of increasingly complex social structures, it is doubtful that many political or economic problems will be found which do not bear some relationship to others. Personal affairs, like "Which car in the $1500 price class represents the best buy for me?" may often be singled out, but even such a problem as "Will I get further ahead by going to graduate school or by getting a job?" depends greatly upon an evaluation of the college senior's economic, social, and professional objectives.

To discuss the settlement of a strike at the Blank Plant by a ten-cent hourly wage raise, for example, may be oversimplifying the situation; the issue of increased wages may be tied closely to other problems. The Blank Plant may already be losing money, and a higher labor cost might force it to close down. Or the whole industry may be highly competitive, and a wage raise might force a price raise which would be disastrous to Blank sales. Or a raise in freight rates may so increase the cost of raw materials that a decrease in wages seems the only way to keep the Blank Plant in business. The relationship of wages to these problems is obvious: instead of assuming that the initial problem is single, or can be isolated, it may be necessary to investigate general business conditions, transportation costs, competition, and so on. How are all of these problems related? What bearing do they have on the wage problem? What effect would granting a wage increase have on these related problems? And would a wage increase create new problems?

II. STATING THE PROBLEM

When the specific problem has been isolated, the next step is to state it in clear and definite language, not only that it may be understood but that it may not be misunderstood.

A. How May the Problem Be Stated?

The way in which a problem is stated usually depends upon how far thinking about it has progressed and the general purpose for which it is being discussed or debated. To illustrate, consider the question of raising dues which confronts the members of the Iota Club.

1. *To locate and define the problem.* At the outset the members are concerned primarily with obtaining information about club finances. Stated simply, their problem is "Why do we need to have dues?"

2. *To explore the problem.* When the need for dues is clarified, the Iota Club may consider this question: "Are present dues high enough to meet our needs?"

3. *To examine suggested solutions.* If the exploration of the problem indicates that more income is necessary, it can be restated: "How can we raise more money for club needs?"

4. *To choose the best solution.* After consideration of various ways to raise money the Iota Club is likely to discuss this question: "Which of these suggested methods is best?"

5. *To secure acceptance of the selected solution.* One member, anxious to settle the problem, begins final debate with a motion: "I move that we levy a special assessment of one dollar per member."

The nature of the group holding the discussion or debate will determine whether the problem is to be stated as a question, a motion, or a resolution. In a public discussion meeting the question form is commonly used; in the business meeting of an organization the motion form is appropriate; in a legislative body or in intercollegiate debate the resolution form is traditional. Here are examples of each form:

Are tax-free coöperatives a threat to private enterprise? (question)
I move that this organization endorse the proposal to tax consumer coöperatives. (motion)
Resolved, that coöperatives should be subject to the same taxes as other businesses. (resolution)

B. What Principles Govern the Phrasing of the Problem?

In the interest of clarity and accuracy, the following general principles should govern the exact phrasing of a problem, whether it is designed for discussion or for debate.

1. *The statement should not be too broad.* Even for exploratory discussions a topic ought to be stated in the narrowest form possible and in precise terms. For pure dialectical amusement a group might discuss "Are we better off than our grandfathers?" but it would be difficult to debate seriously, "Resolved, that civilization has advanced further in the past ten years than during the preceding century." The statement is broad, vague, and unwieldy. To improve it by making it more specific and limiting its scope to a reasonable area, it might be rephrased: "Resolved, that the advance of civilization, *measured in terms of the control and prevention of disease,* has been greater in the past ten years than in the preceding century." When, as in this case, the problem is difficult to isolate specifically, its limitations or relations with other problems should be made as explicit as possible.

2. *The statement should not employ ambiguous words.* A team from Australia, touring the United States and Canada, debated this proposition: "Resolved, that civilization has more to fear from the intelligentsia than from the masses." While the debate was sometimes amusing the question was heavy with ambiguity: what is meant by "civilization?" What does "more to fear" mean? Who are the "intelligentsia?" Who are "the masses?" Instead of discussing "How can we control advertising?" we should rephrase the question to make clear whether the "we" refers to a government agency, the advertising industry, or individual consumers. A public discussion was once held on this topic: "Are public opinion polls useful?" Much wasted time in the discussion would have been saved by removing the ambiguity of the last word: "useful" to whom, "useful" in what way? Ambiguity inevitably invites misunderstanding and misrepresentation.

Closely allied with the ambiguous word is the question-begging or one-sided word. "Resolved, that the wasteful policy of economic aid to Europe be discontinued," is so prejudiced by the word *wasteful* that any discussion of it would be biased and useless. Always seek an objective statement.

3. *The statement should consist of words that may be clearly defined.* Talleyrand once remarked that language was invented to conceal the thoughts of man. This appears to be true when words which cannot adequately be defined are used in phrasing a problem; clarity is sacrificed and confusion results. Sometimes intercollegiate debate topics or congressional bills seem awkward by the length of their statements when they incorporate definitions; however bulky the result, the good intentions should be commended. Try defining the italicized words in these statements: "Is America ready for *industrial democracy?*" "How can we *get the most* out of this course?" "Resolved, that our armed forces *be increased.*" Problems of definition are treated more fully later in this chapter.

4. *The statement should be a complete sentence.* In the grammarian's terms, the statement should be a single simple or complex declarative sentence, not a compound sentence or a single term. Here is a sample statement: "Compulsory military training is good for some college students, but for most of them it is a waste of time and contrary to their religious beliefs." It really contains three questions: (*a*) Is compulsory military training good for some students? (*b*) Is it a waste of time for most students? (*c*) Is it contrary to the religious beliefs of most students? Any one of them might lead to a good discussion. To make the statement more useful it might be phrased this way: "Although military training is admittedly good for some students, it should not be made compulsory for those whose religious beliefs oppose it."

A single term, such as "compulsory military training," "the UN," or "communism," is also inadequate for discussion or debate; it expresses neither a problem nor a point of view. If we do discuss "communism" it should be in some context, as "Does Russian communism threaten the existence of American democracy?"

5. *For a discussion the statement should be in question form.* Discussion is most easily stimulated by the impartial question which suggests the elements of controversy in the topic: "Is the South the nation's number one economic problem?" "How can human rights be enforced internationally?" "What can be done about the high rate of divorce?" The question form is unprejudiced, yet compelling, it is more provocative than a formal proposition; and by implying "a disease needing a cure," it tends to stimulate a more reflective approach to thinking about it. The leader of discussion may find

these criteria, based upon the experience of those who direct public opinion polls, helpful in formulating questions: [1]

a. The question should be brief and to the point. Long conditional or dependent clauses tend to confuse people.

b. The words and phrases should be simple and in common day-to-day use among all groups in the community.

c. The question should not include words which have strong emotional content.

d. The question must avoid all possible bias or suggestion in favor of or against a particular point of view.

e. The question should include all the important alternatives which may emerge on a given issue.

f. When the individual is being asked to choose between different alternatives, this choice of alternatives must be given as early in the interview as possible.

Those who plan public discussion meetings must make the topic appear significant and attractive if they are to secure hearers. Newspaper headlines attract attention because they tell a complete story in a short and vivid phrase. These same qualities will help catch attention in advance publicity for a discussion. "Is your health the nation's business?" "What's the score on civil liberties?" or "Is the UN out of date?" are attention-getting questions.

6. *For a debate the statement may be in proposition, motion, resolution, or question form.* A specific solution or definite point of view should be stated when a problem has reached the stage for final decision and action. Whether this is best stated in a proposition, motion, or resolution, depends upon the local custom and the circumstances of the debate. An advocate at a public forum might argue the proposition: "The State of Ohio should adopt a gross income tax." A civic taxpayers' association might debate a motion: "I move that this association petition the state legislature to adopt a 2 per cent gross income tax." Two guest speakers before a Rotary Club might phrase a resolution: "Resolved, that a state gross income tax would benefit the businessmen of Ohio."

Traditionally the resolution form is used in intercollegiate debate. Experience indicates, however, that a formal resolution sometimes lacks audience appeal; it appears too formidable and academic. When this is true the resolution may easily be rephrased into a question which still makes clear the controversial proposal. Instead of "Re-

[1] George Gallup and Saul Forbes Rae, *The Pulse of Democracy* (New York, 1940), p. 101. By permission of Simon & Schuster, Inc., publishers.

solved, that the federal government should outlaw the Communist
Party," the question form could be used for a public debate: "Should
we outlaw the Communist Party?"

7. *For a debate the statement should establish reasonable choices.*
We do not demand that a debater "prove" his proposition "beyond
the shadow of a doubt," but we do expect that he can establish the
probability of its validity or non-validity. He cannot do this unless
the statement is phrased so as to permit a reasonable conclusion.
"Resolved, that the Irish have contributed more to the development
of America than the Germans," leads to futile debate. "Is the British
Empire decadent?" appears equally sterile of reasonable conclusions.

The statement which is obviously valid or invalid is equally objectionable for purposes of debate. Any reasonable person knows
that there are many ways to provide better college education; he
should therefore, reject a statement such as "The *only* salvation for
higher education is to adopt the University of Chicago plan."

8. *For a debate the statement should set forth a conclusion that
the affirmative wishes the audience to accept.* "He who affirms must
prove," says the law, and we presume an accused man innocent
until he is proved guilty. The duty of proving any proposition rests
upon those demanding the change; until cause can be shown for
adopting the proposal the present status should prevail. This is the
meaning of the principle of "placing the burden of proof on the
affirmative." The affirmative speakers in a debate must advocate a
change from the status quo; the negative either upholds the status
quo upon the presumption that it is satisfactory or advocates another change. When the statement of a problem for debate puts the
burden of proof upon the affirmative the conflict is immediately
apparent. Thus "Resolved, that socialism should supplant capitalism
in America," is a better statement than "Resolved, that capitalism
should be maintained in America," since capitalism describes the
status quo and the advocated change is socialism.

Occasionally a debate may be held before a group which officially
advocates a change from the status quo; in that case a proposition
calling for a change puts the burden of proof upon the negative
as the audience sees the question. The United World Federalists,
for example, believe in a federal world government; "Resolved, that
a federal world government should be established," for that organization, does not propose a change in policy or belief. It would be
wise, in such a case, to rephrase the proposition so that the affirmative

presents the "opposition" point of view, even though it is the status quo: "Resolved, that the UN meets the world's needs."

C. How Do We Define Terms?

We have said that the statement of a problem for discussion or debate should contain only words that can be clearly defined. This is an important point, for many controversies hinge upon definitions: "Why didn't you say that in the first place? I thought you meant ..." President Truman once made a speech in which he said, "When we talk about planning the things we want to do economically we are charged with being Communists and fellow-travelers. I think that the difficulty is that ... the people who find fault with us ... are thinking about *controlled* economy, not *planned* economy." [2] He was using one method of argument by definition. The latest *Webster's* dictionary defines *control* as "to check or regulate ... to exercise directing, guiding, or restraining power over," and *plan* as "to form a plan ... to devise or project a method or course of action."

First we need to familiarize ourselves with the common methods of definition.

1. *Usage.* This method is particularly fruitful when combined with reference to a good dictionary. If we want to define the word *discussion* we may find that the dictionary defines it as "argument for the sake of arriving at truth or clearing up difficulties." This is an adequate definition if it conforms to the way in which people commonly use the term, but we may have to modify it if common usage is something else. For words not in the dictionary common usage is the only method of definition. This was once true of *jazz*, and is now true of *bebop*.

2. *Derivation.* The dictionary may also provide help in definition by indicating the derivation of a word. A man described as a *quidnunc* may be identified as a gossip columnist when we learn that the word comes from the Latin phrase *quid nunc*, "What now?" Or a *tycoon*, used colloquially to describe a businessman of unusual wealth or influence, may be better understood if we know that it comes from the Japanese *taikun*, or "great lord."

3. *Authority.* Often the best method of definition is to secure a statement from a person who, because of special training or com-

2 New York *Times*, February 13, 1949. (Italics ours.)

petence in a particular field, is recognized as an authority. This is especially true in defining highly technical terms. Leonard W. Doob, professor of psychology at Yale University, for example, is a recognized expert on public opinion and propaganda. He defines *public opinion* as "people's attitudes on an issue when they are members of the same social group. . . . It is not a synonym for people. It presupposes a social organization or group as well as a series of more or less common experiences which people have had." [3] In other cases whole books may be essentially definitions of terms by an expert: Charles A. Beard's *The Idea of National Interest* or Selig Hecht's *Explaining the Atom.* This method of definition should be employed carefully, for an authority may be using a term in a restricted sense for a special purpose.

4. *Comparison.* By this method we compare the word in question with others, nearly synonymous, to discover fine shades of meaning. *Arbitration* might be compared with *mediation* or *conciliation; quid pro quo* with *bargain* or *exchange.* Dictionaries are often helpful in this respect: after defining a word they may refer the reader to others, similar or synonymous. Thus the definition of *discuss* includes a comparison with *argue, debate,* and *dispute.*

5. *Contrast.* This is a procedure for defining what a word does *not* mean, and is especially helpful in differentiating between terms which may easily be confused. Thus a psychologist might define *environment* by saying that "it is that influence upon the individual which comes neither from his own original nature, nor from his present adapted and modified nature." Or a writer may say, "This book is not a handbook of law. It is not a manual for law students. It is not a practical guide of that deservedly reprobated pattern called 'Every Man His Own Lawyer.'. . . All that the book hopes to do is to rid anyone of the notion that law is something with which he has no relation except when he gets into what is called 'trouble.' " [4]

Beyond knowing the general methods of definition, we should understand the requisites for a good definition, as they are significant in discussion or debate.

1. *A good definition should be applicable to all situations or to*

[3] Leonard W. Doob, *Public Opinion and Propaganda* (New York, Henry Holt and Co., Inc., 1948), pp. 35, 42.
[4] Max Radin, *The Law and You* (New York, The New American Library, 1948), preface.

all individuals included in the term defined. That is, a good definition
of the word *animal* must be comprehensive enough to include jaguars
and anteaters as well as horses and elephants.

2. *A good definition should exclude situations or individuals not
included in the term defined.* To define the *National Student Association* as "a national organization of undergraduates devoted to the
furtherance of student interests" would be inadequate; it would
apply equally to the Student Co-op, the Future Teachers of America,
or the National Intercollegiate Athletic Association.

3. *A good definition should not include the term being defined or
any derivative of it.* We learn little about *pragmatism* defined as
"that philosophy which is based upon verification of truths by the
pragmatic test." Even the colloquial "the proof of the pudding is
in the eating" is a better definition.

4. *A good definition should be stated in terms which are simpler
than the term being defined.* Does it help the average person to know
that a *fluoroscope* is "a device for observing, by means of some
fluorescent substance, the shadows of objects enclosed in media
opaque to ordinary light, but transparent to Roentgen rays"? Or
must he still discover the meanings of *fluorescent substance, opaque,*
and *Roentgen rays?*

5. *A good definition should be stated in terms which are suited
to the particular audience.* In the discussion or debate situation this
is perhaps the most important requisite of a good definition; though
all other requisites be met a definition is inadequate if the listener for
whom it is intended cannot understand it. As Poincaré, the brilliant
French mathematician, observed, "No man knows anything about
higher mathematics until he can explain it to the man in the street."
A group of political scientists might approve a definition of a *liberal*
as "one who is unbound by orthodox tenets or established forms
in politics, characterized by an attitude of human sympathy, a recep-
tivity to change, and a scientific willingness to follow reason rather
than faith or any fixed set of ideas." But the average man in a discussion may more easily grasp Max Lerner's definition: "A liberal is a
man who wants both groceries and freedom." To most people, as
President Roosevelt pointed out in a once-famous incident, "termination of the illumination" for a wartime blackout meant simply "turn
out the lights." A specialist, talking to specialists, may speak of a
"cervical myalgia," but to the layman a pain in the neck is a pain
in the neck.

Abraham Lincoln was unexcelled in his ability to define obscure terms in language that was accurate, clear, and meaningful to his audiences. Most of the principles we have discussed are illustrated in this excerpt from Lincoln's speech at a Sanitary Fair in Baltimore, April 18, 1864: [5]

The world has never had a good definition of the word *liberty*, and the American people, just now, are much in want of one. We all declare for liberty; but in using the same word we do not all mean the same thing. With some the word *liberty* may mean for each man to do as he pleases with himself, and the product of his labor; while with others the same word may mean for some men to do as they please with other men, and the product of other men's labor. Here are two, not only different, but incompatible things, called by the same name, liberty. And it follows that each of these things is, by the respective parties, called by two different and incompatible names—liberty and tyranny.

The shepherd drives the wolf from the sheep's throat, for which the sheep thanks the shepherd as his liberator, while the wolf denounces him for the same act, as the destroyer of liberty, especially as the sheep was a black one. Plainly, the sheep and the wolf are not agreed upon a definition of the word *liberty;* and precisely the same difference prevails today among us human creatures, even in the North, and all professing to love liberty.

READINGS

BAIRD, A. C., *Argumentation, Discussion, and Debate* (New York, McGraw-Hill Book Co., Inc., 1950), Chaps. 2, 5.

BLACK, Max, *Critical Thinking* (New York, Prentice-Hall, Inc., 1946), Chap. 11.

GALLUP, George, and RAE, S. F., *The Pulse of Democracy* (New York, Simon & Schuster, Inc., 1940), Chap. 7.

LASKER, Bruno, *Democracy Through Discussion* (New York, H. W. Wilson Company, 1949), Chaps. 12-13.

LEE, I. J., *Language Habits in Human Affairs* (New York, Harper & Bros., 1941), Chap. 3.

McBURNEY, J. H., and HANCE, K. G., *Discussion in Human Affairs* (New York, Harper & Bros., 1950), Chaps. 7, 11.

[5] Philip Van Doren Stern, ed., *The Life and Writings of Abraham Lincoln* (New York, Random House, 1940), pp. 810-11.

EXERCISES

1.* Select a problem which you plan to use as the basis for intensive study during the semester: (*a*) follow the approach outlined in this chapter and draw up an analysis which will isolate the problem; and (*b*) apply the principles suggested in this chapter and phrase the problem clearly and concisely.

2. Collect five newspaper editorials and write out for each one the implied proposition upon which it is based. Indicate also any basic assumptions which the writer apparently made.

3. Write out a statement of each of these problems, and label it as (*a*) a problem for discussion or debate, in terms of your own thinking about it, and (*b*) a problem of fact, belief, or policy:
   a. Subsidies for college athletes
   b. A federal sales tax
   c. National health insurance
   d. A federal world government
   e. Compulsory arbitration of labor disputes

4. Any problem may be phrased differently for each of the five stages in the discussion and debate process. Select three problems and state them for each stage of the process.

5. Here is a list of definitions of the word *liberal,* submitted in a contest conducted by Simon & Schuster, publishers; it appeared in the *Saturday Review of Literature,* April 9, 1949, p. 5. Evaluate each one to determine its adequacy.
   a. A liberal is a man with mind and heart open.
   b. A liberal is not afraid to examine a new idea.
   c. I am a liberal. Agree with me, you're a liberal.
   d. A liberal respects the future as well as the past.
   e. A liberal, Max Lerner. (The best definition I know.)
   f. A liberal is a man who will not tolerate intolerance.
   g. A liberal is a man who is prejudiced only against prejudice.
   h. A liberal believes in the freedom of actions and passions.
   i. A liberal unreservedly gives another person freedoms he demands for himself.

6. Evaluate each of the following statements of problems in terms of its propriety for discussion or debate by members of your class.
   a. Can we eliminate graft in government?
   b. Should the pernicious use of diplomatic appointments as political rewards be continued?
   c. Why not unify our marriage and divorce laws?
   d. What does democracy really mean?

* The first exercise listed after each chapter in Part II will relate to a problem selected by the student for collateral study during the semester. In each case this exercise will be marked with an asterisk. Carrying out these exercises should help the student build a large body of information which will be put into a brief on the problem in the final exercise of the series.

    e. Are we moving toward socialism in America?
    f. Resolved, that Tusca Tech needs more academic freedom.
    g. Juvenile delinquency—whose responsibility?
    h. How good were the "good old days"?
    i. Resolved, that the British Empire is decadent.
    j. I think the government ought to leave business alone.
    7. Prepare a three-minute speech explaining the merits of a topic you think suitable for discussion or debate by members of your class.
    8. Evaluate the definitions, implied or explicit, contained in these statements:

    a. I am firm; you are obstinate; he is pig-headed.
    b. "Progressive education" does not deserve to be called "education."
    c. Democracy is government of the people, by the people, for the people.
    d. Our schools ought to teach more Americanism.
    e. Let the people decide whether they want war.
    f. Poverty is the absence of wealth.
    g. I urge my principles; I respect your opinions; I oppose his propaganda.

CHAPTER 5

Exploring the Problem: Research

"IF A LITTLE KNOWLEDGE is dangerous," asked Thomas Huxley, "where is the man who has so much as to be out of danger?" We are now concerned with the discovery of knowledge about the problem which we have located and defined. This process is basic to a college education, not merely to a course in argumentation, discussion, or debate. An educated man may be defined as a person who knows where to go to discover what he needs to know. He has, in other words, some grasp of research procedure. In this chapter we outline a pattern for exploring a problem: using personal sources of information, discovering published materials, and recording relevant data for future use.

I. PERSONAL SOURCES OF INFORMATION

The average student, we suspect, thinks first of the library card catalogue or the *Readers' Guide*—or perhaps the *Reader's Digest!*—when he begins a research assignment. But we also suspect that he may have a reservoir of personal knowledge that is all too often untapped.

A. Experience and Observation

Are you sure, as you prepare to take part in a discussion on tax policy, that you have no experiences which will help you understand the problem? Have you considered, in planning for a debate on uniform marriage and divorce laws, whether your own observations might be useful? You have never dropped an atomic bomb, but a course in ethics may have given you some basis for discussing the international control of atomic energy. Even though you "know nothing" about slum clearance proposals, your observations of slum areas in any large city must have aroused some thoughts and feelings. The place to begin looking for ideas is in your own mental file. Better still, is to maintain a working file—a cardboard file box, a few tabs for subject headings, and some 4 × 6 cards—in which you record ideas, illustrations, quotations, stories, and experiences, for future reference. The quotation at the opening of this chapter came from such a file; so did these two facts: Ralph Waldo Emerson kept what he called a "savings bank" of ideas in which he deposited daily bits of information which he could draw out later; and Lincoln, in preparing for his debates with Douglas in 1858, arranged a collection of notes on law cases, newspaper clippings, tables of statistics, and other data on the issues, in a small notebook for ready reference.

Sometimes if we have had no personal experience with a given issue, we can acquire it, and special insight into the problem. Benjamin F. Butler once spent days examining all the parts of a steam engine and even learned to drive it to prepare himself to cross-examine witnesses in a railroad accident case. Harry A. Overstreet once took a leave from his teaching post to work as a common laborer in a factory to better prepare himself to write about psychological problems in industry. The student who is to discuss the responsibility of broadcasters to the public can spend a day listening to and analyzing typical programs; the debater who advocates the city manager form of government can shape his ideas by observing what goes on at the city hall.

B. Interviews and Inquiries

People who live on college campuses sometimes take college professors for granted, forgetting that they are experts in their fields of study, not just people who grade quizzes. The student who is preparing to discuss government regulation of industry can probably find someone in the economics department who has both general knowledge and practical experience with regulatory agencies; in the classics department he may find a man familiar with the political rivalries in modern Greece who can contribute to his thinking for a debate on American foreign policy; or if the student seeks information about the electoral college he can turn to a member of the political science department. There are resources in town, too: the local editor knows something about freedom of the press, the banker is alert to general economic conditions, and any official of the local or state government has specialized information. By means of interviews, the student may obtain help in his research. He ought to bear in mind the other demands made upon these people and arrange for an interview well in advance, coming to it with specific questions organized into some kind of pattern.

Inquiries addressed by mail to people unavailable for interviews may also be helpful. Government officials, labor leaders, industrialists, and specialists in various areas are usually willing to reply to simple, direct, brief, and purposeful inquiries. The information concerning the Republican Open Forums reported in a previous chapter, for example, came in response to a questionnaire of twelve items on a single page with space for answers.

C. Conversations and Public Discussions

Too often the person preparing for discussion or debate overlooks the resources available through his friends, room-mates, or dinner-table companions. These people may represent a sampling of his audience; if he will try out his ideas on them he can learn to adapt his arguments to meet audience attitudes. This practice has been common among the effective speakers of our times: Woodrow Wilson, once a debate coach, used to say, "I not only use all the brains I have, but all I can borrow." Thomas Dewey, Franklin D. Roosevelt, Mackenzie King, and Herbert Hoover are among those who have regularly pre-tested their thoughts on their friends before speaking in public.

The radio, the public lecture platform, and dozens of organizations in every community offer the student an opportunity to hear discussions of public affairs. Two rewards await him if he will listen: first, he receives a wider range of information and viewpoints on current problems; second, he may learn much about the techniques of discussion and debate.

In short, we suggest that you first "let down your bucket where you are," then go to the library.

II. PUBLISHED MATERIALS

The list of sources which follows is not definitive; it is suggestive, a sampling of the resources offered the researcher by materials in print. Librarians and research assistants in special fields will be able to suggest additional sources of information.

A. General Indexes

1. The library card catalogue is a fruitful starting point for exploration. Here books and pamphlets are usually indexed under title, subject matter, and author's name. Books not available in your local library, but perhaps obtainable through inter-library loans, may be located in the latest *United States Catalogue of Books in Print*, or in the published catalogue of the Library of Congress.

2. The *Readers' Guide to Periodical Literature*, issued monthly and in an annual cumulation, indexes articles in general periodicals such as *Atlantic Monthly, Foreign Affairs Quarterly, Fortune, Harpers, Nation, New Republic, Saturday Review*, and *Yale Review*. Separate entries are made under the name of the author, the title of the article, and the subject. The *Readers' Guide* has indexed periodicals since 1900; for the period 1802-1906 consult *Poole's Index to Periodical Literature* (1938, revised edition).

3. In specialized fields similar indexes are available, such as the *Educational Index, Agricultural Index*, and *Social Science Abstracts*. A general reference for these areas, since 1920, is the *International Index to Periodicals*.

4. *The New York Times Index*, issued monthly and annually since 1913, is a subject-matter index of that newspaper. For the period 1865-1903 the *New York Daily Tribune Index* provides the same information. One of the most useful functions of these indexes is to help find dates of events, speeches, and so on, which may then be checked in contemporary periodicals and in other newspapers. The *Niles' Register*, a weekly journal of opinion, was first published in 1811 and its files and annual index serve as guides to an earlier period than the *Tribune* index. To discover where files of newspapers published from 1821-1936 are available refer to Gregory's *American Newspapers*. The *Directory of Newspapers and Periodicals* (or "Ayer's Directory") lists geographically all newspapers currently published. For research in English newspapers see *Palmer's Index* to *The London Times* for the period since 1790, and the more comprehensive *Official Index* for the period since 1906.

5. *Time* magazine also publishes an annual index which is valuable in referring to that newsweekly, and can also be used to date events which may be covered in other periodicals.

6. Special bibliographies are published in a number of fields, such as the annual compilation of materials in rhetoric and public address

which appears in the *Quarterly Journal of Speech*. A good general guide is *The Bibliographic Index*, a frequently published bibliography of bibliographies.

7. Graduate theses and research monographs are usually indexed in the professional journals of various fields; *Speech Monographs*, for example, carries an annual list of theses in speech and drama.

B. General References

1. Articles on a wide range of topics may be found in standard encyclopedias, such as the *Encyclopædia Brittanica* or the *Encyclopedia Americana*.

2. Special reference sources are frequently useful in providing factual information as well as aids in composition: dictionaries, such as *Webster's New Collegiate Dictionary* (1949), based upon Webster's *New International Dictionary* (1945); wordbooks, such as Roget's *Thesaurus* or *Webster's Dictionary of Synonyms;* quotation collections, such as Bartlett's *Familiar Quotations* or Mencken's *A New Dictionary of Quotations*.

3. Various yearbooks are valuable in furnishing more up-to-date information than can be provided by encyclopedias. Among them are the *Statesman's Yearbook*, *World Almanac*, and the *Information Please Almanac*.

4. Government publications often contain much information not found in other sources. Among these are the *Congressional Record*, Congressional *Hearings*, the *Statistical Abstract of the United States*, and numerous documents, pamphlets, and bulletins issued by various government agencies. Information about these publications, and free price lists, are available from the Superintendent of Documents, Government Printing Office, Washington 25, D.C. Most libraries subscribe to the monthly catalogue, *United States Government Publications*, which lists current publications of all government agencies.

5. For information on living individuals, whose testimony is being evaluated, a limited amount of biographical data may be found in *Who's Who in America*. The comprehensive *Dictionary of American Biography* contains biographies of thousands of distinguished Americans not now living, and also lists important biographies, periodical sketches, and collections of letters and papers; a regular supplement keeps it up-to-date. A similar work covering Englishmen, the *Dictionary of National Biography*, is also useful. *Webster's Biographical Dictionary* is a convenient single volume identifying

noteworthy persons of all nations. The *Congressional Directory*, published each session of Congress, contains short biographies of all members, as well as lists of personnel in all federal boards, bureaus, courts, commissions, and other agencies.

6. The various public opinion surveys on current issues are another type of general reference material. The best known is the Gallup Poll, published in several hundred newspapers; one of the most reliable surveys is published frequently in *Fortune* magazine. These two polls, and others, are summarized in each issue of the *Public Opinion Quarterly*.

7. Other sources for general reference are organizations such as the American Federation of Labor, the Civil Liberties Union, the League for Industrial Democracy, and the National Association of Manufacturers. A list of nearly nine hundred such associations and societies, many of which furnish free materials in the field of their special interest, is to be found in the *World Almanac*. Since these groups all exist primarily to plead their own causes, special care must be taken in evaluating their materials.

8. Many national organizations, the League of Women Voters, the Farm Bureau, and so on, provide discussion guides on current topics for their local groups; sometimes these may be obtained by non-members. Other discussion guides are available periodically for a small service charge from the *Reader's Digest* and *Time*.

9. Discussion programs and speeches also provide an important reference source, and many are regularly available in print. Some newspapers, like the New York *Times*, publish complete texts of speeches by American leaders, *Vital Speeches* is a semi-monthly journal carrying about a dozen outstanding public addresses; the Columbia Broadcasting System selects significant talks and discussions from its broadcasts for publication in *Talks;* the *U.S. News* frequently carries full texts of important speeches or interviews with leaders in government and business; and the *Congressional Record* publishes verbatim reports of Senate and House debates. Transcripts of radio discussions are published each week: the University of Chicago Round Table, America's Town Meeting of the Air, the American Forum of the Air, and the Northwestern University Reviewing Stand. Two annual publications, *The University Debaters Annual* and *Intercollegiate Debates,* include debates, briefs, and bibliographies on a number of current topics.

10. Many other series of publications, dealing with current con-

troversial issues, are also helpful sources of information. A list of
these will be found in the Appendix.

C. Using Printed Sources

Inefficient reading habits are among the most common wasters
of time. In a recent Air Force experiment it was found that the
average officer read only 292 words a minute, and understood 83.2
per cent of what he read. After six weeks of special training the
average officer could read 488 words a minute, while maintaining
his comprehension at 79.3 per cent.[1] Similar training is available in
college reading clinics and the slow reader may benefit by it. Here
we offer a few suggestions for more efficient reading in research
materials.

1. *Read with a definite purpose.* Efficient reading is not "just for
information" but for *specific* information about a *particular* subject;
we need to narrow our range of attention to material that is relevant
to our problem. The best researcher undergoes a "mental house-
cleaning" before he begins, so that he may be as objective as possible
in his reading, free from preconceived notions, stereotypes, and
prejudices. Then his mind can truly be receptive to the material he
examines. This does not mean that one should read uncritically; the
neutral and receptive attitude is perfectly compatible with careful
analysis and evaluation. Bacon long ago offered this sage advice:
"Read not to contradict and confute; nor to believe and take for
granted; nor to find talk and discourse; but to weigh and consider."

2. *Read systematically and selectively.* Gathering up a dozen
articles listed in the *Readers' Guide* on a particular topic and reading
them in hit-or-miss fashion usually results in a hit-or-miss collection
of information. System makes for success. If you are gathering
material on the subject of a European union, for example, you might
first look for information relating to the legal problems of a union,
then gather information on military aspects, economic considerations, its probable effect upon the United Nations, the attitude of
the United States, and so on. The results of such research will only
be as well-ordered as the method. To read selectively also means
being sure that all points of view are examined. Would the picture
of communism given in the *Daily Worker* alone be complete? Could

[1] *Time*, Vol. 55 (August 1, 1949), p. 51.

we rely solely upon what the Chicago *Tribune* says about communism? Or would we be safe in assuming that we had the whole truth if we read only the confessions of an ex-Communist? One way of assuring balanced as well as systematic research reading on a problem is to follow the outline of the so-called "stock issues:" (*a*) Is there a need for a change from the status quo? (*b*) What are the proposed solutions? (*c*) Will any of the proposed solutions meet the need? (*d*) Are any of the proposed solutions practicable? (*e*) Are any of the proposed solutions desirable? (*f*) Will their advantages offset possible disadvantages? These "stock issues" are described in greater detail in the next chapter.

3. *Read from the general to the specific.* If this process is reversed it is like looking on page 60 for the answers to puzzles on page 30 without first reading the puzzles. Major concepts ought to come first; then details become meaningful. If the problem you are investigating demands an understanding of specific actions of the military government in Germany, for example, you ought first to read enough background material to understand the general purpose and philosophy of military rule. Then specific acts can be examined within an adequate frame of reference. If a large amount of material is to be examined it is usually wise to take it up in chronological order. Occasionally, of course, material becomes "dated" quite rapidly, but a systematic preview of all the sources should help you eliminate those that are no longer current.

4. *Read source material whenever possible.* In an era of digests, condensations, and "five-minute biographies," we are likely to encounter a good deal of information in a second or third retelling. The thorough researcher, however, will want to examine the facts at first-hand whenever possible. The process may be more laborious but it usually pays off in the confidence with which you can reply when you are faced with the inevitable question, "What is the evidence?" Better than reading a newsweekly's account—filtered through the attitudes of the reporter and the policies of the editor— of the Supreme Court decision in the Terminiello "free speech" case is to go to the official records and read the majority and minority opinions in full. There are many times, of course, when source material is not available; in such cases unusual care must be taken in selecting secondary accounts.

5. *Read rapidly.* We have already suggested the value of being

able to read rapidly yet with comprehension. Theodore Roosevelt was an omnivorous reader and he believed that intensive self-training in the art of "skimming" made it possible for him to read much and to retain much of what he read. This process involves a quick glance from the top to the bottom of a page, noting ideas that are new, information that is significant, and passing over the familiar and the irrelevant. Careful experiments have demonstrated that one rapid reading followed by a more particularized reading for specific facts often requires less time and results in greater comprehension than one word-by-word reading.

III. RECORDING THE RESULTS

Selecting the most reliable information is not enough; it must be recorded in some usable form. As in all other aspects of research, there are efficient procedures that may be followed with profit. If you expect to assemble large amounts of material and be able to see the relationship of each item to the whole, you need a systematic technique of recording, organizing, and filing your notes.

A. What to Record

1. Whenever you think that you will want the exact words of a speaker or a writer you should record by *direct quotation*, taking the information you want as it was originally phrased. For example: [2]

Allport, Floyd H., *Social Psychology* (Boston, Houghton Mifflin Co., 1924), p. 289.
"The writer has collected the written opinions of students upon debatable questions before and after a free period of discussion. In the reports written afterward there were instances where facts presented by others, though taken up in a sense different from that intended, had been worked into new and very substantial arguments. Conversation and discussion thus proceed by a series of mutual partial misunderstandings which may produce good results in directing old habits of thought along new channels. This is what is meant when we say that one's genius strikes fire from the words of another. If one is not too impervious to social stimuli, something great and even *new* may be produced by putting two or more heads together.... This stimulation of new ways of conceiving old facts represents the profitable side of discussion."

2. When the general idea rather than the exact phrase is most important, the material should be recorded by *indirect quotation*,

[2] By permission of The Houghton Mifflin Company, publishers.

putting into your own words what the speaker or the writer said.
For example:

Rickard, Paul, "An Experimental Study of the Effectiveness of Group
Discussion in the Teaching of Factual Content" (unpublished Ph.D.
thesis, Northwestern University, 1946).

Experimented with basic speech course, using discussion method in
some sections, lecture method in others. Tested for knowledge of factual
content at end of semester and six months later. Found that average
student learns 17 per cent more factual content through discussion
method; inferior student learns 25 per cent more. (Average and inferior
classifications established before experiment by I.Q. and aptitude tests.)
Average student's ability of indirect recall improves 18 per cent more
after discussion than after lecture; ability to demonstrate functional
operation of his knowledge by giving examples increased 28 per cent.
Six months after semester ended found average student could recall 56
per cent more factual content if he had used discussion method than if
he had used lecture method. Experiment carefully worked out with
adequate control of variables.

3. When you read a book or an article and find nothing pertinent
to the problem you are investigating, but think that you may want
to use it in another connection some day, you record a *commentary*
which will remind you of its general contents and their possible
application. For example:

Benne, Kenneth D. and Sheats, Paul, "Functional Rôles of Group Members," *Journal of Social Issues*, Vol. 4 (Spring, 1948), pp. 41-9.

After observation of a series of group discussions Benne and Sheats
evolved a classification of various rôles played by members of the groups.
For example, the *elaborator*, the *energizer* (group task rôles), the
harmonizer, the *standard setter* (group building and maintenance rôles),
the *blocker*, the *dominator* (individual rôles). Might be worthwhile to
appoint a student observer for a class discussion to see if he could
recognize these rôles. Ought to reread this article in order to brief the
student properly on what to look for. The entire issue of the *Journal*
concerns "The Dynamics of the Discussion Group" and might make a
good reading assignment for students!

4. Sometimes you may wish to have on file a more detailed
summary of a book or article you have read, boiling down the
essence into a *précis*. In the case of a book it may even be useful to
list the chapter titles. For example:

Busch, Henry M. *Conference Methods in Industry* (New York,
Harper & Bros., 1949), 107 pp.

The art of conferring is old, but recent analysis and experimentation

have developed methods for improving its effectiveness in many new
situations. Modern industry, needing new and better ways of dealing
with human relations problems, has adopted the conference method as
an aid in increasing efficiency and morale. Industry now employs the
conference method in the fields of policy making, problem solving,
communication, education, foreman training, multiple management, and
settlement of grievances.

This book, written by a man who has been an industrial consultant
for many years, outlines the procedures he has found effective in
developing conference techniques in various areas.

Chap.   1. How Conference Methods Are Used in Industry
Chap.   2. The Bases of Conference Theory and Steps in Procedure
Chap.   3. Planning and Conducting the Conference
Chap.   4. The Conference Chairman: Suggestions on Leadership
Chap.   5. Conference Method in Policy Making and Management
Chap.   6. Conference Method in Industrial Education
Chap.   7. Conference Method in Communication
Chap.   8. Conference Method in the Adjustment of Conflicts
Chap.   9. Panel Discussion
Chap. 10. "The Spirit Giveth Life"

B. How to Record

1. Each item should be recorded separately, preferably upon
sheets of paper or index cards of the same size. (See 8 below.) If
two items are recorded on the same card, one of them is apt to be
overlooked when using the material.

2. Material recorded should be classified under headings which
are as specific and narrow as the topic will allow; this will make it
easier to file related items and will permit more efficient use of the
material. Notes on discussion might be organized under such headings as "definition of discussion," "purposes of discussion," and "the
panel-forum." In some cases it will be easiest to label the notes after
the material has been gathered, but it is preferable to do the labeling
as you go along.

3. To facilitate future reference the sources of all material should
be clearly indicated in your notes. These items are important: (*a*)
title of the book, speech, or article; (*b*) *name* of the author, editor,
or speaker; (*c*) *biographical note* concerning the author, editor, or
speaker, where this is important to establish his qualifications to
speak with authority; (*d*) *source*, such as name of periodical or book,
place and date of publication, and exact page from which material
is taken. If you might want to refer to the material again you will
save time by recording the library call number. For example:

Dewey, John (professor emeritus of philosophy, Columbia University; progressive educator), *How We Think* (New York, D. C. Heath & Co., 1933), p. 93 [Oberlin College library call number: 153/D515.3]
Allyn, S. C. (President of the National Cash Register Company; University of Wisconsin graduate), "Speech and Leadership in Business," *Quarterly Journal of Speech*, Vol. 34 (February, 1948), pp. 36-9.

4. Always use quotation marks when quoting directly. Rules concerning plagiarism are not easy to define, but it is better to err on the side of caution.

5. Be sure that a selected quotation represents not only the letter but also the spirit of the author or speaker. Carelessly taking a sentence out of its context may distort a writer's true intent.

6. When you want to insert your own words in a direct quotation set them off with brackets [like this] to avoid later confusion.

7. Long direct quotations should generally be avoided. It is usually better to condense. When you omit portions of a long citation indicate the omissions by inserting periods. Three periods [...] means only part of a sentence has been deleted; four periods [....] means the sentence preceding the ellipsis is complete.

8. Record your notes on index cards of a standard size. The most practical are 4 × 6 inches, or 6 × 8 inches. It is helpful to rule off spaces at the top of each card to accommodate items of documentation. For example:

SUBJECT:	TITLE:	AUTHOR:	SOURCE:
Discussion types—preferences of Army men	"Opinions and Information About the Army Orientation Course"	Morale Services Division, Report No. B-95. (No author given)	Headquarters, Army Service Forces, Washington, D.C., 1944

How should meetings be conducted?	Infantry		Air Force	
	Off *	EM *	Off *	EM *
Talks followed by discussion	69%	63%	77%	58%
Group discussion	25	27	11	28
Talks without discussion	2	8	10	11
Other	4	2	2	3

Survey taken in infantry divisions and bomber crews after experience with various types of discussion in the regular orientation course.

* Off (officers); EM (enlisted men).

A cardboard file box, or an expanding file envelope, should be used for keeping your research notes. By inserting tabbed index cards for notes bearing the same general headings (see 2 above) your material will always be relatively organized.

9. Regardless of what procedure you may devise for recording material, be sure that it is systematic, and stay with the system. Knowledge is a highly perishable commodity and an efficient method of collecting and preserving it will help you have it when you want it.

The King in Lewis Carroll's *Jabberwocky* concluded his story by saying "the horror of that moment I shall never, *never* forget!" But the Queen knew better: "You will, though, if you don't make a memorandum of it!"

READINGS

ADLER, M. J., *How to Read a Book* (New York, Simon & Schuster, Inc., 1940), Part 2.
A Manual of Style (Chicago, University of Chicago Press, 1949).
BAIRD, A. C., *Argumentation, Discussion, and Debate* (New York, McGraw-Hill Book Co., Inc., 1950), Chap. 3, App. B.
BREMBECK, W. L., and McLAUGHLIN, T. J., *A Classified Bibliography of Group Discussion* (Madison, Wis., privately published, 1948).
HOCKETT, H. C., *Introduction to Research in American History* (New York, The Macmillan Co., 1948), Chap. 1.
ROGERS, R. E., *The Fine Art of Reading* (Boston, Stratford Co., 1929), Part 2.
SEWARD, S. S., Jr., *Note-Taking* (Boston, Allyn and Bacon, 1910).
THONSSEN, L., "A Selected List of Reference Works for Students of Public Speaking," *Quarterly Journal of Speech*, Vol. 27 (April, 1941), pp. 215-22.

EXERCISES

1.* Draw up a plan for research upon the problem you have selected for intensive study during the semester, suggest the general sequence of study, and indicate possible sources of material in a general bibliography.

2. From what sources, other than library materials, might you gather information about these problems:

  a. The function of your student government.
  b. The admissions policy of your college.
  c. The theoretical limit of the national debt.
  d. Economic conditions in your college community.
  e. The attitude of the CIO toward federal aid for education.

3. Investigate the following matters and record your findings on properly documented reference cards:

   a. The biography of the president of your college.
   b. The population, chief industries, and history of Muncie, Indiana.
   c. The five largest endowments held by American universities.
   d. The places where the Lincoln-Douglas debates were held.
   e. The total foreign trade of the United States last year.
   4. Collect one piece of evidence from each of these sources concerning the naval strength of the United States:
   a. A periodical, 1850-1875.
   b. A newspaper, 1875-1910.
   c. A periodical, 1910-1920.
   d. A newspaper, 1920-1935.
   e. A periodical, 1935-1950.
   5. Select one of the following topics and draw up a bibliography of five primary and five secondary sources, with a brief annotation of each:
   a. The social philosophy of the "New Deal"
   b. The women's suffrage movement
   c. The causes of the Civil War
   d. The history of the United Nations
   e. The presidential election of 1948
   6. What would be the best, and most accessible source of information on each of these topics:
   a. The present circulation of the New York *Times*
   b. Publications of the federal Office of Education
   c. The age of the president of the United States
   d. The name of the editor of the St. Louis *Post-Dispatch*
   e. Books written by John Dewey
   f. Biographical information about Harry A. Overstreet
   g. The address of the American Civil Liberties Union
   h. The location of files of the Lebanon, Ohio, *Western-Star*
   i. The education of Thomas Jefferson
   j. Recent articles on the psychology of group discussion
   k. Public opinion on national health legislation in 1948
   l. The population of Twin Lakes, Wisconsin
   m. United States imports from Argentina in 1950
   n. The justices of the federal Court of Tax Appeals
   o. The vote cast by Senator Seward on the Fugitive Slave Law of 1850
   p. A biographical sketch of David Lloyd George
   q. The date of the sinking of the Lusitania

CHAPTER 6

Exploring the Problem: Preliminary Analysis

WHY DID YOU DECIDE to come to college? How did you happen to pick *this* college? Your decision may have been objective, based on a careful study of the issues, or it may have been rationalization, finding reasons to do what you wanted to do. Ultimately you wound up *here*. Each reader of this page may have used a different process of problem-solution. As one investigator concluded, "problem-solving begins with the initial orientation and ends with the closing judgment, but between these bounds almost anything can happen in sequence." [1]

Whenever we are confronted by a problem, whether it requires group or individual action, we should try to improve the orderliness and comprehensiveness of our analysis. Otherwise we risk the confusion of Columbus: "When he started out he didn't know where he was going; when he got there he didn't know where he was; and when he got back he didn't know where he had been." We need order that we may always steer toward our objective, and retrace our course if necessary; we need comprehension that we may see the whole problem, as well as its component parts. As Brigance has said, [2]

One of the great virtues of discussion and debate is that here we are forced to put behind us all reliance upon hope, charity, prejudice, and faith. We are compelled to analyze in the pure light of reason and reason alone. Indeed we have no option in the matter, for in solving any problem, analysis is the seat of life. If it be in error, or if it be inadequate, no amount of reasoning that follows, or eloquence of speech,

[1] Donald M. Johnson, "A Modern Account of Problem-Solving," *Psychological Bulletin*, Vol. 41 (April, 1944), p. 203.
[2] W. Norwood Brigance, unpublished manuscript.

can save the hour. The case is lost, for it starts at the wrong place and goes in the wrong direction.

It is important to think of analysis as a continuing process; as you explore a problem you may want, or even feel compelled, to alter your analysis. For that reason we stress here the concept of a preliminary analysis. You are not ready to pull the trigger, though you are looking at the target and estimating its distance. The importance of the preliminary analysis is indicated by studies which show that when members of a discussion group can recognize and organize (a) a main objective or goal, (b) specific or enabling objectives and goals, and (c) obstacles preventing the goals from being achieved, the quality of their problem-solving discussion is improved.[3] As aids in making a preliminary analysis we submit six queries.

I. WHAT IS THE IMMEDIATE CAUSE FOR DISCUSSION?

The average listener in a public discussion meeting wants to know what "the shooting is all about." Why should he be concerned with the problem? If it is timely, of vital concern to his future welfare, happiness, or safety, that fact is a proper starting point for a preliminary analysis. Often the statement of the problem, combined with a knowledge of current events, implies the cause. In addition to suggesting the significance of the problem, the immediate cause may also suggest possible solutions.

We do not intend to suggest that the precipitating cause is necessarily the most significant. The immediate cause of American involvement in World War II was Japan's attack upon Hawaii; the ultimate or underlying cause, however, is a matter upon which historians cannot yet agree. In other types of situations, as well, the immediate cause may be but a pennyweight that tips the balance of scales already heavy with tons of accumulated causes.

II. WHAT IS THE ORIGIN AND HISTORY OF THE PROBLEM?

Billy Herndon shared Abraham Lincoln's law office for many years and knew how his mind worked: "Before he could form an

[3] See John W. Keltner, "Goals, Obstacles, and Problem Formulation in Group Discussion," *Quarterly Journal of Speech*, Vol. 33 (December, 1947), pp. 468-73.

idea of anything, before he would express his opinion on a subject, he must know its *origin and history* in substance and quality, in magnitude and gravity. He must know it inside and outside, upside and downside...." [4] Before he shaped his attitudes on slavery Lincoln became an expert on what the founding fathers of the nation had said and done on this issue. In his Cooper Institute speech he demonstrated the importance of understanding the historical backgrounds of the problem before attempting its solution. If we are preparing to discuss the proper powers of the Federal Communications Commission we should first discover how that body came into being, what basic concept underlay the assumption of government control of the airwaves, why radio is presumed to operate in "the public interest, convenience, and necessity," and the history of regulatory action by the FCC. The origin and history of the problem may not only offer a basic orientation toward it, but also provide contextual definitions for important terms, indicate major controversial issues, and suggest clues for an ultimate solution.

III. WHAT ARE THE MEANINGS OF THE TERMS?

Traditionally, "defining the terms" is one of the first steps in analysis; it includes establishing meaning not only for the *complete* statement of the problem, but for *each term* in that statement. Although this matter of definition may seem simple, the semanticist and the logician will agree that it is not always so. "Before the war" is a simple phrase, easy to understand, but to the ex-"doughboy" "the war" means World War I, to the ex-"GI" it refers to World War II, and to some Southerners "*the* war" was between the states. Confusion may also arise because of technical or restricted meanings of words. To the average person, for example, *burglary* may mean simply stealing something from someone's house; but in a court of law it means "forcible entry into the dwelling house of another, in the nighttime, with intent to commit a felony therein." If entry is not forced, if it is not a dwelling, if it takes place in broad daylight, or is not with felonious intent, it is not burglary.

Many difficulties in establishing meanings for terms in the statement of a problem can be eliminated by taking greater care in

---

[4] William H. Herndon and Jesse W. Weik, *Herndon's Lincoln* (Chicago, Belford, Clarke & Co., 1889), III, p. 594. (Italics ours.)

phrasing.[5] Others may be overcome by a common agreement on terms in advance among participants in a discussion or a debate; it may be quite proper, however, to make a definition of terms the first step in the discussion meeting.

IV. WHAT APPEAR TO BE THE MAIN ISSUES?

Only after making sure that we understand the statement of the problem and know something of its background should we attempt to isolate the main issues of controversy. These are the vital points upon which investigators of the problem, participants in a discussion or debate, disagree. They are not merely "important points" but *vital* ones, issues upon which the ultimate choice of a solution will depend; and they are *controversial*, issues upon which there is disagreement. A main issue may be compared with a swinging door: it moves in both directions; over its threshold must pass all points of view, often in opposite directions; and a collision is inevitable. In the great debates on slavery a century ago, for example, one of the chief issues of controversy was what government should control it; those who believed in "states rights" and those who believed in federal supremacy collided on that threshold. In today's discussions of how to maintain world peace there is a similar clash over the main issue of national sovereignty or international authority.

Any determination of the main issues of controversy during the preliminary analysis of a problem must be tentative at this point. Our knowledge is incomplete; as further evidence and argument are discovered we may modify our conception of the basic issues. The unusual nature of some problems may suggest a special approach to discovering the main issues, but for many problems the so-called "stock issues" furnish a general pattern for *preliminary* analysis. We call them "stock" because they represent the broad questions we ask concerning any problem: we want to know whether the present situation is unsatisfactory, if there is a real need for a change, whether the proposed course of action will improve the present situation, if it is the best one to meet the need. Like the doctor, we first want to discover whether the patient has a disease; if he has, we want to find the best remedy to cure him. Sometimes, of course, we may discover

[5] Refer to Chapter 4 for a discussion of "Methods of Definition" and "Requisites of a Good Definition."

no illness, despite the complaints of the patient; or we may conclude
that the condition complained of is incurable. The "stock issues" for
preliminary analysis, as we outline them below, are developed for
the complete diagnosis-prescription cycle. In studying any specific
problem, of course, you will use only those which are appropriate.

A. Is There a Need for a Change?

This query resembles the first step in the analysis suggested earlier
in the chapter: discovering the immediate cause for discussion. Unless it can be answered affirmatively there is no point to further
inquiry. A good deal of discussion may be necessary, however, before even a negative answer is agreed upon. If it is determined that
the status quo is unsatisfactory the reasons should be set forth clearly;
of themselves they may suggest possible changes.

B. What Are the Proposed Solutions?

Though rarely are *all* possible solutions for a problem apparent at
the time of preliminary analysis, *some* of them may easily be discerned. Occasionally it is only through further exploration of the
problem that *any* solutions may be discovered. Sometimes, of course,
as in confronting a proposed amendment to the Constitution, it is a
case of approving a specific solution or none, but when there is
opportunity for further discussion or debate several possible solutions may be considered. If a number of proposed solutions are
apparent at this stage of the investigation the remaining "stock
issues" furnish a guide to uncovering main points of controversy.

C. Will Any of the Proposed Solutions Meet the Need?

The first issue asked if there was a need for a change in the status
quo. Assuming that question was answered affirmatively, we now
measure proposed solutions against that need.

D. Are the Proposed Solutions Practicable?

Although one or more of the proposals may appear to meet the
need certain fixed factors in the situation may make them impossible
or impractical.

E. Are the Proposed Solutions Desirable?

Even though some of the proposals may appear to meet the need,
and seem to be practicable, they may so conflict with established
procedures as to be undesirable.

F. Will Their Advantages Offset Possible Disadvantages?

Almost any solution for a problem may have its disadvantages; here we ask whether the price of change is too great.

G. What Action Should Be Taken?

The final issue of controversy is to determine which solution should be adopted. And one point of view on this issue, of course, may be to take no action at all.

Here is a classic example of determining the main issues of controversy. Read Lincoln's letter to McClellan and see which of the "stock issues" he employed in his analysis: [6]

EXECUTIVE MANSION
WASHINGTON, February 3, 1862

MAJOR-GENERAL McCLELLAN:

My Dear Sir: You and I have distinct and different plans for a movement of the army of the Potomac—yours to be down the Chesapeake, up the Rappahannock to Urbana, across the land to the terminus of the railroad on the York River; mine to move directly to a point southwest of Manassas.

If you will give satisfactory answers to the following questions, I shall gladly yield my plan to yours.

First. Does not your plan involve a greatly larger expenditure of time and money than mine?

Second. Wherein is a victory more certain by your plan than mine?

Third. Wherein is a victory more valuable by your plan than mine?

Fourth. In fact, would it not be less valuable in this, that it would break no great line of the enemy's communication, while mine would?

Fifth. In case of disaster, would not a retreat be more difficult by your plan than mine?

Yours truly,
ABRAHAM LINCOLN

The main issues, as the investigator now sees them, provide guides for further exploration. As he studies the problem further, of course, he must be prepared to alter the issues if new evidence demands it.

V. WHAT ARE THE ESSENTIALS OF ANY DESIRABLE SOLUTION?

In planning a house an architect may have a series of "musts." There must be three bedrooms, seven closets, a fireplace, a down-

---

[6] Philip Van Doren Stern, ed., *The Life and Writings of Abraham Lincoln* (New York, Random House, 1940), pp. 693-4.

stairs lavatory, a living room large enough to entertain twenty people, and the house must cost no more than fifteen thousand dollars. The architect's problem is to draw a plan which will incorporate all of these essentials. Similar minimum essentials, factors, or values must be included, or accounted for, in the solution of most problems. We seek means of opposing aggressor nations "short of war," we want to prevent extreme inflation or deflation in our economy "without interfering with free enterprise," or we want federal funds for local schools "but not federal control."

Alleged essentials of any acceptable solution are not always legitimate; sometimes they must be modified if any solution is to be possible; further exploration of a problem may prove them invalid, unwise, or even undesirable. But if at least a tentative list of minimum essentials can be drawn up during the preliminary analysis of a problem it will provide a useful standard by which to evaluate specific solutions proposed later. One economist investigating the problems of the milk industry, for example, formulated these essentials at the analysis stage: [7]

The minimum essentials for the solution of the problem of the milk industry are: 1. a substantial increase in the consumption of fluid milk (which cannot be achieved without adequate price protection for the consumer), and 2. the maintenance of farm income from milk at its present level or the raising of that level. No solution which accomplishes one of these at the expense of the other could possibly be satisfactory.

On the eve of the Anglo-American financial discussions in 1949 President Truman also took the "minimum essentials" approach to the problem by laying down these four premises in his speech of August 29th:

1. That a sound and expanding economy is essential to world peace.
2. That we are trying to expand the exchange of goods and services among nations. We are not looking for trick solutions to deep-seated problems.
3. That we cannot succeed unless we keep everlastingly at it.
4. That the democratic nations are not proposing to interfere with one another's internal policies.

Of course, conflicting interest groups may disagree on the minimum essentials of a solution even when they agree upon the existence of a problem. The National Health Assembly and the American Medical Association both see a need for more and better medical

[7] Warren W. Shearer, unpublished manuscript.

care, but the former group feels some form of compulsion is essential, whereas the latter believes that participation in any plan should be voluntary. In this instance the establishment of minimum essentials is itself an issue in the controversy.

VI. IN WHAT DIRECTIONS MAY THE SOLUTIONS LIE?

The final step in the preliminary analysis is to survey the directions in which solutions may be sought. It should not be viewed as an effort to predetermine the ultimate choice, but simply as orientation. Only complete discussion of a problem and thorough debate of all alternatives is a proper basis for selecting a solution; but at various stages in the investigative process some possible solutions may be clearly indicated. Here are two places to look for suggested solutions:

1. When the immediate cause for discussion is reviewed it is likely that several possible solutions are self-evident. In the event of a strike, for example, Proposed Solution No. 1 may be the union's demand for an hourly wage increase of twenty cents; management's support of the status quo is Proposed Solution No. 2; and the compromise suggested by a mediation board is Proposed Solution No. 3. The ultimate solution, of course, may be none of these. If it be argued that an investigator loses his objectivity by considering possible solutions during this early stage of inquiry, we reply that however desirable an attitude of complete detachment may be, it is impossible to attain when certain possible solutions are inherent in the problem. The wise investigator will recognize them and subject them to rigorous testing as he explores the problem further.

2. A review of the origin and history of a problem will also indicate directions in which solutions may lie. During the great public controversy over the Supreme Court in Franklin D. Roosevelt's second administration a careful historical study would have revealed that the problem was not a new one and that, since 1789, various ways had been proposed to make the Court more responsive to contemporary needs: depriving the Court of the power to review acts of Congress, empowering Congress to override decisions of the Court by a two-thirds vote, voiding all five-to-four decisions of the Court, enlarging the membership of the Court, providing for compulsory retirement of justices at a given age, and so on. While no one of those solutions may have been desirable, a study of them

did reveal possibilities not apparent merely by examining the immediate cause for the discussion.

Part of this final step of preliminary analysis is to take an inventory of what has been called the "movability" of various elements in the problem.[8] In most problems there are some factors about which nothing can be done, other elements that will yield to intelligent attack. In discussing race relations in America, for example, the side-by-side existence of Negroes and whites is an immovable element; neither race can be exterminated or eliminated by wholesale migration. The existence of attitudes of fear, mistrust, and prejudice, however, are movable elements; though they will be difficult to overcome they can be eventually. It is possible that what appear to be immovable elements in preliminary analysis will later be found flexible. Even with this risk it is profitable to conclude the preliminary analysis by raising these questions: what factors combine to make the problem? which of these can we do something about? which appear to be inflexible?

The procedure outlined in this chapter, it must be emphasized, is for *preliminary* analysis; procedures for *complete* analysis will be dealt with later. We hope this initial orientation will avoid the common complaint summed up in these lines:

> I'm generally fond of the human race,
>   Except for that one guy I hate:
> The friend who inquires, "What's your point?"
>   At the end of an hour's debate.

READINGS

BAIRD, A. C., *Argumentation, Discussion, and Debate* (New York, McGraw-Hill Book Co., Inc., 1950), Chap. 6.

CLARKE, E. L., *The Art of Straight Thinking* (New York, Appleton-Century-Crofts, Inc., 1929), Chap. 7.

Columbia Associates in Philosophy, *An Introduction to Reflective Thinking* (Boston, Houghton Mifflin Co., 1923), Chap. 9.

LASKER, Bruno, *Democracy Through Discussion* (New York, H. W. Wilson Co., 1949), Chap. 14.

WALLAS, Graham, *The Art of Thought* (New York, Harcourt, Brace & Co., Inc., 1926), Chaps. 4-7.

[8] See Henry Miller Busch, "Discussion in the Administrative Process," *Adult Education Bulletin*, Vol. 13 (February, 1949), p. 86.

EXERCISES

1.* Prepare a three-minute speech on the origin and history of the problem you have chosen for intensive study.

2. Examine the questions currently used in intercollegiate debating by your school and write out an analysis of the terms used in them.

3. From a newspaper editorial, a magazine article, or a speech dealing with a current public problem determine the immediate cause for its discussion.

4. Prepare a five-minute speech analyzing the main issues of controversy in a current campus problem.

5. Attend a discussion or a debate, or read the transcript of one from the list given in the Appendix, and study it to discover the attention given to a preliminary analysis of the problem. What steps in analysis were included? What steps were omitted? Was the preliminary analysis adequate?

6. Are the terms in the following statements capable of satisfactory definition? How would you restate them?

a. Should the government suppress the Communists?

b. What are the bases of a durable peace?

c. Resolved, that this house pities its grandchildren.

d. Should Congress or the people have the right to declare war?

e. Semantics—hope or hoax?

f. Resolved, that the basic industries of the United States should be nationalized.

g. I move that we go on record as opposed to the obvious injustices in the labor-management relations at the Widget Corporation.

h. Is the national debt a danger to our economy?

i. Government should stop taxing the necessities of life.

CHAPTER 7

Exploring the Problem: Evidence

WE HAVE DESCRIBED the preliminary steps in analyzing a problem and are ready now to consider the use of evidence in supporting the issues discovered in this analysis. At this point we need to follow our own advice and define three terms: *evidence, reasoning,* and *argument. Evidence* is the body of facts and opinions bearing on the problem under consideration. *Reasoning* is the process of drawing conclusions from *evidence.* When an individual uses *reasoning* to get others to accept his conclusions we have *argument.* To put it another way, *evidence* refers to the materials of *reasoning; argument,* to the purpose of *reasoning.* We also commonly differentiate among various forms of argument in which reasoning may be expressed.

In this chapter we consider the materials of reasoning, or evidence; in the next, argument. We write in the conviction, as Jefferson put it, that "in a republican nation, whose citizens are to be led by reason and persuasion, and not by force, the art of reasoning becomes of first importance." [1]

All evidence should be ultimately based upon facts. It may come from two sources, observations of facts and opinions about the meaning of facts. Therefore we must consider both (1) *evidence of fact,* and (2) *evidence of opinion.* Some confusion between these two often arises because, in one circumstance, a piece of evidence may be evidence of fact, but in another it may be evidence of opinion. Or the same circumstance may lead one man to a statement of fact, another to a statement of opinion reflecting his interpretation of that circumstance. Consider this example: during an air attack on

[1] Jefferson to David Harding, April 20, 1824, in Adrienne Koch and William Peden, eds., *The Life and Writings of Thomas Jefferson* (New York, Random House, 1944), p. 713.

London, early in World War II, a bomb destroyed an apartment house located some distance from any military target. Here is what four observers said:

1st observer: "There isn't a wall of that apartment building left standing." [Evidence of fact.]

2nd observer: "There isn't a depot, a power center, or a soldier within five miles of that apartment building." [Evidence of fact.]

3rd observer: "The destruction of this apartment building proves that the Nazis are deliberately bombing civilian areas." [Evidence of opinion.]

4th observer: "This kind of thing ought to persuade America to get into the war on our side." [Evidence of opinion.]

Or, to take another example, a scientist in his laboratory may repeat an experiment many times. After each test he records a statement of fact describing the result. When he has satisfied himself that the result is always the same, he may publish his conclusion in what he regards as another statement of fact. But some of those who read his statement may not be convinced of its validity; for them the scientist's statement is one of opinion, not fact. Thus ". . . whether a statement is regarded as a fact or as an opinion is a matter of degree dependent on how convincing is the proof or disproof of the statement. It is also clear that what is an opinion for one individual may be a fact for another, depending on the amount of information available to each individual." [2]

In the first example, the evidence of all four observers was first-hand; it was their personal observation or their personal opinion. This is not true of all evidence: we often accept facts observed and reported by others, and the opinions of someone else. A senator in debating a bill may rely upon the facts reported by a dozen witnesses in open hearings; a student in a discussion may supplement his own judgment with the opinions of others, laymen or experts. The senator may never have been in China and the student may never have seen a federal housing project, yet each one is equipped by the evidence of others to speak on his problem. In dealing with (1) *evidence of fact*, therefore, we must recognize (*a*) facts of personal observation,

[2] C. I. Hovland, A. H. Lumsdaine, and F. D. Sheffield, *Experiments in Mass Communication* (Vol. 3 in the *Series in Social Psychology in World War II*; Princeton, N.J., Princeton University Press, 1949), p. 265.

and (b) facts observed by others. In discussing (2) *evidence of opinion*, we must consider (a) personal opinions, (b) lay opinions, and (c) expert opinions.

Each of these varieties of evidence will frequently be found in exploring a problem; we need, then, to be able to recognize them and to be familiar with ways of testing each type of evidence for validity.

I. EVIDENCE OF FACT

Discussions are often opened with the statement, "Now here are the facts of the situation. . . ." If these are honestly conceived and presented they are limited to statements which accurately report, describe, or classify, on the basis of personal observation or authentic testimony of others, some event, circumstance, or phenomenon that has happened or is happening. Their existence is not a matter of opinion; the statements are based upon more than assertion.

"It's outrageous," cried the lawyer, "they can't put you in jail for walking on the grass in the city park!" "Maybe not," replied the client, "but here I am." Evidence of fact is the best answer to assertion.

An objective description, then, independent of judgment or interpretation, constitutes an observed fact. If we say that food prices are too high we are stating a conclusion or an opinion. But if a housewife compares her weekly food bills for the past year and reports that local meat prices have risen 17 per cent, canned goods 11 per cent, and fresh produce 15 per cent, she is stating a fact of her own observation, and it may be verified by anyone who examines the same evidence. The speaker who says, "It is a *fact* that women are more attractive in the West than in the Northeast," mislabels his statement. The Census Bureau reported in 1948 that only 17 of every 100 women were single in the West, whereas 25 out of 100 were single in the Northeast. These were facts, established by careful observation; the statement of the speaker was only an opinion which purported to explain the facts. We must learn how to establish the validity of factual evidence lest we be misled by our own investigations or by those of others.

A. Facts of Personal Observation

It is axiomatic that if one is to think straight he must be able to see straight. Although our senses are sometimes deceived, if they are exercised properly our observations are likely to be accurate. How can we be sure that we will see and see correctly? Much that we will say about the observations of others applies equally to our own; but three special considerations are appropriate here.

1. *To observe accurately we must have a definite purpose.* Just as the first step in the scientific method is recognizing the existence of a properly located, defined, and limited problem, so in observation the first step is to know what we are looking for. We need to narrow our attention area so we can recognize the facts we want when we find them; the umpire, referee, and head linesman at a football game each has his own area of concentration.

2. *To observe accurately we must have an honest attitude toward the problem.* While investigating a problem for relevant facts we need to free ourselves as far as we can from prejudice and preconceived notions. Facts favorable and unfavorable should receive an equal reception. The investigator whose pre-judgments distort his perception is not trying to solve a problem, he is rationalizing his point of view.

3. *To observe accurately we must record rather than remember.* At best, memory is unreliable; it tends to screen out the commonplace and the uncomfortable facts so that we recall best those that are colorful and pleasant. The memoirs of Mrs. Franklin D. Roosevelt, Harry Hopkins, and James Farley often disagree on specific facts concerning events that took place when all three were present. A written record, made at the time of our observation, is not infallible, but it is more reliable than our recollection.

We have no wish to discourage reliance upon facts of personal observation; the world would be far poorer without Franklin's autobiography, John Quincy Adams' diary, or Churchill's memoirs. Indeed, we generally find reports of first-hand observations more interesting than second-hand summaries. We get close attention when recounting what we have witnessed or experienced.

B. Facts Observed by Others

None of us was present at the battle of Gettysburg; what we know about it must be based upon evidence gathered and reported by others. Few of us have seen an atomic chain reaction, interviewed Joseph Stalin, or investigated living conditions among Southern sharecroppers, but we have read and heard the testimony of those who have done these things. Thus in discussion and debate we frequently must rely for evidence upon the observations of others. But we should not accept without qualification the statement that "this is a fact because Mr. Jones, an eminent authority in his field, says it is." Mr. Jones, too, has his limitations as a witness.

In the first place, any testimony by a witness involves three elements: *observation, memory,* and *narration.* We have already suggested that accurate observation is not common: twenty people reporting what they thought they saw in a traffic accident, or in a touchdown play on the gridiron, are likely to disagree on major items as well as upon minor details. In one familiar example, 20,000 people testified as to the physical characteristics of a man they saw commit a crime; on the average they overestimated his height by five inches, his age by eight years, and in 83 per cent of the cases gave the wrong color for his hair.[3] Similarly, the average individual is relatively unreliable in recalling what took place one, two, or five years ago. Who followed you in the diploma line at your high school graduation? Can you name the author of the textbook used in your freshman composition course? In the element of narration we often find even greater inadequacies. "I know just what happened but I can't describe it" is a common phrase; our powers of narration are not always equal to describing what we see. Limitations such as these exist quite apart from deliberate dishonesty or incompetency. Taken together, they demonstrate the need for critical evaluation of all testimonial evidence.

Traditionally the evaluation of "fact" witnesses has followed the patterns set in law courts.[4] In general, the legal standard includes these considerations:

1. *A reliable witness must be in a position to observe clearly.* Accurate observation may depend upon being near enough to the scene to view it clearly, being in time to see an event take place, having enough light to see it, or being close enough to hear.

2. *A reliable witness must be physically able to observe accurately.* A reliable observer must have the sensory qualifications necessary to observe the fact in question. A deaf witness cannot testify as to what was said unless he qualifies as a lip reader; a blind person may give valid descriptions only of objects he can feel or hear.

[3] Freling Foster, "Keeping Up with the World," *Collier's,* Vol. 106 (August 17, 1940), p. 6.
[4] See G. P. Baker, *The Principles of Argumentation* (Boston, Ginn & Co., 1895), pp. 230-37; J. M. O'Neill, C. Laycock, and R. L. Scales, *Argumentation and Debate* (New York, The Macmillan Co., 1917), pp. 107-12.

3. *A reliable witness must be able intellectually to understand and report what he sees.* Inasmuch as accurate observation may involve understanding a witness must have powers of discrimination; he must also be able to report what he has observed in clear, unambiguous language.

4. *A reliable witness must be able morally to report only what he sees.* It may be impossible to secure otherwise competent witnesses who have no personal interest in the facts under discussion, but precautions should be taken to discover whether the moral character of a witness is such that he may be presumed not to falsify deliberately.

C. Testing Facts

So far we have been concerned with checks upon the reliability of our personal observations and those reported by others. The following questions test the validity of the asserted facts.

1. *Is the asserted fact clearly accessible to observation?* The accuracy of an alleged fact cannot be established if the witness was not in a position to observe it clearly. In an early law case Abraham Lincoln is said to have examined a witness who testified that the light of the moon had enabled him to identify a man running away from the scene of a murder. When Lincoln produced an almanac which showed that there was no moonlight on the night in question the asserted fact was disproved. Many people who could not possibly be in a position to observe the facts like to speak with assurance; the necessity of testing military "scuttlebutt" and civilian rumors in wartime is equally important in everyday discussion.

2. *Is the reporting of the asserted fact complete?* If evidence is to be meaningful it must include every relevant aspect of the asserted fact and the circumstances in which it was observed. In the early days of "extra-sensory perception" experiments some people accused Dr. J. B. Rhine of reporting only high scores and omitting low ones, but a review of the original data showed that all scores were properly accounted for in the final report. A team of debaters who broke even in six tournament debates, however, triumphantly reported to the press that they had won three debates, period. To use the courtroom phrase, this assertion may have been "the truth" but not "the whole truth."

3. *Can the asserted fact be checked by other observers?* The famous accounts of "sea serpents" inevitably are traced back to only

one alleged observer; this is their weakness. The best scientific tradition, of course, calls for multiple verification: if X plus Y gives Z result for one observer, it should yield the same results for others. When an investigator is told that *"everybody* knows this is a fact" he should ask whether *anybody* else really knows it. Even when an alleged fact has been observed by a number of witnesses, it is wise to inquire whether they all agree on essential points. This is why lawyers may introduce apparently repetitious testimony by a succession of witnesses; juries are more likely to accept a fact if a number of people give consistent testimony concerning it. If different observers disagree, the investigator must "check and double check" by testing the alleged fact in other ways.

4. *Is the asserted fact consistent within itself?* Asserted facts must not be self-contradictory; they must have "internal consistency" in that their several aspects are compatible with each other. If a debater argues that federal welfare programs should be expanded, he cannot consistently also call for decreased federal taxes; if he submits percentage figures they cannot total more than 100 per cent; if he contends that two groups fail to coöperate on a voluntary basis, it will seem inconsistent to argue that they can work together in an organic union.

5. *Is the asserted fact consistent with known facts?* Asserted facts must also have "external consistency"; they must agree with other definitely established facts. If it is true that all textbooks are dull we should beware the instructor who promises a sprightly one. In some cases, to be sure, valid facts cannot pass this test: most rivers in the United States do run from north to south, but the Red River in North Dakota happens to be an exception. Consistency with known facts, however, usually suggests the probable truth of the newly asserted fact.

6. *Is the asserted fact probably true?* This is not the ultimate test of an asserted fact, but it is the broadest. It might be called the "common sense test." If a police captain is found to have a bank account of $300,000, does it make sense to accept his statement that he saved it from his $5,000 a year salary? Knowing what we do about the laws of physics, is it likely that a perpetual motion machine has been invented? Is it probable that the United States might be importing wheat, or Venezuela, tin? An asserted fact is not necessarily invalidated if it cannot pass the probability test; it once seemed

improbable that a plane could exceed 400 m.p.h., or that the atom could be split. But if an alleged fact seems improbable, the investigator should be slow to accept it.

These tests are not designed to make the reader suspicious of all evidence, but to encourage a healthy skepticism until the asserted facts have been adequately tested.

II. EVIDENCE OF OPINION

We are eternally confronted with other people's opinions: "The Secretary of State believes...." "Hanson Baldwin, the New York *Times* military expert, says...." "The men who know tobacco best say...." If these opinions are honestly arrived at and fairly presented they are statements made by persons who are alleged to have special qualifications for expressing pertinent judgments or beliefs. While opinions may be based upon facts, they should be distinguished from facts per se.

As with evidence of fact, we may cite the opinions of other laymen, or quote the opinions of experts. In the latter case, evidence of opinion comes from the judgments or beliefs of someone who has relatively complete knowledge of the facts, an authority in his field. We therefore frequently refer to an expert's opinion as "argument from authority," and in this chapter we use *authority* as synonymous with *expert*. Let us consider an example of each type of evidence of opinion.

1. In preparing for a debate on the desirability of having your town own and operate the light and power company you may examine a financial statement of the present private utility, investigate the probable purchase price and maintenance cost, and study present utility rates. Upon the basis of the facts you may conclude that public ownership of these utilities would result in very small savings to the consumer-taxpayer. In the debate you properly express your belief: "After a thorough study of the financial aspects of municipal ownership it is my honest opinion...." (Personal opinion.)

2. If you take part in a panel discussion about increasing federal power projects, opinions about the values of the TVA will almost certainly be expressed. Though you may never have visited in TVA territory, you may cite the observations of a friend whose judgment

you respect: "Of course, I've never seen TVA development, but a friend of mine who has tells me . . . ." (Lay opinion.)

3. On another occasion you take part in a group discussion on the powers of the Federal Bureau of Investigation. You may have no direct knowledge of that agency's relation to espionage activities, but you have recently read an article by someone who does. "Just a few days ago," you may say, "I read an article in *This Week* magazine by J. Edgar Hoover, who has been director of the FBI since 1924. On this point he says . . . ." (Expert opinion.)

In our treatment of evidence of opinion we will describe and evaluate (*a*) opinions we hold personally, (*b*) those of other laymen, and (*c*) opinions of experts.

A. Personal Opinions

Plutarch long ago observed that "to err in opinion, though it be not the part of wise men, is at least human." Those who take part in discussion and debate must learn how to formulate their own opinions wisely and express them concisely. Much has been written about this subject in such books as *How to Think Straight, Thinking to Some Purpose, Language in Action,* and *The Art of Straight Thinking.* Indeed, much that you have already read in this book has been concerned with the problem of critical thinking. The three points which follow, therefore, summarize some things that have already been said.

1. *A sound personal opinion is based upon a clear understanding of the problem.* Unless we make a comprehensive analysis of questions on which we express opinions we risk "talking off the top of our heads." The first requisite, therefore, is a distinct and orderly picture of the problem.

2. *A sound personal opinion is based upon a systematic study of available evidence.* In Sir James Barrie's *Auld Licht Idylls,* Bowie Haggart says, "I am of the opeenion that the works of Burns is of an immoral tendency. I have not read them myself, but such is my opeenion." Predetermined notions, stereotypes, traditions, and guesses seldom lead to valid opinions. The only adequate basis for sound judgment was phrased long ago by Isaac Watts: "Let the degrees of your assent to every proposition bear an exact proportion to the different degrees of evidence."

3. *A sound personal opinion is based upon careful testing wherever possible.* One cannot always subject his judgments to a prag-

matic test, but they are better when he can. Next best, often, is to see how our opinions square with those of others who are well informed on the problem.

B. Lay Opinions

A layman is one who is not an expert on the problem about which he speaks; he lacks the professional training, the experience, or the reputation necessary to speak with authority. As Abraham Lincoln once wrote to a man asking for a testimonial on his soap: "Some specimens of your Soap have been used at our house and Mrs. L. declares it is a superior article. She at the same time protests that I have never given sufficient attention to the 'soap question' to be a competent judge." The layman may, however, be in a position to observe facts not accessible to us; at such times, and when expert testimony is not available, he may provide our best evidence. Until better is found it must carry some weight.

The public opinion survey, such as the Gallup Poll, or the *Fortune* poll, is one of the most common devices for gathering lay opinions. While recent experiences throw doubt on their accuracy in predicting what people will do in an election, such surveys are the best methods available for obtaining cross-sections of public opinion on current issues.

Special considerations in evaluating individual lay opinions parallel those suggested for checking your judgments: they should be based upon (*a*) a clear understanding of the problem, (*b*) a systematic investigation of available evidence, and (*c*) careful testing wherever possible.

C. Expert Opinions (   )

Nicholas Murray Butler was perhaps the first to refer to the expert as "one who knows more and more about less and less." Others have attacked experts, especially academicians in government service, as theorists, suggesting that "what we need are practical men." Yet, as Kurt Lewin once remarked, there is nothing so practical as a good theory. The expert, or authority, is a man qualified to give an opinion upon a problem by reason of his special competence. We recognize, for example, Emily Post as an authority on etiquette, Webster on definitions, Trygve Lie on the United Nations, and the chairman of the Federal Communications Commission on radio. We should also recognize, however, that the use of authority is not of itself an argument or a method of reasoning. Expert opinion is evidence; like all other evidence, it furnishes only the material of reasoning.

It has sometimes been the fashion to look with disdain upon the participant in discussion or debate who cites authorities to support his own views. In his *Notebooks* Leonardo da Vinci complained that "Whoever in discussion adduces authority uses not intellect but memory." And today we often hear the college debater assert that "Quotations don't prove anything!" He is very wrong; a quotation from an authority does prove something; at the least it proves that the expert has an opinion. These criticisms of the use of expert testimony are really leveled against excessive reliance upon authorities, and against so-called authorities who really possess no special qualifications for judgment. With such criticism we are in agreement; we believe that those who attempt to solve problems through discussion and debate must select expert testimony with care. In the fabric of proof authoritative opinion should be skillfully interwoven with substantial evidence of fact.

We have already said that the fact witness must be in a position to know the facts, and physically, intellectually, and morally qualified to testify. This is also true of those offering expert opinion. In addition there are special tests which should be applied.

D. Testing Opinions

The following tests are concerned chiefly with the authority himself, rather than with the opinions he expresses, since his opinions will be acceptable as valid evidence only if he is respected. No matter how reliable or competent he may be, his opinions will carry little weight if his hearers do not regard him as an authority.

1. *Is the reference to authority specific?* How frequently we hear these vague references, "according to an eminent authority," "most economists agree . . . ," or "one expert in the field says . . . ." We read in a newspaper that "a source close to the President," "a high government official," or "a usually reliable source" said so-and-so. Whether the authority referred to is eminent, expert, or usually reliable cannot be determined unless the reference is specific: who is he? under what circumstances did he testify? This does not mean that we expect a speaker laboriously to cite date, volume, and page for every statement attributed to someone else, but it does mean that some degree of specificity is essential. A lawyer may express a different view on the powers of the Supreme Court before he is ap-

pointed to the bench; an ex-Secretary of State may speak more freely on some issues than when he held office. We need to know the exact degree of expertness of any alleged authority. And if we are to check a speaker's references we must know his sources.

2. *Is the authority generally qualified to testify?* We cannot accept the testimony of a color blind person concerning the color of a traffic light at the scene of an accident, nor should we put much faith in the opinions of anyone whose powers of observation, memory, or narration are questionable. If, because of his religious or political views, or the nature of his private or public life, a man's character is suspect, his testimony must also be looked upon with suspicion. Even though an individual may be in an unusual position to know the facts he must be generally qualified—physically, mentally, morally, and even psychologically—if he is to be regarded as an authority.

3. *Is the authority in a position to know or interpret the facts?* A common failing is to regard an authority in one field as an expert in others, even where he has little knowledge or experience. Thus a physicist may be quoted on foreign policy, a banker on domestic relations, or a college president on economics. Now it is conceivable that some physicists, bankers, and college presidents may be qualified in these other fields, but unless we can show this to be true, we should not presume it. We should learn the opinions of men who have established their competency in the field in question. A fairly safe generalization, though not without its exceptions, is that a specialist is more likely to know the facts in his field and to interpret them better than the non-specialist. As Plato wrote in *Protagoras*, "even though a man may be a good flute player, this is no reason to consider him an authority on politics."

4. *Is the authority aware of the significance of his testimony?* An expert may sometimes casually hazard a prediction, make a guess, or play with an hypothesis, but to take any of these as deliberate testimony on the facts in his field would be unfair to him and to the audience. "Off the record" remarks are seldom proper evidence. We should also be cautious about taking too literally statements made "in the heat of the moment" and which the maker would no doubt admit were exaggerated. Wendell Willkie's famous confession of the extravagances of his "campaign oratory" is a case in point. The rule of reason must be applied in weighing all testimonial evidence.

5. *Is the authority reluctant to testify?* If an individual's testimony seems against his own best interests or desires, his evidence may be regarded as exceptionally valuable. The Republican who endorses a Democratic measure, the labor leader who admits the virtue of a particular company union, the textbook writer who praises the work of a competitor, fall into this category. Such apparently reluctant testimony must always be examined carefully, however, for the lion may have an ulterior motive in professing friendship for the lamb.

6. *Is the authority free from hidden bias?* It would be unreasonable to expect a truly unbiased judgment from an expert in a given field; his very judgment is a bias, though it may have been arrived at by the most careful and scholarly methods. As Oscar Wilde once said, "One can give a really unbiased opinion only about things that do not interest one, which is no doubt the reason an unbiased opinion is always valueless." But we are asking here whether the alleged expert has a hidden bias, a special interest which he carefully conceals. Several years ago a prominent economist wrote a series of articles for a popular weekly magazine in which he subtly praised a particular industrial corporation. When the praise seemed inordinate, the editor investigated his writer and then publicly apologized because he had learned that the economist was on the corporation's payroll. The objection in such cases is not that the authority is really an advocate, but that he pretends an objectivity he does not have.

7. *Is the authority supported by factual evidence?* Too frequently we hear discussions or debates where reference to authority constitutes all of the evidence. There are situations, such as a layman gathering information on technical medical questions, where all valid evidence must come from specialists. But in general it should be regarded as a dubious practice to rely only upon any one type of evidence. So-called authorities, for example, can be found to "prove" that the world is flat, that capitalism is dead, or that an apple a day keeps the doctor away. "Mark you this, Bassanio. The devil can cite Scripture for his purpose." Recognizing that on some questions evidence other than that of authorities may not be available, we should nevertheless accept with caution any reasoning based solely upon opinions.

8. *Is undue reliance placed upon a single authority?* No matter how competent a man may be, we should be reluctant to accept his word alone if other experts are available. On some personal problems

only the person involved may be qualified to speak as an authority, but when we confront a serious problem we prefer a consultation of experts and their combined judgment. Suppose, for example, that Louis Agassiz, the great Harvard scientist, were the only authority cited on the validity of Darwin's *Origin of the Species*. Expert though he was, Agassiz labeled Darwinism "a scientific mistake, untrue in its facts, unscientific in its method, and mischievous in its tendency." [5] Rather than relying solely upon Hockett, Beard, Turner, Nevins, or Schlesinger on a point of historical controversy we should check the opinions of them all. It may be remarked, in this connection, that not every opinion which achieves the distinction of print thereby acquires value: many foolish as well as wise ideas have been published in large type and fine bindings. A critical mind, combined with a fine sense of discrimination is the best equipment for exploring evidence.

9. *Is the reference to an authority who will be accepted?* This final test is quite different in character from those already suggested: here we ask, "no matter how competent this man may be, will this particular audience accept him as an authority?" There are some matters upon which the president of the National Association of Manufacturers is the best authority available, but it is unlikely that his testimony on wages and hours would impress a labor union meeting. Men like Harry Bridges, Robert Taft, Harry Truman, or Joseph Stalin have special competencies, but prejudices against them are so strong among some groups that they must be used as authorities with great care. In general it is good practice to cite authorities who are not extreme in their views. We agree with Thomas Huxley that "it is the customary fate of new truths to begin as heresies and to end as superstitions," yet we would beware of insisting on quoting the supposed heretic when authorities with more prestige are available.

III. SPECIAL WAYS OF PRESENTING EVIDENCE

Two special ways of presenting evidence are so frequently employed that they deserve attention here. These are (1) *the citation of statistics,* and (2) *the citation of examples.*

[5] "Professor Agassiz on the Origin of Species," *American Journal of Science and Arts,* Vol. 80 (November, 1860), p. 154.

These special methods of presentation may be used for evidence of fact or for evidence of opinion. If, for instance, we have made a personal survey of unemployment in Ohio we may present the observed facts *statistically* in order to conserve time or space. Or, we may wish to pick out one specific city from all those surveyed and present its problems in detail as a typical *example*. We might also present evidence of opinion by these methods. The results of a questionnaire asking opinions on unemployment sent to 150 leading economists might be summarized in *statistics;* we might single out Professor Slichter's reply, after determining that it was typical, and cite it as a single *example*.

We often use these special methods to condense a large body of material so that it may be presented in a brief period. This is particularly true when a few comparative figures may quickly demonstrate the result of investigating a thousand cases. We may also use these devices to make our material more vivid or graphic for the listener. "One out of every ten workers in Rocktown is unemployed" is more graphic than "6,714 workers in Rocktown are unemployed." A case history of Joe Brown may make the unemployment problem much more vivid than enumerating a series of conclusions based upon studying hundreds of cases.

In the following pages we will discuss statistics and examples as methods of presentation and suggest ways of testing their value as evidence.

A. Citation of Statistics

One of the most common conversational clichés is the phrase "Statistics prove. . . ." Thus the fans of the American and National baseball leagues carry on their ceaseless arguments by citing statistics or numerical records which are presumed to prove their respective points. Many persons are inclined to mistrust statistically expressed information: "Figures don't lie, but liars figure," they say, with the air of enunciating a profound truth. Nevertheless, statistics may serve as an effective and reliable method of presentation. "On a nation-wide average basis," says a speaker, "construction costs have risen 134 per cent since 1932; 56 per cent since 1940; 44 per cent since 1943; 28 per cent since 1947." This means that he has taken certain numerical records of facts and placed them in a position of relationship. As a device for presenting evidence, then, statistics offer a method of judging phenomena collectively on the basis of enumeration of single instances. Statistics themselves are reports, numerically expressed, of observed facts.

One of the most common uses of statistics is in presenting evidence gathered by the questionnaire or sampling technique. Originally this procedure was used mainly for commercial purposes. A door-to-door canvass in a selected town furnished examples for a generalization as to how many people used Ivory soap, owned a vacuum cleaner, or planned to buy an electric dishwasher. With the development of commercial radio, sponsors were vitally interested in knowing the size of their listening audiences. Again the sampling technique was used: perhaps a thousand people in St. Louis were chosen at random from the phone book, called, and asked what radio program they were listening to. These folks were regarded as typical of the whole listening public in St. Louis and generalizations were made as to the total number of listeners for a given broadcast. The most recent application of this technique has been the public opinion poll; it attempts to discover mass opinion on specific legislative proposals, governmental policies, and other current problems. In planning discussion meetings this same technique is often useful: a survey of those who usually attend may guide leaders in the selection of topics, a questionnaire may reveal the general character of the forum constituency or be an index to the reactions at a specific meeting. A sample questionnaire of this type is included in Chapter 22.

The most obvious advantage of using statistics is that we may present a descriptive survey of a body of data that would otherwise be difficult or impossible to comprehend. They also enable us to compute averages which are helpful in predicting future phenomena in the same class; this is the purpose of the life insurance actuarial table. Finally, by using statistics we can present large quantities of data more graphically so that relationships and trends become more apparent.

Before using statistics to present evidence we should subject them to certain reasonable tests.

B. Test of Statistics

1. *Are the units compared actually comparable?* It may be said that nation X has twice the naval strength of nation Y, but if the units compared are variable the statistics are unreliable. In one case only fighting ships may be counted; in the other, tankers, minesweepers, and repair vessels may be included. The definition of units

is always basic: what is a crime, a student, a highway, a Protestant, an amateur athlete, an unemployable, or a drunkard?

Care must also be taken to see that the unit has not been changed in the course of investigation. We would have to remember, for example, in surveying the prevalence of crime from 1900-1950, that some actions not considered criminal in 1900 are so classed in 1950. After 1934 it became a criminal offense to fail to register securities offered for sale in interstate commerce; in 1947 it became a crime for an employer to make a gift to a bargaining representative of his employees. These extensions of the term *crime* must be considered in weighing the data collected.

If it is said that divorces in the United States have increased rapidly since 1900 because in that year there were 9.32 divorces *per 1000 population* and in 1949 there were 30.2 divorces *per 100 marriages*, any conclusion is ambiguous. Divorces per 1000 population or divorces per 100 marriages must be calculated for each of the years to establish a valid statistical comparison. In other cases the same test should be applied: in comparing child labor in several states we would have to know that the term is used in the same way in each state. The student who added beans and corn and got succotash had the right answer.

2. *Are the statistics really an index to what we want to know?* We must guard against being trapped by statistics which seem relevant but are not. The hourly wage rates for carpenters in Lewisburg may have little connection with the standard of living in Lewisburg. The number of persons attending a Democratic rally in Yanktown bears little direct relation to the probable success of the Democratic ticket in the next election. Such figures may serve as a partial basis for constructing hypothetical judgments, but they are far from conclusive. Similarly, statistical evidence may be limited in value if it is premised upon an implied analogy between the situation covered by the statistics and the situation we are investigating.

3. *Are the statistics presented in their most significant form?* When statistics are presented in gross numbers or *totals*, they are often apt to be misleading; *percentages* or *rates* may present a truer picture. If, for example, we say that there were 1,007,595 divorces in the United States in 1915 and 1,232,559 in 1929 we cannot conclude on this basis alone that the divorce rate has increased; while the total number increased, so did the total population. On the other

hand, if we examine statistics in terms of percentage of population, we would find that there were exactly 10.14 divorces per 1000 people in both years, and conclude that the divorce rate had not actually increased. Here percentages are more meaningful than gross numbers. If, finally, we present statistics in terms of the number of divorces per 100 marriages we would find the figure at 10.14 in 1915, and 16.3 in 1929, and conclude that the divorces-per-marriages rate had gone up. In this case, statistical rates or ratios are also more meaningful than gross numbers.

Americans seem to like figures, but we frequently err by failing to use them in their most significant form. In 1940 the Republicans took consolation in the fact that Wendell Willkie polled more votes than any previous Republican candidate, but the fact was that on at least three previous occasions a losing candidate had received a greater *proportion* of the total vote. After the same election the Democrats boasted that Franklin Roosevelt received more votes than any previous candidate for the presidency, but the *distribution* of this support gave him fewer electoral college votes than in two previous elections.

Another factor in presenting statistics in their most significant form is the choice between *average, median,* and *mode,* three terms which are frequently confused. Ordinarily we think of *average* as meaning "typical" or "medium," but this is often misleading. If a dozen dub golfers were joined by Ben Hogan or Lawson Little their average score would be lowered considerably, but the dubs would still be dubs. In a mathematical sense *average* means the total of a number of individual items divided by the number of items; thus one extreme item, such as Hogan's score, may change the average figure a great deal and give a distorted picture of the whole group. The *median,* on the other hand, is that figure which stands in the middle of a series. If grades in the argumentation class are 34, 41, 48, 53, 55, 75, 81, 86, 95, 95, and 98, then the middle figure of 75 is the median grade. The average is 69+. What we often refer to when we speak of "average income," "average man," and so on, is the *mode,* or the measure which occurs with greatest frequency. Using the same set of class grades, we say that the central tendency, or modal grade is 95.

The concept of the "average man" as really a "statistical man" is illustrated in the survey of its male readers taken by *Time* magazine in 1949.[6] On the basis of questionnaires returned by 3,041 men it was found that the "average *Time* reading male" has an income of $7,600, holds $20,158 worth of stocks and bonds, carries $30.50 in his pocket, shoots a 95 in golf, entertains eleven guests a week at a cost of $1,000 per year, has 34,859 miles on his car, carries 6.0 keys of which 1.1 are never used, owns 31 ties, and uses 82.6 strokes in shaving. But this average or typical man may have no flesh and blood counterpart in real life.[7]

4. *Do the statistics cover a sufficient number of cases?* The law of statistical regularity indicates that a fairly large number of items selected at random from a very large group of similar items is almost certain to have the characteristics of the larger group, and that the items represent the whole group. The danger in presenting statistical data on this premise is that we may overlook the necessity for a large number of items. The golfer who scored a hole in one his first time on the course, and then swore off the game, makes a pretty story about how every time he played he scored a hole in one. But the man who plays regularly knows better. To be statistically reliable, data must be gathered in large numbers if random selection is used: a survey of 300 out of the 1,000 graduates of Home High School, might be an adequate basis for a conclusion that 50 per cent of the graduates went on to college. However, if a scientific sampling is employed, with known factors of difference among cases properly weighted, a smaller number of samples may be statistically reliable: some polling agencies, for example, use as few as 3,000 carefully selected interviews as a basis for determining national opinion on current issues.

5. *Do the statistics cover a sufficient period of time?* As with the last test, our concern here is with an adequate sample, a period of time that is fair and not exceptional. In the month of September in a given year the average temperature in Chicago might be 76.3 degrees, but this investigation would hardly justify a general rule. If a September survey for thirty years showed 65.2 degrees as the average temperature in that month for that whole period, however, a general conclusion would seem valid. Similarly, we might question the validity of the average monthly sale of automobiles if the data

---

[6] "Your Time Exposure," Research Report No. 1019, Time, Inc., January, 1949.

[7] See also Darrell Huff, "How to Lie with Statistics," *Harper's*, Vol. 201 (August, 1950), pp. 97-101.

were based upon June figures, or the average number of out-of-town visitors to New York City if the data were collected during the World's Fair. In situations where it is highly probable that the operating causes are constant, however, statistics based upon short periods of observation may be acceptable. The batting averages of American League champions from 1916-1950, for example, may be fairly calculated on the basis of any five-year period, or the average cost of living for this year may be accurately estimated by checking figures for the second Tuesday of each month.

The importance of these two tests of sufficiency in number of cases and period of time, may be illustrated by imagining a series of ten individual items ranged along a scale of continuous variation.

Grades	10	20	30	40	50	60	70	80	90	100
Students	A	B	C	D	E	F	G	H	I	J

Let them be the grades of ten students on an examination. If we select at random students A, B, C, and F as bases for a statistical picture of the whole group we would find that the average grade appeared to be 30. An equally misleading result would appear if we chose students D, E, and J, or G, H, and I. It is clear that we must have a sufficient number of cases of *representative character*. If we were to use the same illustration, but substituting "Years" for "Grades" and "National Income" for "Students," we would find that a wide range would again be necessary to derive valid statistical data, in this case to insure a *representative period of time*.

6. *How strongly were the gatherers of the statistics interested in the outcome?* In examining any type of evidence we must be alert to any apparent bias, error, or misinterpretation resulting from the special interests of the person gathering the data. People often, intentionally or unintentionally, find what they are looking for; this seems to be especially true of statistical data. For this reason, professional research agencies are often employed to collect and interpret data. If we are considering the cost of living as a factor in possible wage raises, for example, we might find five different estimates made by the Bureau of Labor Statistics, the CIO, the Republican National Committee, the National Association of Manufacturers, and a presidential fact-finding committee. In each instance, the gatherers of the statistics might conceivably have a strong interest in the outcome of the investigation, and their findings should be judged accordingly. The best procedure, in such a case, is to examine the data of as many

different agencies as possible; this advice is applicable, of course, to the evaluation of all types of evidence.

C. Citation of Examples

To guard against the specious use of examples in presenting evidence requires careful analysis and testing; the device of citing examples is frequently misused. To cite a single example means to select one fact or opinion as typical of a whole class of ostensibly similar instances and to draw from it a conclusion concerning the whole class. After reading one short story by Somerset Maugham, we pass judgment on all of his writing; our neighbor denounces frozen foods in general because one package of beans failed to please; the drivers in Texas are condemned because one reckless Texan was met on the highway. In each of these cases a single example is used unwisely to judge an entire class.

In sound reasoning, of course, an isolated example should rarely be relied upon. Rather, a large group of typical examples should be selected from the whole class and a conclusion based upon them. This judgment we call a *generalization*, a general conclusion based upon a limited number of facts or opinions. If we want to draw a reasonable conclusion about Maugham's ability as a writer, we must observe a large number of samples. We will probably discover some stories that are excellent, others that are fair, and a few quite undistinguished. On the basis of these examples, the only reasonable *generalization* would be that Maugham is very much like other writers: some of his work is better than the rest.

It may seem that the categories of statistics and examples overlap in terms of the methods of selecting them and the purposes for which they are used. There is an essential difference, however, in that examples are more vivid and concrete; they are usually more interesting to the listener, and might well be described as animated, personalized, or vivified statistics.

D. Test of Examples

1. *Have the examples been chosen to support a preconceived conclusion?* There is a proper place for advocacy, but even there we want to feel that examples have been selected honestly; in investigating a problem, of course, we should examine as many examples as possible. Sometimes a newspaper editorial, or a book, reads as though the writer had been told, "Here is our policy; now dig up some

examples to support it!" This is typical for anyone who feels obliged to support any kind of party line; as one Communist leader is reported to have said, "When I am on a speaking trip, I say frankly to questions on current events, 'I can only answer up to last Thursday. I haven't seen the *Daily Worker* since then.' " [8] Examples handpicked to support a predetermined point of view should have difficulty passing the tests which follow.

2. *Are the examples fair representatives of their class?* It may be difficult to determine how representative a single example may be, but it is seldom impossible to discover other examples of the same class so that a valid collective judgment can be expressed. It would be manifestly unfair to judge a whole race of people by an unfortunate acquaintance with one representative, the entire Congress by an experience with one senator, or a newspaper by a single editorial. The way to avoid this error is to study many examples chosen from the same class so that we may be sure those presented as evidence are representative.

3. *Are there contrary examples which have not been considered?* Closely allied with the preceding test is this one which asks whether there are any known exceptions to "the general rule" which appears to govern a whole class of examples. Contrary examples do not necessarily invalidate the rest of the evidence, but they should be recorded and accounted for in the conclusion. Suppose that we poll half the seniors at Hapgood College to find what they expect to be earning ten years after graduation. These might be the results:

1 person	$1,500
8 persons	4,000
9 persons	4,500
6 persons	5,000
1 person	10,000

From these twenty-five examples we might conclude that "as a general rule Hapgood College graduates expect to be earning $4-5,000 ten years after graduation." This conclusion agrees with the evidence, but it would have greater validity if it included the two extremely contrary examples, the men expecting to earn $1,500 and $10,000. These unusual cases help define the extent to which the general rule may be considered valid.

[8] E. G. Flynn, in the *Daily Worker*, quoted in *American Mercury*, Vol. 54 (January, 1942), p. 62.

4. *Do the examples represent a large enough portion of their class to justify a generalization?* There can be, of course, no absolute measure of "enough" in applying this test; the answer depends largely upon the phenomena being studied. In certain areas of physics or chemistry a very few examples may be sufficient evidence to permit a valid generalization: if several properly conducted experiments show that when M is added to N the result is O there is little value in endless repetition of the test. But in other areas, where belief, opinion, prejudice, personal likes and dislikes are concerned, a much larger collection of examples is necessary to justify a generalization. We should not be satisfied with two or three answers to the question "What do the American people think of socialized medicine?" or "Should the student council raise the activity fee?" A good general rule is that "the greater the possible variations in answer to our question, the wider must be the field of observation, in order to justify a generalization." [9]

5. *Are the facts concerning the examples verifiable?* One obvious test of an example is to examine its factual basis or the authority behind it. If we generalize that not one in ten Whitetown voters would support Senator Blank for reëlection we have proved nothing about his chances unless we know whether he carried Whitetown six years ago. Opposition to him may have been even greater in the last election. Sometimes, of course, the factual bases of a generalization cannot be investigated: it took ten years before Hermann Rauschning's example of Hitler's views were verified. But whenever possible an example or a generalization should be tested not only as to the facts underlying it but also as to its real significance for the problem being investigated.

6. *Is there other evidence to support probable validity of the generalization?* This test should be applied to any evidence, no matter how it is presented. If we cite Winston Churchill's 1940 proposal for a union of England and France as typical of British opinion at that time we may put too much reliance on a single example. Before we are satisfied we should look for other observed facts or authoritative opinions which might support the generalization. A high probability of validity is established if a varied body of evidence supports a single example or a generalization; but if it

[9] J. M. O'Neill, C. Laycock, and R. L. Scales, *Argumentation and Debate* (New York, The Macmillan Co., 1917), p. 162.

stands unsupported by other evidence it should be regarded as of at least doubtful value.

IV. USING AUDIO-VISUAL AIDS TO PRESENT EVIDENCE

An old Chinese proverb says that "one picture is worth more than a thousand words." This puts the argument for visual presentation pretty strongly, but it is not without some basis in fact. In Navy training courses, for example, audio-visual aids, such as motion pictures, charts, diagrams, and recordings, when used to supplement more orthodox classroom methods, enabled students to learn up to 35 per cent more information in a given time, and helped them to remember the information up to 55 per cent longer.[10] In the Army orientation program audio-visual aids showed similar results when the object was to influence attitudes: men who saw documentary films not only shifted their attitudes but these shifts persisted in marked degree for at least several months.[11] By and large, this experience has been duplicated in civilian classrooms and in discussion and debate programs. The general caution that applies to the use of all audio-visual aids, of course, is not to make such constant use of them for presenting facts and opinions that their value as *aids* wears off; they cannot replace other methods of presentation. Audio-visual aids in discussion and debate often serve the same purpose as examples, making abstract materials concrete. They may also be used to give a panoramic view that would be difficult to condense into words, or at any time when *seeing* as well as hearing will aid the understanding of the listener.

1. *Documentary films* present facts and opinions gathered by someone else, in pictorial and narrative form. They are particularly useful as part of the introduction to a discussion for arousing interest, furnishing information, and stimulating discussion. The U.S. Department of Agriculture's 24-minute film *Banking on the Land*, for example, is an historical review of the development of credit coöperatives among farmers and might furnish background informa-

---

[10] Bureau of Naval Personnel, *More Learning in Less Time* (Washington, D.C., 1943), p. 3.
[11] I & E Division, War Department, "Attitudes and Orientation Films," *What the Soldier Thinks*, No. 1 (Washington, D.C., 1943), pp. 12-3.

tion for a discussion on that topic. Or a discussion of international control of atomic energy might be stimulated by the U.S. Army's 12-minute film, *A Tale of Two Cities*, which pictures the atomic bombing of Hiroshima and Nagasaki. *Using Visual Aids in Training*, a 14-minute film of the U.S. Office of Education, might arouse interest in a discussion of modern educational methods. A list of sources for films such as these is found in the Appendix.

It is important to remember that no matter how good a film may be, it is only an introduction, not a substitute, for discussion. The film itself should be introduced in a one- or two-minute statement, indicating what it is about, why it is significant, and perhaps suggesting what to look for. After the film has been shown the discussion leader should provide a transition by relating it to the topic, recalling points that may serve to open up the discussion, or filling in with facts the film may not have provided.

2. *Recordings* of significant speeches, discussions, or radio programs may both provide information and dramatize the problem. Roosevelt's 1941 war message to Congress, the America's Town Meeting of the Air symposium on the implications of the last national election, or the CBS radio documentary "Communism in America," may each be useful as springboards into discussion. Recordings such as these may be obtained from a number of sources, some of which are listed in the Appendix.

Recordings should be used in much the same way as films: they should be introduced briefly, and after they have been heard the leader should establish points of contact between the recording and the discussion which is to follow.

3. *Pictures, cartoons, maps, and posters* may impress specific bits of information upon the listeners in ways more vivid than spoken words. A picture of a local slum, an editorial cartoon dealing with Congressional investigations, a map of the Far East, or a poster listing the poll tax states, may offer facts or points of view to members of a discussion group. These same visual aids, of course, lend themselves easily for use in advertising a public discussion or debate meeting. Ideas for these aids can be gathered by any imaginative person from his observations, readings, and conversations.

Sometimes pictures or maps may be useful during the whole discussion, but if they illustrate one specific point it is wise not to present them until that point is made; part of their value lies in their freshness. The use of too many aids of this type may divide the attention of the audience; they should be used with discrimination.

4. *Graphs* are used to present statistical information and to aid the listener in remembering important data. Three types of statistical information are commonly presented in graphs: (*a*) comparisons of the quantity of several things at once, i.e., the relative amounts of education received by the average child in rural and urban areas, (*b*) trends in the quantity of several things over a period of time, i.e., average annual income received by farm and industrial workers in the 1920-50 period, (*c*) combinations of comparisons and trends considered together. The reading list at the end of this chapter includes sources of information on the construction of the common types of graphs: the line graph, the bar graph, the pie graph, and the pictorial graph.

When a series of graphs is used to present statistical data it is usually wise to reveal them to the listeners one at a time; otherwise the profusion of data may lead to confusion. If these aids are used by a team in a debate, of course, the opposition is entitled to refer to charts or graphs in refutation even as they refer to statements made by their opponents.

5. *Charts*, among the most useful visual aids, may be used in developing an outline or listing points, or to clarify complex information, such as the structure of the United Nations organization or the details of parliamentary procedure. The ease with which they may be made also recommends them. Charts may be prepared before a meeting, but they are sometimes most useful if constructed during a discussion and used as a record of progress.

6. *Slides and filmstrips* are simply special ways of displaying pictures, cartoons, maps, posters, graphs, and charts. Instead of handling the original document it is copied on slides or filmstrips (a sequence of pictures on 35 mm. film, and in the order in which they will be shown) for projection in a "magic lantern," opaque projector, or filmstrip projector. The sources listed in the Appendix for films and recordings also handle slides and filmstrips.

Especially useful is the filmstrip. A speaker in a symposium on "What responsibilities do advertisers have to the public?" might select several magazine samples of objectionable advertisements, draw a graph showing the percentage of a product's cost that is charged to advertising, prepare a chart showing the increase in newspaper advertising in the last decade, and so on, and photograph each one to provide a running series of illustrations for his talk. The whole series, of course, will be on a pocket-size strip of film.

7. *Blackboards* are perhaps the most used, and most abused, of the media for presenting information. Yet when technical difficulties prevent the use of other visual aids, a blackboard is generally a possible substitute; many times it has advantages over other devices. Charts, diagrams, graphs, maps, and even pictorial sketches may be used in a "chalk-talk," while a person who draws well may do a series of illustrations, erasing one and sketching another, that perform a function similar to the filmstrip. When any visual aid has served its purpose, of course, it should be removed lest it distract the attention of the audience. It is also wise, and for the same reason, to wait until any particular aid is needed before displaying it.

Because of the frequency with which members of a discussion group may use the blackboard, it may be wise to suggest a few basic cautions: (*a*) Don't try to crowd too many details into your illustration; if you "stick to the skeleton" you can make complex items simple. (*b*) Do make the items in your illustration large enough to be seen by all the audience; use large lettering, even exaggerated proportions if necessary. (*c*) Don't be fussy about artistic details and thereby take the audience's attention off the main point; use circles, straight lines, squares, and other shorthand methods of drawing figures and objects. (*d*) Do use contrast, by size of figures or objects, by color of chalk, or by variety in type of illustration, to add emphasis and clarity. (*e*) Don't let yourself "doodle" on the blackboard, but use it only when you need it, then erase what is no longer significant. (*f*) Do let the audience see the board; stand to one side when commenting on it, using a pointer if necessary. (*g*) Don't talk to the board instead of to the audience. (*h*) Do practice your illustrations ahead of time so that you can make them easily; look at them from the back of the room to test their visibility and simplicity.

As means of presenting evidence audio-visual aids may have great value, but they can do no more than supplement the speaker's words. Carefully planned and efficiently used, they can add interest and variety to the presentation.

V. SUGGESTIONS FOR GATHERING EVIDENCE

In concluding our discussion of evidence three admonitions may be appropriate.

Gather enough evidence. There is no definite answer to the obvious question, "How much evidence do I need?" But it is fair to observe that very few participants in discussion or debate suffer from having too much. Seldom will every piece of evidence gathered be immediately useful but, because every audience situation is different, the more evidence a speaker has gathered the better he can adapt his argument to any specific group.

Seek a variety of evidence. A judicious combination of facts and opinions is usually superior to sole reliance upon either one. Whenever possible, factual evidence should come from personal observation, and evidence of opinion from the most competent authorities available. And it is wise to consider the possible efficiency and interest value of using statistics, examples, or audio-visual aids as ways of presenting evidence.

Document evidence carefully. What was said on this point in the discussion of research techniques deserves reëmphasis: knowing the evidence includes knowing the source of the evidence. Without a proper knowledge of the source it is difficult to evaluate a fact or an opinion. Accurate and complete documentation of each piece of evidence as it is gathered may save many hours of later research and avoid possible embarrassment.

The *World Almanac* has long been recognized as an authoritative reference volume. The late Robert Hunt Lyman, who edited it for many years, used to say "The surer I am of a 'fact,' the more pains I take to verify it." [12] We can think of no better advice.

READINGS

ALLPORT, G. W., and POSTMAN, Leo, *The Psychology of Rumor* (New York, Henry Holt & Co., Inc., 1947), Chap. 8.

BAIRD, A. C., *Argumentation, Discussion, and Debate* (New York, McGraw-Hill Book Co., Inc., 1950), Chaps. 8-9.

BLACK, Max, *Critical Thinking* (New York, Prentice-Hall, Inc., 1946), Chap. 13.

[12] "Bookmarks," *Saturday Review of Literature*, Vol. 31 (October 23, 1948), p. 22.

CANTRIL, Hadley, *et al.*, *Gauging Public Opinion* (Princeton, N. J., Princeton University Press, 1944), Chaps. 5, 12.

DALE, Edgar, *Audio-Visual Methods in Teaching* (New York, Dryden Press, 1946).

DOOB, L. W., *Public Opinion and Propaganda* (Henry Holt & Co., Inc., 1948), Chap. 12.

GALLUP, George, "The Quintamensional Plan of Question Design," *Public Opinion Quarterly*, Vol. 11 (Fall, 1947), pp. 385-93.

HOCKETT, H. C., *Introduction to Research in American History* (New York, The Macmillan Co., 1948), Chap. 2.

LEVINSON, Horace C., *The Science of Chance* (New York, Rinehart & Co., 1950).

McBURNEY, J. H., and HANCE, K. G., *Discussion in Human Affairs* (New York, Harper & Bros., 1950), Chap. 9.

MOUAT, L. H., "The Illustrated Speech," *Quarterly Journal of Speech*, Vol. 31 (December, 1945), pp. 428-30.

SCHREIBER, Julius, *et al.*, *It Pays to Talk It Over* (Washington, D. C., National Institute of Social Relations, 1947), pp. 30-47.

STEBBING, L. S., *Thinking to Some Purpose* (Middlesex, England, Penguin Books, Ltd., 1939), Chap. 14.

THOULESS, R. H., *How to Think Straight* (New York, Simon & Schuster, Inc., 1941), Chap. 9.

WAUGH, A. E., *Elements of Statistical Method* (New York, McGraw-Hill Book Co., Inc., 1938).

EXERCISES

1.* Write out, on properly documented cards, five pieces of factual evidence and five pieces of evidence by authority, all relating to your problem for intensive study.

2.* Develop an outline for a speech dealing with one major issue of the subject you have selected for intensive study, include the evidence in the outline, and note in the margins the types you use.

3. In terms of the material presented in this chapter, what are the meanings of the italicized terms in the following statements?

a. It is a *fact* that income taxes are too high.

b. Why can't you use a little *reason* in looking at this problem?

c. My *opinion* is that the Democrats will win the election.

d. What do you *infer* from these facts?

e. Dr. Smith is an *authority* on forensic medicine.

f. Isn't it *self-evident* that the law is unfair?

g. I can prove my point by *statistics*.

h. Doesn't my *example* show that the plan won't work?

i. I *believe* in equal rights.

4. Select one competent authority on each of the following subjects and be prepared to defend your choice:

a. Benefits of advertising

   b. Federal taxation laws
   c. Values of consumer coöperatives
   d. Desirability of abolishing grades
   e. Threats to world peace
   5. Select ten pieces of evidence used in a class discussion or debate and evaluate them by the tests proposed in this chapter.
   6. Under what circumstances, and upon what subject, would the following persons be considered acceptable authorities?
   a. A college professor
   b. The governor of your state
   c. The manager of your local radio station
   d. The president of the local Chamber of Commerce
   e. The treasurer of your college
   7. Not all authorities testify upon the basis of the same type of information. Cite examples of experts whose valid opinions might be of these types:
   a. Judgments based on experience and repeated observations
   b. Judgments based on information not generally available
   c. Judgments based on data the layman cannot ordinarily interpret
   d. Judgments based on incomplete data
   e. Judgments based on inconclusive data
   8. Describe a problem for which the *average* figure might be the most significant. Do the same for *median,* and for *mode.*
   9. What would be wrong with the statistical procedure followed in these instances?
   a. Calculating the average daily bank deposits in Atlanta, Ga., by checking the records from December 17-24
   b. Comparing the population of America and Russia to determine relative military strength
   c. Determining the popularity of a breakfast food by counting the number of box tops sent in by children to collect prizes
   d. Taking the average grade made by the students in each course to determine the academic achievement of the student body as a whole
   e. Predicting the score of the Wabash-DePauw football game on the basis of statements from the Wabash and DePauw coaches
   10. Select three advertisements for nationally advertised products and write a brief analysis of each to answer these questions: (*a*) How much of each advertisement is statement of observed fact, authoritative opinion, or mere assertion? (*b*) How does the evidence in each advertisement qualify under the appropriate tests? (*c*) What more valid evidence would you suggest for inclusion in each advertisement?
   11. Examine each of the following bits of evidence to determine: (*a*) its type, (*b*) its validity when subjected to the appropriate tests. A useful device may be to rank the statements in terms of your estimate of their validity.
   a. "Ambition is destroyed in a large percentage of the population when all the provisions of socialized medicine are put into effect. . . .

The proposed bill ... makes it possible for the government to take directly ... earnings ... of conscientious moral workmen ... and give them to the lazy, shiftless, immoral individuals for sickness which they may have largely brought on themselves by riotous, immoral living." (Edward H. Ochsner, M.D., Chicago Medical Society, in 1946 Senate Committee hearings on a National Health Program)

b. "It is a fair assumption, based upon all-England sales, that more than 50 per cent of England's statesmen and military leaders carry a Biro—by an overwhelming margin, Britain's favorite pen." (Advertisement in the New York *Times*, 1949)

c. "Dr. Meiklejohn concedes that 'sedition does not fall within the constitutional protection' [of free speech and press]. But what is sedition? According to Blackstone, any utterance was seditious and hence bound by law if it 'tended' to endanger public security. Under the 'clear-and-present-danger' rule an utterance is not seditious unless it urges the doing of something which the government is entitled to prevent and the urging is done in circumstances which furnish a clear and present danger that the forbidden action will follow. ..." (Edward S. Corwin, professor emeritus of jurisprudence, Princeton University, in a letter to the editor, New York *Times*, 1948)

d. "A survey at Washington State College revealed that married students do better scholastically than single students. The married student is glad to listen to the professor for a change." (Columnist in the Cleveland *Plain Dealer*, 1949)

e. "Such frauds like compulsory health insurance ... anticipate the establishment of universal state medical service for everybody. That is socialism as unadulterated as if it came from the sanctified pen of Karl Marx himself." (Editorial in *The Nation's Business*, 1940)

f. "By comparison with the United States, the USSR is young: one-half of her population is under 21, two-thirds is under 30" (Dr. Paul Rowland, lecturer on Slavic peoples, 1948)

g. "In general the people who do not reproduce their numbers are in the upper middle and upper socio-economic levels. If the universities of Princeton, Yale and Harvard and the colleges of Smith, Wellesley and Vassar were to limit their enrollment to children of former students, and if all such children were to attend these institutions, their enrollment would drop to one-half the present size in 50 years and to a quarter in 100 years. That is, enrollments would drop unless their universities did something about educating their students to have more children." (Dr. Robert J. Havighurst, professor of education, University of Chicago, 1948)

h. "Federal Reserve support of Government bond prices inflates our money supply: The banks still hold $65 billions—long and short term—of Government bonds. When the Federal Reserve buys these from the banks and the banks use the proceeds to make loans or to purchase other bonds they increase our money supply. That's one of the reasons we now have $170 billions of money instead of the $150 billions we had just after the end of the war." (Letter to policy-holders from Equitable Life Assurance Society, 1948)

i. "The typical American vacationing family means three people in a car, spending 10 days of a two week period travelling, covering about 3,000 miles, and spending $28 per day." (*This Week*, 1948)

j. "If you really want to be discouraged, go through a boys' or girls' dormitory and see the pictures they have on their walls; look at their shelves and see what they read for recreation; listen to the music they play. The answer is that our college boys and girls are artistically almost illiterate." (Dr. Theodore Greene, Yale University, *Life*, 1948)

k. A survey of Americans revealed that 46% were "very happy," 45% "fairly happy," and 8% "unhappy." But the French replied: 9% "very happy," 52% "fairly happy," and 35% "unhappy." (*Ladies' Home Journal*, 1948)

l. "To my mind, the skyrocketing costs of Government represent the most threatening challenge to our democracy today. In 1929 our Government spent three billion eight hundred million. In 1938, under the free spending, anti-depression program of Roosevelt, we spent seven billion three hundred million. Today, in the year of our Lord 1949 our budget is forty-one billion nine hundred million. And this does not include sums for the new housing bill, already approved, and for socialized medicine, socialized education, the new farm program, expanded social security, rearmament of Europe and parts of Asia, and many other programs. These will add at least twenty billion to the cost of Government to the tax-payer. Ask yourself, can you afford a 50 per cent increase in your taxes?" (Congressman Wingate Lucas, of Texas, 1949)

m. "A Supreme Court decision has already declared that the federal government may control that which it subsidizes. Consequently, only a directive would be necessary at any time to establish federal control over the public schools of the nation after they have once become subsidized by the federal government." (Dr. George S. Benson, Chairman, Arkansas Public Expenditures Council, in House of Representatives hearing on aid to education bill, 1945)

n. "Most of the papers are owned by people who are anti-social and anti-liberal, and who are getting money out of advertisers who do not want us to pass beneficent legislation." (Senator Claude Pepper, of Florida, 1946)

o. "In the last twenty-five years the march toward monopoly control of American business has been rapid. There are 3,000,000 businesses today in America. And yet 455 corporations, totaling one-eighth of one per cent of all corporations, now control 51 per cent of American business assets. If the decline of competition proceeds during the next few years at its present rate, and if the economic (and, therefore, political) power of the United States continues to be concentrated in fewer hands, then we shall find ourselves face to face to an increasing degree with fixed prices, directed mark-ups, inferior products, a wholesale destruction of small business, and eventually a regimented economy." (Governor Chester Bowles, of Connecticut, in New York *Times*, 1947)

12. Abraham Lincoln once explained to a jury the meaning of the phrase, "the *preponderance* of evidence." Read his statement, evaluate its extended example, and apply its principle in evaluating an intercollegiate debate.

"Gentlemen of the jury, did you ever see a pair of steel yards or a pair of store scales? If you did I can explain, I think, to your satisfaction the meaning of the word. If the plaintiff has introduced any evidence, put that in the scales and have it weighed. Say it weighs sixteen ounces. If the defendant has introduced any evidence in the case, put that in the scales; and if that evidence weighs sixteen ounces, the scales are balanced and there is no preponderance of evidence on either side. There are four witnesses on each side of this case. If the plaintiff's evidence weighs one grain of wheat more than the defendant's, then the plaintiff has the preponderance of evidence—his side of the scales go down, is the heaviest. If this defendant's evidence weighs one grain of wheat more than the plaintiff's, then the defendant's side of the scales goes down, is the heaviest; and that movement of the scales tells what is the preponderance of evidence. Now apply this illustration to the state·of your mind on weighing the evidence for the plaintiff and defendant." (Account by William Herndon, in Emanuel Hertz, *The Hidden Lincoln*, pp. 98-9)

13. Select several audio-visual aids that might be useful in explaining these topics:

   a. Educational inequalities in the United States
   b. A federal conservation program
   c. How to lead a group discussion
   d. Strategy on the gridiron
   e. The origins of World War II

CHAPTER 8

Exploring the Problem: Argument

"PEOPLE GENERALLY QUARREL," observed G. K. Chesterton, "because they cannot argue." By this he meant that two persons holding opposite views are likely to assert, rather than prove, denounce instead of analyze. The logical results of this illogical procedure are often name-calling and recrimination, vices which Quintilian long ago recognized when he wrote: "No one can exhort my admiration for mere fluency and flux of words lacking *argument*, a thing in which any two quarreling women super-abound." Sound argument, we have already said, is based upon reasoning, or the process of drawing conclusions from evidence. Thus we follow our chapter on evidence with a discussion of argument. The two go hand-in-hand: argument without evidence is mere speculation or non-logical thinking. It is like an automobile without a steering-wheel—the car will run, but aimlessly.

Much has been written about the "mental discipline" value of studying argumentation; this emphasis unfortunately gives rise to the notion that the primary aim of such study is knowledge of the forms and categories of argument. These same writers often appear to assume that mere skill in the manipulation of abstract symbols can be transferred to the solution of specific problems. But no such mystical powers come automatically with a knowledge of argumentation. Argument is only a working tool in the process of logical and purposeful thinking; knowing the tool's name does not insure facility in using it. We do not announce that our remarks in a discussion arc arranged in the form of categorical syllogisms. Indeed, we should have few hearers if we did! But we can use a knowledge of argument and the method of reasoning in reaching our own conclusions and in testing those reached by others.

In this chapter we consider the process of argument under these four headings: (1) deductive argument; (2) inductive argument; (3) argument by analogy; and (4) argument by causal relation.

I. DEDUCTIVE ARGUMENT

Deductive argument is what results when we proceed from two propositions, or premises, to a conclusion based upon those propositions. The argument is that which bridges the gap between the premises and the conclusion. To keep the figure, it is as if the premises form one bank of a river and the conclusion the other bank. If the premises are structurally sound they will be strong enough to carry the argument across to the conclusion on the opposite bank. The test of the validity of the entire argument is whether the premises are strong enough to support it to the conclusion.

Deductive reasoning always proceeds from the general rule to the particular case. Thus we may have this argument:

All courses taught by Professor Brown are interesting.   (general)
History 5 is being taught by Professor Brown.
Therefore History 5 is an interesting course.   (particular)

Inductive reasoning, on the other hand, always proceeds from the particular case, or cases, to the general rule. By induction we might develop this argument:

Brown's History 3 was interesting. ⎤
Brown's History 7 was interesting. ⎬   (particular)
Brown's History 9 was interesting. ⎦
Therefore all of Brown's courses are interesting.   (general)

In each argument we sought to find a valid conclusion, based upon evidence we accepted. The difference between the two was that in one case we began with a general rule; in the other, we tried to establish one. It must not be supposed, however, that deduction and induction are unrelated. In the arguments just cited the general rule applied deductively in the first example had been established inductively, as shown in the second example. Thus each of these arguments might be described as both deductive and inductive, the designation depending upon the viewpoint of the observer.

A. The Syllogism

A complete deductive argument is commonly set forth in the form of a syllogism for the sake of clarity and convenience in analyzing it. Like other argumentative forms, a syllogism is not reasoning in itself, but only a device for expressing alleged reasoning in such a way that it may be tested. We take an argument, break it down into its parts, and force it into a pattern for analysis in much the same way we measure an object of unknown size to determine its dimensions.

The syllogistic pattern is an argument in which three propositions, each stated in subject-predicate form, are related in such a way that one of them (the conclusion) follows from the other two (the premises). The premises are designated as a major premise and a minor premise. The major premise usually states a broad and general rule, a generalization applicable to particular cases, while the minor premise brings the particular case being investigated into the scope of the general rule. The conclusion contains the inference to be made from the premises. Because the conclusion is considered a "reasoning together" of the premises, it is usually preceded by the word *therefore*. Thus the typical syllogistic argument takes this form:

All good citizens exercise the right to vote.	(major premise)
John Small always votes.	(minor premise)
Therefore John Small is a good citizen.	(conclusion)

Another characteristic of any syllogism is the presence of three terms, each one constituting a separate class. The major and minor terms appear in the conclusion, and one of them appears in each of the premises either as subject or predicate. The middle term does not appear in the conclusion since it serves only as a link between the major and minor terms, usually placing the minor term within the class of the major term. If we add designations of these three terms a syllogism may be labeled thus:

middle term major term All democracies are peace-loving.	(major premise)
minor term middle term The United States is a democracy.	(minor premise)
minor term major term Therefore the United States is peace-loving.	(conclusion)

B. Testing a Syllogism

The following rules govern the construction of the categorical syllogism; to test the valid form of such a syllogism, but not the validity of each of its premises, the rules should be applied. The syllogism cannot be valid if it violates any one of them.

1. A syllogism must contain exactly three terms, each of which appears twice in the syllogism, and each of which is used in the same sense each time.

2. A syllogism must contain exactly three propositions.[1]

3. The middle term must be distributed (take in all members of the class) in at least one premise.

4. A term may be distributed in the conclusion only if it is distributed in the premises.

5. If one premise is negative (contains a negative statement) the conclusion must be negative. (A negative conclusion is impossible without one negative premise.)

6. If both premises are negative no conclusion can be inferred.

7. If one premise is particular rather than universal (refers to "*some* . . ." rather than to "*all* . . .") the conclusion must also be particular. (A particular conclusion is impossible without one particular premise.)

8. If both premises are particular no conclusion can be inferred.[2]

It should be emphasized that these rules test a syllogism only for its logical form and the consistency of the relationships of its several propositions; they do not test the premises themselves. If the form and relationships of the propositions are logical the argument is consistent within itself, but the conclusion inferred is valid only if the two premises are true. Thus, to test the truth of the conclusion in a syllogism, each premise must be verified.

C. Types of Syllogisms

So far we have considered the syllogism as a single structural form of reasoning. Three types of syllogisms are usually recognized by logicians, however: categorical, hypothetical, and disjunctive.

1. *The categorical syllogism.* All of the syllogisms used thus far in this chapter have been of the categorical type. Here is another:

All students who pay their tuition are eligible to debate.
John Lawson has paid his tuition.
Therefore John Lawson is eligible to debate.

[1] The first two rules do not actually check the validity of a syllogism; without their observance no syllogism exists.

[2] The logician has assigned a special type of fallacy to each specific violation of these rules. These may be found in the logic texts listed at the end of this chapter.

The categorical syllogism is made up of three propositions which relate three terms; because of their relation to the third term, two of them are combined in the conclusion. In this case the major premise is an inclusive statement covering all members of a certain class: those students who pay their tuition. The minor premise indicates that John Lawson belongs to that class: he has paid his tuition. The conclusion applies the general rule of the first premise to the particular case of the second premise: John Lawson, having paid his tuition, is eligible to debate.

To test the formal validity of an argument which can be expressed as a categorical syllogism the eight rules described earlier should be applied. Try them on these two examples of the categorical syllogism:

> Only those who believe in a high tariff are Republicans.
> Homer Busby opposes a low tariff.
> Therefore Homer Busby is a Republican.

> Every lawyer must pass a state bar exam.
> Roger Parke is a lawyer.
> Therefore Roger Parke has passed a state bar exam.

2. *The hypothetical syllogism.* Unlike the categorical syllogism which states an unconditional major premise, the hypothetical syllogism assumes this form: *"If* this is true, then this follows...." For example:

> If we pledge thirteen men we will fill our fraternity house.
> We can pledge thirteen men.
> Therefore our fraternity house will be filled.

Here the major premise is a conditional proposition consisting of two clauses: the conditional clause (*"if we can..."*) is called the *antecedent,* and the second clause (*"we will fill. ."*) is labeled the *consequent.* In order to be valid in form the minor premise in a hypothetical syllogism must satisfy the condition set up in the major premise, either affirming the antecedent or denying the consequent. If the minor premise does either of these two, the conclusion will follow logically. In this example the antecedent has been affirmed: the condition of pledging thirteen men, stated in the first premise, is met in the second premise. When the minor premise fails to satisfy the condition of the major premise by affirming the antecedent or denying the consequent, the conclusion cannot be valid.

Thus a special rule must be added to test the validity of the structure of the hypothetical syllogism: the minor premise must affirm the antecedent or deny the consequent of the major premise. Apply this rule to the following examples:

> If prize fighting were inhumane it would be made illegal.
> Prize fighting is legal.
> Therefore prize fighting is not inhumane.

> If the coal miners go on strike steel production will be cut.
> The coal miners are going on strike.
> Therefore steel production will be cut.

3. *The disjunctive syllogism.* This form of argument is expressed in a syllogism which is neither categorical nor hypothetical; instead it offers a choice of two or more alternatives: "Either ... or. ..." Thus:

> Either John Rutland acquired his wealth honestly or fraudulently.
> John Rutland did not acquire his wealth fraudulently.
> Therefore John Rutland acquired his wealth honestly.

In this syllogistic argument the major premise offers two alternatives; the conclusion is valid since the minor premise rejects one of them, while the conclusion accepts the other. The conclusion would also have formal validity, of course, if the minor premise accepted one alternative and the conclusion rejected the other.

Two special rules must be respected if the conclusion in a disjunctive syllogism is to be considered valid. (*a*) The alternatives set forth in the major premise must be mutually exclusive: if one is true the other must definitely be untrue. Since a man may be both intelligent and dishonest, for example, we cannot assert that he is intelligent and categorically deny that he is dishonest. (*b*) The alternatives set forth in the major premise must be all-inclusive: there must be no choices other than those stated. We cannot say, that is, that either Ohio State or California will win the football game, for there is always a possibility of a tie. Examine these disjunctive syllogisms in terms of the special rules:

> Either democracy or dictatorship must rule the world.
> Democracy cannot rule the world.
> Therefore dictatorship must rule the world.

> Either a man believes the Bible literally or he accepts the theory of evolution.
> A man cannot reject the Bible.
> Therefore a man must reject the theory of evolution.

The *dilemma*, an argumentative device often encountered in debate, should properly be considered in connection with the disjunctive syllogism which we have just described. Technically the dilemma is constructed by making the major premise into two hypothetical propositions and the minor premise into a disjunctive proposition. In practice this usually means that two or more alternatives are proposed, none of which is desirable. For example:

> If a citizen supports machine politicians he gets poor government; and if he opposes machine politicians he throws his vote away.
> But either he supports machine politicians or he opposes them.
> Therefore he either gets poor government, or he throws his vote away.

No matter what he does, this argument alleges, the voter's action is futile. Formidable as a dilemma may appear in its syllogistic form, however, there are three ways in which it may be met. (*a*) One may *slip between the horns* of a dilemma by demonstrating that there is some alternative other than those offered in the major premise. (*b*) One may *take a dilemma by the horns* and accept one of the alternatives of the major premise and demonstrate that the alleged consequences will not necessarily follow. Or (*c*) one may attempt a *rebuttal* of a dilemma by constructing another dilemma, based upon similar grounds, but leading to an apparently contradictory conclusion. Either of the first two methods will usually be more satisfactory than the third, however, for the conclusion of the dilemma constructed in rebuttal may be no more acceptable than the original one. Use one of these three methods to meet each of the following dilemmas:

> If a college professor alters his teaching to conform to a Loyalty Oath he is violating his convictions; and if he does not alter his teaching he is violating his oath.
> Either he alters his teaching or he does not.
> Therefore he either violates his convictions or his oath.

> A people who oppose dictatorship are worthy, but a people who support dictatorship are unworthy.
> Either a people oppose dictatorship or they accept it.
> Therefore they are either worthy or unworthy.

D. Non-Syllogistic Forms

It must be emphasized again that the syllogism is primarily a device for expressing an argument in a way that makes it easy to analyze. Ordinarily this means that we must restate an argument which we wish to test, for in everyday discussion or debate we seldom hear arguments which are formally presented as syllogisms. Instead we encounter arguments which are either abbreviated or expanded from their syllogistic form. In their rhetorical form they may appear to have validity, but when thrown into the logical form of a syllogism for testing purposes their apparent validity may disappear. When an argument is expressed in abbreviated form it is called an *enthymeme;* in expanded form it is a *chain of reasoning.*

1. *The enthymeme.* This term is commonly used to describe an argument that is incomplete in that one of its premises is not expressed. Thus in *Titus Andronicus* Shakespeare writes: "She is a woman, therefore may be won." The major premise ("All women may be won") is omitted, although it is implied by the conclusion. The enthymeme, therefore, is often called "argument by implication." While the enthymeme may often be expanded into a valid syllogism, it may also conceal faulty or shallow reasoning. A speaker may say "We'd better get a Republican administration if we want prosperity." Here the validity of the argument hinges upon the validity of the major premise which has not been stated: "All Republican administrations bring prosperity." Analyze the following arguments, expressed as enthymemes, by expanding them into syllogisms which will include the implied premises:

> Blessed are the meek, for they shall inherit the earth.
> George must have a B average; he's on the football team.
> Our economy is bound to collapse unless the government stops tinkering with it.

2. *The chain of reasoning.* This phrase describes another type of argument, non-syllogistic in form, but frequently encountered in discussion. Actually it is a chain or sequence of syllogisms with all conclusions but the last one suppressed, like this:

> All persons who have been to school can read.
> All persons who can read are intelligent.
> All persons who are intelligent are educated.
> Therefore all persons who have been to school are educated.

To analyze this argument it is necessary to start with the first part of the chain and express each separate link as a complete syllogism; then each syllogism must be tested separately for its validity. Use this approach in analyzing these chain arguments:

All students seek an education.
All education comes through study.
All study is profitable.
All that is profitable is good.
Therefore all students are good.

All Communists must follow the party line.
Following the party line precludes objectivity.
Objectivity is essential for any teacher.
Therefore we should bar Communists from teaching.

E. Using the Syllogism in Reasoning

Again we recall our earlier statement: the syllogism is not an end in itself, but is simply a schema in which reasoning may be expressed. Because an argument may be stated obscurely, or incompletely, in its rhetorical form, we put it into the logical form of a syllogism to test the internal consistency of its structure. If we are satisfied on that score, we must then analyze the assumptions or premises upon which the conclusion is based, for a test of the logical structure of an argument does not test the validity of its parts. Consider this statement: "Harry Derry is just another extroverted actor." Now put it into the form of a syllogism:

All actors are extroverts.
Harry Derry is an actor.
Therefore Harry Derry is an extrovert.

It now appears to be sound structurally; that is, the conclusion follows logically from the premises. But before we can accept the conclusion we must satisfy ourselves as to the validity of each of the premises: Is the general rule of the major premise valid, are *all* actors extroverts? Does the particular case of the minor premise fall within the scope of the general rule? Is Derry an actor? We may conclude that there is not enough evidence to support the general rule; and we may even find that there are conflicting judgments on Derry, or that different people are using different definitions of the term *actor*.

The value of the syllogism in reasoning, therefore, is the clarity with which it exposes the alleged logic of an argument, and the ease with which it permits us to examine each premise individually. The syllogism is thus an aid in improving our own ability to think logically and is also useful in analyzing the reasoning of others.

II. INDUCTIVE ARGUMENT

We have already indicated that inductive argument is primarily concerned with the translation of particular instances into general propositions. Thus we may define induction as the method of systematic investigation—discovering, analyzing, and explaining particular cases or facts, in order to determine the existence, or non-existence, of a general law covering those facts. The complete process of reflective thinking, then, relies both upon the evidence of induction and the inference of deduction.

Historically this relationship may be illustrated by pointing out that logic meant, for Aristotle, the bringing of beliefs into harmony with one another. Hence, Aristotelian logic was concerned primarily with deduction, "the logic of consistency," in which the syllogism was the keystone. In medieval times, this approach to logic was perverted to mean the bringing of beliefs into harmony with dogma. And in our own times we have witnessed in totalitarian states other attempts to force opinion to conform to dictation. With the development of modern science a new phase of logic was developed, the bringing of beliefs into harmony with facts. Thus logic is also concerned with induction, "the logic of investigation." With the union of deduction and induction in a logical system we become concerned that an argument not only be consistent within itself, but that it also be consistent with other known facts.

To determine factual consistency we call upon induction or systematic investigation. Because its development was coincident with that of modern science it is commonly referred to as the "scientific method" or "experimental logic." In an earlier chapter we described this method as one of (1) *inquiry* into the available facts concerning a given problem, followed by formulating a (2) *hypothesis* or theoretical solution, which is used as the basis for (3) *experiment* or practical testing of the theory, from the results of which a (4) *conclusion*, which may or may not validate the hypothesis, is drawn.

If we examine this method of systematic investigation we find that there are really three separate phases, each described by a familiar term. The first phase is that of pure *induction*, the observation of facts and the verification of observations. The second phase is that of *hypothesis*, the formulation of hypothetical relationships among the facts discovered through pure induction. The third and final phase is that of *deduction*, the checking of the implications of the hypothesis or general law with what we know of the particular facts. Thus, as we have tried to show, although induction may be defined as a distinct method of reasoning, in the practice of reflective thinking it is the constant companion of deduction.

A. Applied Induction

In an applied sense, induction means taking the first step of inquiry, observing and verifying relevant pieces of evidence, and then relating them, by means of a general rule, to the problem under investigation. This procedure may be illustrated as we distinguish between *perfect induction* and *imperfect induction*. When we examine *all* particular instances and are therefore dealing with a universal phenomenon, we have perfect induction. But when we examine only *a few, some* or *most* of the particular instances, we have an imperfect induction. The conclusion in perfect induction contains only that which is set forth in the premises; in imperfect induction the conclusion contains more than is covered in the premises. Here is an example of each type:

The attitude of the members of the City Council will determine whether or not the petition of Main Street merchants to have parking meters installed will be granted. While Council will not meet until next Monday, it is safe to predict that the petition will be rejected. A *Daily Mirror* reporter interviewed all members of the Council yesterday, and each one announced that he intended to vote against parking meters. We must therefore think about some other means of solving our parking problems.

In this case each member of the city council was asked the same question, and each gave the same answer. Since all of the evidence was examined, and there were no exceptions, the induction was perfect.

A *Daily Review* reporter yesterday queried 100 students selected at random as to whether they would approve raising the present activity fee from ten to fifteen dollars for each of the 700 students of Conway College. Of those questioned 87 favored the increase and the other 13 expressed indifference. It is therefore obvious that in next Monday's election the Conway student body will approve the proposed increase in fee.

Here only one in seven voters was interviewed, and even they were not unanimous in their opinions. Thus the conclusion went far beyond the evidence of the premises; the induction was imperfect. As you may recall from our discussion of evidence, such an imperfect induction is labeled a generalization. Whenever we deal with a sample of the total evidence, as in a public opinion poll, and even when that sample has been carefully selected to typify all cases, the conclusion must always be a generalization if it is extended to cover all cases.

The inductive method, of course, may be applied in the use of any of the materials of reasoning described in the last chapter: evidence of facts or opinions, and either one when expressed in statistics or examples. The business of inductive reasoning is the observation and verification of evidence. Logicians have established a series of formalized inductive procedures, known as simple enumeration, joint method of agreement and difference, method of agreement, method of difference, and method of concomitant variations. The reader may study these refinements in one of the logic texts listed at the end of this chapter.

B. Proof and Probability

What has undoubtedly been implicit throughout our discussion of the companion processes of deductive and inductive reasoning should now be given explicit statement: deduction attempts *proof*, whereas induction seeks *probabilities*. Deduction attempts proof in the sense that if the premises of an argument are accepted as valid and if their relationships to each other are sound they prove the conclusion. Induction, however, assembles evidence which is the basis for formulating an hypothesis which asserts only a probability. The difference lies in the fact that in the case of deductive argument one begins with a general law which allegedly governs all particular instances, whereas inductive argument begins with particular cases and suggests the probability of a general law. Thus it is possible that a given set of facts, interpreted by different observers, may lead to different or conflicting hypotheses or probabilities. This fact is often illustrated in legal proceedings where the evidence is all circumstantial and the judge or jury can but choose the hypothesis which seems most probable.

The person who develops an inductive argument will do well to understand the difference between proof and probability. He cannot prove that price control will prevent inflation, but by citing the evidence of particular instances in the past he may be able to show a probability. It is equally important that the limits of the probability established by induction be stated clearly. When Professor Paul Witty completed a study of 1500 intellectually gifted children he concluded that "bright children *tend to be* superior in size, strength, muscular control, and general health to other children in the same age group." [3] There were exceptions to the general pattern and hence no proof that bright Johnny Jones will also be strong is possible; yet we can say that it is probable, in the light of Witty's study, that Johnny will excel physically as well as intellectually. We are not attempting to discourage the use of inductive argument by listing these precautions in its use; we are simply emphasizing the hypothetical character of judgments based upon probabilities. As one logician phrased this warning, "Students sometimes toss a coin to decide how the evening shall be spent. Heads we go to a movie; tails we go to the dance: if the coin stands on edge we study. Some day the coin *may* stand on edge!" [4]

III. ARGUMENT BY ANALOGY

An argument by analogy is an assertion that because two things are known to resemble each other in certain observed respects they will also resemble each other in one or more unobserved respects. We have a set of identical twins in an argumentation class: Alpha speaks today and has unusually effective delivery; since Beta resembles Alpha in every observable respect we assume that tomorrow Beta will also have unusual delivery when he speaks. We argue that there are enough similarities between the thirteen original colonies of yesterday and the democratic nations of today to conclude that if the colonies could establish and maintain a federal government the democratic nations can do the same. This type of reasoning is probably as old as human thought for it relies simply upon the application of our experience in familiar areas to problems in unfamiliar areas. When we explore new problems we seek a frame of reference by relating them to old problems. The Wright brothers were offered plenty of arguments by analogy to prove that a flying machine was impossible. Our earliest automobiles carried a buggy whip as standard equipment. We hesitate about reading *Chips Off the Old Benchley* until we reflect that we have always liked Benchley's earlier books.

[3] New York *Times*, July 3, 1948. (Italics ours.)
[4] Roger W. Holmes, *The Rhyme of Reason* (New York, Appleton-Century-Crofts, Inc., 1939), p. 151.

The football coach seeks to build his team's morale before the big game: "Don't be scared of those guys. They put their pants on one leg at a time, just like you do." A speaker warns us not to adopt a government health program like Britain's, lest we also acquire financial problems like Britain's. "Man," Professor Jastrow said, "is primarily analogical rather than logical!"

One of the reasons for the frequency with which we encounter arguments by analogy is their simplicity. When the analogy to something familiar is presented we find it easier to understand the new idea. When General Eisenhower was explaining the rôle of the Army occupation forces after World War II, for instance, he told Congress:

> You see firemen playing checkers some times, but that doesn't mean you fire them and send them home. They may be vitally needed a few minutes later.
> It's the same way with our occupation forces. We must maintain them at a safe level, because we may need them, even though we don't have full work for all of them all of the time.

And when President Truman made his closing address at the San Francisco conference which drafted the United Nations charter he also used a simple analogy:

> Like this Charter, our Constitution came from a free and sometimes bitter exchange of conflicting opinion. . . .
> This Charter, like our Constitution, will be expanded and improved as time goes on. . . .

Many concepts which we have now tested and classified so that we take them for granted were no doubt once reasoned about by analogy. This is true of terms such as *philistinism, anglicized, Quisling,* and *solid as the rock of Gibraltar.* Sometimes names of strange objects are derived from analogical thinking: the American Indian called the locomotive an *iron horse,* and natives all over the world have termed the airplane a *bird machine.* To the Navy pilot his plane is a *ship,* to all of us the common automobile radio aerial is the *buggy-whip,* and one manufacturer calls his recording machine a *Soundmirror.*

A. The Analogy in Practice

In ordinary usage reasoning by analogy may take one of two forms: *literal analogy* and *figurative analogy.*

1. *Literal analogy*. A comparison of two things belonging to the same class is often made by a literal analogy. "You know the popularity of *Cornies*," says the radio announcer, "Well, I can tell you that *Mealies* are good, too, for they are both products of Holsum Breakfast Foods, Inc." As the following illustration suggests, it is in the area of things having to do with nature or natural laws that reasoning by analogy attains its highest probability: [5]

If I attempt to argue that a human being is like a machine and that therefore, like a machine, he is not responsible for his actions, there are many who would question the adequacy of my argument. But if I am walking along a desert waste and see two ostriches with their heads in the sand, an argument by analogy will be in order. I examine what I can see of the two birds. They have the same size bodies, the same color feathers in the same pattern, their legs look alike, and their feet have the same number and type of toes. Every comparison I make of the two shows them to be alike. It is then reasonable for me to argue that when they get over their fright and take their heads out of the sand, their heads will look alike.

2. *Figurative analogy*. Reasoning by figurative analogy is used to establish a relationship between two things belonging to different classes. Thus when a sports writer asserts that "Oswego U. will take Jordan College on the gridiron tomorrow the way Grant took Richmond," he expresses a judgment based upon an analogy between things of two quite different classes. In using the figurative analogy we often rely upon examples, or base conclusions upon limited observation. The value of such an analogy lies in its reference to familiar examples, but this is also its weakness since we may be generalizing, reasoning from inadequate evidence. The oft-quoted argument of Carlyle against representative government illustrates this point: [6]

According to Carlyle, this kind of government is bound to fail, since, as he puts it, a ship could never be taken around Cape Horn if the captain were obliged to consult the crew every time before changing his course. A generalization is implied, something like, "The sharing of power involves a lack of efficiency." Granted that this holds true on ships, is it also true in government? The argument asserts that the two cases are alike, but it offers no proof that the difference in circumstances is immaterial. The apparent difference, however, is so great that caution is advisable. It may be that the lack of efficiency is due to the sharing of power under certain conditions peculiar to the management of ships.

[5] *Ibid.*, p. 211.
[6] B. H. Bode, *An Outline of Logic* (New York, 1910), p. 163. By permission of Henry Holt and Company, publishers.

With these definitions of the two types of analogy in mind it should now be useful to look back to the quotations from Eisenhower and Truman. Which one is based upon a literal analogy? Which one draws a figurative analogy?

B. Testing Analogies

As with any other argumentative form, the analogy should meet standard tests for validity.

1. *Is the analogy relevant?* An analogy must be relevant to the point at issue or the problem being explored. If a ten year old girl asks "Why can't I stay up after nine o'clock if Barbara can?" the analogy is irrelevant when we know that Barbara is fifteen years old. To argue that because two different motor cars were both manufactured in Detroit their performances will be the same, or that two lawyers will be equally effective in court since they were graduated from the same school, is to rely upon a similarity that may be interesting, but certainly is not relevant. Or take the speech of the "big navy" man who denied that an increase in naval strength would increase the likelihood of war: "Just because New York City acquires additional fire-fighting equipment doesn't mean there'll be an increased number of fires, does it?" Of course the answer to his question was "no," but it established nothing since there is little relation between the two circumstances. If an analogy cannot pass the relevancy test it cannot contribute to logical thinking.

2. *Does the analogy disregard fundamental differences?* We meet many analogies which stress superficial points of similarity between two things but disregard fundamental differences. For example: "How can you expect to reform a criminal? A leopard can't change his spots, you know." The statement is factually correct, but because obvious fundamental differences exist in the two cases the argument is invalidated. "Resemblance is only skin deep" is an axiom that may often be used to test analogies. Those who are inclined to accept arguments by analogy at their face value should recall the fable of the blind men who came upon an elephant for the first time. "It feels like a tree," said one, examining a foreleg. "No," cried another who had seized the elephant's trunk, "it wriggles like a snake." "You are both wrong," said the third man as he grasped the animal's tail, "it's just a piece of rope!"

3. *Does the analogy rest upon a valid generalization?* Arguments based upon an analogy are often only generalizations based upon a

single example; before they can be accepted the validity of the generalization must be determined. Recall the figurative analogy used by Carlyle to attack representative government: a ship's course cannot be decided by a vote of the crew, he said, and then generalized that "the sharing of power [always] involves a lack of efficiency." Though the analogy seems innocent, its basis is a single example, inadequate to sustain the alleged general rule. The classic argument intended to prove that Mars is inhabited is open to the same question. It is usually pointed out that Mars is similar to the earth in that it revolves around the sun, gets light alternately from the sun and the moon, is subject to the law of gravity, has temperature changes, and an atmosphere. With all of these similarities, it is argued, is it not probable that Mars and the earth are also similar in having life? The argument rests upon a generalization that whatever planet possesses these enumerated features must also have life, based upon the single example of the earth. But the generalization must be established before the analogy can be considered valid.

4. *Is there a valid causal relationship in the analogy?* In many arguments by analogy the allegedly analogous situation may be viewed in terms of cause and effect, and before the analogy can be accepted the causal relationship must be validated. In the past decade we have often heard this warning:

When economic maladjustment becomes too oppressive for a large part of the population the people will turn to some form of totalitarian government. Such was the case in Russia; it also happened in Germany; and look at the situation today in Britain. Unless we remedy our own economic injustices the same thing will happen in America.

The validity of this argument depends upon the asserted relationship between economic maladjustment and the turn to totalitarianism. Thus it should not be accepted until we ask whether there were not other causes operating which also tended to produce that effect in the countries named, whether the traditional form of government in Russia and Germany was a factor, whether any of these possible causes other than economic maladjustment could be found in America.

An implied causal relationship supported the argument by analogy in Patrick Henry's revolutionary declaration: "Caesar had his Brutus, Charles I his Cromwell, and George III ... may profit by their example." Though Caesar, Charles, and George were dissimilar in their abilities, habits, and desires, an overriding similarity existed in the oppression by which all three governed; and in the cases of Caesar and Charles this oppression caused revolutions. Thus the basic but implied causal relationship strengthened Patrick Henry's argument by analogy.

5. *Are the asserted facts of the analogy verifiable?* Essential to the analysis of a questionable analogy is a knowledge of the facts which underlie it. This is true whether we are constructing our own arguments or analyzing those of others. If we are concerned with the probability of the success of a unicameral legislature in Ohio, we may reason by analogy with the Nebraska experience, but we must be sure that the asserted facts about both states are correct and are fairly presented.

6. *Do other methods of reasoning support the analogy?* As a general rule, the more support given a conclusion by different methods of reasoning the greater is the probability of its validity. Thus we might attempt to confirm the judgment reached by analogy with analysis by deduction, induction, or causal relationship.

IV. ARGUMENT BY CAUSAL RELATION

An argument based upon causal relation assumes that when any two events are associated, one taking place before the other, and one of them the indispensable and invariable antecedent to the other, the first event is a cause of the second.

The assumption which underlies this conception of causal relation is that there are no chance happenings in the operation of natural phenomena. This assumption indelibly stamps the work of the scientist in his laboratory: if a radio transmitter sends out signals which vary from its assigned frequency there must be some explanation, and the technician's job is to locate the cause, then overcome it. The same assumption pertains to human relationships. If the partnership of Doe & Roe is dissolved, if doctors oppose socialized medicine, if Alice Freeland divorces her husband, if George Arnold flunks History 27, and if a union goes on a strike there must be a cause (or a complexity of causes) for each of these happenings.

In discussion and debate where we are primarily concerned with public problems and their influence upon the individual citizen and upon society, the determination of causes and effects is a matter of utmost concern. When confronted with the problem of a depression, high prices, labor disturbances, an increasing divorce rate, discrimination, or juvenile delinquency, we are vitally interested in determining the cause. And when we are debating the advisability of adopting suggested solutions for problems, we are just as concerned with determining in advance the probable effects.

Two general warnings should be issued at this point. First, we should recognize the difficulty, sometimes the impossibility, of determining causes and effects with certainty. Apparent cause and effect may occur almost simultaneously, there may be a multiplicity of causes, and cause and effect may so operate upon each other as to confuse the entire picture. The purpose of this type of reasoning, then, is never to attempt to "force" a causal relationship where none exists, but only to analyze such relationships as are observed and to establish valid probabilities wherever possible.

The second precaution is this: we must recognize that whenever a cause is alleged for a specific result we are making a generalization, and the resulting argument is subject to all the limitations of that process. For instance, if we allege that an icy road was responsible for a particular automobile accident, we imply that whenever the same conditions are present the result will be the same. This is really a generalization based upon a single instance. There are times, of course, when investigation of similar events will always, or usually, show similar causes. Thus we may study fifty strikes and find that in each case the apparent cause was a violation of contract by the employer. The implication of our findings is that a violation of contract will always cause a strike. Despite our broad study, we are still dealing with a generalization; though we may feel that we have investigated a sufficiently representative sample, we should still recognize that our imperfect induction is the basis of our alleged causal relationship.[7]

A. Testing Causal Relations

Three specific types of causal relation are usually recognized: *cause-to-effect*, *effect-to-cause*, and *effect-to-effect*. We believe that descriptions of these types will be clearer if we first set up standards for validity by proposing six tests of all causative arguments.

[7] It is for this reason that some logicians avoid distinguishing the "cause and effect" concept and instead treat it as one of the ways of establishing generalizations. See Max Black, *Critical Thinking* (New York, Prentice-Hall, Inc., 1946), pp. 294-7.

1. *Is the asserted causal relation complete?* This question stems from one of the cautions in using this type of argument which we mentioned earlier: can it be demonstrated logically that the alleged cause actually brought about the effect in question? Most of our popular superstitions break down at this point: there is no way of establishing that finding a four-leaf clover will cause good luck, or that breaking a mirror causes bad luck. Not all superstitions are related to good or bad fortune; we hear that a political party gave us "a chicken in every pot, a car in every garage," that capitalism leads to imperialism, and that personality is the result of heredity. These several effects may be found *after* the alleged causes, but that is not the same as saying that they are direct *results* of the alleged causes. It is natural that there should be a car in every garage; that's what garages are for. But it may be a coincidence that the garages were built during the administration of any particular party.

2. *Is the cause sufficient to produce the effect?* We need to know whether the alleged cause alone could bring about the effect, or whether there are other causes whose influence is more probable. Many everyday maxims are specious in this respect; they cover coincidences, not causes. We may have plenty of will to do something, yet be unable to do it, even though we remember that "Where there's a will there's a way!" The fact that a stone is rolling may be just one of the reasons for its failure to gather moss; moss, after all, doesn't grow everywhere. We may confront similar oversimplifications of the cause and effect relationship when we are told that the failure of a *single* banking house brought on a financial panic, that crime *must* be expected as long as we maintain slum areas, that sitting in a draft is *certain* to produce pneumonia. In each case there are likely to be allied or concurrent causes. If we ignore other possible causes we make the illogical assumption that just because one thing follows another it was caused by the other. The logician labels this the fallacy of *post hoc ergo propter hoc*, "after this, therefore because of this," and warns us that it is one of the most common varieties of specious reasoning.

3. *Are there other factors operating which tend to preclude the asserted relationship?* Often we are so intent upon establishing a simple and attractive causal relationship that we tend to overlook the presence of other causative factors which would effectively block the asserted relation. The application of creosote to a wooden barn,

for example, may not preserve the barn if termites are already in the beams; even twenty hours of concentrated effort the day before an exam may not prepare us for a bluebook if we have neglected to study during the semester. In predicting probable effects, too, we must not overlook the possibility of factors which operate at cross purposes. Establishment of a "fair price code" among manufacturers does not guarantee lower costs to the consumer if unforeseen taxes are imposed on the product, or if a strike causes a short supply. Testing the validity of an asserted causal relation requires a careful search for causes other than the one singled out in the argument.

4. *May the cause also produce other effects?* In testing causal relations, we often discover that, while the cause does produce the alleged effect, it also produces others, equally good or equally undesirable. Thus the elation of the sixteenth-century merchant at discovering a shorter route to the East across the Isthmus of Panama was punctured by the discovery that malaria and savages infested the Isthmus. Those who advocated wartime rationing believed that it would insure an equitable distribution of goods; they may not have foreseen that it would also result in the "black market." On the other hand, a predicted undesirable result may be more than offset by unpredicted benefits. While the dole system may destroy the initiative and self-reliance of some beneficiaries, it is also true that it keeps some people alive who would otherwise starve.

5. *Is the asserted causation verifiable?* Accurate observation and verification of the alleged facts is as important in examining arguments based on causal relation as it is in investigating other forms of argument. If we assume a causal relation between polluted water and typhoid, for example, we must be certain that the bacteria in the water are really typhoid-producing. Or if we hear it said that the last war has resulted in lower moral standards, we must be sure not only that we understand what is meant by the terms involved, and that we are talking about a measurable effect, but that the alleged effect is true.

6. *Is the asserted causal relation supported by other methods of reasoning?* This is by now a familiar injunction: any conclusion reached by one method of argument should be double-checked, where possible, by other methods. The probability of validity for any argument is increased when the same conclusion may be reached by other modes of reasoning.

B. Types of Causal Relations

Now we are ready to consider in greater detail the three forms which causative argument may assume: (1) *cause to effect*, (2) *effect to cause*, and (3) *effect to effect*.

1. *Cause to effect*. This form is sometimes called *a priori* reasoning, since it sets up a conclusion indicating the probable effect of a specified action or circumstance. Thus we say that if McGuire plays, Pomona will beat Tulsa; if Jones gets at least 80 on his final exam, he will pass the course; if we elect Doakes we will get a "fair deal"; if we adopt prohibition, bootlegging will increase; or, if love is true, it will triumph over locksmiths. In each case we assert that C is an indispensable antecedent to E, and that if C takes place E is the inevitable result. That this type of argument really asserts only a probability is apparent when we consider that opposing parties often assert that contrary effects will result from the same cause. When Congress repealed America's neutrality laws, for example, some people argued that it would keep us out of war, whereas others contended that it would be certain to involve us in the war. It is essential, therefore, that the facts contained in any asserted cause-to-effect relationship be evaluated with care. Try the six questions suggested earlier on these arguments:

a. Twenty years ago almost everybody believed that a broken mirror brought seven years of bad luck, a rabbit's foot good luck, and that a high forehead indicated unusual intelligence. Such has been the increased number of those receiving higher education, however, that today almost no one accepts those superstitions.

b. Census records show that for the same age groups the death rate among married persons is lower than among unmarried persons. Doesn't this prove that marriage causes longevity?

2. *Effect to cause*. This type of argument reverses the procedure of cause-to-effect reasoning: it seeks to establish a judgment concerning the probable antecedent cause of a specified circumstance. The argument, often referred to as *a posteriori* reasoning, takes this form: "*E* has taken place. Something caused it. That something was probably *C*." Thus it is argued that present prosperity is the result of the administration's tax policies; "this is a modern house—Frank Lloyd Wright must have designed it!" Or we attribute our success to push and deny that it was pull. This type of reasoning is the stock in trade of the Monday morning quarterback: "Just like I said, the All-

Stars lost again. I told you they were overtrained." Not so long ago college students even sang a song with an effect-to-cause refrain: "You must have been a beautiful baby, 'cause baby look at you now!"

When we discussed cause-to-effect argument we said that there were two views as to what would happen when American neutrality laws were repealed. It should also be pointed out that since America did go to war *after* that action some people believe it was *because* of that action; they look backward from the effect to find a probable cause. Much of the "scapegoating" associated with racial and religious prejudice is developed in the same way; the prejudice is rationalized by pointing to alleged causes.

From this discussion it should be obvious that causation is a concept that works two ways, and it is largely a matter of individual point of view in many instances whether a problem is approached in terms of effect to cause, or cause to effect. The same basic tests may therefore be applied to these effect-to-cause arguments:

a. Fifteen years ago a tariff was adopted to protect the manufacturers of glotches, then developing a new industry. Since that time the Glotch Manufacturing Company has paid off all of its debts, doubled its earnings, and cut its prices in half. All of this was made possible by the protective tariff.

b. We didn't want to go out on strike, but we had to. The boss refused to agree to our just demands.

3. *Effect to effect.* This variety of causal relation reasoning is developed by joining an effect-to-cause argument with a cause-to-effect one in order to demonstrate an alleged relationship between two effects of the same cause. The argument leads to a conclusion that one specified action or circumstance is related to another by virtue of their both having the same cause. Thus: "E is the result of C. C is also the cause of E'. Therefore E and E' are related effects of the same cause, C." If we are looking for shelter during a hunting trip we may see smoke in the distance and reason that it is caused by fire; then we conclude that where there is fire there is heat, and head for the smoke. Or we discover that a prominent radio announcer (E) received his first training at Union University (C), and so we enroll at Union, assuming that our training there (C) will start us on a successful radio career (E'). In another field we may follow the same reasoning process and contend that unemployment results from decreased business activity, and that decreased

business activity also creates a glutted money market; therefore we assert that a definite causal relationship exists between unemployment and a glutted money market.

The same test questions applied to the other forms of causative argument are appropriate here. In addition we may find it helpful to analyze an effect-to-effect argument by putting into syllogistic form, since effect-to-cause-to-effect reasoning actually involves two syllogisms. Using our last example, we would develop these two arguments:

> Whenever unemployment exists there has been a decrease in
>   business activity.   (effect
> There is unemployment today.   to
> Therefore there has been a decrease in business activity.   cause)
>
> Whenever there has been a decrease in business activity the
>   money market becomes glutted.   (cause
> There is decreased business activity.   to
> Therefore the money market will become glutted.   effect)

By adding this new testing procedure to those already indicated examine the following arguments for validity:

a. When he campaigned for election last fall Congressman Conk promised to support any legislation that would help veterans, and this helped him win. The veterans' bonus bill comes up for a vote today and I'm sure we can count on Conk.

b. I'm afraid we'll have to call off the picnic we planned for tomorrow—there's a ring around the moon tonight and that always means rain.

C. The Argument from Sign

We conclude our discussion of arguments from causal relation by considering the argument from sign. As its name implies, this type of reasoning assumes that whenever two or more circumstances invariably accompany each other, the observed presence of one of them is a sign that the other is also present. Thus the argument is usually phrased this way: "X and Y always seem to go together, and I can see X. Therefore Y must be coming." Our attention is then focused upon Y, and we consider Y in terms of effect-to-cause or effect-to-effect relationships. If we see a storm signal while sailing we attend not to the signal but to the coming storm which causes it to fly; our reactions are set off by the signal but it is the approaching storm that impels us to head toward shore. Words may also be signs: "Communist," "cop," or "Catholic" may set off a whole series of causal relationships in our minds. A more common form of the argument from sign, however, rests upon a simple association of two events or circumstances rather than upon a causal relation between them. We may say "the team that's ahead on the 1st of August will win the pennant," or believe that "as Maine goes so goes the nation." In each of these examples the argument from sign is really based upon a generalization: because sometimes the pennant winner has been apparent as early as August 1st we generalize that whenever a team holds first place on that date "it's a sign" that it will still be ahead in October. The argument from sign may therefore be tested as an example or a generalization.

D. Using Causal Arguments

The investigation of asserted causal relationships may often be our main concern in a discussion or debate when we are attempting to determine probable causes for problems or probable effects of proposed solutions. Legislative actions, personal beliefs, organizational policies, and group actions are all commonly considered and evaluated in terms of their causes or effects. Because frequent use often results in careless use, the argument based upon alleged causal relation bears close examination.

V. CONCLUSION

Justin Miller, former justice of the U.S. Court of Appeals for the District of Columbia, once observed that "a case well argued is half decided." We subscribe to that notion, and therefore emphasize the importance of the material in this chapter. The reader who wants to improve his skill in logical thinking or to present his reasoning to others in discussion or debate needs to master the content of this chapter, not just to pass an examination, but to equip himself with tools for everyday use.

We know that assertion, suggestion, transfer, diversion, denunciation, and sheer emotionalism are sometimes effective devices of persuasion in the short run. But we also know that wise decisions are reached, in the long run, by reflective thought, honestly and persuasively expressed. Careful attention to the methods of reasoning will not only improve our skills of problem-solving but the quality of the arguments we present in discussion and debate. A New York lawyer once closed a jury appeal with these words: "And these, ladies and gentlemen, are the conclusions upon which I base my facts." This statement is the very antithesis of logical thinking.

READINGS

BAIRD, A. C., *Argumentation, Discussion, and Debate* (New York, McGraw-Hill Book Co., Inc., 1950), Chaps. 10-13.

BLACK, Max, *Critical Thinking* (New York, Prentice-Hall, Inc., 1946), Chaps. 2-3, 8.

COHEN, M. R., and NAGEL, Ernest, *Introduction to Logic and Scientific Method* (New York, Harcourt, Brace & Co., Inc., 1942).

Columbia Associates in Philosophy, *An Introduction to Reflective Thinking* (Boston, Houghton Mifflin Co., 1923), Chaps. 4-5.

DEWEY, John, *Logic: The Theory of Inquiry* (New York, Henry Holt & Co., Inc., 1938), Chaps. 21-22.

HOLMES, R. W., *The Rhyme of Reason* (New York, Appleton-Century-Crofts, Inc., 1939), Chaps. 2-3, 6.

McBURNEY, J. H., and HANCE, K. G., *Discussion in Human Affairs* (New York, Harper & Bros., 1950), Chap. 8.

MAYER, Milton, "How to Read the Chicago Tribune," *Harper's*, Vol. 198 (April, 1949), pp. 24-35.

STEBBING, L. S., *Thinking to Some Purpose* (Middlesex, England, Penguin Books, Ltd., 1939), Chap. 9.

THOULESS, R. H., *How to Think Straight* (New York, Simon & Schuster, Inc., 1941), Chaps. 7-8.

EXERCISES

1.* Prepare an outline of the arguments to be used in developing one issue of the problem you have selected for intensive study.

2.* Write a 500-word argumentative statement on the problem for intensive study and marginally annotate the forms of argument employed.

3. Select from past class discussions or debates, or from some other source, one example each of deduction, induction, analogy, and causal relation; write a paragraph of analysis of each argument.

4. How would you define the italicized words as used in these statements?

a. What is the *cause* of the present problem?

b. My *cause* is just.

c. I can't believe such a wild *generalization*.

d. He made a *categorical* statement.

e. Don't take that *analogy* too *literally*.

f. That fact is immaterial, *irrelevant*, and inconsequential.

g. What affects you has no *effect* upon what I do.

h. That's simple *deduction*, my dear Watson.

i. Try to talk yourself out of that *dilemma*.

j. Corn knee high on the 4th of July is a *sign* of a good crop.

5. Restate the following arguments in complete form, supplying the missing premises or conclusions, and determine the probable validity of each:

a. Of course Johnson can't win the election—he's a crook!

b. Is he rich? Look at his clothes!

c. I'll bet my bottom dollar that the Republicans win the next election.

d. Can a man be a success in more than one field? Well, Eisenhower was a successful general and then became a college president; but of course Truman failed in business before he succeeded in politics. Maybe it all depends....

e. Until we can change human nature we can't prevent wars.

f. Naturally the sun will rise tomorrow.

g. If people in the slum areas aren't used to decent housing they probably wouldn't appreciate it if they had it.

6. Clip a current newspaper editorial on a controversial subject and write a brief analysis of it covering these points: (*a*) Does the evidence cited stand up under appropriate tests? (*b*) Does the editorial use a variety of forms of argument? Which ones? (*c*) Do the arguments used stand up under appropriate tests? (*d*) On the basis of the evidence and argument explain your acceptance or rejection of the conclusion.

7. Read a discussion or debate from the list in the Appendix, and evaluate five arguments made by the speakers.

8. Identify the following examples of argument and test their validity:

a. "A university is either a kindergarten, a reform school, a club, a political party, an agency of propaganda, or it is a community of scholars devoted to immutable truths. Of course it cannot be any of the former; it must, therefore, be the latter." (Chancellor Hutchins, University of Chicago)

b. "What sign is there that co-eds are not too keen about domesticity? Three hundred and eighty-eight colleges and universities report that only 11½ per cent of the women students this year specialized in home economics." (*This Week*, August 28, 1948, p. 24)

c. "The best way I can describe hitting is to say that it is like swinging an ax at a tree.... I do not say that it is as easy to hit a baseball, which is a rapidly-moving object capable of being made to do a lot of tricks, as it is to hit a large and stationary tree. But I do know that if hitters could swing a bat as easily and naturally as a woodsman does an ax, they would make life much more unpleasant for pitchers." (Frank "Lefty" O'Doul, *Louisville Slugger Yearbook, 1948,* pp. 3-4)

d. "Victory in a great war is not something that you win once and for all, like victory in a ball game. Victory in a great war is something that must be won and kept won. It can be lost after you have won it—if you are careless or negligent or indifferent." (President Truman, August 9, 1945)

e. There are "three basic principles necessarily related to an effective system of international control: No control without power. No power without law. No law without government." (Norman Cousins, *Modern Man Is Obsolete*, p. 33)

f. "Drink... is the first step away from religion, and atheists are the most likely to become Communists." (Mrs. D. Leigh Colvin, president, W.C.T.U., in *Time*, May 17, 1948, p. 40)

g. "Let these truths be indelibly impressed on our minds, that we cannot be happy without being free; that we cannot be free without being secure in our property; that we cannot be secure in our property, if, without our consent, others may, as by right, take it away—Let us take care of our rights, and we therein take care of our prosperity. 'Slavery is ever preceded by sleep.'" (John Dickinson, *Letters from a Pennsylvania Farmer*, 1768)

h. "It is reasonable to suppose that a grade-school pupil of average memory and unimpaired hearing would derive as much benefit from the Army method [of teaching foreign languages] as anyone else, and if a grade-school pupil could do it, it's not university work!" (Arthur S. Bates, letter to editor, *Time*, January 26, 1948, p. 4)

i. Question: "Are any officers of the United Electrical Workers Communists?" Answer: "I don't think that makes any difference. A door-opener for the Communist party is worse than a member of the Communist party. When someone walks like a duck, swims like a duck, and quacks like a duck, he's a duck." (James B. Carey, secretary-treasurer, CIO, testimony before House labor committee, in New York *Times*, September 3, 1948)

j. "The reasonable man adapts himself to the world; the unreasonable one persists in trying to adapt the world to himself. Therefore all progress depends upon the unreasonable man." (George Bernard Shaw)

k. "...Even a just war must not be waged by immoral means. Under modern conditions, however, war can be waged only by such aerial bombing as must involve the slaughter and maiming of innocent civilians.... To kill the innocent is not a lawful means to any end, however good. Therefore, under modern conditions, no war can be waged without employing immoral means. *Therefore it must be unjustifiable.*" (Edward Ingram Watkin, *Time*, May 10, 1948, p. 56)

l. "*When Is a Telephone Like a Market Basket? When the Cost of Providing Telephone Service Is Compared with the Cost of Filling the Market Basket.* Every Ohio homemaker realizes the cost of living has gone up each time she buys the food to fill her market basket. So too, we find the cost of providing telephone service has gone up each time we install a telephone or handle a call.

"Our income is larger from the increased number of telephone customers but falls far short of meeting the tremendous rise in operating costs—due to wages and prices. If we are to serve you efficiently—we must operate on a paying basis. This is the fair

way, the American way. We know you will agree." (Northern
Ohio Telephone Company letter to subscribers, July 1, 1948)

m. " 'We don't want subsidies,' said William T. Faricy, president of
the Association of American Railroads last week, 'but if the government persists in subsidizing our competitors, we may have to accept
them.' If that threatened socialism, he added: 'You could also have
socialization by simply running out of money.' " (*Time*, November 28, 1949, p. 74)

n. "Of late years some folks, very well-meaning, I am sure, have been
inclined to deride patriotism. They claim we owe allegiance not
to any nation but to the world.

"I cannot agree with them at all. I consider their thinking fuzzy.
I do believe that every American worthy of the name is concerned with the welfare of the world, the good of all humanity.
That is what the Apostle Paul meant when he wrote about charity:
interest in the well-being of other folks. And we all know that
charity begins at home. In other words, we shall be able to do more
for the whole world if we first take a deep interest in our families,
our communities, our state, and our nation.

". . . There is an old hymn that says, 'Brighten the corner where
you are.' When each of us follows that sound advice, he is brighten-
ing the United States, and, for that matter, the whole world."
(Senator Arthur Capper, of Kansas, in *Household*, February, 1948,
p. 4)

o. "Communism is a science, and science is the same everywhere.
H_2O is water in Moscow and H_2O is water in America. We are
not against water because it happens to be H_2O in Moscow. It is
ridiculous." (Councilman Benjamin J. Davis, of New York City,
in *Time*, January 26, 1948, p. 18)

p. "We are right now within 8% of full-fledged state socialism, truly
and in fact.

"No country in history has been able to maintain a capitalistic
democratic government after 40% of the country's income has been
siphoned off through taxation for the support of that government.

"Today our government spends 32% . . . only 8% from the breaking point, and there are legislative programs currently under consideration in Washington, which if adopted, would easily eat up
that 8% gap.

"To continue to pour billions of American taxpayers' dollars into
support of the socialism of Great Britain is a downright betrayal
of public trust. It is high time to tell half the nations of the world
that the United States can no longer afford to arm and support
them." (Congressman Jesse P. Wolcott, of Michigan, to convention
of National Association of Real Estate Boards, Nov. 21, 1949)

CHAPTER 9

Exploring the Problem: Fallacies

LOGICIANS AND social psychologists approach the subject of fallacies from different backgrounds and arrive at different conclusions. The traditional logicians classify as a fallacy "any unsound mode of arguing which appears to demand our conviction, and to be decisive of the question in hand, when in fairness, it is not." [1] This definition seems to assume that reasoning, and the evidence on which it should be based, can be objectively classified as *sound* or *unsound, fair* or *unfair.*

Social psychologists, as we have noted in earlier chapters, hold that our habitual reactions are often based on emotion, not necessarily on logic. We tend, they say, to believe what we want to believe: we see things through glasses colored by our interests and desires. As a result, we are quick to detect weaknesses in our opponent's evidence and reasoning, but slow to admit weaknesses in our own. We may disagree with our opponents just as vigorously on whether a certain argument is fallacious as on the main issue.

We hasten to add that the logicians admit, though they often deplore, the influence of emotions on decisions; and that the social psychologists welcome such evidence as they find of logical thinking. In this book, we teach the methods of discussion and debate, and the detection of fallacies, because we believe that decisions based on the careful analysis of conflicting evidence and arguments are likely to be better than those made under the influence of strong emotions.

Writers on argumentation have traditionally employed a complex set of Latin labels for various types of fallacies. Schopenhauer thought, "It would be a very good thing if every trick could receive

[1] Richard Whately, *Elements of Logic* (London, J. W. Parker and Son, 1859), p. 168.

166

some short and obviously appropriate name, so that when a man used this or that particular trick, he could at once be reproved for it." The value of this approach suffers, we believe, when the list is so long, and the Latin names are so unfamiliar, that attention is focused on naming the trick rather than on the alleged weakness in the evidence or argument. For this reason, we use a simple classification of fallacies under two main captions: (1) fallacies of evidence and (2) fallacies of argument, and list only the special types that are likely to appear in everyday discussion and debate.

I. *Fallacies of Evidence*
   A. Reliance upon inadequate *facts*
   B. Reliance upon unqualified *opinions* } *sources of evidence*
   C. Use of inadequate *statistics*
   D. Use of unrelated *examples* } *presentation of evidence*

II. *Fallacies of Argument*
   A. Faulty *deduction*
   B. Faulty *induction*
   C. Faulty *analogy*
   D. Faulty *causal relation*

If these tests of argument and reasoning were rigidly applied, nearly everyone would be guilty of frequent, though often unintentional, fallacies. Sometimes we must make decisions that are based on very little evidence. Sometimes we reason from premises that we later discover to be wrong. For centuries, it seemed logical to the learned that the earth must be flat; if it was round, they reasoned, oceans, ships, and everything movable, would run to the bottom and drop off into infinite space.

We are taught to avoid personalities, attacking the argument, not the individual. Suppose we know that the individual whose opinion is quoted frequently makes extravagant or unfounded statements. Would mentioning this habit be a fallacy or a proper testing of the authority? Is the statement, "I wouldn't believe anything X said" an unwarranted attack or a legitimate method of refutation?

The fact that a community is prejudiced against Candidate X may not prove that he is unqualified to hold a position, but it may be an adequate reason for choosing someone else. Thus an unfounded, and logically irrelevant appeal to prejudice may be an adequate reason for some decisions. People nod their heads knowingly and pronounce an oft-used sentence beginning, "Where there is so much smoke. . . ."

There is no clear line of demarcation between inadequate and adequate evidence, between faulty and acceptable inductions. The individual, faced with the necessity of immediate action, must act on the basis of what he knows and believes. He cannot properly be charged with a fallacy if he states that his conclusion is tentative and may be changed when more evidence is available.

I. FALLACIES OF EVIDENCE

A. Reliance upon Inadequate Facts

This common type of fallacy relies upon facts which are inadequate to support the conclusion, or even upon facts which may be acceptable but bear no relation, or an improper relation, to the conclusion. So often is this true in testimonial advertising that it has become known as "Sponsor's Logic." In practice it means that someone, usually a pretty girl, is presented in a magazine advertisement or on the television screen battling a sailfish, performing high dives, or swinging a tennis racket. Then the logic of the advertiser insists that the girl's athletic prowess is associated with her preference for a particular brand of cigarettes. This *non sequitur* reasoning is not limited to advertising. A candidate for office may be perfectly honest when he declares himself in favor of home, religion, mother, and country, though these facts may have little bearing on how he will vote on questions of taxation, social security, or anti-trust legislation.

After rechecking the tests of facts suggested in Chapter 7, examine the following arguments to determine the adequacy or relevancy of the evidence used:

Less than half of the teachers in the United States are married, according to a recent survey. This shows what education does for women!

Fifteen per cent of the members of this faculty are listed in *Who's Who;* almost every one is a recognized scholar in his field. You are certain to get a good liberal education from such men as these.

Students in Section 1 used Blank's textbook, and those in Section 2 used Crank's book. Blank's book is undoubtedly better, for the students using it received higher average grades than those who used Crank's.

B. Reliance upon Unqualified Opinions

This fallacy may take one of two forms: citing an alleged authority who is *not qualified to testify as to the validity of asserted facts,* or citing an authority who is *not qualified to interpret facts whose validity has been established.*

In the first class are those whose testimony is of dubious value because of their known bias. The negative views of Governor Dewey on the merits of the Truman administration, or the uncomplimentary judgment of the president of the Ford Motor Company on the merits of the new Chevrolet, would be examples of testimony by men whose positions disqualify them as experts. In this same category fall those who may be free of bias, but who simply have not been in a position to observe the facts in question. The man who last visited Soviet Russia in 1930 is hardly qualified to speak with first-hand knowledge of contemporary facts; and those who have not read the Kinsey Report cannot speak with authority about its contents.

The second class of fallacies of opinion includes testimony by those who may know the facts but are yet unable to interpret them. Some students may master the contents of a textbook in ethics and write an excellent examination on the facts it contains, yet lack consistent moral judgments of their own. The census taker may be familiar with the data he has collected, yet not be able to interpret it in terms of population trends, just as the worker in a factory may know how many machines come off the assembly line, yet not know whether his employer is making a profit.

To determine other ways in which expert or lay opinion may be misused, reëxamine the tests suggested in Chapter 7; then evaluate these statements:

"Only the victory of the Republican party this fall will return America to the ideals of its founders," asserted Lyman Haskell, chairman of the state Republican committee, in an interview yesterday.

Believe me, if a Ford is good enough for the president of the First National Bank, I'm satisfied that it's the best car on the market.

I've been pretty doubtful about the need for a new law regulating strikes, but now I'm convinced; the Gallup Poll this week reported that more than half the people think we need a new law.

C. Use of Inadequate Statistics

The most frequent fallacy involving statistical information is that in which the data cited does not provide valid grounds for the conclusion. The speaker who asserts that "millions of our citizens must belong to un-American organizations, for figures show that there are over 800 such groups in existence," offers us a *non sequitur*. His figure of 800 subversive organizations may be quite correct, but it

does not follow that millions of people must belong to them. Nor
can we accept the publisher's claim that just because 71,693 copies
of a particular book have been sold it must be a good book. Indeed,
we cannot even assume that all the people who bought copies of the
book read them.

Too often there appears to be an assumption that the citation of
precise figures results in precise conclusions when, in fact, the implied causal relationship never has been proved. We are reminded of
an old campus wisecrack which illustrates this kind of fallacious
thinking: "You must be an awful grind," says the first student, "I
see you've got a dozen library books on your desk." "Sure," replies
the second student, "and I've got a dozen nickels in my pocket. But
that doesn't prove I'm a street-car conductor, does it?"

This type of fallacy may take many other forms, as a review of
the tests of statistics in Chapter 7 will indicate. After you have
recalled these tests, apply them to these statements:

Between 1871 and 1940 the Third Republic of France changed its
cabinet 106 times, or about once in every eight months. Since the end of
World War II the rate of turnover has increased nearly 20 per cent. This
demonstrates the basic instability of the French people.

A recent survey of American psychologists shows that another war
is unlikely, for 92 per cent of them deny that human nature possesses any
ineradicable, instinctive factor that makes international wars inevitable.

Germany is the most peace-loving country on earth. In the last three
centuries England has waged 145 campaigns; France 90, but Germany
only 40, of which 14 were against Austria and 16 against Bavaria, to
establish the unity of the Reich.

D. Use of Unrelated Examples

Fallacious use of examples usually takes the form of illustrating
one idea with another not sufficiently related, or of using one concrete instance that does not properly represent its general class.
Because a generalization, even though based upon a dubious example,
may be vivid and dramatic we often speak of it as a "Glittering
Generality." The one Negro we have known may have seemed irre-
sponsible, so we jump to the all-inclusive conclusion that "all Negroes
are lazy." From similarly narrow bits of evidence we may make
broad generalizations about "sly Japanese," "avaricious Jews," "slick
New Yorkers," or "absent-minded professors." Strangely enough, the
person who tends to base his judgments on single instances is often
quick at denying contrary evidence with "Oh, but that's just *one*

example!" It is important, therefore, to encourage members of a discussion group to pool all of their information on a given point, and then draw conclusions from all the examples submitted.

Often the faulty example is used as a basis for a special type of argument. During Hitler's rise to power, some people said, "Of course his methods are brutal, but we need to remember that when all reasonable approaches are closed, force must be resorted to. Charlemagne, Frederick the Great, Lenin, and Lincoln all had to build unity by means of force." Here, of course, the examples were cited in an effort to construct an argument by analogy. In every such use of examples the entire argument must be analyzed for possible fallacy. The tests of examples suggested in Chapter 7 will be helpful in evaluating such statements as these:

Surely the example of the thirteen colonies joining together in one federal union proves that it is not impossible for the nations of the world to create a federal union today.

I'd never take a chance on walking under a ladder. Why, my uncle did that once and he had all kinds of bad luck the next week!

Just remember you can't ever trust a Russian after knowing how the Russians broke all the agreements they made at Potsdam.

E. Guarding Against Fallacies of Evidence

The best protection against arguments which use evidence fallaciously will be found in following these three steps: first, determine whether the evidence itself is valid; second, examine the relationship of the evidence to the argument to see whether it is relevant; third, remind yourself that if you want to believe the conclusion suggested by the evidence, you are inclined to scrutinize it much less closely.

II. FALLACIES OF ARGUMENT

A. Faulty Deduction

The argument based upon faulty deduction usually involves inadequate correlation of a general law with the particular instance it is alleged to cover. For example, in 1949 the Senate refused to approve the appointment of a man to the Federal Power Commission because, among other things, he had once expressed himself in favor of nationalizing railroads and other basic industries. Communists, the opposing Senators argued, believed such things and if this man believed them, too, that made him look very much like a Communist. While the general rule—that Communists believe in nationalization of basic industries—is undoubtedly true, it does not follow that all people holding this view are necessarily Communists. The incident was faintly reminiscent of Horace Greeley's tongue-in-cheek dictum that "All Democrats may not be saloon keepers, but all saloon keepers are Democrats."

As suggested in Chapter 8, the best procedure for testing such arguments is to throw them into syllogistic form, then apply the tests for a valid syllogism. In the present instance, the syllogism would appear this way:

> All Communists believe in nationalizing basic industries.
> The proposed appointee believes in nationalizing basic industries.
> Therefore the proposed appointee is a Communist.

The minor premise fails to place the proposed appointee within the class described in the major premise; hence the conclusion is not valid. It *could* be valid if one could establish a major premise reading "*Only* Communists believe...." Here are three other deductive arguments for analysis:

> The recent refusal of the city council to approve the mayor's proposal for reducing municipal expenses is proof that the present form of city government should be replaced by the city manager system.
> It is perfectly obvious that Communists follow orders from Moscow. If we let Communists hold public office or teach in public schools, it is just the same as giving Russia a voice in our government.
> A student, upon learning that a classmate received a higher grade on an examination, asked him: "Did you use crib notes or did the instructor make a mistake in grading your paper?"

B. Faulty Induction

The most common form of this fallacy is the hasty generalization, basing a conclusion concerning a whole class upon an examination of selected representatives of that class. One might argue that all wars are the result of imperialistic ambitions, and cite Italy's invasion of Ethiopia, Japan's invasion of China, Germany's invasion of Poland, and Russia's invasion of Finland. The error is apparent in the small number of instances cited, and it could be documented with contrary examples, not considered in the generalization, where imperialistic motives were not apparent: the War of 1812, the war with Tripoli in 1815, and so on. Indeed, one investigator has listed 256 causes of war other than imperialism. It should also be pointed out that where value judgments are involved, even a numerical majority which appears from a perfect induction may not have the right answer, and a "second sober thought," plus more evidence, may reverse the decision.

It must not be assumed, however, that an induction which does not examine all instances is always unacceptable: an imperfect induction, based upon a sufficient number of properly representative instances may be valid. The tests of inductive procedures, outlined in Chapters 7 and 8, establish standards by which to evaluate these arguments:

It's true that the English people voted for the socialist government, but I just can't believe they are really in favor of it. I know hundreds of Englishmen, and there isn't a real socialist among them.

Cigar smoking is an unhealthy habit; every time I smoke one I get a headache.

We've polled the warehousemen and the professional tobacco buyers—and with the men who know tobacco best, it's Luckies, ten to one.

C. Faulty Analogy

Figurative analogies, "not to be taken literally," usually wear their fallacies openly: "Looking for an easy course in this college is like fishing in the ocean—you never know what you'll come up with." The two procedures are not the same, and even the speaker only pretends that they are. Literal analogies, on the other hand, attempt to show that two objects or circumstances are alike in certain unexamined aspects because they are alike in certain examined aspects. The fallacy in such an argument may come because the two circumstances are not alike in the observed aspects, or because they are not alike in the unobserved aspects. In an intercollegiate debate one speaker urged that the federal government be given the power to enforce compulsory arbitration in labor disputes: "A similar plan was adopted in Australia where labor conditions are the same as in the United States, and it proved successful there." Examination of this alleged analogy reveals that the *differences* between the two countries are greater than the *similarities:* the proportion of union members to the total population is much lower in Australia, labor unions are incorporated in Australia, there are no jurisdictional strikes in Australia, and so on. As an *example* of how compulsory arbitration has worked elsewhere, the Australian reference might be valuable evidence, but as an *analogy* it is unsound.

Significant considerations in testing alleged analogies are found in Chapter 8. After reviewing them, examine these analogies for possible fallacies:

Of course the federal government could run the railroads. Doesn't it do a good job of running the post offices and the inland waterways?

You claim we don't need compulsory conscription to fill our armed forces because there are enough patriots to volunteer. But I say that's just a theory, and a lot of theories don't work out in practice.

What right have Americans to object to Russia's exploitation in China and Korea? Didn't the United States do the same thing in Nicaragua and Haiti?

D. Faulty Causal Relation

Fallacies of this type occur because mistaken relationships are assumed between causes and effects: when one event takes place *after* another or *with* another it is argued that the second event occurs *because* of the first. Many of our everyday adages and superstitions are of this sort. "A bad dress rehearsal," it is said, "makes a good performance." Sometimes good performances do follow bad rehearsals, but that is not evidence enough to prove the asserted cause-to-effect relationship.

In an earlier edition of this book we used this example of fallacious cause-to-effect argument:

The President of the United States elected in 1840 [Harrison] died in office. So did the Presidents elected in 1860 [Lincoln], in 1880 [Garfield], in 1900 [McKinley], and in 1920 [Harding]. Therefore the President elected in 1940 and in all even-numbered decades thereafter will die in office.

It happened that Roosevelt, who was elected in 1940, also died in office, thus extending the "proof" over a period of 100 years, without a single exception. But, as in this case, even continued repetitions of an apparent causal relationship do not make it valid.

Similar fallacies are also frequently encountered in alleged effect-to-cause and effect-to-effect relationships. Apply the appropriate tests for causative arguments in Chapter 8 in analyzing these samples:

Don't blame me for getting a low grade; somebody had to be at the bottom of the class.

If man has a soul it must be in his body, yet thousands of bodies are dissected every year without any doctor discovering a soul. Man has no soul.

To a friend who wasn't feeling well a woman recommended her own physician. "But is he a good doctor?" asked the friend. "Is he good?" she replied, "Would I have been going to see him twice a week for twenty years if he wasn't?"

E. Guarding Against Fallacies of Argument

Arguments relating to problems which have personal significance for us are the most difficult to test; our desires or beliefs often color our analysis. But, on all problems, analysis is the great foe of fallacy in argument: first, analysis to determine whether the evidence upon which the argument is based is valid; second, analysis to determine whether the evidence cited is relevant to the argument; and third, analysis to determine whether the argument has logical consistency.

No discussion of fallacies can be complete, for there may be as many varieties as there are vagaries of the human mind. In concluding this chapter we list several other types of specious reasoning, each of which has received attention elsewhere in the book.

1. *The fallacy of ambiguity* is a name often given to errors of argument that have a linguistic basis. Sometimes the meaning of certain terms may be changed or distorted in the course of a discussion in such a way that meanings are not clear. (Some writers on argument prefer to call only unintentional distortions *fallacies of ambiguity*, labeling intentional shifts in meaning *fallacies of equivocation*.) A midwestern governor once testified before a legislative committee: "I'm interested in what is good for the masses. If this bill is good for the masses I'm for it, and I know it's good for the masses." The chairman of the national Townsend Clubs used this refutation of his critics: "We are not members of the lunatic fringe because crazy people don't organize." And one anti-prohibitionist argued that "Prohibitionists object to drinking. But we know that men will die of thirst if they stop drinking." In each of these instances ambiguity resulted from a shift in terms or a subtle distortion of meaning. Basically these are problems of definition, and the reader may guard against fallacious argument of this kind by following the advice on definition in Chapters 4 and 6.

2. *The fallacy of diversion* is an attack upon propositions held by an opponent which do not have a direct bearing on the issue in question. The speaker attempts to divert attention from the real issue. In discussing the question of revising federal radio regulations to permit more non-commercial FM stations, for example, an opponent may find himself unable to attack your basic premises. But, if

somewhere in the discussion, you have observed that you admire the British broadcasting system, he may attempt to divert the listeners by attacking that incidental statement. In a sense this might be described as a psychological rather than a logical fallacy, and we shall have more to say about it in later chapters dealing with the ethics of persuasion and participating in discussion.

3. *The fallacy of emotionalization* is a term which includes deliberate appeals to the emotions of the hearer, or the use of ridicule or "name calling" in an attack upon the character or beliefs of an opponent. The purpose is to sway listeners without reference to the logic of the case presented. A speaker might say, for example: "The theory of evolution is absurd. Look at the chief spokesman for evolution—Charles Darwin—a man who believes that his ancestors were apes, who openly admitted that he did not believe in God!" Such psychological diversions from the logical issues cannot be defended; the man who uses them betrays to a thoughtful opponent the weakness of his own position. In the chapter on persuasion we have more to say about such tactics.

Finally, we would warn the reader that the best defense against fallacious reasoning is familiarity with the patterns of valid argument.

READINGS

BAIRD, A. C., *Argumentation, Discussion, and Debate* (New York, McGraw-Hill Book Co., Inc., 1950), Chaps. 14-15.

BLACK, Max, *Critical Thinking* (New York, Prentice-Hall, Inc.), Chaps. 10, 12.

BURTT, E. A., *Right Thinking* (New York, Harper & Bros., 1946), Chaps. 5-7.

CLARKE, E. L., *The Art of Straight Thinking* (New York, Appleton-Century-Crofts, Inc., 1929), Chaps. 2-3, 13.

HOLMES, R. W., *The Rhyme of Reason* (New York, Appleton-Century-Crofts, Inc., 1939), Intro., Chap. 4.

HUFF, Darrell, "How to Lie with Statistics," *Harper's*, Vol. 201 (August, 1950), pp. 97-101.

JASTROW, Joseph, *Effective Thinking* (New York, Simon & Schuster, Inc., 1931), Chaps. 8-10.

McBURNEY, J. H., and HANCE, K. G., *Discussion in Human Affairs* (New York, Harper & Bros., 1950), Chap. 10.

MAYER, Milton, "How to Read the Chicago Tribune," *Harper's*, Vol. 198 (April, 1949), pp. 24-35.

STEBBING, L. S., *Thinking to Some Purpose* (Middlesex, England, Penguin Books, Ltd., 1939), Chap. 12.

THOULESS, R. H., *How to Think Straight* (New York, Simon & Schuster, Inc., 1941), Chaps. 2, 4, 11.

EXERCISES

1.* Find three fallacies you have discovered in your research on the problem selected for intensive study; state them, and explain why they are fallacious.

2.* Select the most common fallacious argument presented on the other side of the subject you are studying intensively, and write out a refutation of it.

3. Read a printed transcript of a discussion from the list in the Appendix and explain any fallacies you find.

4. Select an editorial or an advertisement which you think contains fallacies of evidence and argument, and reproduce it with your refutation included as footnotes, following the pattern of Milton Mayer in the article listed in the readings above.

5. The following statements have been selected from current newspapers, magazines, speeches, books, and radio broadcasts. Test each one for a possible fallacy, describe the fallacy if you find one, and present your analysis of it.

   a. "After taking two bottles of Rumdum, I felt better than I had for years. There is no question but that Rumdum has done wonders for me." (A testimonial advertisement)

   b. "A recent study of children living in Los Angeles showed that they were almost an inch taller, age for age, than children living in San Francisco. Since San Francisco is noted for its cold and foggy weather it has been claimed that the 'golden sunshine' of Southern California is responsible for the difference in development." (A newspaper medical column)

   c. "Is it so bad, then, to be misunderstood? Pythagoras was misunderstood, and Socrates, and Jesus, and Luther, and Copernicus, and Galileo, and Newton, and every pure and wise spirit that ever took flesh. To be great is to be misunderstood." (Emerson's *Essay on Self-Reliance*)

   d. "A despotism may almost be defined as a tired democracy. As fatigue falls on a community, the citizens are less inclined for that eternal vigilance which has truly been called the price of liberty, and they prefer to arm only one single individual to watch the city while they sleep." (G. K. Chesterton, *Everlasting Man*)

   e. "Tasty Tea! The name itself tells you how good it is!" (From a radio commercial)

   f. "The Socialist party had the smallest campaign fund in the last presidential election; that explains why their candidates received the smallest vote." (A news commentator)

   g. "The people of Nevada are more law-abiding than the people of New York State. According to the *World Almanac*, Nevada has twice the area of New York, and yet averages only four murders a year, while New York has more than four hundred in the same period." (A student debater)

h. "You look prosperous, Bill." "Yes, and I feel prosperous . . . an Aroma cigar is a prosperity smoke, and it's only ten cents." (A newspaper advertisement)

i. "Is it because of poverty that you get sick? There is a direct relationship between poverty and living conditions. There is a probable relationship between living conditions and disease. Therefore there can only be an indirect relationship between poverty and disease. Poverty of itself does not cause disease." (A public address by a medical school dean)

j. "Nobody can be healthful, without exercise, neither natural body nor politic; and, certainly, to a kingdom, or estate, a just and honorable war is the true exercise. A civil war, indeed, is like the heat of a fever; but a foreign war is like the heat of exercise, and serveth to keep the body in health; for in a slothful peace, both courages will effeminate and manners corrupt." (Francis Bacon, *The True Greatness of Kingdoms*)

k. "It is because we want this new cold tablet to be available to everyone that we have cut the price to only fifteen cents a box." (A radio commercial)

l. "Many of the revelations of recent sex studies are symptoms of an ailing society. But let us not confuse the ailment with the desired state of health, or change the temperature scales on the thermometer to make the fever 'normal.' " (A public speech)

m. Bernard Baruch, elder statesman, lost a roll of twenty-two $100 bills while watching the horse races at Belmont Park. When a track employee found the money and returned it Baruch "leaped to the season's most charitable conclusion." "This proves," he said, "that everybody around a race track is honest." (Reported in the daily press)

n. "Dr. Garfield was born in China and is eminently qualified to tell us about that country." (Introduction for a public speaker)

o. Moslem leaders in Arabia protested when King Ibn Saud had the first telephone line installed; it was, they said, a work of the Devil from the land of the Infidel. After hearing their complaint Ibn Saud gave judgment: "If the telephone is really a work of the Devil, the holy words of the Koran will not pass over it; if the holy words do pass over it, it assuredly cannot be the work of the Devil. So we will appoint two mullahs, one to sit in the Palace and one in the telephone exchange, and they are to take turns reading a passage from the Holy Book, and we will see." (Magazine account)

p "Logic, like whiskey, loses its beneficial effect when taken in too large doses." (A logic textbook)

q. "I should like to read from an official booklet issued by the Department of Commerce. It shows that our former enemy, Germany, has received in assistance from the United States two billion, 624 million dollars. It shows that the former Axis partner, Italy, has received from the United States Government one billion, 846 million dollars in postwar aid. It shows that Japan, our former enemy in the Pacific and an Axis partner, received one billion, 716 million dollars. On the other hand, it shows that China, our wartime ally and friend, who went through the entire wartime period, received considerably less than either Germany or Italy received, and received approximately what Japan received, or one billion, 755 million dollars, which is considerably different from the testimony on the floor by the Senator from Texas. Therefore had China been our wartime enemy instead of our friend, it would have fared much better." (A speech in the U.S. Senate, 1950)

CHAPTER 10

Examining Suggested Solutions

"ONE MAN'S MEAT," we say, "is another man's poison." Though we follow with diligence the logical succession of steps in investigating a problem we may not all agree upon the best solution. This is not only possible, it is quite natural, and not altogether undesirable. In any organization or society based upon the democratic process each man draws his own conclusions and has an opportunity to persuade others to accept them. Perhaps the most that can be asked is that we feel reasonably sure that we have honestly and conscientiously explored every aspect of the problem, leaving no important evidence undiscovered and no argument unweighed. If, after that, disagreement is still apparent, our task is to examine all of the suggested solutions. Final judgment should be suspended until all views are expressed.

In World War II Leo Pasvolsky, now a director of the Brookings Institution, was a special assistant to the Secretary of State. In that capacity he prepared a "policy paper" outlining a specific course of action in American foreign policy and took it to President Roosevelt. After examining the document Roosevelt said, "This plan you propose is fine. But what do I reject?" What, in other words, are the competing proposals which we turn down in favor of this one? This attitude of recognizing that most problems may have multiple solutions is a healthy one. The "either accept my plan or perish" attitude, though much more common, is seldom justifiable and frequently illogical. As Count Alfred Korzybski expressed it, "We are all products of a civilization which emphasizes always black or white, hot or cold, day or night. Always it is either-or, where more-or-less is a better explanation of the facts." [1]

[1] *Time*, Vol. 55 (August 1, 1949), p. 51.

Our next step, then, is to organize the results of exploring the problem, and the varying interpretations of those results, to examine possible solutions. This can best be done by raising old questions for a new purpose; the general pattern followed in making a preliminary analysis can be used again.

I. WHAT DO WE NOW KNOW ABOUT THE PROBLEM?

We located and defined the problem before we undertook the search for evidence and argument. Do we need to modify our first judgments?

A. What Is the Problem's Present Status?

We can now decide whether the question has passed the discussion stage and whether we are dealing with a proposition of fact, belief, or policy. If we are ready to consider alternative solutions, we should arrange a panel or symposium where each solution is presented or a debate between advocates of two courses of action. If we find that we are analyzing a question of fact we should secure the needed information and conclude the discussion. In dealing with a current issue, what was originally a question of belief may have become one of policy. Or legislative action may have put a policy into operation. In that event, we must decide whether to accept the adopted solution or to advocate other action at the next legislative session.

B. What Type of Problem Is It?

Here we may modify our preliminary analysis considerably. We may have first regarded the use of the atomic bomb as a question of personal or national ethics. We now find that military strategy, international politics and religious beliefs are involved. Many originally considered the repeal of the prohibition amendment as simply a matter of restoring a personal liberty. We now know that it was also a problem in governmental administration (establishing proper controls over public taverns, sale of liquor to minors), tax policy (added revenue from liquor taxes), agriculture (new markets for certain farm products), and so on. While we must have recognized new classifications of the problem during the search for evidence and argument, they should be specifically noted now for their possible significance in considering alternative solutions.

C. What Basic Assumptions Are Important?

It is probable that, during our research on the question, our original ideas about the underlying assumptions have changed. If so, the new assumptions should operate in examining possible solutions. When, for example, the British parliament first considered recognizing the Confederate States of America, it was thought that the major concern of the English cotton mill worker was the embargo on Southern cotton. But the issue involved other factors: it became apparent that the English worker was also vitally interested in abolishing slavery, the question of recognition took on a new aspect. We may approach the problem of providing adequate medical care on the assumption that the individual must be free to choose his own doctor. Further study may reveal that more basic assumptions are the desire for security and freedom from worry about ill health. If this be true, quite different types of solution may be considered.

D. What Are Its Relationships to Other Problems?

Our present analysis is apt to differ most from our original answers to this question. Research is often begun under the illusion that a problem is single, unique, and unrelated to others. "We can consume all that this nation can produce. It's *simply* a matter of price adjustment!" declares a radio commentator. But investigation reveals that the matter of price adjustments is neither simple nor isolated from other problems. It is complicated by factors of production, distribution, purchasing power, and general economic stability. The man with the "one cause mind" is dangerous in society and a nuisance in a discussion group. Only rarely do we find a problem that is unrelated to others. Usually we must ask ourselves: What are the limits of this problem? With what others is it related? Specifically how is it related to them? What does it have in common with them? What effect will the solution of this problem have upon related problems?

II. WHAT NOW APPEAR TO BE THE MAIN ISSUES?

In the preliminary analysis we listed the possible main issues. Now the inquiry should be repeated, this time as a review of the evidence and argument we have accumulated. It is probable that some issues we thought important now appear insignificant, and that our evidence may have brought into focus some new points of controversy. Checking these two possibilities is an important step in further analysis of the problem.

A. Applying Standard Inquiries

One of the best ways to assess the possible areas of controversy is to apply again the stock issues described in an earlier chapter:

1. Is there a need for a change?
2. What are the proposed solutions?
3. Will any of the proposed solutions meet the need?
4. Are the proposed solutions practicable?
5. Are the proposed solutions desirable?
6. Will their advantages offset possible disadvantages?
7. What action should be taken?

B. Principles Governing the Selections of Issues

The character and scope of each problem will determine the number and nature of its main issues of controversy. Five general principles, however, should govern the determination of issues:

1. The points at issue should be vital.
2. They should concern points of controversy between advocates and opponents of a given solution.
3. They should not refer to waived or irrelevant material.
4. They should be phrased as questions to indicate points of disagreement.
5. They should be phrased clearly, simply, and precisely.

C. Establishing Non-Controversial Areas

It is just as important to find areas of agreement among those concerned with a problem as to find where they differ. In the courts this is done by "stipulation." For example, if a prosecuting attorney charges that a murder weapon belongs to the defendant, the defense may concede the point and it is stipulated as an established fact. In collegiate debating it is customary to waive the constitutionality of a proposed action, since both sides must agree that if enough people approve the action the Constitution can be amended to make it legal. In the discussion of everyday affairs we often concede ethical arguments by saying "ideally this isn't the thing to do, but the present circumstances demand it." In similar vein, debaters may agree that the controversy is whether a given course of action *should* be followed, and that argument as to whether people *would* now approve it is irrelevant. The desirability of such a stipulation is indicated in this summary of the views of experts in argumentation: [2]

...We may conclude that the word "should" includes the word "could." Whether or not Congress or the people "would" adopt a particular reform at the present time is beside the point. The merit of a measure is not necessarily shown by popular disapproval. A plan "should" be adopted if it is wise, good, desirable, and practicable; if, of all the alternate courses of action, it will most adequately remedy the existing or threatened evils.

The establishment of non-controversial areas may be effected by general agreement among those planning a discussion or a debate, by a realistic appraisal of circumstances, or by the rule of relevancy.

III. WHAT ARE THE POSSIBLE SOLUTIONS?

A tentative answer to this question was made during the preliminary analysis: exploration of the problem may have opened new avenues and closed others. We need to remind ourselves that this often happens when different people investigate the same problem, even when each one tries conscientiously to follow the pattern of reflective thinking. Different investigators may not be equally impressed by the same facts, they may have observed the problem from contrasting vantage points, or they may have relied upon conflicting authorities. Knowing all of the available evidence and argument is important; interpreting or evaluating evidence and reasoning are equally so.

A. Three Types of Solutions

In general, suggested solutions fall into one of three categories: (1) they may be similar with variations only in minor points, (2) they may be unrelated yet reconcilable, or (3) they may be mutually antagonistic. Here are examples of each sort.

1. Five college students recently held a symposium on the question "How can we best insure adequate medical care for all citizens?" Each speaker took for granted that private medicine would not suffice without some government intervention and financial support. Two

[2] F. W. Lambertson, "The Meaning of the Word 'Should' in a Question of Policy," *Quarterly Journal of Speech,* Vol. 28 (December, 1942), p. 421.

of the speakers presented similar arguments, but one concluded that the federal government should establish free medical service whereas the other favored state services. This same division was apparent when the next two speakers advocated systems of health insurance; one wanted the state, the other the federal government, to establish the program. The fifth speaker favored federal aid only in building hospitals, training doctors, and conducting medical research. The five solutions were similar in their basic premise; they differed in important details.

2. In a panel discussion on "How can our college best contribute to the program of UNESCO?" the three participants advocated different plans which were neither irreconcilable nor mutually exclusive. One suggested a public information bureau which would provide talks and printed materials about UNESCO for interested groups. Another proposed a book collection campaign to help rebuild European libraries destroyed in the war. The third advocated raising funds to help finance the education of foreign students in American universities. Ultimately, in this particular situation, all three proposals were incorporated into a program carried out by the student body.

3. A recent intercollegiate symposium on "What should we do to end the threat of war?" developed a series of alternatives that were neither similar nor compatible: put all of our efforts and confidence in the United Nations; attempt to form a union of North Atlantic democracies; establish rapport, and an alliance, with Russia; create a defensive confederation of Western Hemisphere nations. Logically it would seem difficult to adopt one of these policies without rejecting the others.

B. Testing Suggested Solutions

The investigator should apply the tests of evidence and argument as he studies the problem and examines proposed solutions. When he is taking part in discussion or debate the pressures of time will prevent him from applying as carefully as he would in his own study each appropriate test to every analogy, causal relation, or quotation of authority. He may, however, find these five tests of belief in a proposition a convenient yardstick for measuring what he hears:

1. *Clarity*. A good belief is unambiguous. We know unmistakably what it means.

2. *Consistency with the facts.* A good belief is founded on extensive and accurate observation. It is not contradicted by experience.

3. *Consistency with other beliefs.* There is a presumption against a belief that conflicts with other beliefs well certified by experience. Sometimes, however, it is the latter beliefs rather than the former that need to be revised.

4. *Utility.* A good belief is often distinguished by its usefulness in suggesting further good beliefs.

5. *Simplicity.* Other things being equal, that belief is best which makes the fewest assumptions.[3]

These tests cannot be properly applied unless those who listen do so effectively. Skill in listening is just as important in discussion and debate as skill in speaking. In addition to factors of intelligence, interest in the topic discussed, and proper physical conditions, efficient listening requires: (*a*) ability to make inferences, to apply the principles of sound reasoning; (*b*) ability to structuralize a speech, to see the organizational plan, and the connection of main points; (*c*) ability to see significance in the subject discussed, to relate it with real problems, practical situations; and (*d*) ability to listen for main ideas as opposed to specific facts.[4]

READINGS

BURTT, A. E., *Right Thinking* (New York, Harper & Bros., 1946), Chaps. 9-11.
CLARKE, E. L., *The Art of Straight Thinking* (New York, Appleton-Century-Crofts, Inc., 1929), Chaps. 9-10.
Columbia Associates in Philosophy, *An Introduction to Reflective Thinking* (Boston, Houghton Mifflin Co., 1923), Chaps. 9, 13.
LASKER, Bruno, *Democracy Through Discussion* (New York, H. W. Wilson Co., 1949), Chap. 15.

EXERCISES

1.* Prepare an outline of the problem you selected for intensive study and indicate (*a*) the exact status of the problem, (*b*) the main points of controversy, (*c*) the minimum essentials of any solution, and (*d*) the possible solutions.

2. Listen to, or read, a transcript from the list in the Appendix, of a Town Meeting of the Air broadcast in which several speakers propose

[3] Columbia Associates in Philosophy, *An Introduction to Reflective Thinking* (New York, 1923), p. 334. By permission of Houghton Mifflin Company, publishers.

[4] Ralph G. Nichols, "Factors in Listening Comprehension," *Speech Monographs,* Vol. 15 (1948), pp. 161-2.

different solutions for a problem. Evaluate the discussion in terms of
(a) apparent understanding of the status of the problem, (b) agreement
among the speakers on the main issues of controversy, (c) the presentation of all points of view or all possible solutions, and (d) the nature of
the evidence used.

3. Select three current public questions and outline a plan for a symposium on each one.

4. Select a current problem being discussed on your campus and devise
a series of tests to be applied to suggested solutions in order to discover
their respective merits.

5. Observe a discussion by a local policy-making group, such as the
student council or the city council, to discover whether the participants
are agreed upon the main issues of controversy and the essentials of any
possible solution? What effect does their agreement, or lack of it, have
upon the progress of the discussion? Can you explain their agreement or
disagreement on these points?

6. Prepare an eight-minute speech proposing one possible solution for
a current campus, or national, problem.

CHAPTER 11

Choosing the Best Solution

"WE ARE THINKING just now with our emotions and not with our minds; we are moved by impulse and not by judgment.... The world is governed now by a tumultuous sea of commonalities made up of passions, and we should pray God that the good passions outvote the bad passions." Contemporary as these sentences may sound, they were spoken nearly a half-century ago by Woodrow Wilson. This pessimistic note has been heard in every generation. We believe, however, that as we learn more about the democratic process we can also learn to "think with our minds" in solving democracy's problems. Otherwise this book would not have been written.

So far in our treatment of logical thinking we have emphasized the need for exhaustive inquiry into the facts, careful weighing of all arguments, and judicious examining of all possible solutions. There comes a time, however, when decisions must be made. The juror must affirm or deny his belief in the innocence of the defendant. The legislator must vote for or against the motion. The citizen must choose between *A* and *B*. At such times we properly turn to some form of debate for a thorough presentation of the advantages and weaknesses of the proposed solution.

One of the chief values of debate as a method of making final decisions is that it permits both sides to obtain an equal hearing; this is true even though one viewpoint may be held only by a minority. Of even greater significance is the fact that debate compels men to hear arguments both for and against a given proposal, and the arguments are laid side by side, point by point, so that they may be compared. Only when competing choices are equally represented is freedom of choice important. George Bernard Shaw typically overstated an important point when he said "The way to get at the merits of a case is not to listen to the fool who imagines himself impartial, but to get it argued with reckless bias for and against." It is better to say that if two men investigate the same problem, starting with the facts and working toward a conclusion, and come out with conflicting conclusions, we may assume that there is some truth on both sides; in a confrontation of conclusions we can best determine where the greatest truth lies. When it is time for decision it is time for debate.

Occasionally the best solution for a problem may be chosen after alternatives have been presented in a symposium, but a debate in which the negative advocates its own solution as preferable to the affirmative proposal, or defends the status quo, achieves the same end. Or a debate may be held on each proposed solution. This is essentially what happens in a legislature: under parliamentary procedure one proposed solution is offered as a main motion, alternatives are submitted as amendments or substitute motions, and each proposal is debated in its turn.

At this point of choosing the best solution the method of discussion and debate differs markedly from the scientific method. Since it is impractical to try one old-age pension scheme after another upon a section of our population as a scientist would do with laboratory subjects, we substitute an intensive analysis of each proposal. This procedure can be followed in the area of social problems, we believe, with an attitude of objectivity and rationality equal to that commonly found in the handling of scientific problems.

I. THE PROCESS OF SELECTING A SOLUTION

If it appears that there are three possible solutions for our problem we should analyze each of them thoroughly. This process is relatively objective. The first step is to determine the order in which we shall consider the alternatives. If there are no apparent reasons for doing otherwise we will usually begin with what we believe is the most likely solution, then take up the others. To each we apply the same tests.

A. Does It Include the Minimum Essentials?

In our preliminary analysis we gave the minimum essentials for any acceptable solution. Now in our final analysis we ask whether these minimum essentials are included or accounted for. If so we have a tentative presumption in favor of that solution. If not, we must inquire whether our exploration of the problem has shown any of the presumed minimum essentials to be unsound, contradictory, or unimportant.

Suppose we decide that any plan to alleviate unemployment must incorporate these points: (a) unemployed people must not be permitted to go hungry or homeless, (b) they should be cared for efficiently and economically, and (c) they must be reëmployed as quickly as possible. Each proposed solution, such as a federal public works project, unemployment compensation insurance, or a reduced work week to share employment, must be tested to see if it meets these standards.

B. Does It Solve the Basic Problem?

There is a difference between eliminating symptoms and curing a disease. Enacting "dry" legislation may prevent the open sale of alcoholic beverages but not reduce the amount of drinking. We must ask whether the proposed solution can do what is expected of it.

Sometimes, however, this question cannot be answered categorically. We believe, or hope, that increased taxes will slow down inflation, but we are not sure that this or any other proposal will fully solve the problem. That does not mean that the proposal should be discarded; perhaps we must be satisfied with a plan that does no more than make substantial progress toward a solution. The establishment of new industries, for example, is not likely to solve entirely an unemployment problem, but it may help. Just as we rarely find debate propositions that can be conclusively *proved*, so we seldom discover *perfect* solutions for everyday problems. In debate, whether judicial, legislative, or intercollegiate, we may establish only a *probability;* we may also have to adopt proposals which make only *reasonable progress* toward a complete solution.

C. Is It Feasible?

Note the difference between this and the first two questions. We must sometimes postpone, or even reject, proposals that pass all tests but this one. Your college may need a center for extracurricular activities. The administration might decide that a student union building would be the ideal solution, but be compelled by lack of funds, or greater needs elsewhere, to adopt a less desirable expedient. The best solution in any instance should mean doing the best we can with what we have. Inability to adopt the ideal solution should not be used as an excuse for doing nothing.

Some proposed solutions are not feasible in a different sense: the results may be more objectionable than the problem they are designed to solve. If an offending eye is plucked out we can see less. Over-emphasis on athletics may be cured by abolishing intercollegiate sports competition, but many people would regard the cure as worse than the disease.

D. Will It Create New Problems?

When one head of Hydra, the mythical water serpent, was cut off two new ones grew in its place. The same multiplication of problems may result from the adoption of solutions which are otherwise acceptable. The increase of an amusement tax, some cities have discovered, discourages patronage of theatres, night clubs, and sports events to such an extent that the total tax revenue has actually decreased. Some manufacturers have discovered that when they increased prices to increase profits, they "priced themselves out of the market." And some nations have recently found that aggressive imperialism to relieve alleged overpopulation brings even worse evils. If there is a possibility that a proposed solution will introduce new problems in place of the old it must be regarded with suspicion. Final decision should be withheld, however, until it can be determined whether one of two possible mitigating circumstances exist.

1. *The advantage of the proposed solution may offset the disadvantages of the newly created problems.* It may be true, for example, that the best way for a city to expand its transportation facilities is by establishing a municipal bus line, but going into debt to finance the proposal may seem to create a greater problem. Investigation might show, however, that better transportation facilities would encourage new industries to locate in the town and the taxes they would pay would make the debt less burdensome than it appears.

2. *The newly created problems may be met by an extension of the proposed solution.* Labor unions claim, for example, that the best way to obtain higher wages is to organize the worker. When that solution resulted in a new unemployment situation as some industries migrated to the South to escape the unions, the original solution was extended by organizing Southern labor.

When these four tests have been applied we should be prepared to choose the best solution and to defend our choice on rational grounds. It should not be assumed, however, that decisions will always be clear-cut. One solution may recommend itself because it is the most feasible. Another may create the fewest new problems. A third may offer the best hope for a permanent solution. In addition, it may be necessary to develop particularized tests appropriate to each situation. Even then the result may not be a sharp distinction among alternatives, but a belief that one is somewhat better than the others.

II. ANALYZING THE PREFERRED SOLUTION

When the best solution for a problem has been tentatively selected it is time for the final analysis. This differs from the preliminary analysis in two significant ways: (*a*) the final analysis is made in the light of a more thorough study of the problem, the evidence and argument pertaining to it, and all suggested solutions; (*b*) the final analysis is made in terms of the solution which has been selected. The purpose of the final analysis is also different. Here we make preparations for the last stage in problem-solving: securing the acceptance by others of the selected solution. This process of securing acceptance, which we call persuasion, is described in Chapter 14. Here we are concerned with the necessary preparations for persuasion: organizing the results of our study into major contentions supporting the solution we have chosen, and organizing the evidence and argument supporting each major contention.

A. What Major Contentions Support the Solution?

Any well-ordered speech is a unit made up of smaller units, each intended to support, elaborate, or prove the main thesis or proposition. The advantage of breaking up the whole body of evidence and argument into smaller, compactly organized units is that it makes the total argument easier for an audience to understand. "If I can free this case from technicalities," said Lincoln, "and get it properly swung to the jury, I'll win it." In discussion and debate we "swing" our point of view for the judgment of the listener, first, by building a series of *major contentions*, primary arguments which tend to support our proposition. If they are accepted as true by the listener he may feel that we have proved the case.

One simple method of identifying major contentions is to review the results of your exploration of the problem in terms of the "stock issues," described in the preceding chapter.

Not all problems can be neatly stereotyped and the "stock issue" formula must be applied with caution on two counts: (*a*) *Not all of the "stock issues" are always important.* Sometimes the need for a change is apparent and the controversy will center on the specific change most likely to meet the problem. Or it may be agreed that a certain plan seems desirable but there will be conflicting judgments of its practicability. Occasionally the special nature of the problem may require new standards for selecting major contentions. (*b*) *The phraseology of major contentions should not copy the "stock issues."* They are guides to the discovery of major contentions in any problem; because they are general they are not good models for the precision of phrasing that ought to characterize major contentions.

In a debate on the proposal of a city-manager form of government for Glenrock the first main issue, stated in question form, and following the "stock" approach, would be: "Is there a need for a change from the status quo?" Those who support the proposal would answer "yes" and those opposed "no." But each side would phrase its own major contention. The major contentions presented by the affirmative might be:

1. Continued corruption in the city hall can be met only by abolishing the system which encourages it.
2. The city-manager form of government in Glenrock would insure honest and progressive management of public business.
3. The city-management form of government in Glenrock would be more efficient and offer more services than the present system.
4. The city-management form of government in Glenrock would provide these increased services at less cost to the taxpayer.

The negative might recognize the same issues and phrase a series of major contentions in exact opposition. There would thus be a direct clash between supporters and opponents of the proposition and the listener could reach his own conclusions.

How many major contentions should usually support a proposition? There can never be less than two: if there were but one it would necessarily be identical with the proposition and not a support for it. There are also good reasons why there should rarely be more than three or four major contentions. First, it is logically possible to resolve most arguments into relatively few component parts. Indeed, an argument loses its logical and coherent arrangement if it is divided into too many parts. When one debater proclaimed "twenty-three major contentions in my case," he was not only guilty of elevating a number of subordinate arguments into major contentions, but he also destroyed the unity and coherence of his whole case. Second, audiences have limited powers of perception and memory. They cannot take away a clear picture of a multitude of minor arguments, even though they be labeled "major" contentions. Three or four succinctly phrased and logically related contentions have the best chance of influencing the average listener.

B. What Evidence and Argument Supports Each Contention?

In the chapter on research we urged that each fact or opinion recorded be labeled with a general heading which would fit it into a broad classification of information on the topic. One purpose is to make easier the assembling of evidence and argument relating to each major contention. In taking notes on the city-manager plan of government for Glenrock, for example, we may have used these general headings: "corruption in present government," "lack of services," "cost of services," "values of non-partisan administration," "political appointments," and so on. When the time comes to analyze the selected solution we may easily organize this material under appropriate major contentions. The guiding principles in this task are the simple ones of orderliness and relevancy.

For the same reasons that we suggest the use of few major contentions we also urge that the number of subordinate arguments supporting each contention be limited. In considering each one for possible inclusion we should ask: Is this subordinate argument essential to the establishment of the major contention, or is it merely interesting, colorful, or distantly related? Unless it is essential it should not be used.

What general principles govern the choice of evidence to support each subordinate argument? As we said in the chapter on evidence, there cannot be too much. We should include all of the available relevant evidence on each point when we are analyzing the selected solution. When we are planning a speech of a prescribed length we will choose from the available evidence that best suited to the audience and the occasion. We should remind ourselves that those audience members who listen for specific facts tend to comprehend less than those who listen for main points.[1] The convinced listener, for example, may not remember the specific bits of evidence supporting each main argument. He may recall only that there seemed to be enough valid evidence to prove each point. This consideration makes the careful analysis of all available evidence and argument of utmost importance.

III. BRIEFING THE SOLUTION

One of the most widely read books in recent generations is General Lew Wallace's story of the Holy Land in the time of Christ. Remarkable as are the descriptive passages in *Ben Hur* which clearly and accurately picture the setting, it is even more remarkable that Wallace could write them without visiting the Holy Land. The secret of his accomplishment was the meticulous care with which he planned and organized his task. He drew topographical maps of the country; he plotted the streets, squares, walls, temples and buildings of Jerusalem and other cities important in his story. He sketched floor plans of the Jewish and Roman houses in which his characters lived and pictured the clothes they wore. Only after he had thus thoroughly prepared himself did Wallace feel ready to begin to write.

Participation in discussion or debate should be preceded by this same type of careful planning and organization. This is best done by drawing up a *brief*, a documented record of our judgment and of the evidence and argument which supports it. By virtue of its careful arrangement the completed brief pictures the relationships of the background explanation, evidence, and argument, and their contributions to the proof of the basic proposal. Thus the brief distinguishes the conclusion we reach from the reasons upon which it is based; it represents *what* we think and also *why* we think it.

The term *brief* comes originally from the law. The lawyer for the plaintiff prepares a brief of his case against the defendant, while the latter's attorney builds a brief supporting his plea of "not guilty." In some cases both attorneys submit their briefs in advance to the trial judge so that he may more easily follow the courtroom debate. The technique of briefing has also been adopted by the military services; we speak of pilots being briefed for a mission with a detailed

[1] See Ralph G. Nichols, "Factors in Listening Comprehension," *Speech Monographs*, Vol. 15 (1948), p. 160.

analysis of target, weather conditions, enemy aircraft, bomb loads, and so on. In preparing for debate the making of a brief is usually a coöperative task, undertaken by the members of a team. Occasionally all members of a debate squad on each side of a question will prepare a common brief. There is some precedent for this practice, since several members of a law firm may coöperate in drawing up a brief, each working on a section where his knowledge will be most useful.

A. Distinguishing Characteristics of a Brief

Two characteristics of a brief distinguish it from other written records made in the investigation of a problem.

1. *A brief is complete.* By definition a brief includes *all* background material, valid evidence, and sound argument supporting or relating to the selected solution for the problem. The brief is a virtual storehouse of information about the proposal, so arranged that anyone can look at it and get a "bird's-eye view" of the whole case. In this respect briefing a case is like arranging a bridge hand. Thirteen cards grouped only by chance may present no pattern, but when they are grouped by suits and in sequence they present a clear pattern enabling the player to make his bid and play the hand with greater ease. By an orderly arrangement of evidence and argument in a brief the proper relationship of each separate item is apparent, and the testing of each link in the chain of evidence and argument is made easier.

It should be kept in mind that a *brief* is more than an *outline;* it is prepared by a different method and serves a different purpose. The outline makes no pretense of including all of the evidence or argument relating to a proposal. It is simply a plan for the presentation of a proposal to a particular audience and thus includes only the evidence and argument suited to that group. In later chapters dealing with techniques of participation in discussion and debate we will consider the problem of outlining.

2. *A brief is impersonal.* A brief is prepared with no particular audience in mind; it is impersonal in that it is a reservoir of data from which can be drawn appropriate materials for different audiences. It is also impersonal in its language: such phrases as "we ought to . . . ," "I think . . . ," or "our interest . . ." should be avoided. In short, the author of a brief does not personalize it by planning it for a particular audience, nor does he project his personality into

it. The brief is an objective chart of a particular course of thought, based only upon evidence and argument.

B. General Rules for Constructing a Brief

A systematic procedure, based upon a few simple rules, is necessary for the construction of a good brief. Here we first consider five general principles, then those that apply specifically to each part of the brief.

1. *Phrase a clear and accurate title.* Rather than titling a brief "Civil Rights," with no indication of your point of view or the scope of the topic, be precise and descriptive: "A brief supporting the proposition 'Resolved, that Congress should enact into law the recommendations of the President's Commission on Civil Rights.'"

2. *Construct the brief in three parts: the introduction, the proof, and the conclusion.* Include essential background or explanatory material and a statement of the main issues of controversy in the introduction; present the evidence and argument supporting the major contentions and the proposition in the proof; summarize the major contentions in the conclusion.

3. *Arrange the individual items with uniform symbols and indentations which indicate their relationship.* The most convenient pattern of symbols is the one used in this book: Roman numerals, capital letters, Arabic numerals, small letters, Arabic numerals in parentheses, and small letters in parentheses. They may be indented as follows:

I. Major contention...
   A. Primary argument...
      1. Supporting argument...
         a. Evidence...
         b. Evidence...
         c. Evidence...
            (1) Sub-argument...
            (2) Sub-argument...
               (*a*) Evidence...
               (*b*) Evidence...
      2. Supporting argument...
         a. Evidence...
         b. Evidence...

   B. Primary argument...
      1. Evidence...
      2. Evidence...

4. *Let each item contain only one point.* The inclusion of more than one point in an item may result in ambiguity and confusion. If, for example, a proposal is opposed because it is too complex and too costly each argument should be entered separately.

5. *Phrase each item in a succinct, complete, declarative sentence.* Incomplete sentences or entries in question form become ambiguous; to the casual reader they may appear as a secret code which hides the meaning. Each item should be so phrased that a person unacquainted with the subject can follow the argument.

C. The Introduction

Any necessary explanatory material or background information should appear in the introduction. This will be of a non-controversial nature and require no proof; an affirmative and a negative brief might properly be identical in their introductions. The general outline of the introduction should resemble that of the preliminary analysis, including these topics and in this order:

1. The immediate cause for discussion
2. The origin and history of the problem
3. The meanings of the terms of the proposition
4. The minimum essentials of any acceptable solution
5. The main issues of controversy

D. The Proof

1. *The major contentions should correspond to the main issues.* One main issue may have been stated as "Will legislation outlawing the Communist party eliminate its influence?" The major contention derived from this issue by the affirmative is an elaboration of "yes," i.e., "The way to eliminate the influence of the Communist party is to outlaw it by federal legislation." The negative response, an elaboration of "no," is a major contention reading "Outlawing the Communist party will only drive it underground." In some instances, of course, the two sides will not select the same issues; but the major contentions on each side should correspond to the main issues as stated by that side.

2. *Make every subhead support the preceding point.* The purpose of the proof is to erect a pyramid-shaped structure, with the proposition at the apex, supported by major contentions which are supported, in turn, by subsidiary arguments and evidence at the

pyramid's base. These structural relationships may be made clear by adding connective words such as *for*, *and*, or *because* to the major contentions.

I. Municipal ownership of local public utilities means lower rates, *for*
   A. Cities which have municipally owned utilities can cut overhead costs, *because*
      1. Present city officials may be able to administer the utilities, *and*
      2. The city can buy power from itself without paying a profit. *For example*
         a. Both of these savings have been effected by the city of St. Preston, *and*
         b. Both of these savings have been effected by the city of Millersville.

Note that there are at least two primary arguments to support each major contention, at least two subsidiary arguments to support each primary argument. This must be the case if we are to maintain logical unity: if *I* above, were supported only by the primary argument *A*, then *I* should be rewritten, as "Cities which have municipally owned utilities can maintain lower rates by cutting overhead costs."

3. *Include the evidence supporting each argument.* Evidence in the mind of the investigator cannot be evaluated by someone reading the brief. In the illustration above items *a* and *b* are bits of evidence which support arguments *1* and *2*.

4. *Give the source of all evidence.* We have deliberately omitted the source of the evidence in the above illustration to show the questions that still remain: Where was the evidence found? How good is it? etc. The debater who cites pieces of evidence should be able to document them. One efficient procedure in briefing is to record the source in parentheses immediately under each statement of evidence.

   A. Collegiate interest in forensics is widespread today, *for*
      1. The national honorary forensic fraternities have chapters on 335 college and university campuses.
         a. Delta Sigma Rho has 72 active chapters, *and* (*The Gavel*, Vol. 31, March, 1949, p. 56.)
         b. Tau Kappa Alpha has 81 active chapters, *and* (*The Speaker*, Vol. 31, May, 1949, pp. 25-6.)
         c. Pi Kappa Delta has 172 active chapters, *and* (*World Almanac*, 1948, p. 172.)

2. West Point and the Naval Academy have added debate to their postwar curriculum, *and*
(William J. Thompson, "Speech Instruction at West Point," and William S. Shields, "An Integrated Speech Program at Annapolis," *Quarterly Journal of Speech*, Vol. 34, December, 1948, pp. 489-93.)

3. Seventy-eight per cent of the debate coaches whose opinions were surveyed in a recent study testified that on the campuses debate was enjoying a "renaissance" or at least holding its own in the postwar period.
(E. L. Pross and John Shirley, "Debate Coaches View the Post-War Situation," *Speech Activities*, Vol. V, Summer, 1949, p. 56.)

5. *Include opposing arguments and evidence to refute them.* Any careful student of a topic, though he may hold one view on it, will know the more obvious or significant arguments of the opposition. These he should incorporate in his brief, together with material for refutation.

A. The argument that monopolies are not a threat to free enterprise is open to question, *for*

1. The Federal Trade Commission reports that at the end of 1947 almost half of the net capital assets of the U.S. was controlled by 113 corporations, *and*

2. There were thirteen industries at the end of 1947 where more than 60% of all manufacturing facilities were owned by three companies in each industry, *and*
(*Time*, September 5, 1949, p. 53.)

3. During World War II 17% of the business organizations of the U.S. went out of business, *and*

4. During the war 5% of the largest corporations became employers of a quarter of all the workers who before the war were employed by the other 95% of the corporations.
(Carroll Kilpatrick, "Monopoly Marches On," *The Progressive*, September, 1949, p. 14.)

E. The Conclusion

The purpose of the conclusion is to restate the major contentions and to assert that they, and the supporting evidence, prove the author's position on the question. The issues stated in the introduction should appear as major contentions, and in the same order both in the proof and in the conclusion.

This chapter concludes our study of problem-solving as a basic element in discussion and debate. We have described a methodology for applying the processes of logical thinking to the democratic method. If we have achieved our purpose the reader should conclude that neither faith, hope, nor charity are adequate substitutes for rigorous and continuous analysis.

READINGS

BAIRD, A. C., *Argumentation, Discussion, and Debate* (New York, McGraw-Hill Book Co., Inc., 1950), Chap. 7.

Columbia Associates in Philosophy, *An Introduction to Reflective Thinking* (Boston, Houghton Mifflin Co., 1923), Chap. 13.

HOLMES, R. W., *The Rhyme of Reason* (New York, Appleton-Century-Crofts, Inc., 1939), Chap. 14.

LASKER, Bruno, *Democracy Through Discussion* (New York, H. W. Wilson Co., 1949), Chap. 16.

STEBBING, L. S., *Thinking to Some Purpose* (Middlesex, England, Penguin Books, Ltd., 1939), Chap. 14.

EXERCISES

1.* Draw up a complete brief advocating a specific solution for the problem you selected for intensive study, following the general rules for constructing a brief as suggested in this chapter.

2. For practice in brief construction, select a magazine article dealing with a current problem and construct a brief (necessarily incomplete since it is limited by the scope of the article) of it.

3. Read a transcript of a Town Meeting of the Air broadcast which proposed alternate solutions for a problem, and test each solution by the procedure outlined in this chapter.

4. Using the complete brief prepared in exercise 1 above, construct three different outlines of the material you would select from it for presenting a speech before (*a*) the student body of your school, (*b*) a labor union, and (*c*) the Chamber of Commerce.

Part III

THE LISTENER

CHAPTER 12

How Individuals in Groups Think

OUR STUDY OF THE techniques of analyzing the problem must be balanced by a study of the listener or participant in discussion and debate. It is not enough to know the subject; we must also know people, their ways of thinking and their general pattern of behavior in group situations.

In an earlier chapter we considered how individuals think in isolation. We are now concerned with how they think in groups. Generally we distinguish two types of group situations: (1) the *face-to-face group* where the individual members are reacting primarily to each other, and (2) the *co-acting group* where the individual members are reacting to an outside and common stimulus. Typical of the face-to-face group is the informal discussion or the committee meeting. The co-acting group is exemplified by the usual audience listening to a public speech, a debate, or any other type of public discussion. In these chapters dealing with the listener we are concerned with both types of groups; where our observations are limited to one, we shall be explicit.

I. GENERAL CONSIDERATIONS

A. The Unorganized Group

In the unorganized group we may have many individuals, but little or no polarization; the individuals are not paying attention to the same stimuli. In consequence, the group, without a leader, tends to be fickle and random in its actions; bewildered, highly emotional, and extreme in its judgments. Its members tend to lose a sense of personal responsibility. Such groups may easily be led to become a crowd, a mob, or, on some occasions, an audience.

In any event, the group either disbands, or effects some sort of temporary organization. In psychological terms, the heterogeneous group becomes homogeneous and polarized when attention is focused on a common stimulus. It may and usually does disband when this stimulus is removed. A sidewalk orator, for example, may climb upon his soap-box to proclaim the coming of revolution. The casual passersby, an unorganized group, may stop and listen to the orator. To the extent that they are polarized for the moment they have become a crowd, "a collection of individuals who are all attending and reacting to some common object, their reactions being of a simple, prepotent [predominant] sort and accompanied by strong emotional responses." These reactions are in part the result of social facilitation or interstimulation—the interplay between members of a group which tends to canalize and make more intense their aims, feelings, and responses. What takes place is not a complete blending of personalities, but rather "an increase in response merely from the sight or sound of others making the same movements [responses]," says Allport.[1]

This phenomenon of social facilitation serves to release the reactions for which the individual is in readiness, and to increase those reactions once they have been initiated. It does not develop from any "group mind" as a mystical entity apart from the individual minds. Rather, the concept of social facilitation suggests that when a group is organized there are many minds which at that particular time are organized in a special way and for a special purpose. Such is the case when a heterogeneous group gathers for a common purpose, such as hearing a speech, protesting a city ordinance, or deciding how to solve a problem of mutual concern.

B. The Audience

In referring to co-acting groups we commonly use the term *audience*, sometimes described as "a form of institutionalized crowd." This phrase means simply that an audience is usually more formal than an unorganized group because it has a predetermined reason for assembling, a specific place of meeting, regular seating arrangements and, normally, a predisposition to attend to a common stimulus, usually a leader. Those sociologists who employ the term *crowd*, however, usually suggest that the behavior of audiences is similar

[1] Floyd H. Allport, *Social Psychology* (Boston, Houghton Mifflin Co., 1924), pp. 262, 292.

to that of crowds, or unorganized groups, differing in degree of response rather than in kind.

The extent of polarization present is the most obvious difference between the unorganized group and the audience. That is, to develop an unorganized group into an audience it is necessary to establish the leader, or speaker, and the listeners as two separate entities, but with enough in common to make interaction possible. Polarization then develops through such conditions as these: the lighting, which may be adjusted to center attention upon the platform; the seating arrangement, which directs attention upon the platform and establishes a degree of social unity in the audience; the auditorium, which in itself suggests not only social unity but purposiveness in the gathering; the platform, whose elevation may attract immediate attention to those upon it; the ritual, which tends to merge the individuals into a social unit; and, finally, the speech or performance itself.[2]

"Circular response" is another important phenomenon which appears in the polarized audience. It begins with the response of the audience to the speech or performance. Signs of this response may be the relatively restrained action of approving smiles, nods of agreement, or frowns of disapproval, or the more vigorous action of applause and shouts of approval or disapproval. The speaker is affected by these visible and audible responses and is stimulated to release new energy and effort. In turn, this elicits new responses from the audience; the speaker and his hearers continue to play upon each other and to heighten each other's responses.

Circular response may also operate among members of the audience. One's own responses are stimulated and increased by those of persons sitting nearby, and these serve to stimulate further responses in his neighbors. In sum, this interplay of stimulation or circular response tends to heighten the reactions of individuals beyond what would be normal outside of the audience situation.

C. Types of Audiences

Though all audiences may have certain general characteristics, no two are exactly alike. The integration of the listeners with each other, and with the speaker, varies with the degree of polarization. Hollingworth has devised a simple classification of audience types, based on these five sequential tasks the speaker must perform in

[2] See Jon Eisenson, *The Psychology of Speech* (New York, Appleton-Century-Crofts, 1937), pp. 200-4, for an analysis of the psychological audience.

persuading his hearers: (1) securing attention, (2) establishing interest, (3) making an impression, (4) convincing the audience, and (5) directing the action of the audience.

If a speaker wishes only to create an awareness of a problem, he needs only to secure attention from his hearers. He may need to perform the second task also if his purpose is to arouse interest in seeking a solution. In a symposium to inform, however, the speakers must also consider the third task of impressing their hearers. Should a speaker want to convince his audience, as in a debate, he must also assume the fourth task; and if he calls for action by his hearers he must perform the fifth. It is Hollingworth's classification of audiences in terms of these tasks [3] that is the basis for our discussion.

1. *The pedestrian audience* may be best exemplified by the casual or transient group which gathers on the midway to hear a sideshow barker. As the audience is casual in its gathering so its degree of orientation toward the speaker is slight. Hence he must begin with the basic task of *securing attention*. A group of strangers who sit together on a subway, or a chance luncheon meeting of several faculty members may also constitute a pedestrian audience.

2. *The passive audience* is typically a face-to-face discussion group or a committee meeting. Here the audience is already partly oriented by having a meeting place; this orientation may shift to an integration of individuals with each other, and move finally to a degree of polarization toward the speaker. As various members of the group participate this polarization shifts. Since a partial orientation exists, any participant should probably begin with *establishing interest* in what he has to say.

3. *The selected audience* is one that has gathered for a common and specific purpose, such as a professional convention, or a legislative session. The common purpose increases the initial degree of integration and polarization and makes less essential the first two tasks of the speaker; he may be able to begin with *making an impression*. Often a college class might be labeled a selected audience.

4. *The concerted audience* consists of individuals who have gathered with a definite and mutually shared interest in a specific enterprise. A church congregation or the audience at a political rally might be called a concerted audience. Here polarization is almost

[3] H. L. Hollingworth, *The Psychology of the Audience* (New York, American Book Co., 1934), pp. 18, 21-5.

complete and the speaker may begin immediately to *convince the audience*, or even with the final task of *directing the action of the audience*. It may be noted that this type of audience has a characteristic almost opposite that of the typical discussion group where the degree of polarization is so slight that it shifts from time to time as different members participate.

5. *The organized audience*, such as the football team listening to the quarterback's signals, is polarized to the ultimate degree. The individuals have not only a definite and mutual interest in a specific enterprise, as in a concerted audience, but have also previously indicated their acceptance of the quarterback's authority. In public speaking situations one occasionally finds such extreme circumstances: a state of apparently perfect polarization existed in the early Nazi rallies in Germany and may also be found in some highly regimented political or religious meetings in America. In such circumstances the leader need not be concerned with convincing his audience, but must perform only the final task of *directing its action*.

II. INTENSIFIED TENDENCIES IN INDIVIDUAL BEHAVIOR

In Chapter 3 we discussed seven related aspects of non-logical thinking; here we are interested in knowing the group's influence upon those individual tendencies. In general, whenever an individual exhibits these tendencies in group situations they are both intensified in degree and increased in number. As has often been said, "the individual in a group tends to behave just as he would behave alone, *only more so.*"

A. We Tend to Increase Our Random Thinking

In an organized group the individual's attention is likely to be focused upon a leader; thus his tendency toward random thinking would seem to be restricted by the degree of his rapport with the leader. In cases of extreme polarization and under conditions of intense interstimulation among audience members, however, it is this very rapport which encourages the individual to "follow the leader," whether his appeals are logical or non-logical. In this sense the individual's own thinking is not deliberate and purposive, but random and haphazard.

B. We Tend to Rationalize Even More

We observed earlier that because of the considerable social pressure upon us to "be rational" we may often inhibit our normal responses. In the group situation, however, if "everybody is doing it" this inhibition is lessened, and we tend to rationalize actions which we would not take as isolated individuals. The individual often occupies a relatively anonymous position in a group and this also may encourage behavior that is not normal: "All doubt or worry as to one's course of action disappears when one finds that one is acting with the other members of the crowd. The fact that others approve of what one wants to do by doing the same thing themselves gives a comfortable sense of moral sanction." [4] This attitude is in itself a form of rationalization.

C. We Tend Further to Confuse Desire and Conviction

While man commonly desires to believe that he is guided in his thinking by logical considerations, other competing desires may be so much stronger that he accepts certain beliefs in spite of contrary evidence. In a group situation certain dormant desires often come to the fore and are expressed freely if we find that our fellows share them. Thus is begun the process of circular response: the demand for the satisfaction of our desires is intensified and we are therefore more likely to accept those beliefs which offer that satisfaction.

D. We Tend to Be Even More Suggestible

Suggestion, we have said, operates most successfully when there is a state of excitement and when there are no equally strong competing suggestions. Both of these special conditions are likely to be present in groups in addition to the normal play of social facilitation. As Bogardus says, "A heightened state of suggestibility is characteristic of a crowd. The preponderance of feelings over reason heightens suggestibility. The excitement that frequently prevails in a crowd throws persons off their guard. The force of numbers is overwhelming." [5] We might also add that in a group with an acknowledged leader, his prestige may give additional force to his use of suggestion. Beyond these factors is the consideration that all

[4] Allport, *op. cit.*, p. 312.
[5] Emory S. Bogardus, *Fundamentals of Social Psychology* (New York, Appleton-Century-Crofts, Inc., 1950), p. 387.

individuals have what the sociologist calls reserve behavior potentialities. These are immature attitudes or ideas which may find their first expression as a result of suggestion by a group leader. The average audience members, suggests Professor L. Guy Brown, may have enough fear, hate, and prejudice in their reserve behavior potentialities to be aroused to the lust of war. At the same time they may have enough altruism and charity in reserve to be aroused, by different suggestion stimuli, to donate to the Red Cross or the Community Chest. Thus we see that the group situation often lends itself to the use of suggestion for the release of these behavior potentialities.

E. We Tend to Succumb More Readily to Personal Appeals

Three facts about group behavior lead us to this conclusion. First, groups tend to be more susceptible than individuals to personal appeals when they come from one with group status, who can speak with authority or prestige. Second, there is heightened susceptibility to personal appeals when a speaker "links himself to the audience," not only by stressing such terms as *we*, *you*, and *us*, but by appealing to common experiences, backgrounds, and interests. Propagandists label these as "plain folks" or "togetherness" devices. Finally, circular response contributes to this susceptibility to personal appeals and increases their effect in a group situation. Even though an individual may not initially be impressed by, or react favorably to a speaker, he may be stimulated by the favorable reactions of other members of the group to modify his own behavior.

F. We Tend to Accept Specious Argument More Readily

This conclusion is implicit in almost all that we have said concerning the effect of the group upon individual thinking: specious arguments are even more readily accepted. The explanation, of course, lies in the fact that many group influences encourage the individual to drop his critical defenses, to follow the crowd rather than to doubt alone. A speaker's non-rational appeals have not only their own initial impact upon his hearers, but are facilitated and reënforced by the reactions of the group.[6]

[6] It is equally true, of course, that a generally hostile audience may also influence a receptive member to change his attitude toward a speaker, but that does not alter our general conclusion; the group's hostile behavior may be based upon specious arguments.

G.   We Tend Even More to Ignore Intellectual Appeals

This is an obvious corollary of our previous observations. When the members of a group are led to rationalize, to substitute desire for conviction, to be suggestible, to respond to personal appeals, and to accept specious arguments, they are accepting substitutes for intellectual appeals. Logical thinking yields to non-logical thinking. "Crowds act quickly via the feelings, but via reason exceptionally if at all, for feeling tends to submerge reason." [7] Membership in a group, and especially in a co-acting group, tends to give the individual a temporary and partial release from his usual inhibitions; he develops a sense of emotional freedom which leaves him free to ignore intellectual appeals.

We do not mean to say, however, that all groups act alike. There are obvious differences among them which may modify the tendencies we have presented. These tendencies occur more frequently in co-acting groups. Even concerted and organized audiences may, for one reason or another, resist effective polarization and social facilitation. In face-to-face discussion groups, these tendencies may be less apparent, primarily because the smaller number of group members, and their purpose in meeting, decrease the effectiveness of the circular response and make the shifting of polarization easier. This makes more difficult the continued dominance of the group by one individual. And in some small groups, composed of individuals skilled in coöperative thinking, there is less non-logical thinking than would be apparent in those individuals when alone. In general, however, the individual's tendencies toward non-logical thinking are intensified in the group situation, and it is this fact which makes desirable proper training in the skills of group problem-solving.

III.   DISTINCTIVE TENDENCIES IN GROUP BEHAVIOR

In addition to the intensified individual tendencies just described, there are also certain distinctive tendencies in man's thinking which appear most markedly in group situations. They deserve mention here.

[7] Bogardus, *op. cit.*, p. 386.

A. We Tend to Conform to Group Standards in Belief and Action

One of the more common stimulus-response patterns in the behavior of a member of a group is his reaction to the apparent standards of other group members. A fundamental human drive is the tendency to behave in ways that will gain group recognition, admiration, respect or approval. This tendency is in itself a learned response: we discover through trial and error that if we are amenable to group pressures and standards our group relationships are happier. Thus it is not an aspect of our personality alone that causes us to act in certain ways, or refrain from acting, but the group situation itself. If we are to retain our status in the group we do what the others do. If our fellows put money in the collection plate, sign the pledge, or cheer the speaker, we tend to conform to the group standard which they set. [8]

The tendency to conform is most apparent in co-acting groups. It may be so strong under certain conditions that freedom of speech is restricted, the audience being unwilling to hear anyone speak against the prevailing belief. In this respect the group tends to be conservative. As Weaver observes, "If we define conservatism as a reluctance to do anything different, then, clearly, by very definition, the crowd being a group of individuals acted upon by one another and responding in uniform fashion is conservative. From the point of view of the particular crowd itself this uniformity is conservatism. Who is the conservative, really, but the one who is fearful of breaking the social code and is eager to do what everyone else is doing?" [9]

B. We Tend to Intensify Our Prejudices

Prejudice may be defined as a prejudgment or an opinion formed without due examination of the facts. Some wit has suggested that what we call thinking is largely a re-arrangement of our prejudices, and there is at least a touch of truth in the remark. Our prejudices

[8] Some psychologists find that on certain items in behavior the tendency to conformity is so great that a J-curve, with the majority of members of a group lumped at the upper end and the rest indicating deviations as they are ranged on a sharply dropping curve, must be substituted for the more common bell curve distribution. See F. H. Allport, "The J-Curve Hypothesis of Conforming Behavior," *Journal of Social Psychology*, Vol. 5 (May, 1934), pp. 141-83.

[9] Andrew Thomas Weaver, *Speech: Forms and Principles* (New York, Longmans, Green & Co., 1942), p. 347.

are based upon culturalized values and attitudes, they grow out of our cultural status in society, and create "blind spots" in our thinking. The "all Negroes are lazy," "all aliens are radicals," or "all Wall Street men are crooks" type of thinking is usually based upon such prejudgments rather than upon the evidence. As a rule we are not willing to admit our prejudices; indeed, much of our rationalization comes from a desire to find rational justification for our biases and prejudices.

In the group situation, particularly in co-acting groups, these latent prejudices are intensified; normal inhibitions upon their expression are often removed by social facilitation, the notion that other folks feel the same way. Thus even the expression of a self-acknowledged prejudice may occasion no feeling of shame. Many groups in the concerted or organized audience, indeed, are assembled specifically for the purpose of activating these prejudices, as in meetings of the Ku Klux Klan or the formation of a lynching mob.

In face-to-face groups prejudices are by no means eliminated, but by the exchange of views in such groups prejudices are more likely to receive critical examination. And it is true that, in some situations, face-to-face discussion may serve as a therapy for eliminating prejudice. Success in this respect depends, of course, upon having trained leadership and participants who are skilled in using the techniques of the group process.

C. We Tend to Become Susceptible to Propaganda

It is impossible to conclude this discussion of how individuals in groups think without using the much-abused term *propaganda*. In some circles propaganda always has "bad" connotations ("I educate, but he propagandizes!") although it simply designates a technique or medium for the expression of either non-logical or logical thinking. Thus propaganda, like persuasion, or education, is a device that may be used for good ends or for bad.

Doob has defined propaganda as "the attempt to affect the personalities and to control the behavior of individuals toward ends considered unscientific or of doubtful value in a society at a particular time." [10] And Lasswell offers a useful distinction between propaganda and education: "propaganda is the manipulation of symbols to control controversial attitudes; education is the manipula-

[10] Leonard W. Doob, *Public Opinion and Propaganda* (New York, Henry Holt & Co., Inc., 1948), p. 240.

tion of symbols (and of other means) to transmit accepted attitudes (and skills)." [11] The symbols manipulated by the propagandist may include speeches, printed material, stories, broadcasts, rumors, insignia, and other forms of social communication. These are usually employed to influence large publics, rather than small groups, to accept predetermined ends. Propaganda should no more be denounced out of hand just because it may plead a culturally doubtful value than should editorial writing just because it may sometimes be used for evil purposes. As Doob indicates, propaganda functions where there is no science or when people's values are in conflict; the way to eliminate propaganda is to eliminate the unscientific and controversial areas in society.

So long as propaganda is a commonly used technique, it is important to note that individuals, especially when they are in groups, tend to become susceptible to it. Some efforts have been made to teach techniques of analyzing propaganda, but the best antidote, we believe, is training in the use of logical thinking for solving our problems.

We may now summarize what has been said about how individuals in groups think. As groups of people are increasingly oriented and polarized toward a specific stimulus, e.g., a leader, their tendency to think logically decreases; and with an increase in social facilitation the tendency toward non-logical thinking increases. This result appears to be caused by an intensification in group situations of non-logical thinking, plus the appearance of certain distinctive tendencies in thinking when individuals become members of groups. In sum, individuals when placed in group situations tend to relax their discrimination, to respond non-logically rather than logically.

READINGS

BLACK, Max, *Critical Thinking* (New York, Prentice-Hall, Inc., 1946), Chap. 13.
DOOB, L. W., *Public Opinion and Propaganda* (New York, Henry Holt & Co., Inc., 1948), Chaps. 5, 11.
LaPIERE, R. T., and FARNSWORTH, P. R., *Social Psychology* (New York, McGraw-Hill Book Co., Inc., 1949), Chap. 23.
LEE, A. M., and LEE, E. B., *The Fine Art of Propaganda: An Analysis of Father Coughlin's Speeches* (New York, Harcourt, Brace & Co., 1939).

[11] Harold D. Lasswell and Dorothy Blumenstock, *World Revolutionary Propaganda* (New York, Alfred A. Knopf, Inc., 1939), p. 10.

Lippmann, Walter, *Public Opinion* (New York, The Macmillan Co., 1923), pp. 79-156.

Lowenthal, Leo, and Guterman, Norbert, *Prophets of Deceit: A Study of the Techniques of the American Agitator* (New York, Harper & Bros., 1949), Chaps. 1-2, 10.

Krech, David, and Crutchfield, R. S., *Theory and Problems of Social Psychology* (New York, McGraw-Hill Book Co., Inc., 1948), Chap. 9.

Stebbing, L. S., *Thinking to Some Purpose* (Middlesex, England, Penguin Books, Ltd., 1939), Chaps. 7-8.

EXERCISES

1. From campus groups with which you are acquainted select five to illustrate the five types of audiences discussed in this chapter. With what types of problems might each be concerned?

2. Write a 300-500 word case history of an occasion in which you have observed the operation of one of the distinctive tendencies of the individual in the group situation as they have been discussed in this chapter.

3. Find examples of three of the individual tendencies in thinking which are often intensified in the group situation.

4. Prepare a three-minute speech of explanation and analysis of a sample of propaganda by an individual or agency such as one of the following: (*a*) a newspaper editorial, (*b*) the publicity director of your college, (*c*) advocates of federal world government, (*d*) a political party, (*e*) an advertiser, (*f*) a fund-raising campaign.

5. Organize a class symposium on the nature and extent of propaganda, dealing with such topics as these:
   a. Propaganda in the news
   b. War propaganda
   c. Propaganda of alien groups in America
   d. Propaganda in commercial advertising
   e. Propaganda in the schools

6. Organize a class-discussion unit on propaganda. This assignment may be carried out on four successive days, one third of the class participating in each of the three panel-forums, and the whole class taking part in the concluding formal group discussion. The four discussion topics, and the purpose of each discussion, might be:
   a. Locating and defining the problem (panel-forum):
      What is propaganda?
   b. Exploring the problem (panel-forum):
      How does propaganda influence our thinking?
   c. Examining suggested solutions (panel-forum):
      How may we as individuals best deal with propaganda?
   d. Choosing the best solution (formal group discussion):
      How should democracy deal with propaganda?

CHAPTER 13

Analyzing the Audience

IN THE LAST CHAPTER we considered some aspects of the thinking processes of the individual in a group situation. Now we continue our analysis of the individual by describing his role in significant aspects of group relationships, and making general observations upon his understanding and his beliefs. Finally, we summarize this discussion by outlining a procedure for analyzing a specific audience.

I. PRELIMINARY CONSIDERATIONS OF GROUPS

A. Society Is Built upon Group Organization

Our society is built upon group organization, formal or informal. Contrasted with other forms of government, democracy respects the status and the integrity of the individual, but even a democratic society functions largely in terms of group organization. Every person, no matter how individualistic, belongs to one or more groups, and his behavior is conditioned by that membership. Thus an individual may be a laborer, a businessman, or a professional man, and belong to a large informal group of those similarly employed. At the same time, he may also be a member of a smaller, but parallel group, such as a labor union, a manufacturer's association, or a medical society. These group rôles are separate from purely social groupings, although these may be similarly homogeneous.

B. Each Individual Belongs to Many Overlapping Groups

People not only belong to formal or informal groups based upon the way they earn their living, but to other groups as well: religious, racial, national, social, political, fraternal, cultural, and so on. As Harold J. Laski has said, "Whether we will or no we are all bundles of hyphens." Thus in a public discussion audience, itself a special group, we may have a listener who belongs to a carpenter's union, the Catholic Church, the Knights of Columbus, the Fourth Ward Democratic Club, the American Legion, and the Sons of Italy, as well as to a general social-economic-cultural class. To each of these groups he makes his personal intellectual, emotional, and/or financial contribution. In their turn, each of these groups has its effect upon the individual, determining the creed he accepts, the way he votes, the prejudices he holds, and the way he thinks on personal and public problems. Because of his multiple-membership, however, he finds it difficult to give total allegiance to any single group; the group also finds it difficult to enforce anything comparable to military discipline upon its members. As Walter Lippmann describes the situation, "when men strive too fiercely as members of any one group they soon find that they are at war with themselves as members of another group." [1]

C. Each Individual Is Also Apart from All Groups

It would be inaccurate to say that an individual always thinks, believes, and acts in terms of the groups to which he belongs. Rather, as we have indicated, the individual must continuously adapt his personality to all of these groups. The very multiplicity of his group affiliations makes it unlikely that there is any single and uncontroverted pressure upon him to follow a specific course of action or to accept a given belief. In consequence the individual is not only *of* certain groups but he is also *apart from* all groups. It is from this position that his adjustments must be made. Says Grace Coyle, "Within the mind of each member as he participates in the group, there goes on continuously an intricate adjustment of psychological forces. He is affected not only by pressures that reach him from his associated activity in this organization, or that rise from his own consciousness, but also by the necessity of adjusting his relationships to a variety of groups." [2]

In summary, our whole society is built upon group organization, and the groups to which a man belongs influence his behavior. What Graham Wallas characterized as *The Great Society* is in reality a

[1] Walter Lippmann, *A Preface to Morals* (New York, The Macmillan Co., 1929), p. 269.
[2] Grace Longwell Coyle, *Social Process in Organized Groups* (New York, 1930), p. 35. By permission of Farrar & Rinehart, Inc., publishers.

collection of lesser societies or groups. To the leader or participant in discussion and debate, this group basis of society is significant. We may observe that pure democracy is a vertical community, including everyone. When society becomes too large for pure democracy we organize horizontal groups, on lines of culture, class, creed, and so on. We then all belong to many horizontal groups, and because they are so diverse in their base, there must be compromises and adjustments to accommodate that diversity. One way in which necessary accommodations are made is through discussion and debate. Thus a particular audience may be a select one, composed of members of a specific group, such as a labor union, or a church. Or an audience may be a general one, made up of members of many groups who are gathered for a common purpose, such as hearing a public lecture, or a campaign debate. In either case the leader, speaker, or participant, is dealing not only with the ideas of the individuals present, but also with the beliefs, doctrines, and prejudices of the horizontal groups to which the individuals belong. These must be discovered and analyzed if participants in discussion and debate are to be fully effective.

II. GENERAL ASPECTS OF ORGANIZED GROUPS

A. Groups Are Usually Built Around a Common Characteristic

The American Medical Association is limited to members of the medical profession; the League of Women Voters is composed of women electors; the Boy Scouts have age qualifications; and the Union League Club attracts only men holding a particular economic and political philosophy. On other counts the individuals making up a group may be most inharmonious, but within the particular group and for its particular purpose, a large number of heterogeneous individuals have become temporarily homogeneous. As we have said, "there are many minds which at that particular time are organized in a special way for a special purpose."

B. Groups Commonly Determine Their Own Membership

In the 90's the Ladies New York Club was open only to "gentlewomen whose social status is beyond question." Today the Inter-Varsity Fellowship and the Communist party are alike in that both require a "confession of faith" from prospective members. Membership in the so-called "white collar class" is determined by occupation and economic status, but in smaller and more formally organized groups, membership is determined by the group itself, according to its purposes or interests. Membership restrictions, of course, tend to maintain group unanimity.

C. Groups Tend to Be Dynamic Rather than Static

Dynamic group character is manifested in two ways. (1) In groups whose principles undergo but slight modification from one generation to another, there is a dynamic quality apparent in the changing methods by which these principles are maintained and furthered. (2) There are some groups in which the principles themselves may be changed as a result of changes in membership. These may result from sudden shifts in income status, the change in a political balance of power, or merely the change in age and energy reflected in the old French proverb: "He who is not a radical at twenty has no heart, but he who is not a conservative at forty has no head."

D. Groups Transmit Cultural and Social Values

Presumably the Descendants of the Mayflower, the Daughters of the American Revolution, or the Daughters of the Confederacy, exist not only to maintain certain social distinctions, but because they transmit to succeeding generations certain cultural values. Within family, church, or political groups, the same may be true; and it is also unhappily true of other types of groups with strong racial or religious biases, such as the Ku Klux Klan, or the Silver Shirts. In general it may also be said that one of the reasons for studying history is that accepted and traditional values may be perpetuated.

E. Groups Are Important in Determining "Life's Chances"

Significant sociological studies have shown that groups play a major role in "life's chances" for an individual, i.e., his normal expectations in health, education, wealth, occupation, and basic ideologies and values. It is more than mere accident that our conversation often includes such phrases as "he was born to..." or "he isn't likely to rise above...." The formal or informal groups in which an individual matures provide a fairly reliable basis for predicting the opportunities that will be open to him, what he may become, and what he may think.

F. Groups Encounter Obstacles in Inter-Communication

In intragroup communication individuals seldom face serious obstacles, but in intergroup contacts there are limiting factors which make communication difficult, or even impossible. This is a special aspect of organized groups which the discussion leader or the persuader must recognize. Among the obstacles to intergroup communication are these:

1. *Groups vary in ways of thinking.* The recent immigrant from an Old-World nation often has difficulty in contacts with Americans; a New Englander may have the same experience with a Midwesterner. Different social mores, cultural values, educational standards, economic opportunities, and even different desires and interests are apparent in each of these particular environments. Thus the frame of reference for the thinking of one individual may be quite different from that of his new neighbor.

2. *Groups are influenced by varying traditions.* The state of Wisconsin has traditionally encouraged liberal experiments in government; farmers as a group are said to be traditionally conservative; and graduates of Teachers College, Columbia University, have traditionally encouraged "progressive" education. Members of any of these groups may find difficulty in discussions with those who do not share their traditions; indeed, the respective group traditions may be mutually irreconcilable.

3. *Groups are influenced by diverse experiences.* Scientists whose experiences are primarily concerned with controlled laboratory experiments may have difficulty in understanding public opinion experts whose experiences are with predicting probabilities of human behavior. The members of each group may be well versed in their own areas and their own methods, but have difficulty in comprehending each other's experiences. Such obstacles are frequently encountered in employer-employee relations; sitting together around the same table is not equivalent to sharing the same experiences.

4. *Groups vary in cultural status.* As the economic, social, or political status of groups vary, the difficulties of intergroup communication increase. For the so-called middle-income class there usually exists a culture and a body of information and attitudes derived from that culture which differ from that of the so-called lower-income class. Different information and attitudes are reflected

even in approaches to problems: thus we may characterize groups as liberal or conservative, autocratic or democratic, Jeffersonian, Hamiltonian, or Marxist.

5. *Groups differ in degrees of expert or lay status.* The problem of establishing adequate common understanding between the expert and the layman often presents another obstacle to intergroup communication. The expert in taxation does not easily divest himself of research terminology so that he may speak in non-technical language; and the layman does not easily acquire a facility for understanding technical language. Walter Lippmann and Graham Wallas have each emphasized this lack of a common vocabulary for experts and laymen; it frequently results in delayed application, if not loss, of research findings about social problems. If discussion and debate are to provide effective means of problem-solving, these obstacles to intergroup communication must be understood and dealt with by leaders and participants.

G. Groups Reach Agreement by Different Methods

Even those organized groups concerned only with research, exploring problems rather than finding and applying solutions, must have some procedure for reaching agreements. In policy-determining groups, from family councils to national legislatures, effective methods of making decisions are of prime importance. Students of group relations are generally agreed that *consensus* or *integration* of different viewpoints, is the ideal method of resolving conflicts. This method should be distinguished from other common procedures.

1. *Authority.* It is actually paradoxical to include this method in a list of ways in which groups reach agreement, for it amounts simply to group acceptance of a decision made by a person in authority. Its virtue lies in the outward appearance of a "united front," but it is usually only pseudo-unanimity, with divergent opinions concealed. Those who have what Ralph Linton calls "ascribed" rather than "achieved" leadership make such decisions for their groups: national dictators, army generals, and football captains. The discussion leader who adopts such an autocratic rôle, of course, defeats the very purpose of the discussion method.

2. *Enumeration.* When this method is followed, without an opportunity to use the discussion-debate sequence, it simply substitutes the vote of the group for the single authority. Even so, it is often

a better method than that of authority, as shown by the researches of Knight and Gordon, cited in Chapter 22 on evaluating discussion. When enumeration follows some sort of discussion or debate, other research cited in the same chapter shows, the method has greater merit. The chief weakness of simple enumeration is that while differences may be registered in the process of decision, they are not reflected in the result.

3. *Compromise*. When groups state their positions *before* they meet in conference, as in the case of many labor-management disputes, the method of compromise, though not ideal, may be the only way of settling a controversy. A compromise solution may give the appearance of formal unanimity, but in fact it means that different members of the group yield part of their positions for the sake of a settlement. The original differences of opinion may remain untouched. Sometimes such sacrifices are imperative if any decision is to be reached; legislative action is often based on compromise.

4. *Integration* or *consensus*. This method of agreement is the ideal one; it can result most easily when group members begin the analysis of a problem *before* their opinions are firmly set. Consensus is possible even when there are basic differences among members, if discussion can integrate the differences into a new solution which is a synthesis of the views of all members of the group. This type of agreement is the goal of labor-relations conciliators who are fortunate enough to enter a dispute before conflicting views are publicly announced. Integration is not a likely result, however, where external pressures operate on a group, where tensions are high within a group, or where a deadline for decision must be met.

The democratic, as distinguished from the authoritarian, leader will regard these general aspects of organized groups as significant. He will realize that he must inevitably deal with individuals in discussion and debate as group members, and that much of their behavior may be determined by the accepted values and procedures of the group. Before intelligent and effective problem-solving can result, both leaders and participants must understand the psychology of group behavior and develop the sensitivities and skills appropriate to democratic group action.

III. THE UNDERSTANDING OF AUDIENCES

A. The Orientation of the Speaker

Those who take part in discussion and debate must not only be aware of the general characteristics of organized groups but also of the general understanding of audiences: What, in short, can the speaker expect of his hearers' ability to learn, or to perceive facts and to use them in reasoning and imagining? If understanding is thought of as a capacity for incorporating social experiences into adaptations to new situations, what can we say of the understanding of audiences?

Obviously any comments must be quite general; only the speaker's own analysis of his specific audience will prepare him to meet it. The most commonly accepted index of an audience's understanding is its educational level. Even this criterion must be used with care: some pretty poor minds have been exposed to four years of college education, and some brilliant ones have developed without much formal training. The men and women who served in World War II provide a very broad sampling, within a limited age group, of our population. Here are the figures on their educational attainments: [3]

College

4 years	3.6%
3 years	2.0
2 years	4.0
1 year	6.3
	15.0

High School

4 years	23.3
3 years	11.2
2 years	10.9
1 year	7.8
	53.2

Elementary School

5 to 8 years	27.4
4 years or less	3.5
	30.9

[3] *Time*, Vol. 45 (February 19, 1945), p. 4.

Working from similar figures Rudolf Flesch has studied the implications of educational attainment in terms of ability to understand verbal communication. On the basis of his findings he has established general norms for different levels of spoken and written style, and has correlated them with different levels of educational attainment.[4] As a rather general guide in such matters as vocabulary, length and complexity of sentences, the Flesch formulas arc worth examination. We shall have more to say on the matter of adapting spoken style to the audience in Chapters 16 and 26.

Regardless of the educational attainments of his listeners, the speaker should recognize that there are always certain psychological barriers to effective communication. They arise primarily because of the symbolic nature of our formal language; our words are often inadequate to convey the complexity, fluidity, and multidimensional character of the real world. Daniel Katz has suggested four of these psychological obstacles: [5]

1. *The failure to refer language to experience and reality.* There is often an inability to grasp the difference between a symbol and its reference, a failure to check back constantly from language to the experience it represents.

2. *The inability to transcend personal experience in intergroup communication.* Members of different groups, e.g., labor and management, may become so involved in presenting their experiences in their own symbols that they cannot make themselves clear to each other. Katz observes that there is more likely to be a common psychological core of reality between people than their language indicates.

3. *The assimilation of material into familiar frames of reference.* Stereotyped thinking often leads us to "fill in the blanks" as we listen with preconceptions, extensions of limited attitudes, and cultural superstitions. Thus we add an improper emotional coloration to what we hear, and consequently misunderstand it.

4. *The confusion of percept and concept.* Listeners sometimes forget the proper distinctions between words referring to percepts, or aspects of perceived experience, and terms which designate concepts and abstractions. As a consequence they often personify abstract concepts, or speak metaphorically and analogically, rather than literally. The result is oversimplification, which lacks exact, scientific description.

[4] Rudolf Flesch, *The Art of Plain Talk* (New York, Harper & Bros., 1946), esp. pp. 134-40.
[5] Daniel Katz, "Psychological Barriers to Communication," *Annals of the American Academy of Political and Social Science,* Vol. 250 (March, 1947), pp. 17-25.

The speaker in discussion or debate should, as part of his basic orientation, recognize these limitations upon the understanding of his audiences. In meeting a specific audience he may find Abraham Lincoln's advice helpful: "I always assume that my audience is in many things wiser than I am, and I say the most sensible things I can to them. I have never found that they did not understand me."

B. The Effects of New Information

Raymond Clapper once stated this basic rule: "Never underestimate the intelligence of your audience; and never overestimate its information." This is sound advice; it suggests, as we have said explicitly many times in this book, that intelligent problem-solving is based upon knowledge and understanding of relevant evidence. There is sometimes a danger, however, that we may confuse exposure to information with absorption of it. "I can't understand the group's decision," says a forum leader, "they had heard all the facts." But hearing and understanding are very different things, and discussion leaders must distinguish between them.

What audiences understand, regardless of the amount of their formal education, we have just noted, depends in large measure upon certain psychological aspects of communication. Katz' theoretical discussion of this problem has been made specific in a number of studies to determine the correspondence, if any, between the nature and amount of material presented and its absorption or understanding. Two investigators of this problem made a careful examination of surveys of the National Opinion Research Center and reached these conclusions: [6]

1. *There exists a hard core of chronic "know-nothings."* "There is something about the uninformed which makes them harder to reach, no matter what the level or nature of the information."

2. *Interested people acquire the most information.* "The widest possible dissemination of material may be ineffective if it is not geared to the public's interests."

3. *People seek information congenial to prior attitudes, and tend to ignore uncongenial information.* "Merely 'increasing the flow' is not enough, if the information continues to 'flow' in the direction of those already on your side."

4. *People interpret the same information differently.* It is "false to assume that exposure, once achieved, results in uniform interpretation

[6] Herbert H. Hyman and Paul B. Sheatsley, "Some Reasons Why Information Campaigns Fail," *Public Opinion Quarterly*, Vol. 11 (Fall, 1947), pp. 412-23.

and retention of the material." Memory and perception are distorted by wishes, motives, and attitudes.

5. *Information does not necessarily change attitudes.* Informed people do react differently from uninformed, "but it is naïve to suppose that information always affects attitudes, or that it affects all attitudes equally. . . . There is evidence . . . that individuals, once they are exposed to information change their views *differentially*, each in the light of his own *prior* attitude."

Some of the implications of these conclusions are treated elsewhere in this book. Our purpose in referring to them here is to emphasize the complexity of the problem of evaluating the understanding of audiences, and to encourage participants in discussion and debate to undertake careful analysis of the specific audiences to which they speak.

IV. THE BELIEFS OF AUDIENCES

A. The Nature of Belief

It is usually said that our beliefs are socially determined, that is, they are based only in part upon our personal experiences, and depend largely upon the advice, testimony, and influence of others. Even when beliefs are based upon tradition, as many are, they have a social character in that they have been transmitted from person to person or group to group. When analyzing an audience perhaps the most important observation to make about belief is that all men tend to formulate some kind of belief about situations they encounter. That is, men perceive with meaning and interpretation, even though they do not have all the evidence. "We cannot help doing this," social psychologists say. "Man is an organizing animal. . . . We cannot say to ourselves, 'Hold off any interpretations until you collect all the facts.' As soon as we experience any facts, they will be perceived as organized into some sort of meaningful whole. This is a universal characteristic of the cognitive process and not a weakness of the impatient or prejudiced individual. . . ." [7]

It is not surprising, therefore, to observe relatively small numbers of people who answer "don't know" in public opinion surveys. Men tend to think they know; they generally have convictions on controversial questions. In part these convictions are held because of men's group relationships.

[7] David Krech and Richard S. Crutchfield, *Theory and Problems of Social Psychology* (New York, McGraw-Hill Book Co., Inc., 1948), p. 86.

What a man states to himself as his argument or reasoning or thinking about a national issue is, from the more exact point of view, just the conflict of the crossed groups to which he belongs. To say that a man belongs to two groups of men which are clashing with each other; to say that he reflects two seemingly irreconcilable aspects of the social life; to say that he is reasoning on a question of public policy, these all are but to state the same fact in three forms.[8]

Lund asked a number of individuals to rate a set of propositions on a scale of belief strength and to indicate in each case the source of his belief. When the indicated determinants of belief were analyzed they fell into these categories and with these frequencies: [9]

Determinants	Frequencies
A. Teaching and training	326
B. Personal experience	151
C. Personal opinion	116
D. Personal reasoning	92
E. Desire and satisfyingness	58
F. Authoritative opinion	46
G. Public opinion	44
H. Axiomatic principle	6
(Individual responses)	125
(No response)	86
Total	1050

It is significant to observe that fewer than one third were attributed to "personal" factors. Again we see evidence that our beliefs are byproducts of social influences. Through many agencies, and throughout his life, the individual is influenced by the beliefs, habits, and values of society. And these beliefs, in turn, provide him with a basis for his behavior. It is important for the leader or participant in discussion and debate to recall, as Krech and Crutchfield observe, that these beliefs, right or wrong, are the natural result of man's experience; they do not necessarily reflect impatience or deliberate prejudice.

B. The Determinants of Belief Strength

As a working principle in discussion and debate we should recognize the chief factors in determining the strength of our beliefs.

[8] Arthur F. Bentley, *The Process of Government* (Chicago, University of Chicago Press, 1908), p. 204.

[9] F. H. Lund, "The Psychology of Belief," *Journal of Abnormal Psychology,* Vol. 20 (April, 1925), pp. 174-96.

For not all beliefs are held with equal conviction: a voter may be more certain of his preference for Candidate *A* over Candidate *B* in the gubernatorial race than of his preference for Candidate *Y* over Candidate *Z* in the senatorial race. Experimental studies have demonstrated the significance of the following factors in determining the strength of a belief.

1. *Length of time held.* Some investigators have found a very high correlation of belief-strength with the length of time the belief has been held. As Marple reports, "whether measuring changes in belief due to chance or those which occur in the presence of a group or expert preference, there appears to be a decline of suggestibility with increasing age." [10] As we grow older and hold our beliefs longer they tend to become stronger, and we are less likely to relinquish them.

2. *Influence of group and expert opinion.* Marple's experiments also tend to indicate a positive correlation between personal belief and group opinion: "Group opinion, with these groups, is more powerful in affecting individual agreement than is expert opinion." [11] While this conclusion has generally been confirmed by other studies,[12] there is occasional evidence to support the predominant prestige of the expert.[13] It is probably true that group opinion is strongest; but the subject under discussion and the prestige of the expert may make for exceptions.

3. *Ability to influence beliefs of others.* A study of individual influence in discussion tends to indicate that those who are the most influential are the least influenced by others.[14] Belief-strength, in other words, may be greater for those individuals possessing

[10] C. H. Marple, "The Comparative Susceptibility of Three Age Levels to the Suggestion of Group versus Expert Opinion," *Journal of Social Psychology*, Vol. 4 (May, 1933), pp. 4, 176-86.

[11] *Ibid.*

[12] H. E. Burtt and D. R. Falkenberg, "The Influence of Majority and Expert Opinion on Religious Attitudes," *Journal of Social Psychology*, Vol. 14 (November, 1941), pp. 269-78; David Wheeler and Howard Jordan, "Change of Individual Opinion to Accord with Group Opinion," *Journal of Abnormal and Social Psychology*, Vol. 24 (July-September, 1929), pp. 203-6.

[13] D. H. Kulp, "Prestige, as Measured by Single-Experience Changes and their Permanency," *Journal of Educational Research*, Vol. 27 (April, 1934), pp. 663-72; Irving Lorge, "Prestige, Suggestion, and Attitudes," *Journal of Social Psychology*, Vol. 7 (November, 1936), pp. 386-402.

[14] Ray H. Simpson, *A Study of Those Who Influence and of Those Who Are Influenced in Discussion* (New York, Teachers College, Columbia University, 1938), p. 87.

attributes which are effective in influencing the beliefs of others.

4. *Degree of involvement.* There is some evidence to suggest that the degree of personal involvement is important in determining the strength of beliefs and the resistance to new beliefs. When both sides of a fairly academic controversial question are presented, for example, already existing beliefs and prejudices will be intensified. But when the issue is judged closer to reality by the listener more open-mindedness is apt to follow.[15] It is also significant in this connection to note that when reacting to speeches that are neutral on the issues being discussed, the listener tends to interpret what he hears as favorable to his own beliefs.[16]

5. *Desirability of belief.* The studies by Lund, referred to earlier, involved ratings of several hundred propositions on scales of "belief strength" and "desirability," and gave a positive correlation in rank between the order for belief and the order for desire of over $+.80$.[17] This, of course, is also a "common sense" conclusion. The person who does not believe in the income tax will find that belief strengthened every time he pays his taxes, and the student who believes in abolishing the grading system will have his belief strengthened every time he receives a low mark.

C. Results of Belief Surveys

The beliefs of any specific audience can be discovered only by close acquaintance with its members or by taking a poll. Only the latter method is possible, of course, when we are dealing with larger publics than, say, a discussion group whose members we know personally. As an example of the type of data that may be collected in a national poll, we reproduce here the findings of the American Institute of Public Opinion in a survey made March 13, 1948, on this issue: "There are now certain taxes and fees which dealers who handle margarine have to pay which they do not have to pay on butter. A bill has been introduced in Congress to do away

[15] R. L. Schanck and C. Goodman, "Reactions to Propaganda on Both Sides of a Controversial Issue," *Public Opinion Quarterly*, Vol. 3 (January, 1939), pp. 107-12.

[16] A. L. Edwards, "Political Frames of Reference as a Factor Influencing Recognition," *Journal of Abnormal and Social Psychology*, Vol. 36 (January, 1941), pp. 34-50. See also Howard Gilkinson, "The Influence of Party Preference Upon the Responses of an Audience to a Political Speech," *Sociometry*, Vol. 5 (January, 1942), pp. 72-9.

[17] F. H. Lund, "The Psychology of Belief," *Journal of Abnormal Psychology*, Vol. 20 (April, 1925), pp. 194-5.

with these taxes and fees on margarine. Do you favor or oppose this bill?" [18]

NATIONAL TOTAL	REMOVE TAXES 69%	KEEP TAXES 15%	No OPINION 16%
By Occupation			
Professional and business	78%	9%	13%
White collar	72	13	15
Farmers	39	37	24
Manual workers	75	10	15
By Education			
College	75%	15%	10%
High school	72	13	15
Grammar school	66	16	18
By Sex			
Men	67%	18%	15%
Women	72	11	17
By Geographical Section			
New England and Middle Atlantic	74%	11%	15%
East and West Central	64	20	16
South	68	10	22
West	75	18	7
By Type of Fat Used			
Butter-users only	58%	22%	20%
Margarine-users only	84	7	9
People using both	71	13	16

As this example indicates, public opinion pollsters attempt to take into consideration all possible group orientations that might be significant in interpreting responses. On other issues it might be important to consider age, religion, military service, and so on. In any event, an effort is made to include among the people questioned the appropriate proportion for each of these significant categories. If the question involves religion, for example, and 15 per cent of the total population is Baptist, that same percentage of the sample must be Baptist. It should also be noted that this sample poll takes account of those people questioned who had no opinions. In some surveys of public opinion those questioned are also asked to give

[18] *Public Opinion Quarterly*, Vol. 12 (Summer, 1948), pp. 358-9.

the reasons for their beliefs; this type of questioning adds considerably to the significance of the results for those who expect to deal with the same topics in discussion or debate.

V. A METHOD OF AUDIENCE ANALYSIS

Before we speak, wrote Thomas Wilson in his *Arte of Rhetorique* (1560), we must "aduisedly marke the men before whom we speake, the men against whom we speake, and all the circumstances which belong.unto the matter." So far we have dealt with audiences in general; now we turn to the specific audience. What questions are important in analyzing "all the circumstances"?

A. The Audience and the Problem

1. *What is the relationship of the problem to the specific audience?* Few audiences are, or can be, equally interested in all phases of a problem; thus the first task in analysis is to discover what phases of the problem are of greatest concern to that audience. If the problem is one of procuring cheaper electrical power, the local Chamber of Commerce may be interested in learning how cheaper power would affect local industries; a general audience of voters may want to know how candidates for office stand on the question; the high school assembly may be most interested in the general social implications of the project. It is important to find out whether the audience has only an academic interest in the problem, or is motivated by real needs or wants. Does the audience have a direct responsibility for the outcome of the discussion (as a city council debating a proposed ordinance), or will its conclusion be advisory only (as a city forum discussion of a pending council ordinance)? Another approach is to ask how far the audience has progressed in thinking about the problem: (*a*) Is the audience aware of the existence of the problem? (*b*) Has the problem been located and defined? (*c*) Has the problem been fully explored and investigated? (*d*) Has the audience already considered suggested solutions? (*e*) Has any one solution been definitely or tentatively chosen? (*f*) Is the audience primarily concerned with securing general acceptance of a selected solution?

2. *What information does the audience have on the problem?* The speaker needs to find the proper course between the extremes of telling his audience what it already knows and of neglecting to

give it information essential to understanding the problem. It is also useful if speakers can determine the probable sources of their audiences' information, such as newspapers, radio reports, academic studies, rumor, personal experience, or propaganda agencies.

3. *What beliefs or prejudices does the audience have concerning the problem?* It is as important to find the answer to this question as it is to discover the extent of an audience's knowledge of the problem, for people act on prejudices as well as upon facts. The speaker may also learn more about his hearers if he can find the sources for their beliefs and prejudices.

4. *What is the attitude of the audience toward the problem?* In a general way we should observe that most speakers have two audiences: those individuals who have already made up their minds about the problem under discussion, and the so-called "marginal voters" who have yet to reach a decision. Specifically, the speaker may characterize his hearers as (*a*) *favorable*, (*b*) *neutral*, or (*c*) *unfavorable* toward his point of view. It may sometimes be impossible to reach a definitive conclusion on the proportion of those in an audience who hold each attitude, but previous inquiries should help the speaker make at least a generalization which will guide him in planning what he will say. As the speaker summarizes this portion of his audience analysis, he would do well to make a list of the specific objections and difficulties he may expect to meet. Planning his presentation in terms of these obstacles should increase his effectiveness.

5. *What is the speaker's specific purpose in presenting the problem?* The speaker's *general* purpose should be clear in his mind even before he tries to analyze his audience; his *specific* purpose can be determined only after studying his hearers. In a civic forum on the problem of cheaper electric power, the specific purpose may be simply to inform the audience of the possible benefits, or it may be to gain support for a municipal bond issue to procure the power. As all speaking has a purpose, the speaker must determine it in advance, and in terms of those who will hear him.

6. *How much time is available?* This question, frequently overlooked by discussion leaders, is extremely important. In a half hour, for example, no speaker or speakers could hope to make an adequate presentation of the need for cheaper power, its social and economic benefits (and possible disadvantages, in terms of initial plant cost, and so on), and the most desirable method by which cheaper power

could be obtained. In terms of his study of the audience the speaker must decide which of these aspects of the problem seems most important and arrange his presentation to fit his allotted time. The same considerations are important in informal discussions; the group must not undertake a problem too big for the time available.

B. The Audience and the Speaker

1. *To what general group does the audience belong?* The audience may be made up largely of industrialists, housewives, professional men, skilled laborers, small businessmen, or college students. In any case, the group orientation of the audience may affect its response to the speaker.

2. *To what specific group, if any, does the audience belong?* As the speaker may make certain generalizations about college students or businessmen, so he may make additional ones about more restricted groups like a campus International Relations Club or a Rotary Club. The status of the group in the community may also be of significance.

3. *What are the general characteristics of the audience?* Here we may consider several lines of analysis: (*a*) Is the audience homogeneous or heterogeneous? Do its members have similar or dissimilar cultural and environmental backgrounds? (*b*) Does the audience have an apparent "personality," i.e., cheerful, apathetic, tired, eager? (*c*) What is the probable educational level of the audience and how will that affect the speaker's choice of words and the complexity of his ideas? (*d*) What are the common interests, beliefs, or prejudices of the audience? How can a knowledge of them be used for effective motivation, or for overcoming psychological obstacles in the audience's thinking?

4. *What are the specific characteristics of the audience?* In anticipating probable beliefs and attitudes of his audience a speaker will be aided by considering its special characteristics, such as race, age, sex, religion, political affiliation, and so on. Not all of these factors will be significant for all problems; the speaker must select what he needs to know in terms of his subject.

5. *What is the status of the audience in terms of needs and wants?* Since we know that people tend to act and believe largely in terms of their needs and wants, it becomes important for a speaker or discussion leader to analyze his audience in these terms. He should ask not only whether his audience is drawn from a relatively satis-

fied or dissatisfied community; he should also seek out the specific grounds for any such generalization.

6. *What is the attitude of the audience toward the speaker?* Rhetoricians have long stressed the importance of *ethos* in a speaker, his ethical appeal. One who has the confidence and trust of his audience, for example, can more successfully champion an unpopular cause than one whose competence and veracity the audience questions. Three separate factors are apparently involved in the audience's evaluation of a speaker: (*a*) his qualifications as an authority concerning the facts relevant to the problem, (*b*) his qualifications as an authority concerning the interpretation of the facts, and (*c*) his prestige, or the general feeling toward him, based upon past acquaintance or reputation. A speaker may discover, in his analysis, specific difficulties presented by the attitude of his audience. If he hopes to overcome the obstacles to his acceptance by his hearers a speaker would be wise to summarize these difficulties in advance. Candid self-evaluation will go far in providing a basis for improved speaker-audience rapport.

VI. APPLYING THE METHOD OF AUDIENCE ANALYSIS

The questions suggested above will ordinarily lead to as much information as a speaker needs in preparing to take part in discussion or debate. In some instances there may be other points which are significant, because of the topic, the audience, or the circumstances. Speakers should not hesitate to investigate these points; they cannot know too much about their hearers.

The speaker who is going to address an audience in a strange community may find it difficult to make the complete analysis we have suggested. This does not mean that he cannot participate effectively in discussion or debate, but it means that his task is more difficult. He will have to make more impromptu adjustments and adaptations than would be necessary if he knew his hearers better in advance. The beginner should be warned that the ability to make such adaptations "on the spot" comes only with practice; and he will be wise to avoid the necessity of frequent impromptu adjustments by analyzing his audience as carefully as conditions permit, before he speaks.

The best way of securing the information for an audience analysis is by talking with members of the audience, or at least with people of the same general group from which the audience will be drawn. The local newspapers—editorial columns, and "letters to the editor," as well as the news columns—may be helpful in discovering what people in the community are thinking about and what interests them. The log of a local radio station offers similar reflections of public interest. Check the activities of local organizations: what topics are being discussed at Rotary Club meetings, what subjects are being studied by the League of Women Voters, what issues seem to agitate local political groups?

Even when it is not possible to make a first-hand investigation of public opinion which provides a setting for discussion or debate, the speaker may find it useful to analyze *similar* groups with which he is already familiar. Labor unions, for example, may not follow the same policies everywhere, but certain valid generalizations may be made about organized labor groups in Middletown based upon an understanding of labor groups in Uniontown. Local businessmen may be Republicans or Democrats in a particular community, but businessmen in any town are apt to have about the same attitudes toward certain public questions.

On a broad scale, the several national surveys of public opinion are useful indexes to what audiences are likely to believe. And many local newspapers or polling agencies publish frequent reports of public sentiment in their own communities. This information, like past election results, may be very helpful in giving to the speaker a feeling for the climate of opinion in which he must operate.

In the next chapter we will take up ways in which an analysis of the audience may be applied through the use of persuasion.

READINGS

BAIRD, A. C., and KNOWER, F. H., *General Speech: An Introduction* (New York, McGraw-Hill Book Co., Inc., 1949), Chap. 17.
DOOB, L. W., "Some Factors Determining Change in Attitude," *Journal of Abnormal and Social Psychology*, Vol. 35 (October, 1940), pp. 549-65.
DOOB, L. W., *Public Opinion and Propaganda* (New York, Henry Holt & Co., Inc., 1948), Chap. 8.
HOLLINGWORTH, H. L., *The Psychology of the Audience* (New York, American Book Co., 1935), pp. 126-39.
LAPIERE, R. T., and FARNSWORTH, P. R., *Social Psychology* (New York, McGraw-Hill Book Co., Inc., 1949), Chaps. 23-4.

LASKER, Bruno, *Democracy Through Discussion* (New York, H. W. Wilson Co., 1949), Chap. 4.
LAZARSFELD, P. F., BERELSON, B., and GAUDET, H., *The People's Choice* (New York, Columbia University Press, 1948).
MONROE, A. H., *Principles and Types of Speech* (Chicago, Scott, Foresman & Co., 1949), Chap. 9.

EXERCISES

1. Find examples from campus groups to show the four ways in which group agreements may be reached.
2. Prepare a survey to determine the beliefs and attitudes of the members of your class on a problem you are currently discussing. Analyze this belief-survey to determine probable sources and strength of the beliefs recorded.
3. Select several pairs of groups which have frequent contacts, such as farmers-laborers, Chamber of Commerce-CIO, and examine their past relations to discover specific obstacles in communication.
4. Draw up a careful analysis of your class audience as one step in preparing for class discussion or debate.
5. Listen to an assigned public address given on your campus and write a critical evaluation of the speaker's apparent analysis of his audience.
6. Assume that you are to give a speech advocating the solution you have chosen for your semester problem, and draw up an audience analysis for three of the following groups before which you might speak: your college assembly, a Kiwanis Club, a labor union, the League of Women Voters, the local Republican club, an adult discussion group.

CHAPTER 14

Persuasion

"HE WHO WANTS to persuade," said Joseph Conrad, "should put his trust not in the right argument, but in the right word. . . . Give me the right word and the right accent and I will move the world." Conrad is not alone in his belief that one well-placed emotional appeal is more powerful for most of us than a battery of facts and arguments. C. G. Lange, the distinguished Danish physiologist, wrote: "Emotions are not only the most important forces in the life of the individual human being, but they are also the most powerful force of nature known to us." And H. A. Overstreet, author of *Influencing Human Behavior*, regards as axiomatic his statement that "no appeal to reason that is not also an appeal to a want can ever be effective."

We need only to look about us to see that those whose business is to influence the attitudes and actions of others act on this belief. Advertisers know that appeals to real or fancied wants sell more goods, to all but professional buyers, than objective analyses of their product. Campaign speakers avoid detailed discussions of taxation, international finance, or foreign policy. Instead they urge us to beware of *radicals, reactionaries, warmongers,* or *dictators,* and promise a *square deal* with *peace, prosperity* and *justice* for all. By every available means of communication, these and other persuaders connect their proposal with the known desires of their public. They are after results and these are the ways to get results.

If logic and argument run a poor second in a race with emotional appeal, why are we writing this book on objective thinking and its use in discussion and debate? Because we believe that emotional appeals may be properly used to reënforce evidence and argument. However, we think that emotional appeals are too often substituted

238

for objective analysis and logical thinking. Our system of legislative delays, so irritating to those who are sure they know what ought to be done, was designed to give time for the gathering of evidence and the sober second thought that renders less effective the individual who sways audiences by playing on their hopes and fears.

Our quarrel is with those who use emotional appeals simply because they are powerful. These persons are more dangerous to a democratic society than those who sell worthless stock. But this danger cannot be averted by legal action. The remedy lies rather in a more general understanding of the processes of persuasion, and in training speakers to employ emotional appeals with due regard for their social consequences.

I. A DEFINITION OF PERSUASION

The term *persuasion* occurs frequently in our conversation. We use it to designate our attempts to get others to do what we want them to do. We persuade those whom we have no power to command. The salesman persuades others to buy his goods; the public relations counsel persuades us to like his client; the minister persuades his congregation to follow the good way. In this general sense, a large part of our written and oral communication might be called *persuasion*.

Such a definition is too inclusive for our purpose. There are different methods of securing belief or action. One speaker analyzes the problem, gathers and organizes the evidence on the issues, and then presents his conclusions with a minimum of emotional appeals. This process we call *argumentation*. It demands of the listener the ability and the willingness to weigh the evidence and test the reasoning before he makes up his mind. Another speaker follows almost the opposite course. He states his proposition early in his speech, connecting it immediately, and repeatedly, with his listeners' needs, beliefs, and basic desires. His arguments are presented as established conclusions and supported with vivid illustrations. There is only enough evidence to satisfy those who desire it, and the reasoning is presented in simplified terms. This is *persuasion* in its more extreme form.

Argumentation aims at a delayed, critical acceptance of a proposition, after an examination of the supporting proofs; *persuasion* aims at a more immediate and less critical adoption of the speaker's conclusions. The argumentative speech follows a logical pattern; the persuasive speech is psychological, rather than logical, in arrangement.

Persuasion, then is *the process of securing acceptance of an idea, or an action, by connecting it favorably with the listeners' (or readers') attitudes, beliefs, and desires.* This definition does not exclude the use of evidence and reasoning. But the emphasis is on making the listener want to do what the evidence indicates he should do. Persuasive speeches are properly used to secure acceptance of conclusions reached through study and investigation.

We should note in passing that the processes of persuasion and propaganda are practically identical. Lasswell makes this distinction: "Propaganda is dispersed or concentrated; when concentrated upon a few persons it is persuasion." [1] Merton agrees but notes that "persuasion differs from propaganda in two technical respects. It involves a higher degree of social interaction between 'persuader' and 'persuadee' and it permits the persuader to adapt his argumentation" to the reactions of his listeners. [2] Our negative conditioning to the word *propaganda* arises from the fact that it left the church and fell into bad company in World War I, and into even worse hands since then.

II. THE BASES OF PERSUASION

To be successful, persuasion must reach the main-springs of human motivation. This subject has been treated rather fully in Chapters 3, "How Individuals Think" and 12, "How Individuals in Groups Think." The list presented here is drawn from these chapters and from the writings of psychologists.

A. We Tend to Believe What We Want to Believe

Much of what we call reasoning consists of finding reasons to justify our beliefs and actions. We want to believe that we are underpaid, that a new car is really a necessity, that the other fellow is to blame, that "all is fair in love and war." Our wants are partly physical and psychological, and partly social in origin. We want

---

[1] Harold D. Lasswell and Dorothy Blumenstock, *World Revolutionary Propaganda* (New York, Alfred A. Knopf, Inc., 1939), p. 10.

[2] Robert K. Merton and others, *Mass Persuasion* (New York, Harper & Bros., 1946), pp. 38-9.

food, naturally enough, but we want caviar because Mrs. Jones has some. The interested reader can find in books on influencing human behavior, lists of basic and acquired wants. While the terminology used is variant, the writers agree that, to an extent determined by such factors as the length of time we have held the belief in question and the urgency of the desire, we tend to believe what we want to believe.

B. We Tend to Believe, and to Do, as We Are Told

Unless we have information to the contrary, we tend to accept what we hear and what we read. In psychological terms, we are suggestible. To the psychologist, suggestion means the tendency of an idea to result in an act, or of a stimulus to result in a favorable response, without an interval of deliberation such as would be required for the evaluation of evidence or the weighing of consequences. The listener responds to stimuli created by the speaker, by significant elements in his surroundings, and by fellow listeners. He may also react to stimuli arising within himself, from such sensations as hunger and discomfort, or from his memories of previous experiences.

Suggestion plays a larger part than we like to admit in shaping our opinions and in determining our actions. The advertiser subjects us to a continued barrage of suggestion. The propagandist uses suggestion almost exclusively. Indeed, propaganda has been defined as "a systematic attempt by an interested individual, or individuals, to control the attitudes of groups of individuals through the use of suggestion and, consequently, to control their actions." But the use of suggestion is not confined to advertisers and propagandists. As A. Lawrence Lowell says, "In most of the affairs of life we are constantly acting upon suggestions without being aware of their origins, or, indeed, of the fact that we did not frame our conclusions unaided." [3]

C. We Tend to Act in Accordance with Our
Dominant Attitudes

The word *attitude* is in common usage. We say that a student gets good marks because he has the right attitude toward his work, or that an employer has the wrong attitude toward his employees.

[3] A. Lawrence Lowell, *Public Opinion and Popular Government* (New York, Longmans, Green & Co., 1914), p. 17.

Implicit in such statements is our belief in the existence of tendencies to act in accordance with a pattern, compounded of native desires and acquired beliefs. G. W. Allport expresses this idea in his definition: "An attitude is a mental and neural state of readiness, organized through experience, exerting a directive or dynamic influence upon the individual's responses to all objects with which it is connected."[4] Attitudes may be as specific as interest in football, or as general as satisfaction with the established order. Each individual has a number of attitudes, usually organized, more or less loosely, into general systems or patterns.

Dominant attitudes are those that are active at the moment. Some of these dominant attitudes are easily changed; others can be modified only with great difficulty. The persuader is interested in connecting his proposition favorably with the dominant attitudes of his listeners.

D. We Tend to Make Stereotyped Responses to Stereotyped Stimuli

Walter Lippmann used the word *stereotype* to designate what he calls "the pictures in our heads." From what we are told and what we imagine, we have these pictures of many things we have not directly experienced. Often they bear little resemblance to reality, but they influence our conduct, none the less. For example, we have stereotyped pictures of a burglar, a school teacher, a fraternity man, or a reformer. They are stereotyped because the same pictures remain in our minds unless they are modified by direct experience, and because the pictures are common to large numbers of people. Analysis of the stereotypes held by different individuals in the same general environment indicates that they are more likely to be uniform than to be accurate.

The attempt to analyze any situation anew each time it arises would be fatiguing in the extreme. To avoid this expenditure of energy we learn to make habitual, or stereotyped, responses to stereotyped stimuli. We laugh at the right times, applaud when it is expected of us, and make the usual responses in conversation. Our attitudes tend to become stereotyped: As Murphy, Murphy, and Newcomb point out, "Our attitudes towards races, flags, nations,

[4] Quoted in *Handbook of Social Psychology* by Carl Murchison (Worcester, Mass., Clark University Press, 1935), p. 906.

national anthems, and towards the words which crystallize generally accepted values such as freedom, honor, and democracy, tend to be imprinted upon us in more or less *standardized* form." [5] Much of what we think of as first-hand observation is colored by existing stereotypes; much of what we call objective thinking is influenced by them.

E. We Tend to Respond to the Emotional Connotations of Words

Our experiences are accompanied by feelings of pleasantness or unpleasantness, of pleasure or pain, in varying degrees. By the process of conditioning, words and other symbols acquire the power of arousing the feelings or emotions which accompanied the original experiences. This is true, whether the words refer to objects as specific as roast beef, or to stereotypes as general as *patriotism* or *tyranny*. Thus, we have in our vocabulary two types of emotionally loaded words: those which refer to specific experiences, objects, or persons; and those which designate abstractions, generalizations, judgments, and attitudes.

The use of emotionally loaded words is among the oldest of persuasive methods. The speaker uses "virtue words," to which his listeners will respond favorably, in speaking of his friends or of the cause he is upholding. He refers to opponents and their arguments in terms which arouse unpleasant emotions. He stands for a *righteous* cause, fighting only because he was *forced to do so*, against *cruel, heartless, barbaric* enemies. He is fighting, *without thought of personal gain or glory*, in defense of *justice, human decency*, and *the fundamental rights of man*, against an *unscrupulous aggressor* who does not hesitate to use *lies, to bomb hospitals and churches*, or to *terrorize innocent women and children* in his *selfish lust for power*. His friends are *patriots;* his enemies, *traitors*. It is as simple, and yet as fundamental, as that.

F. We Tend to Yield to the Repetition of Stimuli

Only in rare instances does the first use of a persuasive device produce a favorable response from any large number of listeners. While it is true that we tend to do, or to believe, as we are told,

[5] Gardner Murphy, Lois Murphy, and Theodore Newcomb, *Experimental Social Psychology* (New York, Harper & Bros., 1937), p. 1040.

it is also true that the desired response may require an expenditure of energy, or money, that we are not immediately prepared to make. Sometimes, too, the speaker must overcome not only the listener's inertia but, in addition, an attitude varying from skepticism to active hostility. In such cases, the listener may not pay much attention to a single stimulus; any tendency to respond favorably is inhibited by previously acquired habits of reacting in other ways, or by thoughts of what the desired response would mean in terms of failure to satisfy other conflicting desires.

Succeeding stimuli in a series do not encounter the same degree of resistance as did the first. If the repetition is skillful, the listener's attention is increasingly focused on the advantages of responding favorably and distracted from the disadvantages. Furthermore, by the process which the psychologists call "the summation of stimuli," a number of stimuli, repeated at proper intervals, combine to produce a response when no one stimulus in the series acting alone can do so. Thus, inertia or negative attitudes are finally overcome and the desired response secured.

G. We Tend to Accept Ideas from Those We Like

The reverse of this statement is equally true: We tend to reject equally good ideas from those we dislike. Aristotle observed that, "our judgments when we are pleased and friendly are not the same as when we are pained and hostile." The psychologist uses the term *prestige* to describe the attitudes of one person towards another. For the audience member, prestige means the extent to which he likes or dislikes a speaker, accepts him as an authority, defers to his judgment, attaches importance to what he says or does. In discussing "the immense importance of prestige in suggestion," the authors of *Experimental Social Psychology*, conclude that "two classes of persons appear in general to be effective in giving prestige suggestion, those whom we fear and those whom we love." [6]

H. We Tend to Conform

This tendency includes the beliefs and actions of those about us as well as styles and fashions. Public opinion, we say, favors this idea or opposes that action. In many cases, this is not the result of discussing the idea or debating an issue. It is due, rather, to what we might call "crowd suggestion." Here the stimuli come not from

[6] Murphy, Murphy and Newcomb, *op. cit.*, p. 237.

one source, but from many. If everyone of importance in our community says and does the same thing, we assume it must be right.

The pressure to conform is strongest in large meetings. It takes a considerable effort of the will to remain seated when everyone else stands, to applaud when the rest express disapproval, or to swim against the current of public opinion. The knowledge that a majority of our fellows hold an opinion often influences our beliefs, especially when we know little about the question.

I. We Tend, When Persuaded, to Act Immediately

When our emotions are aroused and we are ready to act, we feel ill-used if the opportunity to respond is denied us. We know what Bishop Buckley meant when he said that "there is no pain like the pain of an undelivered speech." And we will not easily be re-aroused to action on the same problem. The skilled speaker provides something definite for his listeners to do. It should, of course, be something they can do. We could not all enlist in the armed forces but we could save "waste fats," or tin cans, and join the Red Cross. Generalities, like "helping in every way possible," or being ready to act when the time comes, are an unsatisfactory substitute for definite action.

J. We Tend to Regard Our Actions as Logical

We cheerfully admit that others are moved by their emotions, but believe that our decisions are based on objective thinking. Such words as *logical, reasoning, scientific,* and *research* are often used as general complimentary terms. We would not feel flattered if someone told us we had made a very emotional address, that our appeals to self-interest and fear were especially skillful. Daniel Webster knew that the jurors in the White Murder case would be pleased when he said, "I am sure that gentlemen intelligent and just as you are, are not, by any power, to be hurried beyond the evidence."

III. THE PROCESS OF PERSUASION

Four factors combine to determine the success of a persuasive speech: the speaker's prestige, the listeners' attitudes towards his proposal, the skill used in constructing the speech, and the circumstances under which it was delivered. A complete analysis of the process of persuasion requires full information about these four factors. Here we give general principles which the speaker should apply to the specific situation.

A. Acquiring and Using Prestige

We have seen that a speaker's success in persuasion depends, to a considerable degree, on his ability to gain immediate, uncritical acceptance of his ideas. Listeners accept suggestions most readily from speakers who, in their estimation, have prestige or status. Speakers who have already attained prominence do not have the problem of acquiring prestige; they must simply use to advantage what they have. But college students and unknown speakers cannot expect the same degree of uncritical response. They must gain such prestige as they can, from things said about them when they are introduced, and from what they do and say in their speeches.

How can prestige be acquired? Officers or official representatives of any important organization gain prestige because they represent others. We attach importance to the views expressed by the president of a "national" society, though we have never heard of it. Knowing this, propagandists sometimes create such an organization and become its president or executive secretary. To a more limited extent, student speakers gain prestige when they represent their college. Presiding officers often attempt to increase a speaker's prestige by telling what he has done, or by introducing him as a "recognized authority."

Individuals gain prestige when they have unusual experiences, or when they excel in almost any line of endeavor. Managers of political campaigns believe that a short statement by a famous actor, or prizefighter, urging others to vote for X for president, carries more weight than an endorsement by a professor of political science. Managers of propaganda campaigns take advantage of this popular tendency to accept the views of newsworthy or important people, regardless of their knowledge of the question under consideration, by filling their letterheads with big names, and by getting prominent people to take part in their meetings.

Some of these methods cannot be used by college speakers, even if they wished to use them. How, then, may the student speaker acquire prestige?

1. He can learn to speak as one having authority. While he cannot tactfully say that he knows more about his subject than do his listeners, they will draw that conclusion if he presents plenty of evidence, precisely

stated and carefully documented, and if his conclusions do not go beyond
his proofs.

2. He can make use of prestige suggestion by presenting well qualified
authorities in support of his conclusions, and making their qualifications
clear to the audience.

3. He can gain prestige, if he can show that he represents the views of
the majority. If he speaks for the minority, he can gain prestige by admitting it, reminding his listeners that most reforms begin as minority
movements.

4. He can gain prestige by exhibiting, during his speech, those traits
of personality and deportment that his listeners admire.

B. Relating the Desired Response to Listeners' Wants

The first step in planning the persuasive speech, after the information has been gathered, is to decide whether it can be shown that
adoption of the speaker's proposal would lead to the satisfaction
of any fundamental wants or desires. If so, the speech should be
so organized as to make repeated reference to this claim; if no
such connection can be shown, the speech will probably be ineffective. Some desires are regarded as more praiseworthy than
others; the most powerful are those of which we are least proud.
There is an understandable tendency for the persuasive speaker to
refer casually to these powerful, but generally unadmitted, desires
and to stress those that are socially approved.

The next step is to consider both the general attitudes of the
audience and their specific attitudes towards the speaker's proposal.
Whenever possible, the desired response should be favorably associated with those things in which the listener believes most
strongly. If the listeners are already inclined to believe or to do as
the speaker desires, his task is to release and reinforce their favorable
attitudes. If they are hostile, he must devise ways of breaking down
their unfavorable attitudes. He may do this by calling his proposal
by a new name and then proceeding to build a favorable attitude
towards that new name.

The third step in devising ways of relating the desired response
to the listeners' desires and attitudes is to make a list of stereotypes
and emotionally loaded words to which the listeners will respond
favorably, and another list to which they will give a negative
response. The first list is used repeatedly in referring to the speaker's
proposal and those who support it; the second, in speaking of the
opposition. One of the most effective methods of uniting people

in support of a cause is to unite them against a common enemy. Whether we like it or not, the use of emotionally loaded words is a basic method of persuasion.

C. Constructing the Persuasive Speech

We have emphasized the necessity of considering the listeners' attitudes towards the speaker's proposal. For the favorable audience, the speech should be so arranged as to give the listeners frequent opportunities to applaud enthusiastic statements of their beliefs. The hostile audience must be approached more cautiously. Usually, the best method is to begin with references to accepted attitudes and stereotypes. After the habit of responding favorably to what the speaker says has been established, the listeners may accept ideas that would have been rejected earlier in the speech. The material to which they are most hostile should be placed near the end. This is what Overstreet calls the "yes-response technique." For the audience that has no strong attitudes, the logical order of arrangement should be used.

The best information about the style and structure of the persuasive speech can be gained by examining the successful addresses of our great reformers and advocates. The conclusions which follow are the result of such an investigation.

1. The persuasive speaker should talk to his audience on the assumption that he and they are members of a group with like interests and worthy motives, engaged in defeating the efforts of an outsider representing hostile forces. He should address his hearers directly and on a basis of equality. Whenever possible, he should assume that they already agree with him. Franklin D. Roosevelt's, "You and I know. . ." is a familiar example. Note also, the use of these devices in the beginnings of sentences in the second paragraph of Woodrow Wilson's Second Inaugural Address:

We have centered counsel and action . . . We are a composite and cosmopolitan people . . . We are of the blood of all the nations . . . We have drawn closer together . . . We have been deeply wronged . . . We have not wished to wrong or injure . . . We wished nothing for ourselves . . . We stand firm in armed neutrality . . . We neither desire conquest nor advantage . . .

2. When the audience is homogeneous and not hostile to the speaker's purpose, he should use vivid illustrations and emotionally loaded words which refer to specific attitudes and experiences. The

specific is usually more interesting, and more persuasive, than the abstract. When the Red Cross tells of women and little children who are cold, hungry, and homeless, we want to help them because even to imagine the suffering of others is unpleasant.

3. When the audience is heterogeneous, with conflicting interests and desires, the speaker cannot describe his proposal in detail for fear of arousing opposition. Instead he uses stereotyped phrases which refer to generally approved attitudes and ideas. Suppose, for example, that a candidate for office is attempting to secure the votes of a community containing about equal numbers of farmers, small businessmen and employers, and members of labor unions. The opposition of any one of these groups may defeat him. All are anxious to know his views on measures on which the three groups take different positions. In such situations the speaker almost inevitably talks in general terms, using abstract stereotypes such as *justice for all, a fair day's work for a fair day's wage, settling our differences peaceably about the conference table,* and *taxation based on the principle of ability to pay.* Of course, these phrases will be interpreted differently by listeners with various interests. It is easy to criticize this practice, but difficult to suggest an alternative. Moreover, these abstractions are not meaningless; they represent policies or trends. If the speaker uses them carefully, they reveal his general philosophy from which his hearers can judge how he might act in specific situations.

4. The persuasive speaker frequently asserts that people with desirable qualities or attributes believe as he does; or that individuals with undesirable characteristics take the opposing view. Obviously, the listener wants to be among those "intelligent, fair-minded persons" who agree with the speaker, and the way to be so included is simply to accept his conclusions. Such phrases as "most thoughtful people believe," "this is the intelligent thing to do," "those who love freedom more than self," or, "if you believe this accusation you are not as intelligent as I think you are," illustrate the use of this device.

5. The persuasive speaker connects his cause with great names and revered institutions. A quotation from Lincoln, or even a reference to his name, is often more persuasive than a direct statement from a living witness. Washington's supposed views on "entangling alliances" kept thousands from supporting the League of Nations. In most persuasive speeches to popular audiences there

are quotations from the Bible: the name of the Deity appears in nearly all speeches made in times of crisis.

6. The persuasive speech makes great use of all forms of repetition. Emotionally loaded words and stereotypes are often used in groups of three or four in the same sentence. Note the following example from a speech advocating the amendment of the National Prohibition Act, given by Senator James A. Reed of Missouri, February 18, 1929.

> I assert, Mr. President, that it will not be long until the moral sensibilities of all thoughtful people are awakened to the truth that the prohibitory law is the worst crime ever committed within the borders of the United States. It will not be long until the reign of *hypocrisy, cant, chicanery*, and *fraud* will come to an ignominious end.
>
> I characterize the prohibitory law as a crime because it violates the principles of natural justice, has brought widespread disrespect for authority, and has become the facile instrument of *graft, bribery, blackmail*, and *oppression*.

The key phrases, containing the basic appeals to attitudes and desires, are reiterated at frequent intervals. Sometimes, indeed, the main purpose of the speech seems to be that of providing an opportunity to repeat a few simple formulae.

D. Setting the Stage for the Delivery of the Speech

Experienced speakers know that the success of a persuasive speech depends, in large measure, on the surroundings in which it is delivered and on the atmosphere that has been created. Whenever possible, members of the audience should be seated in a compact group so that tendencies to respond may be communicated easily from one individual to another. It is better to have people clamoring for admission than to have a larger audience scattered throughout a big auditorium.

One method of creating a favorable atmosphere is by displaying symbols to which the listener habitually responds favorably. A recent political meeting was held in a hall that was plentifully decorated with American flags, pictures of the candidates, and pictures of great American statesmen of the same political party. On the platform were a number of noted individuals, including clergymen of various denominations. The meeting was opened with prayer. When this had been concluded, three men in uniform—a sailor, a soldier, and a marine—marched to the platform while the band played "Onward Christian Soldiers" and stood at salute during the singing of the national anthem. After these preliminary exercises, which were in reality an important part of the meeting, the candidate was introduced. We have here an illustration of what propaganda analysts call the "transfer device." The object is to transfer to the candidate the favorable emotional attitudes, elicited by the prayer, the flags, the uniforms, and the martial music. The use of the transfer device is not limited to political campaigns. The church has, for centuries, known the effectiveness of religious symbols in creating background and mood for the sermon. The Red Cross, by its very name, transfers to the organization something of the emotions kindled by the religious symbol.

Another method of creating a favorable atmosphere for the speech is to get the members of the audience to do something together. They may join in singing, in reading a ritual, in laughing, or in applauding a familiar sentiment. On secular occasions, community singing, applauding, and cheering are commonly employed. If the program is properly arranged, the speaker is introduced as soon as the habit of responding has been established. He should take advantage of any legitimate opportunities to win applause or laughter in his opening remarks.

IV. OBJECTIVE STUDIES IN PERSUASION

In the chapters on "Evaluating Discussion" and "Evaluating Debate" we report experiments measuring the effects of these types of oral communication on the attitudes of listeners and participants. We are now concerned with what happens when only one side of an issue is stressed. The investigations reported here are representative, both in methods and results, of current studies in this field.

In 1935, Knower reported an elaborate and carefully controlled experiment comparing the effects of logical and emotional appeals on the attitudes of university students toward prohibition. The experimental group consisted of 1,000 students, including some enrolled in evening classes, at the University of Minnesota. Some 300 others constituted the control group. Four speeches of about 2,500 words—dry-logical, dry-persuasive, wet-logical and wet-persuasive —were constructed. The Thurstone attitude tests were administered before and after the students in the experimental groups heard, or read, the speeches. The groups were formed on the basis of initial attitudes, and each speech was delivered to a hostile audience.

The findings on the points in which we are here interested are given below:

CRITICAL RATIOS OF CHANGES OF ATTITUDE [7]

	Oral Presentation	Written Presentation
All initially dry subjects	6.66	3.14
All initially wet subjects	9.38	5.58
Logical appeal to dry subjects	5.47	2.73
Persuasive appeal to dry subjects	4.00	1.33
Logical appeal to wet subjects	6.27	3.81
Persuasive appeal to wet subjects	7.37	4.23

From these data two conclusions are evident: (1) in this instance, there is little difference between logical and persuasive appeals; (2) in every instance, the oral presentation produced greater changes in attitude than did the written. Knower also found that students who heard, or read, the arguments when alone tended to change their attitudes more than did those who heard, or read, the arguments in groups.

The data was analyzed to discover the relationship of initial attitude to the degree and direction of change. Those whose initial attitude was more or less neutral showed the greatest change; those with extreme attitudes tended to move towards more moderate positions, but to remain on the same side of the question; those with moderate attitudes made the smallest proportion of significant changes. In this last group there was a relatively large number of changes in the direction opposite to that of the appeal.[8]

Using the same experimental procedures, Lull studied the effectiveness of humor in twenty-minute persuasive speeches on socialized medicine. Students in thirty-two speech classes at Wisconsin and Purdue constituted the experimental group; four other classes served as controls; seven speakers took part in the experiment.

[7] A critical ratio is a statistical index of reliability. When the critical ratio, computed on the basis of "standard error," is 2 or greater, the difference is considered significant.

[8] F. H. Knower, "A Study of the Effect of Oral Argument on Changes of Attitude," *Journal of Social Psychology*, Vol. 6 (August, 1935), pp. 315-347. See also *Journal of Abnormal and Social Psychology*, Vol. 30 (January-March, 1936), pp. 522-532; and *Journal of Applied Psychology*, Vol. 20 (February, 1936), pp. 114-127.

Attitudes were tested two weeks before the speech was heard, immediately afterwards, and three weeks later. The students also judged the humorousness, interestingness and convincingness of the speech.

Lull found that "attitudes towards socialized medicine were changed significantly, in the anticipated direction," by both humorous and non-humorous speeches. There were no significant differences between the effectiveness of the two types of speeches. The tests taken three weeks after hearing the speech showed some regression towards original attitude but about one-third of the classes "retained attitudes that represent statistically different changes" from their original opinions on the question. The humorous and non-humorous speeches were judged about equal in interestingness and convincingness.[9]

Willis investigated the relative effectiveness of the straight talk, the complete dramatization, and the talk with dramatized illustrations in changing attitudes on three current problems. Nine fifteen-minute scripts, representing each program type for each topic, were prepared and recorded. The subjects were 526 high-school juniors and seniors and 89 University of Wisconsin students. Attitudes were tested immediately before the programs, the day after, and two weeks later. The students also indicated their preferences among the three forms of presentation.

Willis found that "a fifteen-minute radio program can shift the attitudes of high-school and college students significantly, and this influence persists to a significant degree for a period of at least two weeks." The three forms were equally effective in influencing the attitudes of college students. The dramatization was most effective with the high-school students, followed, in that order, by the combined form and the talk. The combined form was preferred by a large majority of the high-school students, with the dramatization second and the talk third. The college students ranked the combined form first, the talk second, and the dramatization third. The relation between intelligence and the shift of attitude was negligible.[10]

In 1946, Dietrich published the results of his study comparing attitude changes produced by conversational and dynamic delivery

[9] P. E. Lull, "The Effectiveness of Humor in Persuasive Speeches," *Speech Monographs*, Vol. 7 (1940), pp. 26-40.

[10] Edgar E. Willis, "The Relative Effectiveness of Three Forms of Radio Presentation in Influencing Attitudes," *Speech Monographs*, Vol. 7 (1940), pp. 41-47.

of the same material. Six speakers recorded a fifteen-minute radio commentary in each type of delivery. A total of 760 university students participated in the experiment. Attitudes were tested one week before, immediately after the broadcast, and again, two weeks later. Both styles of delivery shifted attitudes significantly and the shift, though smaller, was still significant two weeks later. The conversational delivery was more effective than the dynamic; the difference, though statistically significant for the group, was, in the case of some speakers, rather small. Forty-one students regarded the dynamic delivery as propaganda; only two so regarded the conversational broadcasts.[11]

During World War II, the Research Branch of the Army's Information and Education Division, investigated this question: "When the weight of evidence supports the main thesis being presented, is it more effective to present only the materials supporting the points being made, or is it better to introduce also the arguments of those opposed?"[12]

The experiment was conducted when military experts believed the troops in the European theater were under-estimating the time required to defeat Japan. Two radio commentaries were prepared and recorded from materials supplied by the War Department: one, fifteen-minutes in length, gave only evidence supporting one side; the other, added four minutes of opposing arguments. The records were played during the regular orientation period with no officers present. The soldiers were told not to sign their names to the attitude tests which included items on various topics. Both programs resulted in significant attitude changes. In each case 47 per cent of the men increased their estimate of the time required to defeat Japan by six months or more. The authors conclude that giving the strong points for the other side "can make a presentation more effective . . . at least for the better educated men and for those who are already opposed to the stand." The reverse tendency is seemingly true for the less educated, especially those already favoring the proposition.

A striking instance of mass persuasion took place September 21,

[11] John E. Dietrich, "The Relative Effectiveness of Two Modes of Radio Delivery in Influencing Attitudes," *Speech Monographs*, Vol. 13 (1946), pp. 58-66.
[12] Carl I. Hovland, Arthur A. Lumsdaine, and Fred D. Sheffield, *Experiments on Mass Communication* (Princeton, N.J., Princeton University Press, 1949), pp. 201-27.

1943, during the third war loan campaign. Kate Smith spoke briefly
sixty-five times during eighteen consecutive hours. Each talk was
a personal message, given in a voice "often broken, it seemed, by
deep emotion," and ending with the direct appeal: "Will you buy
a bond?" She said nothing about buying bonds as a sound investment
or to help check inflation, but talked of neighbor boys facing death
so far from home and invoked "themes of love and hate, of large
hopes and desperate fears, of honor and shame." [13]

Merton made this classification of the appeals in her talks: sacrifice,
50 per cent; doing one's share, 16 per cent; appeals to families of
service men, 6 per cent; competition, "going over the top" first,
12 per cent; facilitation, "just step to the phone," 7 per cent;
personal references to self, 6 per cent.

When the eighteen-hour campaign was over, the Columbia
Broadcasting System reported $39,000,000 in bond pledges. Ob-
viously this happy result cannot be attributed to Kate Smith's
efforts alone. But when we make allowance for other persuasive
factors, Kate Smith's achievement still seems almost incredible until
we remember that her all-day campaign secured $110,000,000 in
pledges in the fourth bond drive.

The main findings of these studies, and others not reported here,
are summarized in the following statements:

1. Significant changes in group attitudes, even on much discussed subjects, can be produced by fifteen minutes of oral persuasion.
2. From twenty to forty per cent of the listeners changed their attitudes significantly.
3. These changes remained significant when final tests were given two
to nine weeks later.
4. In most instances, the attitudes had regressed toward the original
position at the time of the final tests. However, from a study not reported
here, the Research Branch of the Army's Information and Education
concluded that "changes in opinion of a general rather than specific
nature may show increasing effects with the lapse of time." [14]

V. THE QUESTION OF ETHICS

Ever since Plato, himself no mean rhetorician and persuader,
intimated that rhetoricians were more concerned with winning, even

[13] Robert K. Merton and others, *Mass Persuasion* (New York, Harper &
Bros., 1946), p. 2.
[14] Hovland, Lumsdaine, and Sheffield, *op. cit.*, pp. 182-200.

if it meant making the worse appear the better reason, than with searching for truth, the question of ethics in persuasion has been the cause of misunderstanding and controversy. To Plato's charge, Aristotle replied that persuasion is a skill which can be used for worthy or unworthy purposes. "What makes a man a sophist," he said, "is not his skill, but his moral purpose." The good man should master the art of persuasion, both to enable him to defeat the efforts of unscrupulous opponents and to make him an effective advocate of what he regards as the truth. Aristotle believed that, if the better side of the argument is ably presented, even a skilled persuader cannot long make the worse appear the better reason. "Things that are true," he said, "and things that are better are, by their nature, practically always easier to believe in." [15]

There is recent evidence to support Aristotle's dictum as far as participation in discussion is concerned. From objective studies, cited in Chapter 22, we learn that discussion group members are more likely to accept good suggestions from their fellows than to reject them, more likely to retain right than wrong answers throughout the discussion.

Some of the most frequent comments on the ethics of persuasion grow out of a failure to remember that the persuader is not at the moment searching for truth. He thinks he has already found it and is engaged in the important task of winning converts. As he becomes more engrossed in his cause, he finds it difficult to understand how intelligent people can honestly oppose him. He is sure that his own motives are good; therefore his opponents must either be naïve advocates of the wrong side of the question or, what is worse, individuals who would knowingly mislead others for their own selfish purposes. To him, the difference of opinion tends to become a battle between the forces of right, in which he is enrolled, and the forces of evil which must be exposed and defeated. There can be no compromise; to be neutral is only a shade less reprehensible than to be an actual enemy.

When a speaker believes intensely in his cause, it is useless to expect him to be calm and objective in his advocacy. What he regards as a fair statement will probably seem biased to an opponent; what he regards as logical reasoning may seem to those who disagree with him an unwarranted use of emotional appeals. The reformer inevitably uses the most dramatic and convincing proofs at

[15] Aristotle, *Rhetorica*, Bk. I, 1355a.

his command. If he talks about opposing arguments, he cannot be expected to state them as strongly or as effectively as would someone who believes in them. Only on subjects that do not seem to him vitally important can the persuasive speaker give an argument that minimizes appeal to the basic emotions and desires. And these speeches seem uninteresting to the average listener. To expect what a neutral observer would regard as a logical, objective argument from a speaker who is deeply concerned about the problem, especially in a time of crisis, is to ignore the realities of the situation.

We do not expect a salesman to point out the weaknesses in his product and the merits of his competitor's goods. We know that the representatives of warring nations stress victories and minimize defeats. We know that political campaigners emphasize the achievements of their own party and the failures of others. As long as we know that the speaker is selling an article, representing an organization, or advocating a point of view, we can be on guard against an uncritical acceptance of his conclusions. We want advertisements to be labeled as such; we have the right to expect that the persuasive speaker will tell us whom he represents.

There are certain limits beyond which no persuader, be he advertiser, salesman, or advocate, can go without incurring legal penalties. The advertiser who makes false claims can be prosecuted for fraudulent advertising. The salesman must comply with legislation intended to safeguard the interests of the purchaser. The witness who knowingly makes false statements can be punished for perjury; the speaker who damages the reputation of another, and who cannot prove his charges, can be sued for slander. It is not enough that the speaker stay well within the legal limits in his persuasion. We expect him to be guided by a code of good manners and good morals, to avoid doing anything for which he would criticize an opponent.

The speaker's ethical problems stem, partly at least, from the idea that suggestion and emotional appeals are always ethically inferior to logic and reasoning. This, we believe, is not necessarily so. Both have their proper place in persuasion; both may be improperly used. The speaker who gives only the facts supporting his position, and leads his listeners to believe that he is "telling the whole truth," is just as blameworthy as the speaker who appeals only to their selfish desires and basic fears.

In this situation, as in so many others, there is a middle course.

As Merton writes in *Mass Persuasion*, "Appeals to sentiments within the context of relevant information and knowledge are basically different from appeals to sentiment which blur and obscure this knowledge." [16] He approves the first, criticizes the second, and adds that the speaker should choose his persuasive techniques with an eye to their long-time effects on his listeners.

How far the end justifies the means in a critical situation when people must be roused to immediate action, is a question on which there will always be real differences of opinion. Each speaker must answer immediately to his own conscience, and eventually to those whom he leads or misleads.

It is impossible to formulate a code of ethics as precise as the rules describing and penalizing improper behavior in football. However, there are certain practices which, we believe should not be condoned:

1   It is, of course, unethical for a speaker to distort or falsify evidence.

2. It is unethical for a speaker to use emotional appeals when he lacks evidence to support them, or when he knows his listeners would not support his conclusion if they had the time and the opportunity to investigate the problem for themselves.

3. It is unethical for a speaker to divert attention from weaknesses in his argument by unsupported attacks on his opponent or by appeals to hatred, intolerance, bigotry and fear.

4. It is unethical for a speaker to conceal his real purpose, or the organization he represents, pretending to speak objectively when he is an advocate of one point of view.

5. It is unethical for a speaker to pose as an "authority" when he has only a layman's knowledge of the subject.

No code can be legislated or imposed to relieve the listener of the duty of analyzing the speech and deciding for himself what constitutes valid proof and a legitimate appeal to the emotions. Familiarity with the methods commonly used in persuasive speeches should constitute a valuable part of the listener's equipment for this important task.

READINGS

BRIGANCE, W. N., *Speech Composition* (New York, Appleton-Century-Crofts, Inc., 1937), Chapter 5.

————, "A Genetic Approach to Persuasion," *Quarterly Journal of Speech*, Vol. 17 (June, 1931), pp. 329-39.

16 Merton, *op. cit.*, p. 186.

CHASE, Stuart, *The Tyranny of Words* (New York, Harcourt, Brace & Co., Inc., 1938), Chaps. 1-2.

DOOB, Leonard, *Public Opinion and Propaganda* (New York, Henry Holt & Co., Inc., 1948).

FRIED, Edrita, "Techniques of Persuasion," in H. L. Childs and John B. Whitton, eds., *Propaganda by Short Wave* (Princeton, N.J., Princeton University Press, 1942), pp. 261-302.

HALLE, Louis J., "Raw Materials of Persuasion," *Saturday Review of Literature*, Vol. 33 (March 11, 1950), pp. 9-10, 34-8.

HOLLINGWORTH, H. L., *The Psychology of the Audience* (New York, American Book Co., 1935), Chaps. 8-9.

KAY, Lillian, "An Experimental Approach to Prestige Suggestion," *Journal of Psychology*, Vol. 24 (July, 1947), pp. 71-82.

LEE, I. J., ed., *The Language of Wisdom and Folly* (New York, Harper & Bros., 1949).

MERTON, R. E., *Mass Persuasion* (New York, Harper & Bros., 1946).

MILLER, C. R., *The Process of Persuasion* (New York, Crown Publishers, 1946).

OLIVER, R. T., *The Psychology of Persuasive Speech* (New York, Longmans, Green & Co., 1942), Chap. 1.

SCOTT, W. D., and HOWARD, D. T., *Influencing Men in Business* (New York, The Ronald Press, 1928).

EXERCISES

1. Make a five-minute speech, based on one of the readings listed above. Your purpose is to give information, or illustrations, not contained in this chapter and to comment on any differences of opinion you may find.

2. Make a speech stating and defining your point of view on the advice given, or the ideas expressed, in one of the following quotations. In some instances, you should read the section, or chapter, from which the quotation is taken to be sure that you are interpreting the author's intentions correctly.

   a. "Some imputations we may mitigate by the use of other words: *luxury* will be softened down into *generosity, avarice* into *economy, carelessness* into *simplicity*, and I shall seek to win a certain amount of favor or pity by look, voice, and action." (Quintilian, *Institutes of Oratory*, Book IV, II, 77)

   b. "There is nothing of more importance in speaking than that the hearer should be favorable to the speaker, and be himself so strongly moved that he may be influenced more by impulse and excitement of mind than by judgment or reflection For mankind makes far more determinations through hatred, or love, or desire, or anger, or grief, or joy, or hope, or fear, or error, or some other affection of mind than from regard to truth, or any settled maxim, or prin-

ciple of right, or judicial form, or adherence to the laws...."
(Cicero, *De Oratore*, Book II, CXLI)

c. "In pleading, my usual method is to fix on whatever strong points
the cause has, and to illustrate and make the most of them, dwelling
on them, insisting on them, clinging to them; but to hold back from
the weak or defective points in such a way that I may not appear
to shun them, but that their whole force may be dissembled and
overwhelmed by the ornament and amplification of the strong
points." (Cicero, *De Oratore*, Book II, LXXII)

d. "Wherever you would persuade or prevail, address yourself to the
passions; it is by them that mankind is to be taken.... If you once
engage peoples' pride, love, pity, ambition (or whichever is their
prevailing passion) on your side, you need not fear what their
reason can do against you...." (Lord Chesterfield's *Letters to His
Son*, letter dated Feb. 8, 1746)

e. "We are also to assume, when we wish either to praise a man or
blame him, that qualities closely allied to those which he actually
has are identical with them; for instance, that the cautious man is
cold-blooded and treacherous, and that the stupid man is an honest
fellow, or the thick-skinned man a good-tempered one. We can
always idealize any given man by drawing on the virtues akin to his
actual qualities: thus we may say that the passionate or excitable
man is 'outspoken'; or that the arrogant man is 'superb' or 'impressive.'" (Aristotle, *Rhetorica*, Book I, 1367a)

f. "In most cases, the masses, intoxicated by the speaker's powers, are
hypnotized to such a degree that for long periods to come they see
in him a magnified image of their own ego. Their admiration and
enthusiasm for the orator are, in ultimate analysis, no more than
admiration and enthusiasm for their own personalities, and these
sentiments are fostered by the orator in that he undertakes to speak
and act in the name of the mass, in the name, that is, of every
individual." (Robert Michels, *Political Parties*, p. 72)

g. "*Socrates:*

Shall we then assume two sorts of persuasion,—one which
is the source of belief without knowledge; as the
other is of knowledge?

Gorgias:

By all means.

Socrates:

And which sort of persuasion does rhetoric create in
courts of law and other assemblies...?

Gorgias:

Clearly, Socrates, that which gives only belief.

Socrates:

Then rhetoric...is the artificer of a persuasion which
creates belief about the just and unjust, but gives no
instruction about them?

Gorgias:
> True.

Socrates:
> And the rhetorician does not instruct the courts of law and other assemblies about things just and unjust, but he creates belief about them; for no one can be supposed to instruct such a vast multitude about such high matter in so short a time?"

(Plato, Gorgias)

3. Analyze the use of persuasive devices in a persuasive speech. What basic desires and attitudes are appealed to? What use is made of stereotypes and emotionally loaded words or phrases? You will be expected to use a speech on some current issue. The following paragraphs illustrate the type of material you should use in this exercise.

  a. Here is the conclusion of Woodrow Wilson's war message to Congress in 1917:
  "It is a fearful thing to lead this great, peaceful people into war, into the most terrible and disastrous of all wars, civilization itself seeming to be in the balance. But the right is more precious than peace, and we shall fight for the things which we have always carried nearest our hearts, for democracy, for the right of those who submit to authority to have a voice in their own governments, for the rights and liberties of small nations, for a universal domination of right by such a concert of free peoples as shall bring peace and safety to all nations and make the world itself at last free. To such a task we can dedicate our lives and our fortunes, everything that we are and everything that we have, with the pride of those who know that the day has come when America is privileged to spend her blood and her might for the principles that gave her birth and happiness and the peace which she has treasured. God helping her, she can do no other."

  b. Here is one of Kate Smith's appeals in the Third War Loan drive, September 21, 1943:
  "Early yesterday morning a man who had lost both legs called in and said he wanted to buy a bond. He wanted to buy a bond with the money he had been saving to buy himself a pair of artificial limbs... making the supreme sacrifice, giving up the dream he had cherished for years, the dream of walking once again. As he said himself: 'My limbs can wait, but this war can't'. ...What sacrifice are you or I or any of us making that would in any way compare with the self-sacrifice of this magnificent person? Surely if a legless man can give up his dream of a lifetime, then we can give a little extra money to buy another bond. Don't delay, call Circle 6-4343 and give WABC your order for the biggest bond you can afford, or even more than you can afford. Will you buy a bond?"

c. Here are excerpts from an address given by Dave Beck, executive vice-president of the International Brotherhood of Teamsters, Chauffeurs, Warehousemen and Helpers of America at a meeting of the Minneapolis Chamber of Commerce, March 31, 1949:

"Under free enterprise this country of ours has developed into the greatest nation on earth. The working people of no other country under the sun enjoy as fine conditions of employment, or as high a standard of living, as we enjoy who are members of Labor in the United States. I say to my associates in Labor, and to industry as well, and even to those who would tear our government apart: we have made our tremendous progress in Labor, and our great industrial development, under free enterprise. We cannot have a free country unless we have free men. We cannot remain free unless we merit that freedom by our own intelligent effort. We cannot have free men unless we have a government based on freedom, which accords to all men and women the freedom of expression, freedom of the press, and freedom to conduct themselves in harmony with the dictates of their own consciences. All these rights to freedom must be recognized, unquestioned.

"Above all else, we must respect and defend religion, for if we ever destroy religion, or permit it to be destroyed, we will have lost our safest guide toward progress. If we ever see the time when an oath taken in the presence of the Bible shall be disregarded, then indeed will all our civilization come crashing down."

d. Here is a 25-second "spot commercial":

"An automobile is made, never born. All the skilled craftsmanship in the world could not make a finer car than a Ford. The name Ford means service and dependability. Every feature of the new Ford is designed for your approval. The makers of this smart new automobile are convinced of one thing: when you see and drive the better-than-ever Ford, you'll be convinced for life that there should be a Ford in your future."

4. Now that you have had some practice at detecting the use of persuasive devices in the speeches of others, analyze one of your own speeches from this point of view. If you have not made a speech recently, note your use of persuasive devices in conversation.

5. Hand in a plan for a speech in which you will combine argumentation and persuasion. List the desires and attitudes to which you will appeal and include some of the stereotypes you propose to use.

6. On the basis of the information in this chapter, analyze an intercollegiate debate. Comment on the presence or absence of persuasive methods and on the quality of such persuasion as may be found.

7. Make a list of the stereotypes and persuasive appeals you would use on one of the following occasions:

a. A speech urging Congress to provide low-cost housing
b. A speech urging severe punishment for drunken drivers

c. A speech proposing capital punishment for persons convicted of kidnapping

d. A speech urging everyone to get chest X-rays

e. A speech asking another chance for a student dropped from school because of low grades

f. A speech advocating medical care at public expense

Part IV

DISCUSSION

CHAPTER 15

Discussion: Types, Purposes, and Limitations

DISCUSSION IS NOT NEW; in one form or another it has existed wherever and whenever citizens won the right to make decisions on matters affecting their welfare. The last twenty years, however, have witnessed a widespread adoption of discussion methods by governmental agencies, religious organizations, and groups interested in various types of adult education. A fairly complete survey of the current uses of discussion is found in Chapter 2.

I. TYPES OF DISCUSSION

Because the word *discussion* means different things to different people, we must define its usage in this book. It is difficult, however, to frame a one-sentence definition that is broad enough to include the various types of group and public discussion and sufficiently restricted to exclude other forms of oral communication. For this reason, we begin by describing the general characteristics of discussion meetings.

A. Characteristics of Discussion

1. *"Thought in process."* Participants in discussion should be willing to pool their information and join in a coöperative search for the best solution to the problem before the group. They are, theoretically at least, willing to follow wherever the evidence leads them. Debate, on the other hand, occurs between individuals who have supposedly examined the evidence and arrived at different conclusions. The reformer seldom has time for discussion; he thinks he

has found the right answer and wants others to adopt it as quickly as possible.

2. *Informality*. Discussion aims at organized informality. The degree possible for any occasion depends on such factors as the seating arrangements and the size of the group or audience. The speakers should use the language of conversation.

3. *Opportunity for general participation*. The discussion method assumes that each individual may have something of value to contribute. If the group is small, all who wish to may speak. If the audience is large, only a small percentage of its members can get the floor. However, it should be remembered that active listening is participation.

4. *Purpose*. Discussion is talk with a purpose. Conversations that leap from one topic to another are pleasant and may have social values for those who take part in them, but they are not included in our definition of discussion.

5. *Planning and leadership*. Except for occasional conversations that happen when alert and interested minds meet, discussion meetings require a leader and a plan. The chairman should not put his trust in the possibility of spontaneous combustion.

To summarize, discussion is a planned, but relatively informal, meeting in which those who attend are invited to join in thinking aloud about a topic or problem of mutual interest, under the guidance of a leader or moderator.

B. Types of Discussion

At this point we should make a classification of discussion based on the number of participants, and state what we mean by a *forum*.

1. A *group discussion* includes not more than fifteen or twenty persons, all of whom may take part in the conversation. Members are seated so they may see each other and participate alternately as speakers and listeners.

2. A *public discussion* takes place in the presence of an audience. The program consists of conversation or speeches by designated individuals followed by a forum period in which audience members question the speakers, or enter briefly into the discussion.

3. A *forum* is that part of a public discussion in which audience members may participate.

Discussion may take different forms depending on such factors as the size of the group, the stage group members have reached in analyzing the topic, and the purpose of the meeting. Each type will be described in detail later; these brief definitions serve our immediate purpose.

1. *Informal group discussion.* Not more than twenty people converse, rather than make speeches about a subject of mutual interest.

2. *Coöperative investigation.* The leader divides the subject for discussion into a number of sub-topics, and a member undertakes to present information on each of these points.

3. *Committee meeting.* A small group, appointed by the parent organization, meets to investigate a problem and, later, to formulate its report.

4. *Conference.* Delegates representing various organizations, sometimes coöperative, sometimes hostile, meet to consider a problem and, if possible, to recommend a course of action.

In the types of public discussion described below, there should be a forum period following the formal presentation.

5. *Panel forum.* Three to five people with special knowledge of a topic hold an orderly and logical conversation about it before an audience.

6. *Symposium.* Three to five people with special knowledge of the topic make speeches presenting different types of information or different points of view.

7. *Public hearing.* Meetings called by committees to investigate problems, to carry out a government policy, or to give representatives of various groups the chance to present their views on pending legislation.

8. *Lecture forum.* A speech by a person with special qualifications to talk on the problem before the group.

9. *Debate forum.* A series of speeches of equal length for and against a specific proposal. This type is also considered in the section on debate.

10. *Legislative session.* A series of meetings, demonstrating in miniature the parliamentary procedures and the types of discussion used at different stages of the legislative process.

Those interested in the discussion movement have developed other procedures, most of them variations of the types listed above. One might, for example, have a lecture-panel-forum, or a panel-lecture-forum. The *film forum* substitutes a documentary film for panel or symposium speakers. "Discussion 66" secures full audience participation during the forum period. The audience is quickly divided into groups of six who consider a single pointed question for six minutes and report their findings to those in charge. These methods will be treated more fully in later chapters.

II. PURPOSES OF DISCUSSION

Each discussion should have a specific objective which can be classified under two main headings: (a) training the individual and (b) considering mutual problems.

A. Training the Individual

Discussion provides valuable training for the individual to the extent that it serves one or more of these purposes.

1. *To overcome timidity or stage fright.* The person who has never spoken out in meeting may be encouraged to ask a question or say a few words in response to an inquiry. This may be a first step towards voluntary participation and making a speech on more formal occasions.

2. *To develop a direct conversational manner of speaking.* We converse more frequently than we speak in public. Moreover, developing skill in conversation is excellent preparation for public speaking.

3. *To learn to listen accurately.* Good listening is just as important in discussion as good speaking. Many misunderstandings would be avoided if the persons concerned listened to what was said and reported it accurately.

4. *To learn how to give and take criticism.* We need to learn the difference between refuting an argument and making personal remarks about its proponent. Of equal importance, is the ability to take criticism. We should at least learn to keep silent if we cannot make the answer "that turneth away wrath."

5. *To stimulate the desire for good evidence and straight thinking.* The tests for determining the strength of the evidence and reasoning apply in discussion as well as in formal argumentation and debate.

6. *To learn when and how to compromise.* The person who must have his way at all costs is not a good citizen. We should distinguish between compromise on basic principles and those involving the application of these principles. The former are seldom, if ever, justified; but the success of our democracy depends on our willingness to make and accept compromise of the latter sort.

7. *To train discussion leaders.* A first step in a discussion program of any size, whether in school or out, is to train a sufficient number of discussion leaders.

B. Considering Mutual Problems

The various types of discussion meetings are designed to serve one or more of the following purposes.

1. *To exchange information.* The first step towards understanding a problem should be the pooling of available information. Group discussion should only be used if a number of the members have information to share. Those who plan the meetings should make sure that adequate information is available. They may do this by distributing printed materials, or by inviting people who understand the problem to participate in the discussion.

2. *To form attitudes.* A major function of the church and the school is to change some attitudes and create others. Thus, we may profitably discuss freedom of speech, for example, even though there is no case that requires decision. The assumption is that attitudes thus formed will influence, perhaps determine, action when the occasion arises. Sometimes the discussion topic does not require group judgment or group action. Such questions as, "What should be my attitude toward coöperatives?", "What factors should I consider in choosing a profession?", or "When is a book worth reading?" are examples. In such cases each individual is free to act as he thinks best.

3. *To evaluate possible solutions.* This is the third step in analyzing a problem. Sometimes at this point there is general agreement that one course of action is best. But discussion of vital questions does not usually result in such unanimity. Honest, intelligent people often draw widely different conclusions from the same evidence. In such cases, it is important that the strength and weaknesses of all solutions be thoroughly explored before action is taken. We prefer intelligent and orderly discussion to any other method for reaching group decisions.

This use of discussion is stressed most by students of government. In July, 1945, *Life* magazine headlined that at the United Nations Conference in San Francisco, "a New and Better Charter Came Out of the Reliable Soil of Free Discussion." The discussion lasted nine weeks and was described by President Truman as a "free and sometimes bitter exchange of conflicting opinions," a comment in which the words *free* and *exchange* deserve emphasis.

When different opinions as to the proper course of action persist, our parliamentary procedure calls for a debate on a motion to adopt what seems to be the best solution. When each side has presented its arguments, a vote is taken and the will of the majority becomes the official action of the group.

4. *To release tensions.* Sweetness and light do not always prevail between factions, or among members of an organization. Tensions are likely to increase; each side assures its members of the justice of its views and attacks the motives of opponents. When such a situation prevails the rational consideration of the controversial issue is impossible. The first step in breaking through such an emotional log jam is usually to organize a discussion among leaders of the opposing factions. The meeting should first consider points on which agreement is likely. Then, as members of the opposing groups discover mutual beliefs and interests, they should be less emotional and more objective when they proceed to the crucial issues.

Discussion is immediately valuable when it gives people an opportunity to express their emotions which, if long repressed, might explode in violent acts. This is what the Greek writers called *catharsis*, what we have in mind when we say, "I feel better since I've got that off my chest." But discussion that stops here has, at best, a sort of negative value; the group should continue its deliberation until it has agreed upon at least a temporary solution to the problem. Otherwise, the tensions are likely to build up again.

5. *To indoctrinate.* We do not ordinarily associate discussion with efforts to "sell" a belief or to make propaganda for a predetermined course of action. A great many organizations are created to do just that. The membership consists of persons who believe in the organization's goals and purposes; doubters and un-believers are not likely to join or to be welcomed if they should. Group members could not be expected to produce an unprejudiced discussion on questions involving the association's basic beliefs. They might, however, profitably discuss differences of opinion that exist within the group, and the best ways of getting their beliefs accepted by non-members. Discussion in a missionary society is not expected to question the validity of the gospel but to consider the best ways of spreading it.

This is a legitimate use of discussion when the situation is clearly stated. We cannot continually begin at the beginning and reëxamine the validity of our ideas and ideals. We may, for example, announce our belief in democracy and discuss what a democracy should do in a specific situation.

III. LIMITATIONS OF DISCUSSION

Enthusiasts often overstate the values of discussion; critics often overstate its weaknesses. There are occasions when it should be used and times when it should not. As long as humans are prone to error the techniques they develop will have faults and limitations. Some people are disappointed in the outcome of discussion, however, because they do not understand its nature and its use. Some of the more common misconceptions are considered in the following paragraphs.

1. *Agreement is no sure test of success.* Too often it is assumed that if people just talk things over they will agree with one another. The extent of agreement is assumed to measure the value of the discussion. But there are good discussions in which people disagree vigorously. Indeed, when agreement on a controversial subject comes too easily, one suspects that the thinking has been superficial, or that members avoided points of disagreement. In the latter case, the real discussion takes place when people gather in small groups after the meeting.

2. *There may be silent participation.* Some are inclined to measure the success of a meeting by counting the number who said something. This criticism overlooks the fact that listening is an active process, that intelligent listening is participation. One person speaks and other group members who are paying attention are "talking back," formulating ideas into sentences that may be spoken if they get the chance. In public discussions only a small proportion of those present can speak during the forum period. If those who have ideas and information do the speaking the others will learn from them.

3. *Discussion may not "settle" anything.* In many discussions the primary objective is not to settle anything. Sometimes, indeed, the aim is to unsettle people so they will do some thinking about the problem. Until we have taken the steps involved in the thought process we are not ready to take action. When that stage is reached, we count the votes and follow the judgment of the majority.

4. *Even small groups are important.* We Americans have a liking for statistical information. We measure yield per acre, tally runs per inning and judge performance by the applause meter. That people often measure the success of a meeting by the number in attendance

is understandable, but sometimes unfortunate. The value of the San Francisco conference which created the United Nations should not be measured by the number of delegates present. The personnel of the group may be more important than its size. Information gained and opinions formed in discussion meetings may be passed from person to person through the entire community.

A. Limitations of Group Discussion

Group discussion has these fundamental weaknesses which may also be found in some public discussions.

1. *Discussion is a slow process.* It should not be used when immediate action is required. In such cases, even the most democratic organizations give their leaders broad emergency powers.

2. *Group discussion is inefficient for new problems.* If group members know little about a topic, they should not begin discussion until they have a background of information. They should read, attend lectures, listen to public discussion.

3. *Discussion is a poor method for considering questions of fact.* So, for that matter, is debate. The group should not spend its time guessing about facts; someone should look them up and report them.

4. *Discussion seldom provides an orderly analysis.* The informality makes a careful statement of the issues or a sustained presentation of an argument, difficult. The listener is not usually offered a clearcut alternative on which to base his decision.

B. Common Faults

These faults occur with such frequency as to warrant special attention.

1. *Lack of immediate preparation.* Discussion participants do not have the incentive to prepare as thoroughly as they would for a speech or a debate. Each counts on the others to present information he lacks and to carry on until the discussion reaches a point on which he wishes to speak. Invitations often stress the fact that "there are to be no speeches. We're just going to talk things over informally." The result is often impromptu thinking as well as impromptu speaking, and our first thoughts are not always our best thoughts.

2. *Concealing real differences.* The idea that conflict is bad often leads discussion groups to avoid sore spots on which there are vital differences of opinions. But this does not resolve the conflict. On the contrary, says John Dewey, " . . . it keeps the realities of the situa-

tion out of sight. . . . In consequence the triumph of the views of one or of a faction is a sham victory. It has been gained by failing to bring underlying conflicts out into the open . . ."[1]

3. *One-sidedness.* In spite of carefully laid plans, discussions are often dominated by advocates of one point of view to the comparative neglect of others. Moreover, discussion is easier to "rig" than most other meetings. A half-dozen individuals, acting in concert, can take over almost any discussion, except the debate.

READINGS

AUER, J. J., "Discussion Programs and Techniques in the Armed Forces," *Quarterly Journal of Speech,* Vol. 32 (October, 1946), pp. 303-10.

BEARD, C. A., *The Discussion of Human Affairs* (New York, The Macmillan Co., 1936), Chap. 2.

DICKENS, Milton, "Discussion, Democracy and Dictatorship," *Quarterly Journal of Speech,* Vol. 33 (April, 1947), pp. 151-8.

ELLIOT, H. S., *The Process of Group Thinking* (New York, Association Press, 1928), Chap. 1.

ESTES, C. T., "Speech and Human Relations in Industry," *Quarterly Journal of Speech,* Vol. 32 (April, 1946), pp. 160-9.

KELTNER, J. W., "Goals, Obstacles and Problem Formulation in Group Discussion," *Quarterly Journal of Speech,* Vol. 33 (December, 1947), pp. 468-73.

LASSWELL, H. D., *Democracy Through Public Opinion* (Menasha, Wisconsin, Banta Publishing Co., 1941), Chap. 2.

LEYS, W. A. R., "Can Forum Discussions Be Reasonable?" *Journal of Adult Education,* Vol. 10 (January, 1938), pp. 61-6.

LIPPITT, Ronald, *Training in Community Relations* (New York, Harper & Bros., 1949), Chaps. 1-2.

OVERSTREET, H. A., and OVERSTREET, Bonaro, *Town Meeting Comes to Town* (New York, Harper & Bros., 1938), Chap. 2.

SATTLER, W. M., "Socratic Dialogue and Modern Group Discussion," *Quarterly Journal of Speech,* Vol. 29 (April, 1943), pp. 152-7.

WIENER, P. P., "Scientific Method and Group Discussion," *Journal of Adult Education,* Vol. 9 (April, 1937), pp. 136-40.

EXERCISES

1. Make a five-minute oral report on one of the suggested readings.
2. Prepare to lead a ten-minute informal discussion on ideas expressed in one of these statements:
   a. The National Opinion Research Center used this question in its

[1] John Dewey, quoted in A. D. Sheffield's *Training for Group Experience* (New York, The Inquiry, 1929), Intro.

November, 1947, poll: "Do you happen to belong to any groups
or organizations that discuss national or international problems?"
Of those queried, 16% said, "Yes"; 84%, "No". Of those who
answered "Yes", 32% had attended college; 15%, high school
only; 7% had not gone beyond the eighth grade.

b. "In the United States the importance of organizing intelligent discussion of broad public policies is greater than in more centralized
states, because no one government has full power. Effective action
involves the coöperation of 49 governments in many cases, as
well as cities and other local authorities.... Modern methods of
intercommunication present alternative procedures for discussion,
but the dramatic character of a congressional debate has not yet
been superseded by forums or polls of whatever kind and value."
(Charles E. Merriam, *Systematic Politics*, pp. 142-3)

c. "Tolerance is learned in discussion and, as history shows, is only
so learned... One of the greatest pains to human nature is the
pain of a new idea. It is, as common people say, 'so upsetting'; it
makes you think that after all your favorite notions may be wrong,
your firmest beliefs ill-founded... If we know that a nation is
capable of enduring continuous discussion, we know that it is
capable of practicing with equanimity continuous tolerance."
(Walter Bagehot, *The Age of Discussion*)

d. "Let us converse together and open our minds freely to each other.
Let every Town assemble. Let Associations and Combinations
be everywhere set up to consult and recover our just rights."
(Samuel Adams, 1772)

e. "Who does the thinking? The notion that 'the group thinks'
deserves to be put by the side of the great freaks of philosophy
which have been put forth from age to age. Only the elite of
any society, in any age, think, and the world's thinking is carried
on by them by the transplanting of ideas from mind to mind,
under the stress and strain of clashing arguments and tugging
debate..." (William Graham Sumner, *Folkways*, p. 206)

f. "The ideal aim for a group of speakers is to create a 'consensus' on
the matter discussed—that is, a conception to which each has contributed and on which all are disposed to act." (Alfred D. Sheffield,
Joining in Public Discussion, p. 14)

g. "When men are brought face to face with their opponents, forced
to listen and learn and mend their ideas, they cease to be children
and savages and begin to live like civilized men. Then only is
freedom a reality, when men may voice their opinions because they
must examine their opinions." (Walter Lippmann, "The Indispensable Opposition," *Atlantic Monthly*, August, 1939, p. 190)

h. "... All losing sides dread discussion, for it shortens their lease on
life. Silence is for them a kind of reprieve. Their instinct, then,
is to choke off discussion at all hazards... Seeing that no great
wrong can long survive open discussion, we may characterize free
speech, free assemblage, and free press as the rights preservative

of all rights. Safeguard these fundamental rights, and the rest must come." (E. A. Ross, *Social Psychology*, p. 307)

3. Attend a discussion meeting or listen to one of the network discussion broadcasts. Write a 300-word analysis, applying the information in this chapter.

4. Make a four-minute speech in which you state and defend your opinion on one of the following topics:

a. Discussion and propaganda
b. How free should discussion be?
c. What is a good discussion?
d. Discussion or compulsory arbitration?
e. Discussion causes conflicts
f. Discussion or debate?

CHAPTER 16

Organizing and Leading Discussion

THERE IS MORE to arranging a successful discussion program than inviting some speakers and hiring a hall. While the detailed preparations depend on such factors as the sponsorship of the discussion, the nature of the topic, the size and makeup of the expected audience, there are certain steps that should be taken before all types of discussions.

I. ORGANIZING FOR DISCUSSION

Someone must analyze local interests and needs, choose and phrase a topic to fit those interests and needs, decide which type of meeting should be used, choose the leader or moderator, arrange for the best available meeting place, and advertise the event. There is plenty of work for a committee. In the case of public meetings, the committee should include representatives of various community groups.

A. Analyzing the Local Situation

The first step is to think about the people who are likely to come to this particular meeting. Some information can be gained by noting the organizations that sponsor the discussion. Members of a Parent-Teacher Association, for example, are brought together because of their mutual interests in the schools. Delegates to a labor-management conference meet to consider the needs and desires of the groups they represent. To a considerable extent, the audiences at public meetings also have a mutual interest and purpose. Only those concerned with international problems are likely to attend a symposium on the future of the United Nations. Beyond this common ground, however, members of public audiences probably have different backgrounds and may have diverse interests. These questions illustrate the type of information that should be considered in analyzing the local situation. Are those likely to attend of the same age level? Are they from the same social and economic backgrounds? Do they include different racial groups? What are their religious affiliations? Have they had similar amounts and kinds of education? Not all of these factors will be important for every discussion. Racial backgrounds, for example, would probably not be important in considering the purchase of fire fighting equipment; they might be in discussing housing or zoning laws.

B. Choosing the Topic

Sometimes it is the existence of a problem that initiates the discussion. However, for groups that have regular meetings and those planning a series of public discussions, the selection of the topic is important. It is desirable to choose topics of general interest; the danger is that those in charge may choose questions that interest only themselves, or problems that they feel *should* interest the public.

A questionnaire, carefully designed and widely circulated, is the best method of choosing discussion topics. The sample on page 280 was designed for a particular group; its general pattern may be adapted to meet any local situation.

A final word: Don't avoid local problems on which the community is divided. These are the topics on which discussion is most needed. The fear that nothing but controversy will result is without much foundation. Speakers who differ violently are likely to be more courteous and coöperative in face-to-face conversation than in partisan meetings with the opposition absent.

C. Phrasing the Discussion Topic

The next step is to phrase the topic in a manner that attracts attention and is susceptible of discussion. This is especially important for public meetings where the well-worded topic is useful in advance publicity. Some suggestions follow:

1. *Use question form.* The question is more likely to attract attention, and less likely to seem biased, than a statement.

2. *Avoid ambiguity.* This goal is difficult to achieve, but we can phrase questions in familiar words and avoid terms that are sometimes used because they do mean different things to different people.

3. *Narrow it down.* Fruitful discussion seldom results from such

DISCUSSION PLANNING QUESTIONNAIRE

The Madison Civic Forum is planning a series of meetings for the discussion of current affairs. The committee needs your help in choosing the type of meeting and the topics in which you are most interested. Please return this questionnaire to _____.

1. Would you like to attend meetings of this sort?

    _____ yes   _____ no

2. Which type of meeting would you prefer? (Check only one.)

    _____ a talk, followed by a question and answer period.

    _____ several talks on different points of view, followed by a forum period.

    _____ a debate, followed by a forum period.

    _____ an informal group discussion with a trained leader.

3. Which of the following subjects would you personally be most interested in having discussed or in discussing yourself? (Check three.)

Current affairs:

_____ the United Nations organization.

_____ the future of Japan.

_____ the future of Germany.

_____ the future of world peace.

_____ labor legislation.

_____ public health insurance.

_____ the problem of minorities.

_____ freedom of the air.

_____ price and wage control.

_____ relations with Russia.

_____ control of atomic energy.

_____ guaranteed full employment.

_____ the problem of broken homes.

_____ streamlining Congress.

Civic problems:

_____ new zoning laws.

_____ juvenile delinquency.

_____ need for new school buildings.

_____ city-manager form of government.

_____ housing programs.

_____ city vs. state tax programs.

_____ the future of our city.

_____ how to reduce traffic accidents.

Personal affairs:

_____ coöperative societies.

_____ life insurance protection.

_____ owning your own home.

_____ social security.

_____ installment buying.

_____ choosing a vocation.

_____ religion in your life.

4. If there are any subjects in which you are interested, but which are not listed above, write them in below: _____

_____

5. What other suggestions do you have that would be helpful in planning a discussion meeting that would interest you? _____

_____

Name (if you wish) _____

questions as: "What about our young people?" or "Atomic power?"
The second topic has the added defect of being incomplete.

4. *Give it headline value.* Newspaper headlines catch attention
and focus it on a story. Discussion topics should have the same qualities and for the same reasons.

D. Choosing the Type of Discussion

In the preceding chapter we listed and described briefly the more
familiar types of discussion. The choice for any meeting should be
made after considering these factors: the topic, and how much the
listeners know about it; the size and personnel of the group or audience; the purpose of the meeting; the degree of formality desired;
and whether the group members can be expected to adopt new procedures. The transition from formal to informal procedures should
be made gradually.

E. Publicizing the Meeting

A good discussion program, once established, will run for a while
on its own momentum. Even so, experience has repeatedly shown
that discussion will be more lively, and more to the point, if the
members have advance notice of the topic. They will probably not
make much special preparation but they will be ready to contribute
any information and arguments that they chance to read or hear.

Starting a public discussion program requires the skill and ingenuity needed to launch any new enterprise. The meetings should
be held in a public building. Members of labor unions will not freely
attend a discussion on a labor problem held in the Chamber of Commerce hall; members of one church, or members of no church, may
feel hesitant about attending meetings held in churches with widely
different creeds. To keep the meeting from turning into a propaganda affair requires special invitations to representatives of supposedly hostile groups. If possible, leaders of these organizations
should be members of a sponsoring committee.

The public should have advance information about the procedure.
For the first meetings at least, the "rules of the game" should appear
on programs distributed as people enter the hall.

II. LEADING DISCUSSION

The most important person in any discussion is the leader or moderator. This is not always apparent to the casual observer, for when the leader is most effective he keeps the spotlight of attention on others. He announces the topic and the purpose of the meeting, encourages the expression of minority opinions, checks those who want to talk all the time, encourages timid members to take part, summarizes individual comments into some sort of unity, and in dozens of unobtrusive ways keeps the discussion from "scattering all over the place."

A. The Discussion Leader vs. the Presiding Officer

One way of explaining the duties of the discussion leader is to contrast his position with that of the presiding officer.

At regular meetings of an organization the president serves as presiding officer. Ability to get elected, some knowledge of parliamentary law, are essential qualifications. If he can gracefully introduce those who are to appear on the program, so much the better. He may not know until he arrives what the program is to be. He is the official announcer of what comes next.

Sometimes mass meetings are called to arouse interest in a cause. For such occasions, the chairman is chosen for his prestige. His skill in presiding is of secondary importance as long as he endorses the purpose of the meeting. In such cases, the chairman may in effect be an advocate for one point of view. Those who deal with public assemblies know it is a great advantage to have a chairman ready to give them the benefit of the doubt.

The proper rôle of the discussion leader is quite different. He need not be president of the organization, nor should he be chosen just because he is prominent. Most certainly, he should not be partisan on the issue. He should be chosen for his ability to help others to think coöperatively.

Lasswell suggests the need for a "clarifier" in discussions. "The job of the clarifier," he says, "should be to make words make sense. ... He will not express personal preferences. ... He will·ask the questions that every member of the audience would ask if he were able to think of them promptly and to ask them consecutively. The clarifier aids in the process of creative thought." [1]

[1] Harold D. Lasswell, *Democracy through Public Opinion* (Menasha, Wisconsin, Banta Publishing Co., 1941), pp. 90-1.

B. Qualifications of the Discussion Leader

It is easy to generalize about the qualities of successful leaders in any field, but difficult to be concise. "The precise nature of leadership," wrote Charles E. Merriam, "is one of the most difficult problems in the domain of politics, or, indeed, in social action; yet it is one of the most real phenomena in political or social behavior." [2] He listed these "attributes commonly found in a variety of leaders": social sensitivity, facility in personal and group contacts, skill in "dramatic expression" by voice or pen, and "an unusual degree of courage."

Zeleny compared leaders and non-leaders in student discussion groups, and found leaders superior, in varying degrees, in these characteristics: finality of decision, forcefulness, participation, self-confidence, prestige, insight, steadiness of purpose, intelligence, knowledge, quickness of decision, tact, pleasant voice, self-control and appearance.[3]

It would seem, at first thought, that the discussion leader must be something of a superman. It is true that comparatively few people have the happy combination of personality, knowledge and skill needed to lead a great public discussion, or to act as conciliator in disputes between large organizations of labor and management. But it is equally true that in any group there are members who are sufficiently qualified to lead discussions in local meetings. Moreover, with the possible exceptions of the ability to think and act quickly, these skills can be learned. The informal discussion group is a good place to learn them.

In choosing leaders, or moderators, these abilities and skills should be considered.

1. *Ability to think and act quickly.* The unexpected is always happening in a discussion meeting, and the leader must be able to adjust his plans on a moment's notice. The person who insists on following a pre-conceived plan should not try to become a discussion leader. The leader must also be able to make quick decisions and to reverse them with equal firmness if he finds that he was wrong.

2. *Ability to get along with others.* The leader tries to get people to think together instead of listening passively to each other. The

---

[2] Charles E. Merriam, *Systematic Politics* (Chicago, University of Chicago Press, 1945), pp. 107-8.

[3] Leslie D. Zeleny, "Characteristics of Group Leaders," *Sociology and Social Research*, Vol. 24 (November, 1939), pp. 140-9.

conference chairman often has the added task of composing differences and soothing ruffled tempers. These tasks are difficult enough when the leader is well liked and emotionally stable. If he is inclined to "fly off the handle" he will be in continual trouble.

3. *Respect for the opinions of others.* The leader must be a good listener, genuinely interested in what others know and believe. The individual who believes people should be told what to think and do is irritating enough as a group member or forum speaker. Certainly he should not be the leader. Nor should the leader show impatience when the discussion moves slowly and the members prefer a plan of their own to his. If he shows he doesn't like what the group members are doing, they will respond by not liking him.

4. *Willingness to remain in the background.* The leader who cannot resist the temptation to parade his own knowledge, or to point out the mistakes of others, will be about as popular as the quarterback who elects himself to carry the ball whenever there is a good chance for a touchdown. This does not mean that the leader should let others take control of the meeting. He keeps attention focused on what others know and think about the topic. Whenever possible he asks the group to decide matters of procedure but he guides the progress of the meeting none the less.

The prospective leader's knowledge of the discussion process, his attitude on the topic, and his skill in speaking should also be considered.

5. *Knowledge of the discussion process.* This is the most important qualification of the successful leader. He must also know the objectives and the procedures agreed upon for the discussion he is to lead.

6. *Knowledge of evidence and reasoning.* The fact that discussion is often as informal as conversation does not justify assertions without proof or conclusions not warranted by the evidence. This is another way of saying that the leader should have a good working knowledge of evidence and argument.

7. *Knowledge of the topic.* The leader should have a general knowledge of the topic but he should represent the interested layman who raises pertinent questions, not the expert who answers them. If he has stated or published his conclusions on the problem he may be open to a charge of prejudice. In this event, he can better serve the group as a source of information or as an advocate for his point of view.

8. *Freedom from prejudice.* It would be impossible to find a leader absolutely free from prejudice on the controversial topics considered in discussion meetings. The practical question is whether these prejudices exist to a degree that would make the proposed leader unacceptable to the group. Individuals should not lead public discussions on topics touching their personal or professional interests. A football coach is prejudiced on the values of football; a professor, on faculty salaries; a labor leader, on strikes. While these persons may lead discussions within their own groups, they should participate in public meetings as sources of information or spokesmen for their point of view.

9. *Skill in speaking.* The group discussion leader does not need to be an accomplished public speaker; indeed, as we have said, he should resist the temptation to make speeches. But he should have some proficiency in clear and direct conversation, which is not a simple thing. It requires, among other things, ability to speak the language of the group, to use short sentences and familiar words, and a voice that can be easily heard.

The moderator of a public discussion needs, in addition, the "skill in dramatic expression," mentioned by Merriam, and ability to command attention.

III. THE LEADER'S PART IN THE MEETING

The leader should be chosen well in advance of the discussion. In some instances he will be a member of the planning committee. In any case, he should know what has been done in arranging the meeting. His special duties in preparing for and leading each type of discussion will be described in later chapters. Here we give instructions that apply to all types.

A. Getting the Meeting Started

The leader should set a good example by the precision and brevity of his opening remarks. They should include: a statement of the topic; an explanation of the procedure so each person will know when and how long he may speak; and, in the case of public discussions, introductions of the speakers or panel members, stating their knowledge of the topic and what point of view they represent. If the meeting begins with talks the leader then introduces the first speaker; if it begins with conversation, he asks a question that he hopes will start the discussion.

B. Keeping the Discussion on the Track

Discussion tends to wander off the main road and into bypaths. Sometimes these excursions are interesting and fruitful; sometimes they lead into unrelated fields. The leader constantly wonders how closely he should hold the discussion to the prearranged plan. If those present feel that he is too "bossy" they will resent his directions; if he lets the discussion go too far afield, he isn't really a leader.

The problem is to find the golden mean. The leader should be slow to announce that the discussion is off the subject. Rather, he should raise the question and let the group members decide whether it is and what they want to do about it.

C. Making Occasional Summaries

Internal summaries may be used to check needless repetition, to get the discussion back to the problem, or to record points of agreement and disagreement. They should be brief and in the language of the group. The leader should not, of course, play up one point of view or assume agreement where none exists. He can guard against prejudiced or inaccurate summaries by asking those present to check him and supply missing items.

D. Encouraging General Participation

Although only a few members of a public discussion audience can be given opportunity to speak, it is important that anyone with something to say be encouraged to say it. The leader who begins the forum period by asking "Does anyone have anything to say?" is not making it easy for anyone to speak. If he says it as though he does not really expect anyone to respond, no one will. But if he says, "I know a great many of you want to speak, who will be first?" the forum is more likely to get off to a good start. Sometimes he plants the first question to make sure there will be one.

Usually, the leader should not, without previous arrangement, put questions to individuals in the group. They may have nothing to contribute and resent having to say so. He may, however, encourage timid members to speak by asking for information he knows they possess. He should ask for comments from those who have not spoken and recognize them in preference to more vocal members.

In opening the forum period, leaders sometimes ask only that audience members question the speakers. This implies the listener-learner relationship instead of coöperative thinking. The listeners may have additional information or opinions that they want to express. The invitation should be broad enough to include these types of participation.

E. Keeping the Discussion from Becoming One-Sided

In spite of careful planning, it sometimes happens that one point of view is more skillfully presented than the others, or is upheld by a majority of the speakers. Then, the minority, feeling themselves outnumbered, are likely to increase the one-sidedness by keeping silent. The leader should do his best to correct this situation. He may even find it necessary to abandon his rôle as leader and question the majority's views or present the other side as well as he can on the spur of the moment. This is a makeshift expedient, but justified if it keeps the discussion from becoming a propaganda meeting.

F. Testing the Information and Reasoning

The leader should not be concerned about the conclusions reached through discussion, but he should be constantly concerned about the quality of the evidence and reasoning. He can best guard against faulty reasoning and poor evidence by raising questions such as those in the following list. Also included in this list are questions directed at other situations needing attention:

1. *To call attention to a point not yet considered:* "Has anyone thought about this phase of the problem?"
2. *To question the strength of an argument:* "What reasons do we have for believing this argument?"
3. *To get back to causes:* "Why do you suppose Doakes takes this position?"
4. *To question the source of information or argument:* "Who gathered these statistics that you spoke of?" "Who is Mr. Gish whose opinion has been quoted?" "Do you know that as a fact, or is it your opinion?"
5. *To suggest that the discussion is wandering from the point:* "Can someone tell me what bearing this has on our problem?" "Your point is an interesting one, but can't we get back to our subject?"
6. *To suggest that no new information is being added:* "Can anyone add anything to the information already given on this point?"
7. *To call attention to the difficulty or complexity of the problem:* "Aren't we beginning to understand why our legislators haven't solved this problem?"
8. *To register steps of agreement (or disagreement):* "Am I correct in assuming that we all agree (or disagree) on this point?"

9. *To bring the generalizing speaker down to earth:* "Can you give us a specific example on that point?" "Your general idea is good, but I wonder if we can't make it more concrete. Does anyone know of a case...?"

10. *To handle the impatient, cure-all member:* "But would your plan work in all cases? Who has an idea on that?" "Hadn't we better reserve judgment until we all know more about this problem?"

11. *To suggest that personalities be avoided:* "I wonder what bearing this has on the question before us?"

12. *To suggest that some are talking too much:* "Are there those who haven't spoken who have ideas they would like to present?"

13. *To suggest the value of compromise:* "Do you suppose the best course of action lies somewhere between these two points of view?"

14. *To suggest that the group may be prejudiced:* "Is our personal interest in this question causing us to overlook the interests of other groups?"

15. *To draw the timid but informed member into the discussion:* "Spelvin, here, lived for quite a while in China. Suppose we ask him whether he ever saw...?"

16. *To handle a question the leader can't answer:* "I don't know. Who does?"

17. *To encourage a speaker to talk with the group, not at the leader:* "Don't you think you'll be heard better if you face the rest of the group?"

18. *To cut off a speaker who is too long-winded:* "While we're on this point, let's hear from some of the others. Can we save your other point until later?"

19. *To take the play away from a verbose member:* "You've raised a number of interesting points which should keep us busy a good while. Would anyone else like to comment on them?"

20. *To help the member who has difficulty expressing himself:* "I wonder if what you're saying isn't this...?"

21. *To encourage further questions by friendly comment:* "That's a good question. I'm glad you raised it. Anyone have an answer?"

22. *To break up a heated argument:* "I think we all know how Jones and Smith feel about this. Now who else would like to get in on it?"

Leaders sometimes phrase their questions so that a simple "yes" or "no" answer will suffice. In most cases, this type of question tends to stifle discussion; when a man says "yes" he may not be inclined to say more. Occasionally such questions may be used to get an expression of opinion that can be used as a basis for discussion. Questions that are too broad baffle the members. Start with "what" to get facts and opinions, "who" or "where" to get sources, "why" for reasons or causes, and "how" or "when" to get down to specific cases.

How, one may ask, can a leader do all these things and yet remain in the background? The answer lies in the manner of his participation rather than in the amount. In a People's Platform broadcast, for example, there were 132 participations in thirty minutes. The moderator spoke 43 times; of the four panel members, Mr. *A* spoke 37 times; Mr. *B*, 21 times; Miss *C*, 16 times; Mr. *D*, 15 times. A discussion training conference conducted by the Institute for Group Dynamics, had three sections with skilled leaders. Group *A* averaged 161 participations per hour and the leader occupied 24 per cent of the time; group *B*, 243 participations with the leader speaking 35 per cent of the time; group *C*, 162 participations with the leader speaking 30 per cent of the time.[4] The proportion of time used by the leader should vary with the type of meeting.

IV. THE LANGUAGE OF DISCUSSION

The language and style of the speeches given in discussion are treated at some length in Chapter 26, "The Debate Speech." Here we are concerned with the various types of informal discussion and with the speaking that takes place during the forum period.

A literal transcription of an informal discussion, even among experienced speakers, usually reveals things that would be regarded as weaknesses in written style. There are incomplete sentences, loose-jointed sentences, and words whose antecedents are grammatically doubtful. There are sentences that start off strongly, reverse themselves in mid-field, and trail off into silence. We do not condone slipshod statements or obvious grammatical errors. The speaker should attempt to avoid them in his everyday talk as well as in more formal communication. But good talk has a rhetoric of its own; it should not be judged by the standards commonly applied to written style. The speaker who "talks like a book" is just as bad as the book of unedited extemporaneous talk. The language used in plays and radio scripts, except for the fact that it is written and edited by experts, illustrates the style of informal discussion and may serve as a guide for language in discussion.

Here are the main differences between the languages of informal discussion and formal writing:

1. The discussion speaker makes more use of the personal pro-

[4] Ronald Lippitt, *Training in Group Relations* (New York, Harper & Bros., 1949), p. 158.

nouns, *I*, *you*, *we*, *our*, etc., than is usually regarded good form in writing.

2. The discussion speaker can properly use fragmentary sentences when the meaning is clear. "Second" is just as meaningful as "I second the motion." Note the incomplete sentences in this excerpt from a discussion on propaganda:

Leader: Now for some examples of propaganda...
Mr. A: Campaign speeches...
Mr. B: Sermons, raising money for missions...
Mrs. C: Many movies...
Mrs. D: Gossip...
Mrs. E: Aren't we all...
Mr. A: I think so, at one time or another...

3. The discussion speaker properly uses more repetition than would be acceptable in writing. The reader can vary his rate to suit his mood or the difficulty of the subject matter. He can reread a paragraph or stop reading to ponder the meaning or the importance of an idea. The listener can do none of these things. He must attempt to adapt his listening rate to the speaker's speed of utterance. When his attention wanders, as happens with the best of listeners, he may miss important sentences that are not repeated. One advantage of informal discussion is that participants may interrupt the speaker when they missed the point or do not fully understand his meaning.

4. The discussion speaker often uses colloquial language that would seem inappropriate in formal speeches. The more nearly the speaker uses the everyday language of his listeners, the more nearly will they understand what he says. The oft-printed advice to use short, Anglo-Saxon words is sound, not because of the length or origin of these words, but because the average listener has known and used them since childhood.

5. The discussion speaker uses questions more frequently than he would in formal address. The leader uses questions in introducing the topic and in making transitions. The speaker is questioned on what he has said. Members of the group question each other. The question and answer is one of discussion's most common rhetorical devices.

Aside from these differences, the language of discussion should be that appropriate for speaking or writing where the communication of ideas, and a calm consideration of their importance are the main objectives. There should be a liberal use of definitions, explanations, and typical examples. The summaries and transitions should be clear enough to keep the listener from getting lost. There is no place in discussion for the rhetoric of display or for the more extreme appeals to the emotions.

V. HANDLING SPECIAL SITUATIONS

A. What About the Overly Talkative Member?

There are three types: (1) the individual who talks easily and knows a great deal about the topic; (2) the long-winded member who doesn't realize how long he has spoken; (3) the irrelevant member who tries to make a speech on his pet theme.

The best way to handle such situations is to prevent them. The rules of the game should be made clear before the meeting begins. The leader should stop the first member who attempts to speak overtime. He should ask the irrelevant member to connect his speech with the issue under discussion. The person who speaks not too long but too often usually responds to an indirect suggestion about the desirability of hearing from those who have not spoken. The leader, like the judge or umpire, must enforce the rules without favoritism.

B. What About Personal Remarks?

The best solution is to create an atmosphere in which personal attacks will seem out of place. An occasional comment of this sort should probably be ignored. The group will usually deal with a member who persists in attacking individuals rather than arguments. One leader of considerable experience remembers only two occasions when he had to make direct rulings that speakers were out of order. One persisted in questioning the good faith of an opponent; the other referred to the race of an audience member who had cross-examined him quite effectively.

Discussion audiences often express surprise that speakers who oppose each other vigorously seem to respect, even to like, each other. It is sometimes difficult to get active opponents in a controversy to appear on the same platform. Once there, they usually carry on the discussion in the spirit set by the leader's opening statement.

C. Should Votes Be Taken?

A good many groups announce that they will neither pass resolutions nor take votes on the issue. One purpose is to keep pressure groups from attempting to stack the audience and secure endorsement of their cause. Another purpose is to avoid hasty or ill-considered action. An even more fundamental reason is that discussion is not the best method of lining up arguments for and against a motion; this is best done in debate.

We do not say that votes should never be taken. Members may properly be asked to vote on questions of procedure. There are occasions when they are prepared to vote on the issues at the close of a good discussion. We should learn to withhold decisions until we have heard the evidence; but it is equally important that we learn to evaluate evidence and to make tentative decisions. The perpetually open mind is just as bad as the mind that has closed too soon.

READINGS

BAIRD, A. C., *Argumentation, Discussion, and Debate* (New York, McGraw Hill Book Co., Inc., 1950), Chaps. 21, 23.

CAMPBELL, C. M., "The Rôle of the Chairman in Leading Discussion," *Adult Education Bulletin*, Vol. 9 (June, 1945), pp. 135-40.

ELLIOTT, H. S., *The Process of Group Thinking* (New York, The Association Press, 1928), Chap. 2.

HANNAFORD, E. S., *Conference Leadership in Business and Industry* (New York, McGraw-Hill Book Co., Inc., 1945).

HEYEL, Carl, *Standard Business Conference Technique* (New York, Funk and Wagnalls Co., 1948), Parts 1 and 2.

LASSWELL, H. D., "The Clarifier of Public Discussion," *Quarterly Journal of Speech*, Vol. 34 (December, 1948), pp. 451-5.

LEVINE, Sol, "An Approach to Constructive Leadership," *Journal of Social Issues*, Vol. 5 (Winter, 1949), pp. 46-53.

McBURNEY, J. H., and HANCE, K. G., *Discussion in Human Affairs* (New York, Harper & Bros., 1950), Chaps. 15, 16.

MILLER, S. M. "Planning for Participation," *Journal of Social Issues*, Vol. 5. (Winter, 1949), pp. 33-41.

NICHOLS, Alan, *Discussion and Debate* (New York, Harcourt, Brace & Co., 1941), Chap. 7.

SHOEMAKER, C. C., "Management of Group Discussion," *The English Journal*, Vol. 36 (December, 1947), pp. 508-13.

UTTERBACK, W. E., "The Moderator's Function in Group Thinking," *Quarterly Journal of Speech*, Vol. 34 (December, 1948), pp. 455-8.

————, *Group Thinking and Conference Leadership* (New York, Rinehart and Co., 1949), Chaps. 7, 10.

WILLIAMSON, Ralph, "Training Volunteer Lay Leaders in Rural Parishes," *Religious Education*, Vol. 40 (March, 1945), pp. 78-82.

WITMAN, S. L., "Selecting and Phrasing the Discussion Subject," *Library Journal*, Vol. 72 (May 1, 1947), pp. 700-5.

ZELENY, L. D., "Experiments in Leadership Training," *Journal of Educational Sociology*, Vol. 14 (January, 1941), pp. 310-2.

EXERCISES

1. Make a four-minute speech on one of the suggested readings.
2. Hand in your plan for an informal class discussion.
3. Find out as much as you can about the methods of organizing one of the network discussion programs.
4. Plan a discussion for your home community. Tell why you chose the topic and the method.
5. Your instructor will give you one of these assignments as an observer of a group discussion:

a. Pay attention to the logic of the discussion:
   (1) Does the group follow a logical plan?
   (2) If the group gets off the beam, can you tell why?
   (3) If the group gets off the beam, how does it get back on?
   (4) Are the contributions (qualitative) evenly distributed?
   (5) Does the group really get somewhere?

b. Observe the work of the leader:
   (1) Does he seem to know where he's going?
   (2) How does he keep the group on the beam?
   (3) What special leadership devices does he use?
   (4) Is he generally authoritarian, democratic, or laissez faire?
   (5) How might he have done his job better?

c. Classify the types of participation by each member; such as:
   (1) The elaborator (who wants to add further explanations)
   (2) The energizer (who continually urges the group along)
   (3) The harmonizer (who tries to smooth over conflicts)
   (4) The standard setter (who wants to measure group decisions)
   (5) The blocker (who impedes group progress)
   (6) The dominator (who tries to take over the discussion)

d. Make a chart of the discussion, following these directions:
   (1) Draw small circles on a large sheet of paper to represent the position of each member.
   (2) After the leader's opening remarks, draw a line from his circle to that of the next person to speak; then draw a line from that circle to the one representing the next speaker, and so on.
   (3) The result should be a "spider web" diagram of the discussion. (You may want to start a new diagram at several points, so you can tell whether the pattern changes as the discussion progresses.) Then consider such questions as these:
      (a) Do most of the lines converge upon the leader, or is there a fair amount of "cross-talk"?
      (b) Are the most loquacious people sitting together, and the relatively silent ones also?
      (c) Does the diagram reflect real *group* discussion, or a series of little monologues?

e. Keep a record of the participations of each member. Count not only complete statements, but also such interjections as "That's right!" "No!" or "Explain what you mean!" which indicate the participant's point of view.

At the end of the discussion have each member write down the names of three members of the group, plus his own, who in his opinion contributed most to the discussion.

By making a ranking of the quantitative participations (your record) and a ranking of the qualitative participations (group ballots), you can see whether there seems to be a correlation between the amount and value of participation.

CHAPTER 17

Special Discussion Techniques

LINCOLN, so the story goes, labeled one pigeon-hole in his desk, "If you can't find it anywhere else, look here." Much the same thing can be said of this chapter. Included are such seemingly miscellaneous items as "rôle-playing," the "buzz technique," the film forum, and the forum period. These cannot be classified as special types of discussion; they are devices to increase the effectiveness of various forms. Included also are descriptions of the discussion team and the self-evaluation period that may be used to improve the quality of discussion. Finally, there is a section on intercollegiate discussions to show how the method is being adapted for use in forensic programs.

While these techniques are not types of discussion, most of them can be classified in terms of objective or purpose. They were developed to create interest in the discussion method or in a specific problem; to secure more audience participation in the forum period; to improve the quality of discussion; or to develop interschool discussions.

I. CREATING INTEREST IN DISCUSSION

We are not thinking here of the usual publicity methods, posters, displays in local libraries and bookstores, and announcements in the newspapers and on the radio. We assume that appropriate publicity will be given to all meetings. We are thinking of ways to interest people both in the method and in the problems discussed.

A. Film Forums

The film forum uses motion pictures, strip films, or slides, to arouse interest and present the problem in its broad outlines. But the film forum should involve more than looking at a picture and asking questions afterward. The *Film Forum Guide*, published by the University of Wisconsin Extension Division, suggests this outline for the meeting:

> 5 minutes to introduce topic and pictures
> 20 minutes to show pictures
> 20 minutes for panel or symposium on problem
> 20 minutes for audience forum
> 10 minutes for conclusions and planning ahead

The panel or symposium should supplement the information contained in the pictures, consider the local aspects of the problem, and suggest possible solutions. The Wisconsin Extension Division service to discussion groups provides, in addition to the pictures, a package of pamphlets, articles and clippings, and a discussion outline.

The program committee should not choose the film forum as an easy way to arrange a discussion meeting. The tasks of finding suitable pictures, getting the proper device for showing them, making sure that the needed electrical connections are available, and that someone knows how to operate the equipment, are superimposed on the work involved in organizing the usual discussion meeting. In addition, there are the rental charges for the pictures and projectors.

But, in many cases, the values of the film forum more than compensate for the difficulties in arranging it. The prospect of seeing pictures attracts people who would not otherwise attend the meetings. The process of looking at the pictures gives a more vivid realization of the problem than the average audience member is likely to get from any but highly skilled speakers. This is especially true of eye-minded individuals to whom seeing is believing.

B. Rôle-Playing

This device, sometimes called "socio-drama" or "psycho-drama," is not new. Youngsters have used it for generations, "playing school" and reënacting funerals, weddings, and church services. The writer was once invited to be "the pause in the day's occupation" in a highly dramatic presentation of "The Children's Hour"! But rôle-playing has its grown-up uses, too. With more advance planning and rehearsal, it is employed in such diverse situations as sales demonstrations, mock trials, model sessions of the United Nations, documentary broadcasts and morality plays. Its purpose parallels that of the illustration in the speech. The fact that rôle-playing is not new may enhance, rather than lessen, its value in discussions. The participants are more likely to know what is expected of them.

Rôle-playing, as used in discussion, is the "spontaneous acting out of problems or situations."[1] It is employed partly to add variety to the meeting and partly to portray the situation more vividly than would usually be done by straight narration or description. The actors are told to give the opinions and portray the actions of the characters they impersonate. They are allowed a few minutes to agree on the points to be made in the episode; beyond this there is no rehearsal. The "acts" are usually not more than five or six minutes in length. They may occur at any point in the discussion where an illustration is needed. The rôle-players must have imagination, and willingness to enter whole-heartedly into the characterization.

The discussion leader who uses this device should first make sure that the actors understand the nature and purpose of their assignment. They must resist the temptation to be merely entertaining or to give impersonations that raise laughter at the expense of group members. In Miss Fenner's words, "Rôle-playing should be a stimulant to thinking, not an escape from the discipline of learning." Its value should be measured in terms of its contribution to the process of group thinking. When poorly done, it might better have been left undone.

II. CONDUCTING THE FORUM

The forum provides the only opportunity for audience members to speak in public discussion meetings. It is, therefore, an essential element in group thinking. In meetings of any considerable size, only a small percentage of those present will participate. Many feel that they have nothing to say; others are too timid to speak. Some keep silent because they don't know how to take part. There can be nothing but praise for those who refrain from speaking when they really have nothing to contribute to the discussion. From those who intend to speak and from those would like to if they dared, the leader attempts to build a meaningful forum period.

A. The Rôle of the Leader

In opening the meeting, the leader should announce when, how long, and how often, audience members may speak. Better still, he

[1] Mildred S. Fenner, *Educational Trend* (October, 1949).

may provide mimeographed or printed programs containing, in addition to this information, significant facts about the panel or symposium speakers, and a questionnaire to get such audience reactions as may be desired.

The rules usually specify that forum speakers should rise and be recognized by the chairman before they speak, that speeches cannot exceed one or two minutes in length, and that members who have not spoken will be recognized in preference to those who have. The leader should see that the time limit is enforced from the start. If he lets the first audience member speak overtime, he will have to give others the same privilege.

In large meetings, the leader often repeats questions from the floor to make sure everyone hears them. He may, with the questioner's consent, rephrase questions that are not clearly stated. When the audience is not familiar with forum procedure, the leader may have a few individuals prepared to ask questions or contribute information to get the discussion started. To make sure that the discussion ends well, he may have an audience member raise an important issue two or three minutes before the time set for adjournment. Or he may call on each panel or symposium speaker for a thirty-second summary of his position on the discussion topic.

In a panel-forum, with audiences of moderate size, the leader should encourage both panel members and listeners to discuss any important audience questions or comments. The result should be a sort of expanded conversation in which everyone is free to take part. This procedure cannot be followed in large meetings.

The symposium or debate forum that aims to draw out conflicting opinions presents special problems. The leader must see that these different points of view have a fair chance. He may ask for questions directed to each speaker in turn, call attention to various aspects of the problem, or ask all speakers to comment on questions put to one of their number.

The best procedure in the forum following a lecture is to ask the speaker to take a seat in the audience after his talk. This makes it easier for the listeners to discuss points raised in the lecture and harder for the lecturer to make a short speech in response to each audience contribution. In the debate-forum, questions and comments can be discussed pro and con by the opposing debaters. The moderator should keep this discussion brief to allow as much audience participation as possible.

Occasionally the leader will have to deal with irrelevant questions, *ad hominem* remarks, and requests for information that has already been given. Of course, irrelevant questions will be asked as long as there are muddle-headed individuals. In such situations, the leader may suggest that, since the question does not seem closely related to the discussion, it be taken up with the speaker after the meeting. He may advise audience members to make sure, before asking a question, that they can relate it to the discussion in progress. *Ad hominem* questions, those that attack persons, violate one of the basic assumptions of discussion: that intelligent people can discuss each others' ideas without discussing each other. The leader must rule such questions out of order. When audience members ask for information already given, he can again suggest that they question the speakers after the meeting. George V. Denny's methods of dealing with some of these situations in Town Meeting forums are shown in the exercises at the end of this chapter.

B. The Rôle of the Audience Member

The question is the most frequent form of audience participation, at least in the larger public meetings. The questions fall into four categories.

1. *Requests for further information.* The largest number are in this classification. Especially is this true when the speakers are recognized as authorities on the problem under discussion. The listeners naturally want to learn as much as they can while they have the opportunity. If the speaker has the information, he welcomes the chance to give it; if he doesn't, that fact may be significant.

2. *Requests for the speaker's opinion.* When the speaker has prestige, listeners ask for his opinions almost as frequently as they ask for information. They want to know what he thinks about a particular argument, or what he would advise them to do in a specific situation.

The questions in the third and fourth categories may also seek information or opinions, but they differ in that they indicate the questioner's attitude toward the speaker.

3. *Friendly questions.* Asked by friends of the speaker or those who share his opinions, these questions give him the chance to present further information or to amplify his arguments. Sometimes the questioner hopes to win public approval by getting the speaker to endorse one of his pet ideas.

4. *Hostile or challenging questions.* These may be intended to re-

veal weaknesses in the speaker's evidence or reasoning, or to "put him on the spot" by challenging him to state his position on a controversial issue. The effectiveness of a single well-phrased question was demonstrated in the Town Meeting broadcast of February 18, 1937, on "Can Democracies Avoid Dictatorships?" Much has happened since then but the issue is not outdated. Mme. Agresti, of Italy, praised Mussolini's Guild State, arguing that it protected the liberties of the average citizen. This is what happened in the forum period.

> Man from the audience: "Can such a thing as America's Town Meeting take place in Italy?"
> Mme. Agresti: "No."

An observer called this question "the 'No' heard round the world."

Another example of hostile questions occurred in the debate-forum broadcast on the American Forum of the Air, January 19, 1941. It is included here to illustrate the effectiveness of repeating a hostile question, even though the speakers were not audience members. The topic was "Should Congress Adopt the Lend-Lease Program?" Congressman Andrew J. May, Chairman of the House Military Affairs Committee and Ernest W. Gibson, Chairman of the Committee to Defend America upheld the affirmative; Senators Gerald Nye of North Dakota and Wayland Brooks of Illinois, the negative. The first negative speaker asked: "What aid, short of war, will this Lend-Lease bill permit that we have not given, or cannot now give?" The advocates could give no real answer. Commenting on this forum, J. Calvin Callaghan wrote eight years later, "I can still recall my empathic embarrassment as I listened that evening to Brooks' reiteration of that damning question, thirteen times asked, never effectively answered." [2]

Thus far we have considered what the typical audience member does in the forum period; we now offer suggestions about the manner of his participation.

1. Those wishing to speak should rise and be recognized by the chairman. This practice serves a double purpose: it avoids the confusion that would result if others try to speak at the same time, and it enables the audience to identify the speaker. Those who want to remain anonymous should remain silent also.

2. While he is talking to the moderator, or to one of the speakers on the platform, the forum participant should remember that he

[2] J. Calvin Callaghan, *The Lend-Lease Debate*, unpublished Ph.D. thesis, University of Wisconsin, 1949, p. 353.

ought also be speaking to the entire audience. Conversation between speakers on the platform and audience members on the front row should be audible to those in the back seats.

3. The forum speech must usually be extemporaneous, but it need not be impromptu. Knowing that he has only a minute or two in which to make his point, the speaker should make every sentence count. He should make a brief outline and probably write out any questions he wishes to ask. Those who speak without thinking are likely to land beside the chap who leaps without looking.

4. The forum participant should be persuasive rather than aggressive in manner. Unless he is sure of his ground and his skill, he should avoid heckling a speaker; the odds are against him in any such interchange.

C. "Discussion 66"

Also called "the buzz technique," for reasons that will become apparent, this is a method of getting every audience member to take part in the forum period. Here is a general outline of the procedure:[3]

1. A single, carefully-worded question is presented to the audience. Depending on the nature of the question and the purpose of the meeting, Discussion 66 may either precede or follow the panel or symposium.

2. Committees of six are formed either by rearrangement of chairs, or, in rooms having immovable seats, by grouping three members in row one with the three just behind them.

3. Each committee quickly chooses a chairman and a secretary-spokesman. The chairman encourages each member to speak in the brief discussion. The secretary-spokesman is provided with a 5″ x 8″ index card on which to keep a record of the meeting.

4. When the organization is complete, the question is again announced and the chairman asks each member to give his answer. The secretary-spokesman records these answers omitting the names of members.

5. After each member has spoken, the chairman asks the group to choose the most valuable suggestion or idea. When there is time, the secretary-spokesman reports the group decision orally; in the case of large meetings, the written reports are collected and synthesized for later presentation to the audience.

[3] See J. Donald Phillips, "Report on Discussion 66," *Adult Education Journal*, Vol. 7 (October, 1948), pp. 181-2.

The name, "Discussion 66," implies that groups of six discuss the question for six minutes. Actually, the time allotted depends on the nature and importance of the question. In any event, the time consumed in organizing, electing officers and making sure the groups know what to do, is not included in the six minutes.

Phillips reports that Discussion 66 has been successfully used on the following occasions: A state meeting of 700 Four-H Club members; a national convention with 2000 in attendance; an assembly of 400 junior high school students; and a management-supervisor conference conducted by the Michigan Bell Telephone Company.

A representative of the American Telephone and Telegraph Company who observed Discussion 66 in action wrote:

... There is no limit to which the "66 Plan" can be used in bringing to light pertinent questions. ... The anonymity of the questioner is a vital factor. Without doubt questions are asked ... which would not be asked if an individual had to state them. In fact, the groups seemed to enjoy asking questions which they thought were ticklish. ... The method has been used very successfully as a means of developing individual and group thinking on problems and their solutions. ... [4]

III. IMPROVING THE QUALITY OF DISCUSSION

Though discussion has been talked about, praised, and sometimes practised, for a good many years, the average citizen still doesn't know just what is expected of him in various types of discussion meetings. His experience has been generally limited to membership in the passive audience which, as Lasswell remarks, "is supposed to hold its tongue, sit on its hands, relax its feet, and never squirm." [5] To improve the quality of discussion, especially in public meetings, conventions and conferences, members need instruction in what to do and leaders need assistance in keeping the discussion clear, informed and relevant.

A. The Clarifier

In 1941, Lasswell proposed that the discussion leader be assisted by a clarifier who might interrupt the conversation at any time in the interest of clarity.

[4] Report published by the Information Department, American Telephone and Telegraph Company (October, 1948), p. 10.
[5] Harold D. Lasswell, "The Clarifier of Public Discussion," *Quarterly Journal of Speech*, Vol. 34 (December, 1948), pp. 451-4.

The clarifier differs from the judge, who applies a body of legal rules to the words presented before him. He differs from the "chairman" who looks simply to the rules of order. The clarifier is not a "moderator," if by the moderator we mean one who tries to keep the discussion advancing toward clarity, but who holds his own intervention within modest bounds.[6]

The clarifier is neutral as far as the question is concerned. His function is sometimes performed by the examiner of a House or Senatorial Committee in his questioning of witnesses and frequently exemplified in public hearings before such agencies as the Federal Trade Commission and the Federal Communications Commission.

"The clarifying function," says Lasswell, "calls for poise, alertness, and experience." The clarifier can play his part successfully only when audience members and speakers understand what he is trying to do and accept, though they may not welcome, his interruptions. "The willingness to be interrupted, to be challenged for explanation, is a virtue befitting a democrat in pursuit of enlightenment." Lasswell predicted, in the *Quarterly Journal of Speech* article, that "Teams of chairmen and clarifiers will gain local, and then larger, renown and gradually improve the level of public discussion."

B. The Discussion Team

Lasswell's team idea has been developed and adapted to the needs of conventions and "work conferences," lasting two or three days, that bring together delegates who do not know each other and are often equally unfamiliar with discussion methods. The current procedure is to form discussion teams that work with the same group of delegates throughout the conference. The personnel of the teams and the duties of team members are still matters for experimentation.

Teams consisting of a discussion leader, a content recorder and a process observer were used in the 1947 San Francisco Conference on Nursing Education.[7] The duties of the discussion leader have been stated in preceding chapters; those of the other two team members are paraphrased here:

The functions of the *content recorder* are to get the major issues discussed, with pro and con arguments indicated, the major agreements

[6] Harold D. Lasswell, *Democracy through Public Opinion* (Menasha, Wisconsin, Banta Publishing Co., 1941), pp. 90-5.

[7] Watson Dickerman and Marjorie Davis, "The San Francisco Nursing Education Conference," *Adult Education Bulletin*, Vol. 12 (February, 1948), pp. 82-7.

reached, and the recommendations for action. The recorder reports his group's thinking, in general sessions and in public statements. The *process observer* records, not the content, but the procedures of group thinking. He notes such things as the nature and extent of group participation, the way the leader functions, the dead spots in the discussion, and the morale of the group. He uses this information to help group members evaluate their performance and increase their efficiency.

Bradford believes that every conference needs certain *resource persons*, with "specific information, experiences, skills, or points of view, useful to the group."[8] Usually these individuals should not be members of a team; instead, they should be available to all groups, on request. After noting that information may also be supplied in special information sessions, Bradford concludes that "few conferences have succeeded in successfully using resource persons."

A training session for members of the discussion teams is essential to the success of the conference. The session usually includes a restatement of each member's duties; the rôle-playing of a discussion meeting, followed by an evaluation of each member's part in it; and a briefing session on what to do in typical situations. Even though a full day was devoted to "dress rehearsal" preceding the Nursing Education Conference, Dickerman and Davis felt that the meetings suffered from the "too sketchy training of leaders, observers, and recorders." They advise more advance practice, and more meetings of, and with, the teams between the conference meetings. However, they believe "that these important and educative assignments can be assumed by delegates to a conference and need not be performed by scarce and expensive experts."

C. The Evaluation Session

The last ten or fifteen minutes of a discussion meeting should be reserved for an evaluation session. The leader turns the chairmanship over to the observer, who makes suggestions or leads a discussion on how the process of group thinking could have been improved. To avoid hurt feelings or embarrassment the observer should rarely single out members of the group for adverse comment. He should usually call attention to not more than two or three weaknesses or difficulties he has observed, suggesting, in question form, what might have caused them. Group members can then decide whether the shoe fits. Those

[8] Leland P. Bradford, "Planning the Work-Group Conference," *Adult Education Bulletin*, Vol. 12 (February, 1948), pp. 68-73.

desiring individual comments and suggestions for improvement should consult the observer after the meeting.

It is also desirable to have evaluation periods at general conference sessions to acquaint members of one group with what is happening in the others. When the number of groups is small, the observers and recorders can make individual reports. A better procedure is to arrange two panels; one including all observers; the other with the recorders as panel members.

The rôle of the observer in evaluation sessions is quite similar to that of the critic judge in forensic contests. Both try to help the speakers to do better next time; both aim to help listeners recognize varying degrees of skill in a special type of performance. The main difference is that the observer does not usually present awards or declare winners.

IV. CONDUCTING DISCUSSION CONTESTS

In early attempts to adapt discussion to the intercollegiate forensic program, the contest element was generally omitted. The purpose was to divert the participant's attention from winning (winning was supposedly bad) and free him to think coöperatively about the discussion problem. Unfortunately, this freedom often resulted in inadequate preparation. The student knew that he was free to speak only when he wanted to; in some cases he could sit through a session without saying anything if he so desired. Students who made adequate preparation, as far as studying the topic was concerned, had no yardstick by which to measure their performance and received no recognition for their contribution to the success of the discussions.

To meet this situation, those who conduct intercollegiate discussions usually provide an observer-judge who offers suggestions on the discussion procedure and rates each participant on a scale similar to the Discussion Evaluation Blank shown on page 306.

The Evaluation Blank can be used in both non-competitive and contest situations. In conferences and tournaments where each speaker engages in a number of discussions, recognition can be given to those with the highest cumulative scores. The ratings should be distributed after each meeting, so that participants can try to remedy their weaknesses as the series progresses.

Elsewhere in this book, we describe legislative sessions and intercollegiate conferences that usually combine discussion and debate.

306 DISCUSSION AND DEBATE

There are, however, a number of intercollegiate forensic events that are limited to discussion. Two examples are included here.

DISCUSSION EVALUATION BLANK

Score each speaker from one to five on each of the five evaluation points described below. The significance of the scores is indicated on the linear scale.

1	2	3	4	5
Poor	Below Average	Fair	Good	Excellent

I. *Information about the problem.* (Breadth, accuracy and use of information.)

II. *Analysis of problem.* (Sensing problem's importance; finding the issues; avoiding irrelevant matters.)

III. *Ability to think coöperatively.* (Open-mindedness; alertness; willingness to abandon weak arguments; ability to synthesize contributions of others.)

IV. *Skill in speaking.* (Adapting voice, action and language to occasion; ability to state ideas clearly and briefly.)

V. *Good manners.* (Listening attentively; quoting others accurately; giving others a chance to speak; general courtesy.)

Speaker	A	B	C	D	E	F
I. Information						
II. Analysis						
III. Coöperative Thinking						
IV. Speaking Skill						
V. Good Manners						
Score						

A. The University of Alabama Discussion Conference

This event begins Thursday evening with a symposium in which prominent authorities speak on the question, and adjourns Saturday noon, after listening to reports from the various discussion groups. Participants are divided into groups of six; each group engages in six discussions on different phases of the central problem. A statement of the sub-topics is sent to each entering school several weeks before the conference. The personnel of the groups remains the same throughout the series. Each member takes his turn at leading the discussion. Critic judges hand in ratings at the conclusion of each meeting.

B. The University of Wisconsin Discussion Contest

This event is a combination of extemporaneous speaking and informal discussion. An outline of the problem is sent to all participating schools a month before the event. Each school may enter four contestants. Each discussion includes six students from as many different institutions. Two hours before the first discussion the speakers draw topics, phases of the central problem on which they prepare four-minute speeches. The meetings resemble the symposium-forum; the six speeches are followed by informal discussion. The personnel of the groups is changed, and the speakers draw different topics for each meeting. Wisconsin students, familiar with the discussion method, serve as chairmen. Critic judges rate the participants; the six with the highest combined scores appear in a final public discussion.

READINGS

ALLEN, H. B., "Film Forums: An Experiment in Community Education," *Quarterly Journal of Speech*, Vol. 31 (October, 1945), pp. 300-3.

BENNE, K. D., BRADFORD, L. K., and LIPPITT, Ronald, *Group Dynamics and Social Action* (New York, Anti-Defamation League of B'nai B'rith, 1950.)

BRADFORD, L. P., "Leading the Large Meeting," *Adult Education Bulletin*, Vol. 14 (December, 1949), pp. 38-50.

———, "Planning the Work-Group Conference," *Adult Education Bulletin*, Vol. 12 (February, 1948), pp. 68-73.

BROWN, J. M., "Are There Any Questions?" *Atlantic Monthly*, Vol. 168 (November, 1941), pp. 605-9.

DICKERMAN, Watson, and DAVIS, Marjorie, "The San Francisco Nursing Education Conference," *Adult Education Bulletin*, Vol. 12 (February, 1948), pp. 82-7.

GUNDERSON, R. G., "Group Dynamics—Hope or Hoax?" *Quarterly Journal of Speech*, Vol. 36 (February, 1950), pp. 34-8.

HERRING, J. W., "Forums and How to Run Them," *Adult Education Bulletin*, Vol. 1 (June, 1936), pp. 7-10.

JENKINS, D. H., "Feedback and Self-Evaluation," *Journal of Social Issues*, Vol. 4 (Spring, 1948), pp. 50-60.

KELMAN, H. C., "Group Dynamics—Neither Hope Nor Hoax," *Quarterly Journal of Speech*, Vol. 36 (October, 1950), pp. 371-7.

LIPPITT, Ronald, "Group Self-Analysis of Productivity in the Work Conference," *Adult Education Bulletin*, Vol. 12 (February, 1948), pp. 74-9.

——, *Training in Community Relations* (New York, Harper & Bros., 1949), Chaps. 1-3.

LASKER, Bruno, *Democracy Through Discussion* (New York, H. W. Wilson Co., 1949), Chap. 7.

PARKER, C. S., "Leading a Horse to Water," *Atlantic Monthly*, Vol. 165 (March, 1945), pp. 101-6.

RAY, R. F., "The Iowa University Student Senate," *Quarterly Journal of Speech*, Vol. 32 (December, 1946), pp. 454-7.

REES, Etta, "Group Discussion Through Motion Pictures," *Educational Screen*, Vol. 24 (May, 1945), pp. 188-ff.

UTTERBACK, W. E., *Group Thinking and Conference Leadership* (New York, Rinehart and Co., 1949), pp. 169-76.

VAN PELT, J. R., "Lantern Slides and Such," *Quarterly Journal of Speech*, Vol. 36 (February, 1950), pp. 44-50.

EXERCISES

1. Analyze these examples of forum participation quoted from the published transcripts of Town Meeting broadcasts. To conserve space, questions requiring longer answers are omitted.

a. On September 13, 1949, the discussion on "What Are Democracy's Best Answers to Communism?" was broadcast from India. The panel members were: Dr. V. K. Rao, director of New Delhi University's School of Economics; Mrs. Renuka Ray, vice-president of the All-India Womens' Conference; Mrs. Edith Sampson, Chicago attorney and president of the National Council of Negro Women; and Mr. Wilson C. Hemingway, past president of the American Banker's Association.

Man: Mr. Hemingway, don't you think that what democracy has achieved in a century, Communists can achieve in ten years?

Mr. Hemingway: I don't think they want to achieve it.

Man: Mrs. Ray, wouldn't it be better if, instead of quantity, quality was to rule the country?

Mrs. Ray: I think it better that quantity should have its say and quality should represent quantity.

Man: Mrs. Sampson, are you alarmed by the spread of communism?

Mrs. Sampson: Not in America. I don't think it has a ghost of a show in America.

Man: Mrs. Sampson, what is America going to do to abolish the veto power of the Big Five.

Mr. Denny: I think that isn't Mrs. Sampson's question. It's probably Dr. Rao's question.

Dr. Rao: I think America is trying her best to do this but she can't succeed as long as the charter of the United Nations stands.

b. The topic on October 11, 1949, was "Should Labor Be Subject to Anti-Trust Laws?" The panel members were: Harry Bridges, head of the Longshoreman's Union, C.I.O.; Almon Roth, president of the San Francisco Employers Council; Shelden Elliot, dean of University of Southern California's Law School; and Alexander Schullman, A. F. of L. attorney.

Man: Dean Elliott, what would you substitute for the right to strike?

Dean Elliott: I wouldn't substitute anything for the right to strike. I would simply make it subject to reasonable regulation in the public interest.

Lady: Mr. Bridges, are you in favor of any regulation of labor unions? If so, what regulations?

Mr. Bridges: It would depend.... That's a general statement and pretty hard to answer generally. But I certainly am in favor of some regulation. If you ask me to spell it out, I might get stuck at the moment. For example, I certainly believe that labor unions should be so regulated that someone couldn't steal all of the funds out of the treasury....

Mr. Roth: I'd like to ask Mr. Bridges very pointedly whether he believes that the longshoremen who went up from Portland to The Dalles and threw the pineapples into the bay and injured three men, should be subject to the law....

Mr. Bridges: I think the law is still functioning in Oregon. I understand that proper investigations are being made. You're not going to get me up here to attack my own organization. I've got to be elected you know, once in a while.

c. The Town Meeting discussed "What Should Be the Liberal Program Now?", November 15, 1949. The panel members were: Paul H. Douglas, Democratic Senator from Illinois; Dore Schary, vice-president of Metro-Goldwyn-Mayer; John D. Lodge, Republican Congressman from Connecticut; and Philip Willkie, representing the Republican Senatorial Campaign Committee.

Man: Mr. Schary, I'd like to ask you should not liberals oppose all attempts at censorship of the movies by organized pressure groups?

Mr. Schary: Yes, I think that the liberals should oppose, and have constantly opposed censorship.

Mr. Denny: The gentleman wants to talk back. Yes sir?

Man: In that connection, I wonder what your stand would be in reference to the Hollywood ten who were fired and blacklisted from the movie industry because of the pressure of the House

Un-American Activities Committee. How would you fit that in with your explanation here?

Mr. Schary: Your facts are wrong. I don't think that this discussion has room for a complete discussion of the Hollywood investigation, but your facts are wrong.

Man: Well, that's a matter of opinion.

Mr. Schary: Yes, it is.

Man: My question is addressed to Mr. Willkie. What should be the position of the liberals with respect to future relations with Franco's Spain?

Mr. Willkie: Well, I would say the minimum possible relations.

d. Here is a brief interchange from the October 25, 1949, discussion on "What Should the Free World Do about the Atomic Bomb?"

Man: Since Russia refuses to come to terms with us on the atomic bomb, what is your solution to the problem?

Mr. Denny: Well, that's just what he suggested in his speech.

Man: I want to know more about it.

Mr. Denny: You want to know more—I'm afraid that's putting him on the spot and asking him to make another speech. Let's take the next question up there in the balcony.

2. Make a short speech reporting on one of the suggested readings.

3. Organize a leadership team for one of your class discussions.

4. Use rôle-playing in a class discussion, and give your opinion of its effectiveness.

5. Conduct an informal discussion on the values and weaknesses of special discussion methods.

6. If possible, conduct a film forum on a current problem.

CHAPTER 18

Informal Group Discussion

THE MOST COMMON characteristics of this type of discussion are the limited size of the groups, the comparative absence of set speeches, and the assumption that members share equally in the meeting and in responsibility for its outcome. By informal group discussion we mean the conversation that takes place when not more than fifteen or twenty persons talk about a topic of mutual interest under the guidance of a member serving as leader for that occasion. Members come expecting to take an active part; there are no spectators and no one is set apart as an authority on the topic.

This type of meeting should be held in surroundings conducive to relaxation and informality. The chairs should be so arranged that each member can see every other member. Some typical arrangements are these:

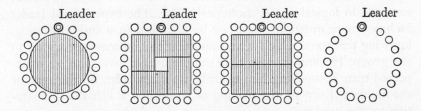

The spirit of informality is emphasized if everyone, including the chairman, remains seated while speaking. Members should refer to each other by name, by first names as they get acquainted. Individual contributions should be short. Unless certain members have been assigned to report on some phase of the topic, the "speeches" should seldom exceed a minute in length. The transcripts of many informal discussions show a little more than three participations a minute. Informal discussions may be profitably held in groups of six or eight interested members. If more than twenty attend it is practically impossible to maintain the spirit of informality and to include everyone in the conversation.

The primary purpose of informal group discussions is to share information about the topic. Members should have some items of information to share with others; thus each member learns from the others and compares his opinions with theirs. If the group finds that it has little or no information on the topic, the discussion should be adjourned until this defect can be remedied. Discussion is informal talk, but it should be informed talk.

Sometimes members of an informal discussion group devote a number of meetings to a problem until they agree on a solution. Sometimes the issue may be one on which only individual action is needed: "Should I join the YMCA?" or "Should I take out more life insurance? Sometimes there may be no immediate need for action; often, the group will have no power to act. In the latter event, it may communicate its recommendations to those who do have such authority.

I. THE LEADER'S PREPARATION

In addition to the general preparation described in the preceding chapter, the leader should prepare a discussion outline, plan for group participation, and prepare his introductory statement.

1. *Making an outline.* The leader should come to the meeting with a plan or outline. Such outlines usually consist of a series of questions, arranged in logical or psychological order. The experienced leader includes more questions than can be discussed in a single meeting, knowing that some which seem important to him may not appeal to the group. He knows, too, that the discussion may take an unexpected turn, compelling him to make up a new plan on the spur of the moment. Even so, the making of an outline is valuable preparation for the meeting.

The experienced leader also knows that the same general procedure can be followed in discussing various questions. Such an outline, based on the normal steps in thinking through a problem, is given below. It is unlikely, of course, that more than one or two of these steps can be adequately considered in a single session.

This general outline may be used in preparing to lead other types of discussions.

GENERAL DISCUSSION OUTLINE

I. *What is the nature and extent of the problem?*
  A. What background information is necessary to an understanding of the problem?
  B. What is the specific question to be decided?
  C. How serious is the problem?
  D. What factors must be considered in deciding on a solution?

II. *What solutions are proposed?*
  A. What are the advantages of each proposed solution?
  B. What are the disadvantages?

III. *What is the group's initial reaction?*
  A. On what points does the group substantially agree?
  B. What are the chief differences?
    1. On matters of fact?
    2. On matters of opinion?
  C. How fundamental are these differences?

IV. *Which solution, or combination of solutions, seems best?*
  A. Can a compromise be reached that will meet with general approval?
  B. If not, which solution, after debate, is favored by a majority?

V. *How may the chosen solution be made effective?*
  A. What can this group do?
  B. What can I do?

On the next page is a sample outline on "What can we do about death on the highway?" It was prepared for a group already familiar with the nature and extent of the problem; it began, therefore, at the stage of examining possible solutions. The leader phrased it in questions which he could throw out to the group. He was prepared to break the outline down into even smaller units or to omit some parts if they failed to interest the participants.

2. *Planning for general participation.* If group members know the procedures, and each other, little advance preparation is needed. Someone will begin talking as soon as he gets the chance. But if the members don't know what is expected of them, they are likely to do nothing for fear of doing the wrong thing. In such cases, the leader

may well take steps to avoid that awkward pause after his opening statement when everyone waits for someone else to break the ice. He may distribute brief items about the topic and have them read at the beginning of the meeting. He may ask two or three members to be ready to volunteer questions or brief comments if the pause develops. Once the conversation starts and the members are convinced that their experiences and opinions are really wanted, group participation is assured.

SAMPLE DISCUSSION OUTLINE

I. *Nature and extent of the problem.*
    A. Two-minute summary of information gained at previous meeting.
    B. Can anyone add anything to this?

II. *How can we tackle this problem?*
    A. What about teaching safe driving in our schools?
    B. How can we best approach adult drivers? Men's luncheon clubs? Women's organizations?
    C. What about our local traffic laws? Are they adequate?
    D. Are our traffic laws properly enforced?
    E. Can we suggest other ways of reducing traffic accidents?

III. *What steps should be taken?*
    A. Do we agree on what ought to be done? On the best place to begin?
    B. What can this group do?
    C. What can we do as individuals?

---

3. *Getting discussion started.* A discussion group is seldom equipped with a self starter. The leader should consider how he can get the general discussion started in the first few minutes. What he says, and how long he speaks, depends on the familiarity of the group with the topic and with discussion procedures. Certainly, he must state the topic; he probably should add two or three sentences about its nature and importance. If the members are quite unfamiliar with the problem, the leader, or someone else, should sketch its history. If members don't understand the discussion method, the leader should explain it so they will know what is expected of them, and when. Leaders are more likely to talk too long in getting the meeting started than too briefly.

II. CONDUCTING THE MEETING

Most of the suggestions in the preceding chapter are applicable here. A word of caution about concluding the discussion may be needed. The leader should not wait until everyone is talked out so the meeting adjourns with an anti-climax. He should note the tempo and spirit of the discussion and adjourn while the interest is still high. It is generally advisable to announce the length of the meeting in advance and stop at the time set for adjournment.

A concise summary will help send the members away with a feeling that the experience has been fruitful, and that it might be a good idea to attend the next meeting.

III. PARTICIPATING IN INFORMAL DISCUSSION

Since members of informal discussion groups may speak or keep silent as they choose, they do not have the incentive to prepare for the meeting that would result from a definite speaking assignment. They may read newspaper stories or magazine articles on the topic that come their way but will probably not make a trip to the library. They may even jot down any ideas that occur to them but are not likely to think much about the question.

The absence of specific immediate preparation, however, does not necessarily mean the lack of real materials for discussion. If the topic is well chosen, some members may have had first hand experiences of importance. Parents of college students do not have to go to the library for materials on the effects of college on their children. Things that the individual has observed, articles or books that he has read months before, may constitute real preparation. When Webster said that he was twenty years in preparing his reply to Hayne he meant he had been thinking about the relation of the states to the federal government for twenty years; the immediate preparation for the speech was limited to a very few hours. Preparation may be no less real because it is not immediate; not all evidence of value is to be found neatly catalogued in the *Readers' Guide*.

The next step is to consider what takes place during an informal discussion. From a general picture of the meeting, the role of the individual can be determined. The usual procedure at informal discussions is apt to follow a sequence of events something like this:

The first person to speak after the leader's opening statement is likely to do one or more of these things:

a. Ask a question about the meaning of some term used in introducing the problem, or about the meaning of the problem itself.

b. Ask a question about the purpose of the meeting, or what type of evidence is sought.

c. Give a bit of information or state his own position on the point raised by the leader.

d. Ask someone in the group for his opinion on the first point.

Simpson says that each comment made by the second, and by all subsequent speakers, will fall into one of these categories:[1]

a. A rebuttal of the preceding point of view.

b. The introduction of new information or evidence.

c. The reiteration of an opinion previously stated by someone else.

d. The admission of a changed point of view or shift of opinion.

e. The recognition of evidence presented by a member of the group, but accompanied by a different conclusion.

f. A question concerning the accuracy or meaning of a particular bit of evidence.

g. An expression of a desire to crystallize the group decision and conclude the discussion of the particular problem involved.

h. A citing of the opinion of an expert.

i. The citing of some case favoring the viewpoint of the speaker.

This outline tells what the individual may contribute to a discussion. It does not tell him when to speak, how long or how often. Only the most general advice can be given on these points. It seems obvious that the proper time for a member to speak is when he can add something to the point under discussion. It seems equally obvious that the member who knows a good deal about the topic should speak more often than his neighbor whose knowledge is more limited. The spirit of equality need not extend to equal time allotments.

Transcripts of informal discussions indicate that the average length of individual "speeches" is from fifteen to twenty seconds or from thirty to fifty words. This does not mean that each individual contribution is just that long; some are single words or fragments of sentences; others are a minute or more in length. It does mean that each statement should be as brief and concise as the speaker can make it on the spur of the moment.

[1] Ray H. Simpson, *A Study of Those Who Influence and of Those Who Are Influenced by Discussion* (New York, 1938), p. 8. By permission of Bureau of Publications, Teachers College, Columbia University.

Members of informal groups can add greatly to the clarity of the discussion by using phrases or sentences relating what they are about to say to what has just been said, or by making it plain that they are shifting the conversation to another point, for example:

"I disagree with Mr. Blank's statement about the effect of capital punishment on other criminals, I believe..."
"Here is another definition of propaganda. Professor Lasswell says..."
"I wonder if I may go back to the first part of what you said..."
"Do you mean by that statement that a teacher must be a person without any convictions at all?"
"That leads me back to a question we raised at the beginning of the hour..."
"I don't know whether this is quite on the point, but I was thinking..."
"Not only do we have the right to object to propaganda whose source is hidden, but..."

Professor Sheffield has listed some of the individuals who are not popular members of discussion groups:[2]

1. The member who is always quoting one source, i.e., her husband, the Constitution, Karl Marx....
2. The person with an emotional fixation on some idea or panacea which turns him off the main line of thought whenever the pet idea is touched on.
3. The nervously loquacious person who keeps adding to what he (she) has said, seemingly unable either to improve on the first statement or to stop.
4. The silent member who sits glumly through the meeting and pronounces judgment to all who will listen after the meeting is over.
5. The watch-in-hand member, and the person who gets up and leaves in the middle of the meeting.
6. The person with a prejudice against discussing a certain subject, using a certain word.
7. The historically minded member who wants to read all the history into the record.
8. The member who constantly urges people to "be simple" in approaching the most complicated problem.

IV. THE COÖPERATIVE INVESTIGATION

How can members of a discussion group profitably consider topics on which they have little information? Of course, the first step must be to provide this information in a manner that will not too greatly

[2] A. D. Sheffield, *Training for Group Experience* (New York, The Inquiry, 1929), pp. 81-2.

interfere with the informality of the meeting. One way of doing this has been called the "coöperative investigation." [3]

The subject is chosen well in advance of the meeting. The leader meets with several members who have agreed to take part in a preliminary investigation. The subject is divided into a number of subtopics, and each member undertakes to find information on one of these points. The discussion meeting then begins with a pooling of this information in the form of brief reports, so arranged as to provide an orderly consideration of the problem. The leader asks other members of the group to add any information they have gained from their own reading, observation, or direct experience. Aside from the reports of the investigators, the procedure is the same as for the informal group discussion.

Experience indicates a word of caution. It is easy to provide more information than the group can assimilate. A discussion that begins with masses of undigested evidence may fail just as completely as one that lacks information. The investigators should present their findings in a form as simple as is consistent with accuracy. The leader should first make clear the need of information on various points and then introduce the person who has that information. Group members may be given an opportunity to ask questions after each report, but the main body of the discussion should come after all of the reports have been given. At least half of the time should be reserved for this part of the discussion.

READINGS

BACON, F. L., "Improving Secondary Education Through Group Discussion," *School and Society*, Vol. 44 (December, 1936), pp. 236-41; also Vol. 46 (August, 1937), pp. 225-31.

BAIRD, A. C., *Discussion: Principles and Types* (New York, McGraw-Hill Book Co., Inc., 1943), Chap. 14.

BOGARDUS, E., and WILLIAMS, Chester, *Democracy by Discussion* (Washington, American Council on Public Affairs, 1942).

CAMPBELL, C. M., "The Rôle of the Chairman in Group Discussion," *Adult Education Bulletin*, Vol. 9 (June, 1945), pp. 135-ff.

CHAMBERLAIN, N. W., "Group Discussion and Collective Bargaining," *Adult Education Bulletin*, Vol. 9 (June, 1945), pp. 135-ff.

FANSLER, Thomas, *Discussion Methods for Adult Groups* (New York, American Association for Adult Education, 1934), Part 2.

[3] A. F. Wileden and H. L. Ewbank, *How to Conduct Group Discussion* (Madison, University of Wisconsin Extension Division, 1935).

GARLAND, J. V., and PHILLIPS, C. F., *Discussion Methods* (New York, H. W. Wilson Co., 1940), pp. 17-64.
HARDY, R. Q., "Group Discussion," *Education*, Vol. 68 (September, 1947), pp. 24-8.
Learning Through Group Discussion (Columbus, Ohio, Junior Town Meeting League, 1949).
The Story of A Discussion Program (New York, New York Adult Education Council, 1946).
UTTERBACK, W. E., *Decision Through Discussion* (New York *Times*, 1946).
———, "The Political Significance of Group Discussion," *Annals of American Academy of Political and Social Science*, Vol. 250 (March, 1947), pp. 32-40.
WAGNER, R. A., and ARNOLD, C. C., *Handbook of Group Discussion* (Boston, Houghton Mifflin Co., 1950), Chaps. 6-8.

EXERCISES

1. Make a four-minute speech based on one of the suggested readings.
2. Prepare to lead an informal group discussion. Hand in your choice of topic and your plan for the meeting.
3. Do the same for a coöperative investigation.
4. Record an informal discussion. Analyze the types of group participation, noting especially the leader's rôle in the meeting.
5. Make a short persuasive speech designed to secure members for a discussion group.
6. Make a four-minute speech on one of the following topics:
   a. The socialized recitation
   b. The Socratic dialogue
   c. The use of evidence in informal discussion
   d. What is a good discussion?
   e. The members who don't take part
   f. The New England town meeting

CHAPTER **19**

Committee and Conference Discussion

EXCEPT FOR occasional public hearings, committee and conference sessions are *private*, rather than *public* meetings. They resemble group discussion in the limited number of participants and the informality of procedure. They differ in that members represent organizations and are chosen to discuss a specific problem. They differ from each other in respects that will be considered in this chapter. The conference, especially, should play an increasingly important rôle in our society as we learn to substitute reason for force in settling our controversies.

I. COMMITTEE DISCUSSION

Every organization, from the days of the New England town meetings to the present, from the community club to our national legislature, makes frequent use of committees. Appointing a committee is the parliamentary procedure of assigning to a few members of an organization tasks that cannot be efficiently performed by the entire group. It would be a waste of man power for a hundred people to attempt the drafting of a constitution or for our House of Representatives to frame a tax bill in general session. Any member may make suggestions to the committee and join in the debate when its report is before the organization for action.

The essential facts about committee procedure are these: (1) the committee is authorized by the parent organization and is responsible to it; (2) the committee's powers and duties are defined in the legislation creating it, or by the organization's constitution and by-laws; (3) these powers range from supplying information about a problem, or recommending a course of action, to acting for the group within limits set by the parent organization.

A. Committee Membership

Committees that represent organizations are either appointed by the presiding officer or elected by the membership. The first method should result in a better-balanced committee; the second may be more democratic.

Committees with power to act are appointed to carry out a plan or project already authorized by the association. They should usually consist of not more than three persons chosen from those who favor the project. Members should be selected on the basis of their efficiency and dependability, as well as their ability to work together.

The deliberative committee, authorized to investigate a problem and recommend a course of action, should be set up on a different basis. Certainly it should include representatives of various interests and points of view; sometimes geographical considerations are important. For some problems there should be a combination of men and women, of youth and age, of new members and those who know the organization's history and traditions. Depending on the task assigned, it may be wise to have representatives of various political, social, racial, and religious organizations.

The deliberative committee should be large enough to represent the different groups interested in the problem. This may mean as many as nine or eleven members. Qualifications for membership should include knowledge of, or interest in, the investigation, willingness to do the work and to coöperate with other members. Trouble is likely to develop if the committee includes individuals who actively dislike each other, or too many who would like to be chairman.

In 1945, our State Department appointed a committee to formulate a policy on the use and control of atomic energy. The committee devoted its first session to a discussion of committee procedures. One member wrote, ". . . even before we studied the problem of atomic energy we studied committee techniques" and what the reasons were which made the committee system "fail so often or come up so frequently with sterile compromises." The committee noted that committees often fail because "members come to their job with fully formed conclusions . . . and spend their time proposing and exhorting rather than listening and considering." To avoid this, the members agreed that they would liberate all discussions from "idea possessiveness." Questions were considered as coming from the group as a whole; objections to any one point were regarded as something that troubled the entire committee. The committee virtually lived together during the two months required to produce the report. One member wrote, "You might call this a sort of research for individual and group objectivity.... We were trying to create a collective wisdom."[1]

The sponsoring committees have a still different purpose. They are mainly useful for their publicity value, on the theory that, if names make news, big names make big news. To that end, members are chosen for their prestige and their willingness to endorse the project. Their chief duties are to advise the smaller working committee and sometimes to make public appearances in support of the undertaking. Their names appear on stationery and in publicity releases. Sponsoring committees may be much larger than deliberative or action committees, large enough to include representatives of all important groups and interests.

B. The Committee Chairman

When he appoints the committee, the presiding officer usually designates the chairman. If he does not, the individual whose name appears first may serve in that capacity. When the committee is elected, some organizations provide that the chairman is the one receiving the largest number of votes. In other groups, the committee elects its chairman.

Whatever the method of choice, the chairman should be selected quite as much for his knowledge of the problem under investigation as for his mastery of discussion methods. The chairman who retains his position for a number of years, as in the case of many legislative assemblies, comes to have great influence over legislation. The seniority rule whereby the member of the party in power who has served longest on a committee automatically becomes its chairman does not necessarily insure an able leader. Nor does the practice of some organizations in naming as chairman the maker of the motion creating the committee.

1. *Preparing for the committee meeting.* The committee chairman's first official duty is usually to call an organization meeting. If

---

[1] Norman Cousins and Thomas Finletter, "The Beginnings of Sanity," *Saturday Review of Literature*, Vol. 29 (June 15, 1946), pp. 5, 38.

the members are not acquainted with each other, some type of social gathering should precede the business sessions.

In preparation for his duties the chairman should (*a*) get a copy of the legislation creating the committee so he will know the nature and extent of the assignment, (*b*) draw up a tentative outline of the work required to complete the project, and (*c*) learn the interests and abilities of each member. His plan should not be imposed upon the committee. It should be offered as a suggestion, along with others, for consideration by the committee. In many cases individuals or sub-committees, will be appointed to conduct different phases of the investigation. The chairman should be willing to do his full share of the work and to study aspects of the questions that do not interest other members.

2. *Conducting the committee meetings.* Committee meetings should be informal, following the pattern described for the informal group discussion. The chairman speaks on equal terms with the others. He should not attempt to dominate his colleagues or to run the meeting to suit himself. He should see that the committee keeps working toward its goal, that due attention is given to the contributions of each member and to the consideration of each proposal. Members should not commit themselves on controversial points until they have examined the available evidence. When this has been done, differences of opinion as to the action to be recommended should be discussed frankly. If these differences are not resolved, the final report will be formulated after debate and a vote in which the will of the majority determines the action of the committee.

While the committee meeting should properly be conducted as an informal discussion, there are certain specific steps that must be taken if the committee is to fulfill its assignment. In outline form these may resemble the agenda for a more formal parliamentary meeting, but they may also be adapted informally to committee discussions. In some instances, committees hold several meetings before accomplishing their tasks, as is implied by some of the items in the agenda which follows.

1. Call meeting to order; roll call, etc. (Appoint a secretary if it is the first meeting.)
2. Reports of subcommittees. (Not applicable at the first meeting.)
3. Review of committee objectives: a statement of purpose and the scope of inquiry.

4. Establishment of committee procedure: the plan of attack.
5. Analysis of the problem for discussion, including consideration of "movable" and "immovable" factors, i.e., those about which something may be done, and those factors which are fixed.
6. Establishment of criteria: minimum essentials for any acceptable solution.
7. Examination of possible solutions.
8. Evaluation of proposed solutions by applying established criteria.
9. Decision: committee action.
10. Planning method of presenting the committee report.
11. Preparation of the committee report.
12. Review of the committee's procedure: analysis and evaluation for future guidance.
13. Adjournment.

To avoid action without the consideration of majority and minority opinions, the rules of legislative assemblies provide for representation of both major parties on committees. This procedure should be followed by other organizations. It can then be assumed that the committee report represents an effort to harmonize different interests and points of view. If this effort has failed, the minority may propose amendments or offer a minority report when the matter is considered in the assembly.

The committee should appoint a secretary to summarize discussions and record any tentative conclusions that may be reached. These reports serve the same purpose as the summaries made by the leader in informal group discussions. Actual voting on sections of the report should be deferred to the last committee session. With the exception of the motion to adjourn, the motion to adopt the report is the only formal parliamentary action required of the committee.

3. *Reporting committee action.* The report to the parent organization is usually given by the committee chairman who explains it and moves its adoption. He may call on committee members to explain and defend sections with which they are most familiar. By giving credit to others he will gain more favorable recognition than if he tries to claim it all for himself.

II. CONFERENCE DISCUSSION

The term *conference* has been used to include such diverse occasions as an interview with the boss on "When do I get a raise?" and public gatherings with a program of speeches dealing with different aspects of a topic. Neither of these represents the type of meeting we are here considering. The conference, as we use the term, consists of delegates representing various organizations who meet to consider a mutual problem and, if possible, to agree upon a course of action. Sometimes the delegates have power to act within fixed limits. More often they are instructed to present a point of view and to report the conference findings to the groups they represent.

The purpose of a conference may be (*a*) to settle disputes, (*b*) to formulate a joint course of action, or (*c*) to share information without regard to its immediate use. Delegates from churches, schools and governmental agencies might confer on the causes of juvenile delinquency and conclude with a statement of their findings. Delegates from various religious denominations might hold a conference that produces a plan for combined operations in rural areas. We may have local conferences on improving the public schools; national conferences on our treatment of minority groups; and international conferences on ways of increasing understanding among nations.

A. Calling the Conference

Conferences do not just happen. Someone must sense the need and be willing to do a great deal of preliminary planning. The person who furnishes the motive power may be called the organizer, to distinguish him from the chairman, who is usually chosen at the first conference session. If the organizer belongs to one of the groups invited to participate in the conference, others may feel that he and his organization will try to claim the lion's share of the credit for the enterprise. This may be avoided by forming a voluntary committee, with representatives of various groups, to participate in the planning and join in issuing a "call" for the conference. This call should include the reasons for the meeting, a statement of the problem, the bases for inviting organizations and selecting delegates, and a tentative outline of the program. The tentative nature of the outline should be emphasized. Conference members may wish to amend it as the discussions progress, but even in its preliminary form it gives the invited organizations a basis for deciding whether they wish to accept and, if so, the type of delegate that will best represent them.

B. Determining the Size

The purpose of the meetings and the number of organizations interested in the problem should determine the size of the conference. Although it is true that not more than twelve or fifteen people can think together efficiently without a tendency for the less vocal members to become an audience, it is equally true that other considerations often make it advisable to invite a much larger number of delegates. Conferences to settle specific disputes are usually organized in multiples of three, representing equally the two parties in controversy and the public, with nine or twelve as the maximum membership. On the other hand, a state rural leaders' conference has been known to run efficiently with forty-five to fifty delegates. Conferences of United Nation's organizations cannot be small even if each nation sends a single delegate. The best procedure in such case is to form committees, and even sub-committees, assigning each a specific task.

C. Qualifications of Conference Members

Before the conference members or delegates are chosen, the officers of the participating organizations should be sure that they understand the nature and purpose of the meeting. If the conference is to make a preliminary investigation of a problem, knowledge of the subject should be the most important qualification. If the purpose is to agree upon a policy or to draw plans for a joint enterprise, delegates should also be familiar with the traditions and practices of the organization they represent. If the conference is called to settle a controversy, delegates should be emotionally stable. The ability to state an argument and maintain a position without calling names or questioning the good faith of opponents is of the greatest importance. Otherwise the meeting may increase the hostility and ill will instead of laying the foundation for mutual understanding.

In accepting their assignment, the delegates should inquire into the nature and extent of their authority. When the conference is to make a preliminary investigation of a problem, there is little occasion for misunderstanding. The delegates will contribute the information at their disposal and will join in the discussion as to possible next steps. But if the conference prepares a formal report or plan of action the situation is different. Unless the delegates are specifically authorized to act for the association, they will present the conference report at the next meeting of their association and move its adoption. In the discussion on the motion they should present the arguments for and against the conference proposal. In this respect their duties resemble those of the deliberative committee.

A successful conference is more likely if the delegates are about equal in prestige, knowledge of the problem, ability to think quickly, and skill in extemporaneous speaking. These qualifications should be accompanied by willingness to consider opposing arguments and a desire to arrive at a solution acceptable, if not satisfactory, to all.

D. The Rôle of the Conference Chairman

The chairmanship of a conference is often the most exacting assignment confronting a discussion leader. Even when there is no particular hostility among the groups represented, there is the problem of getting them to work together. The opening sessions may well require all the skill the discussion leader possesses, plus tact and a willingness to make haste slowly.

Conferences that attempt to settle disputes offer both the greatest challenge and the greatest difficulty. This is likely to be true when the delegates have no experience with the discussion method of talking things over and arriving at a conclusion based on the evidence. It is especially true when the conflict has reached the fighting stage, with each side announcing its demands and denouncing the opposition. When this happens, even the most skilled leader may be able to do little until emotions subside and the groups are willing to accept a face-saving solution that each can claim as at least a partial victory.

The United States Conciliation Service notes that there are three stages in management-labor relationships: the organizational stage, the fighting stage, and the coöperative stage. This agency believes that conferences held when the first signs of a dispute appear on the horizon can largely eliminate the fighting stage. To that end, it offers to labor and management the services of skilled conference leaders. The advice to deal early with causes of disputes applies equally to relationships among community groups. The leadership of these local conferences will normally be drawn from the community.

The first order of business at a conference is usually the election of a chairman. The conference organizer normally knows more than anyone else about the purpose and plan of the meetings. If he is equally informed about discussion methods, and skilled in their use, he is the obvious choice for the chairmanship. In the interests of efficiency the conference chairman should preside at all sessions. But sometimes, to avoid charges of prejudice, it is wise to alternate the chairmanship among leaders of the various delegations, even though the thought process is interrupted while the group gets acquainted with the new moderator and he gets acquainted with his task.

E. Preparing for the Conference Meetings

The conference often brings together some who are not acquainted and some who actively dislike each other. Under such circumstances, much depends on what happens before the first business session. These suggestions have been helpful in getting conferences off to a good start:

1. If possible, delegates should be housed in the same hotel with arrangements for taking their meals and their recreation together. What happens between sessions may be fully as important as what takes place in the meetings.
2. Hold the sessions on neutral grounds so the relationship of host and guest will not put either side at a disadvantage.
3. Begin the conference with a luncheon or dinner. Arrange the place cards so the members of a delegation will not sit together. People find it harder to hate each other after they have eaten together.
4. The organizer should see that the conference room is so arranged that hostile groups do not sit on opposite sides of the room facing each other. If the group is small enough to be seated about a table, such a tendency can be overcome by the use of place cards. If the table is round, no one can complain that he is seated at the foot and his favorite enemy at the head.

A large conference, such as the UNESCO meeting at San Francisco, May 13-15, 1948, requires careful advance preparation. The convening committee met in all-day session, April 19, phrased the conference theme, "How can I help meet the world crisis with understanding?" and decided that it should be a working rather than a listening conference. To that end, the plans called for sub-conferences on Education, Communication, Human and Social Relations, Cultural Relations, and Natural Science. Information on these problems was sent to each delegate. The schedule included a series of three discussion meetings on each topic, periods when the discussion sections were divided into small groups in which everyone could speak, and plenary sessions to act on reports from the five "sub-conferences." Discussion teams were chosen, each consisting of a leader, a recorder, an observer and a subject matter specialist. The topics for the three discussion meetings were: (1) analyzing and defining the problem; (2) considering available methods or tools; (3) discovering ways of using these effectively. Suggestions on participating in group discussion were distributed to each delegate. What is most important, the teams met for a full day's training and rehearsal the day before the conference convened. Martin Andersen wrote concerning the use of the discussion method: "Most of the folks who were skeptical about the possibility of developing informal discussion in large groups came away from this conference completely sold on the methods used." [2]

F. Conducting the Conference

Conferences on difficult or controversial issues usually require a number of sessions. In such cases, the first meeting should be devoted to getting acquainted, deciding on procedural matters, and exploring points of agreement. The conference should choose a secretary, whose duties will be to prepare an objective summary of what takes place at each session, to be read at the beginning of the next. Any conclusions recorded should be regarded as tentative. All formal voting on conference findings should be withheld until the last sessions to guard against hasty action and the necessity of reconsidering decisions that no longer seem wise.

At the proper point in the first session the chairman should call for discussion on the tentative outline contained in the call for the conference. This may be amended by the group so long as they do not put the cart before the horse and start considering answers before the questions are understood. The delegates might be encouraged to adopt the general plan with the right to amend it as the situation warrants.

Here, for example, is a general outline, prepared by the United States Conciliation Service, for use in labor-management conferences:

Step I. What is the grievance (or dispute)?
Step II. What are the points of agreement and disagreement (dividing the latter into less controversial and more controversial)?
Step III. Discussion of the less controversial points.
Step IV. Discussion of the more controversial points.

In the case of serious differences, several sessions may be required to arrive at acceptable solutions. The conciliator's life is not always a happy one.

[2] Personal letter, dated November 19, 1948.

The plan for "educational" conferences, like the UNESCO meeting described above, will be quite different. Most of the time may be spent in exchanging information and opinions, leading to recommendations for action to be considered at the last session. The delegates may then urge that the recommended action be taken by the proper agencies.

The procedure at small conferences should be that of the informal group discussion or committee meeting. The larger meetings should be divided into committees or discussion units for at least half of the sessions. The chairman's rôle is that of the discussion leader rather than that of the committee chairman. He must be keenly sensitive to the feelings and prejudices of delegates, willing to spend what seems a disproportionate amount of time in lessening tensions and building good will. He must convince everyone of his fairness and his willingness to follow the facts, wherever they may lead. And when he has done his best only to have the conference end in disagreement, he should remember that results are not always immediately apparent. The meetings may have started the formation of public opinion that will eventually result in favorable action.

III. THE TRAINING CONFERENCE

Within recent years, the "conference method" has been widely adopted by business and industry for employee training programs. Zelko reports the results of a survey he made in 1947:[3]

Of over 100 major industries and 25 large governmental agencies surveyed, at least 90% indicated the conference method as that most used in employee training, and *all* said that the training or instructional conference was the basic method for developing supervisors.

As its name implies, a main purpose of the training conference is to share information, to compare methods of doing a certain job or of handling a difficult problem. Cooper says that the conference method "is universally accepted as the best method available... for training any group of people in subjects in which they have already had practical experience."[4] Beckman agrees, adding that "the conference, properly conducted, provides training which is not

[3] Harold P. Zelko, "The Place of Speech Training in Industry and Government," *Journal of Industrial Training*, Vol. 2 (April, 1947), p. 9.
[4] A. M. Cooper, *How to Conduct Conferences* (New York, McGraw-Hill Book Co., Inc., 1942), p. 5.

usually regarded as such and is therefore welcome...because all share in the teaching as well as in the learning process." [5]

The phrase "properly conducted" should be given special emphasis. Beckman believes that the failure of training programs is "so patent as to suggest the imperative need of intensive attention to problems of discussion technique." The Maryland Department of Education believes that well-trained conference leaders are "as essential to a prosperous and secure America as new materials, new inventions, better labor relations, or any other single factor affecting industry today." [6]

The techniques of the training conference are largely those of informal group discussion, with the added requirement that the leader must know the problems and use the language of the group. Workers in industry tend to be uncomfortable in the presence of "those theoretical professors," and to resent the efforts of youngsters fresh from college to tell them how to do their jobs better.

READINGS

Busch, Henry M., *Conference Methods in Industry* (New York, Harper & Bros., 1949).

Cooper, A. M., *How to Conduct Conferences* (New York, McGraw-Hill Book Co., Inc., 1942).

Cushman, F., "The Conference as an Educational Procedure," *Journal of Educational Sociology*, Vol. 12 (September, 1938), pp. 32-8.

Fansler, Thomas, *Creative Power Through Discussion* (New York, Harper & Bros., 1950).

Garland, J. V., and Phillips, C. F., *Discussion Methods* (New York, H. W. Wilson Co., 1940), pp. 61-74, 315-9.

Hannaford, E. S., *Conference Leadership in Business and Industry* (New York, McGraw-Hill Book Co., Inc., 1945).

Heyel, Carl, *Standard Business Conference Technique* (New York, Funk and Wagnalls, 1948).

Maclin, R. S., and McHenry, P. T., *Conference Leader Training* (Deep River, Conn., National Foreman's Institute, 1945).

Poole, D. C., "The Conference Method," *Educational Record*, Vol. 17 (August, 1936), pp. 169-79.

Sorenson, Roy, *The Art of Board Membership* (New York, The Association Press, 1949).

Utterback, W. E., *Group Thinking and Conference Leadership* (New York, Rinehart and Co., 1949), Chaps. 13-14.

[5] R. O. Beckman, *How to Train Supervisors* (New York, Harper & Bros., 1942), p. 15.
[6] *Manual for Conference Leaders* (Baltimore, Dept. of Education, 1945), p. 6.

WALSER, Frank, *The Art of Conference* (New York, Harper & Bros., 1945).

YOUNG, H., "Conference Process," *American Journal of Sociology*, Vol. 46 (March, 1941), pp. 408-17.

ZELKO, H. P., "Training Conference Leaders for Industry and Government," *Southern Speech Journal*, Vol. 14 (March, 1949), pp. 246-57.

EXERCISES

1. Give a four-minute speech based on one of the suggested readings.
2. Prepare a written analysis of a committee you have observed in action.
3. If possible, attend and evaluate a training conference session.
4. Organize the class as a conference on some local problem. Each participating member should represent an organization or an existing point of view.
5. Let four or five members of the class meet as a committee to select topics and leaders for a series of discussions. If possible, have the committee sit at a table in the middle of the room, with the rest of the class in a circle around them. After half an hour, stop the committee discussion and let the observers answer such questions as these: Was there a logical progression of ideas? Did committee members share equally in the meeting? Did the chairman use any special devices to keep the meeting going?
6. Attend a meeting of the city council, the board of education, or some policy forming group, and evaluate their discussion in terms of the principles suggested in this chapter.

CHAPTER 20

Panels and Public Hearings

PANELS AND PUBLIC hearings are types of public discussion. They are held before audiences of varying sizes, most of whose members will be listeners only. Not more than twelve or fifteen participate in the usual forum period. Audience members come because they are interested in the topic or because they want to see what happens when hostile panel or committee members question each other. Both types provide the opportunity for spirited interchanges among participants.

I. PANEL FORUM

The panel was developed by Harry A. Overstreet and first publicized at the 1932 convention of the American Association for Adult Education. The "cast" includes a chairman and from two to four persons with special knowledge of the topic. Seated on a platform so they may be seen and heard by the audience, they carry on a conversation among themselves. They remain seated while speaking and in other ways attempt to create the spirit of informality that characterizes the University of Chicago Round Table and the Northwestern Reviewing Stand. As in informal group discussion, the leader guides the conversation, but in this case the discussion follows an outline previously agreed upon by the participants and, presumably, moves in a more logical fashion. When the panel has established a pattern of discussion, the leader, usually after a brief summary, invites audience members to join in the conversation. It is possible to maintain the spirit of conversation with audiences of about a hundred. The panel is useful with larger groups, though the speaking inevitably becomes more formal.

The panel may be used either to give the audience a better understanding of the problem or to weigh the advantages and disadvantages of proposed solutions. Although it does not give any speaker an opportunity for a unified statement or defense of his position, the panel is an excellent device for creating audience interest and a desire for further information about the issue. One of its chief values lies in giving the audience the experience of witnessing vigorous, but good-tempered, conversation among people with decided differences of opinion, and the opportunity to judge the importance of these differences. Listening to good panel-forums is valuable preparation for those wishing to take part in informal group discussions.

A. Preparing for Panel Discussions

Someone, usually a program committee, must make the usual arrangements for a public meeting. The panel chairman should either be a committee member or be consulted during the advance preparations. His qualifications and duties are, in many respects, similar to those of the leader of informal group discussion. We shall confine ourselves here to the chief differences.

1. *Choosing panel members.* Panel members should be chosen well in advance of the meeting, but after its objective has been determined. They should represent different sources of information or different points of view about the problem. Otherwise, the discussion may be one-sided. They should expect to spend some time in special preparation, including attendance at a preliminary meeting. After this meeting, they should be sure that they have sufficient factual information to support their own contentions and to enable them to comment intelligently on points made by other panel members.

Panel members should have some skill in extemporaneous speaking. Fansler says that those chosen "should be ready thinkers, quick witted, and have the ability to express themselves easily and clearly. The slow, considering type of thinker, the dominating dogmatist, and the facile chatterbox should be avoided." [1] To avoid "loading the panel," the members should have about the same prestige and the same degree of skill in this type of speaking.

2. *Explaining the procedure.* It is important that each panel member have a clear understanding of this type of meeting and of his part in it. This should be item one on the agenda of the planning ses-

[1] Thomas Fansler, *Discussion Methods for Adult Groups* (New York, American Association for Adult Education, 1934), p. 105.

sion, mentioned earlier. Those in charge of the University of Chicago Round Table publish a "Round Table Memorandum" which is sent to all participants in that broadcast series. It contains a statement of objectives, a description of procedures, a list of "do's and don'ts" and a sample outline.

The following rules should be presented and explained at the planning session:

a. There are no formal talks. The method of public conversation is used throughout the meeting.

b. Individual contributions to the conversation should be brief. Four thirty-minute Northwestern Reviewing Stand broadcasts, in 1949, had 71, 73, 87, and 91 separate "speeches," ranging in length from three to about two hundred words.

c. Address your remarks to each other, but speak loudly enough so those in the rear of the room will hear and feel included in the conversation. In this respect, you have the same problem that confronts the actor.

d. You must listen as well as speak. Show by your facial expression and manner that you are paying attention to other panel members. You can hardly expect audience members to be interested if you and your colleagues seem bored or indifferent.

e. Don't sit back and wait to be called on. If two of you try to speak at once, the leader will decide who is to speak first.

f. If you have three points to make, label them, "1, 2, 3."

g. Sometimes direct your remarks to another panel member: "Jones, what would you say about this situation," or "I'll have to disagree with you, Smith, . . ."

h. Help establish your colleagues (and yourself) as authorities on the question: "Jones, you're our expert on labor relations . . . ," "From your ten years in China, Brown, what conclusions . . . ?", "I speak as the only fraternity member on this panel."

The panel members should also be informed in advance about these general procedures:

a. *Seating arrangements.* A seating arrangement similar to that indicated in the diagram is recommended. It enables the panel members to speak to each other and yet seem to speak to the audience. Timid members should not be placed in the end positions, lest they find themselves excluded

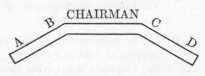

from the conversation. Nor should members holding the same point of view be placed at one side of the chairman.

b. *Length of meeting.* It is difficult to conduct a panel-forum in which there is considerable audience participation in less than an hour. It is hard to hold the attention of audience members for more than an hour and a half. For public meetings, it is wise to set an adjournment time in advance, publicize it, and stick to it.

c. *The forum period.* About half of the time should be reserved for the forum. Panel members should resist the temptation to answer questions at length, or to say something about every speech from the floor.

3. *Preparing the discussion outline.* The rest of the planning session should be devoted to an informal discussion of the topic. As the discussion progresses, the leader should note the points made and the proofs advanced by each panel member. From these, he prepares a tentative outline of the main points which he presents to the group for revision and approval before the meeting adjourns. He assumes responsibility for expanding the outline and sending a copy to each panel member. The outline should be fastened to a larger sheet of paper on which members make notes of data they wish to present, or questions they plan to ask. It is desirable for the panel team to hold a brief session just before the public meeting to re-check the outline, making changes to bring it up to date, and to review the leader's plan for getting the discussion off to a good start.

Below is a sample outline, prepared for a discussion of the housing problem. An approximate time allotment is stated for each major sub-topic and the name of the panel member who is responsible for introducing each point is given.

WHAT CAN BE DONE ABOUT NEW HOUSING IN MIDDLETOWN?
Participants: Brown, Smith, Jones
Total Time: approximately 36 minutes

I. *Introduction* (not more than 5 minutes).
   A. Conversation recently overheard (Jones).
   B. Results of Chamber of Commerce survey of present housing (Smith).
   C. Future development of the community depends upon new housing (Brown).

II. *Is the principal need for privately-owned homes or for rental property?* (about 8 minutes).
   A. Depends upon who needs housing (Smith).

1. Professional people and Main Street merchants generally expect to be permanent residents and want their own homes (Jones).
2. Factory employees are less certain of permanency and would prefer to rent desirable apartments and houses (Brown).
B. This question also depends upon income levels; cite data from Chamber of Commerce survey (Smith).
C. But, most of all, it depends upon the cost of home-building (Brown).

III. *What has happened to housing costs?* (about 8 minutes).
A. Costs have skyrocketed; give figures comparing today with ten years ago (Jones).
B. Summarize the effect of housing costs upon the desire for new housing; this means little hope for the building of as many new homes as Middletown needs and wants (Brown).
C. Effect of higher costs on building apartments and other rental property (Smith).

IV. *What are the possible answers to this problem?* (about 12 minutes).
A. Prefabricated housing is a possibility (Brown).
B. Possible modifications of trade agreements and trade-union policies which have kept costs high (Smith).
C. Attraction of idle investment capital into apartment building (Jones).
D. Alteration of building codes to lower costs and still maintain public health and safety standards (Smith).
E. Government assistance: FHA, GI Bill, and latest public housing developments (Brown).
F. Opening of new developments on the outskirts of town to find lower land costs (Smith).

V. *Summary* (about 3 minutes). (All three, but Jones winding up).

Panel members often ask whether they should hold a practice session. The director of the Chicago Round Table writes that participants "go through a practice session which is recorded and played back.... The experience of the Round Table is that preparation is the necessary basis of spontaneity."

B. Conducting Panel Discussions

The leader should review what has been said about his duties in earlier chapters. The suggestions which follow apply particularly to panel discussions.

1. *Getting the meeting started.* The leader should prepare a

program for distribution as audience members arrive. It should include: the question for discussion; the names of the panel members and their qualifications to discuss this topic; and the rules governing audience participation. The program may also include definitions, summaries of plans under discussion, and statistical data that the listener can consult during the meeting. When a program containing this information is distributed, the leader can begin with a sentence or two about the nature and importance of the problem before the house and ask a question to start the discussion. Each panel member should get into the conversation within the first two or three minutes. The audience is just as impatient when the leader spends too much time getting the discussion under way as they are with a slow first act in the theater.

Note how quickly the moderator gets the discussion started in these thirty-minute broadcasts. The first example is the Northwestern Reviewing Stand broadcast of October 2, 1949.

Topic: Are We Losing the Cold War in Asia?
Panel: Captain Michael Fielding, author and commentator
F. S. Marquardt, Ass't. Foreign Editor, Chicago Sun-Times
Wm. M. McGovern, Professor of Political Science, Northwestern University
Moderator: Dean J. H. McBurney, School of Speech, Northwestern University
Mr. McBurney: Are we losing the cold war in Asia?
Mr. Fielding: Yes, definitely, as of this moment. The setback in China has given tremendous impetus to Communist movements throughout Southeast Asia and the Hindu Pakistan sub-continent, and unless the West takes a positive stand soon, its prospects of prevailing ultimately will have been irreparably damaged.
Mr. Marquardt: I think the evidence is clear that we are losing the cold war in Asia. But I also think that the tide can be reversed.
Mr. McGovern: Yes, we are losing the cold war—but it is not yet lost —and the situation can be remedied if we adopt a more realistic foreign policy towards the Asiatic continent.
Mr. McBurney: Last week the Reviewing Stand analyzed *The Cold War in Europe.* We agreed that our situation in Western Europe is greatly improved, thanks to the Marshall Plan and the Atlantic Pact.
Asia remains the big question. Our speakers today are far from optimistic about Asia.
Captain Fielding has just said rather flatly that we are losing the cold war in Asia. Why do you believe that, Fielding?

The second example is from the Chicago Round Table broadcast of October 16, 1949.

Topic: France and the Future of Europe.
Panel: Louis Gottschalk, Professor of Modern History, University of
    Chicago
    André Philip, economist, Socialist member of the French Chamber
    of Deputies
    Louis Wirth, Professor of Sociology, University of Chicago
Mr. Wirth: The world is accustomed to frequent changes in French
government. Last week occurred the first cabinet crisis in France in
over a year. It was something of a record for one cabinet to endure
that long. A new government was authorized to be headed by the
Socialist, Jules Moch. What does this new government, if it is formed,
mean for France, for Europe, and for the world?

We are looking today at France not merely because we are interested
in France but for what it means as a symbol of Europe and of the
emerging new world. Philip, does this recent change in government
in France mean that France is on the road to disintegration or on the
road to recovery?

Mr. Philip: I think that France is on the road to recovery. In the last
two years a great deal of progress has been made in economic and,
I would say, even political stability. This is possible because, even
when we change the government, one has to remember that the
policy and the administration remain the same. The majority of
the members of the new government are the same people who have
been in all the governments since the liberation. The only members
changing are the prime minister and the minister of finance.

Mr. Gottschalk: I think that the instability of the French governments
can easily be exaggerated. At the same time, at the present moment,
it seems to me that France's political stability is determined by the
fact that the parties in the center have common enemies. That is
to say, they are afraid of the Communists on the left and of the
De Gaullists on the right. Within the center forces there are real
problems which may at any time split them. Therefore political
instability is a real problem from the point of view of American
policy.

Mr. Wirth: You take it, Gottschalk, that the Socialists who are taking
the lead here, belong to the political center. This is something of a
revelation to many Americans, is it not?

Mr. Philip: As for the center, it is simply the people who are in favor
of the French constitution. Since this constitution is challenged by
two authoritarian parties—the Communists on the one side and the
De Gaullists on the other—there must be in power a coalition of people
who are very different from each other, including Socialists, Catholics,
and the Conservatives. There is a majority only if the Socialists, the
Catholics, and the Conservatives are put together.

Mr. Gottschalk: The center parties constitute a majority, fortunately, at
the present moment. How long it will remain a majority is a question
which remains to be seen.

Mr. Wirth: There is now a majority of just one vote.

In both instances the moderator had the assistance of the announcer who stated the question and gave the names of the panel members. These introductions illustrate different techniques. Dean McBurney asks the question already announced as the problem for discussion and the panel members state their positions briefly. Professor Wirth, who serves both as panel member and discussion leader, begins with a 120-word statement about the timeliness and importance of the problem, ending with a direct question to Mr. Philip.

2. *Keeping the discussion going.* Since each panel member has a copy of the outline, the discussion is not likely to wander off the track. The leader's main duties are to keep the conversation moving from point to point, to see that each panel member has a fair chance to express his views, and to ask questions intended to clarify points for the audience. On rare occasions, he must break up disputes between panel members.

In the Reviewing Stand broadcast, Mr. McBurney spoke 14 times; Mr. Fielding, 23 times; Mr. Marquardt, 21 times; Mr. McGovern, 16 times. The participations average about 25 seconds in length. Here are typical examples of the moderator's speeches:

"Before we go on with this analysis of your positions, there are two assumptions which appear to run through this discussion and I am anxious to examine them just a bit. First, that Asia is vital to American interests. Why is this the case? Why risk American men and money in this area?"

"What should be our policy in China, McGovern? Do you think we ought to recognize Communist China?"

"What is this Hindu Pakistan sub-continent?"

"Do you men expect that we are going to get any substantial aid in Asia from England and other European countries?"

"Then, in conclusion, what do you men recommend for policy in Asia?"

In the Chicago Round Table discussion, Mr. Wirth spoke 26 times; Mr. Philip, the guest from France, 35 times; Mr. Gottschalk, 18 times. Here are examples of the moderator's speeches:

"There is a French proverb, Philip, 'The more it changes, the more it is the same thing.' Does that apply to the French government?"

"In other words, as you see it now, the Marshall Plan cannot terminate as planned in 1952?"

"What are the problems which this Council of Europe is going to solve? Is it going to solve any economic problems?"

"Do you mean Western Germany or all of Germany?"

"Let me ask one further question about this European Consultative Assembly. If it really works, do you think it could constitute a real third force, standing as something of a balance between the United States, on the one hand, and the Soviet Union, on the other?"

Our illustrations have been drawn from panels with three or four members, including the leader, or moderator. When the number is larger, each speaker has correspondingly greater difficulty in getting his ideas before the group. Fansler gives this report on the contributions of each person in a seven-member panel: [2]

Mr. A.	Mr. B.	Miss C.	Leader	Miss. D.	Mr. E.	Miss F.
17	23	26	49	1	12	6

There may have been equality of opportunity but there certainly was not equality of participation. There were 66 contributions from the leader's right and only 18 from his left. He spoke too often in a frantic effort to keep the discussion going. The moral, probably, is not to have seven members on a panel.

The report of the 1939 Institute for Education by Radio contains the transcript of a forum in which the audience questioned three veterans of Chicago Round Table discussion about the lessons they had learned from experience. The following excerpts from their replies contain valuable advice for all panel members, and, when followed, valuable help for the leader:

"We learned quickly not to emphasize ourselves what somebody else is adequately emphasizing."

"My strategy is to play up what others play down... to give a balanced picture out of our joint participation."

"We make no pretense of trying to give full information on any specific point of view, or to reach any definite conclusions."

"You cannot cite long statistics. You cannot use technical terms without defining them explicitly..."

"If one of us makes a *faux pas*... another will invariably say 'you mean so-and-so,' and make it possible to smooth it over..."

"The excellence of the spontaneity depends in large measure upon the intensity of preparation." [3]

C. Concluding the Panel Discussion

When the time allotted to the panel has expired, the leader must conclude that section of the program, and invite audience participa-

[2] Fansler, *op. cit.*, p. 113.
[3] Josephine MacLatchy, ed., *Education on the Air, 1939* (Columbus, Ohio State University Press), pp. 18-38.

tion in the forum. The leader either makes a brief summary or calls on each panel member to state in a sentence or two the points he regards as most important. Whatever the method, the summary should be brief. Witness the moderator's statements in the two broadcast discussions that have served as examples of panel leadership. Since there was no forum period, these speeches also closed the discussions.

McBurney: "Yes, the cold war in Asia is apparently a fact, whether we like it or not. Our speakers today believe we must strengthen our position in Asia, as we have done in Europe, if we hope to find the means of bargaining with Russia."

Wirth: Europe will continue, for some years to come, to be economically and militarily vulnerable and weak, while the tensions between the United States and the Russians continue. We all must hope, thus, that to aid in this effort of France to live in this very unstable world situation, the international organizations will, in the course of time, be strengthened. We must hope that meanwhile the Europeans, through intelligent action in solving their own internal difficulties, will come to be something of a force to prevent a world conflict.

The leader's rôle in the forum period is considered in Chapter 17.

II. COLLOQUY

Directors of discussion programs believe that members of discussion groups should do their own thinking and make their own decisions. But their decisions should be based on evidence, and the opinions of experts are evidence. Panel and symposium speakers usually provide plenty of evidence, but the listeners tend to be merely listeners, accepting uncritically what they are told. Indeed, they can do little else if they are beginning to think about the problem. This tendency to accept opinions uncritically may be partly overcome if the evidence and arguments for different points of view are presented with equal vigor, but, even so, the thinking of the audience is largely conditioned by the specialist before the laymen have a chance to speak.

There is another difficulty. The longer an authority studies a subject, the more difficulty he has in talking about it in everyday language. Panel and symposium members, especially those unskilled in speaking, are likely to talk to each other in technical terms, and to miss the points in which listeners are most interested.

The colloquy was devised by the American Association for Adult Education to meet these difficulties. The participants include a leader, a panel of audience members, and a panel of authorities on the topic. A seating arrangement, similar to that indicated in the diagram is recommended. The leader and the panel representing the audience begin the meeting as in informal group discussion. The authorities supply information and state their opinions, only on request. Audience members participate 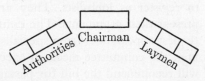 from the beginning of the discussion. They consult the authorities as they would refer to books or other sources of information. The success of the colloquy depends largely on the willingness of the authorities to accept this seemingly subordinate rôle. It is best suited for conventions and conferences where specialists are available and the auditors have an active interest in the problem.

In its original form, the colloquy is not widely used. However, the desirability of having subject matter specialists available to supply information when needed, is generally recognized. As indicated in an earlier chapter, these individuals are commonly called "resource persons." The problem is to have them present only when the group wants to consult them. An unnamed writer in *Educational Trend* for January, 1948, cites with approval the arrangement at the 1947 National Conference on Veterans' Education. A number of resource persons were brought to the conference. Their names and qualifications were made known to the discussion leaders. When a group wanted certain information the appropriate authority was summoned.

III. PUBLIC HEARINGS

Hearings, in which citizens and their authorized representatives may speak, are designed to maintain communication between the people and their government. More specifically, the purpose of a hearing may be to give opportunity for arguments on the merits of a bill that has been introduced in a legislative assembly and referred to a committee, to guide administrative agencies in the performance of their duties, or to investigate a problem that may require legislative action. Committee hearings are standard practice in most legislatures. The chairman, having announced the nature and purpose of the meeting, usually calls, first, on the author of the bill, then on those who favor its passage and, finally, on those who oppose it. The speakers are generally asked to begin by stating the nature and size of the organization they represent. In many states, they must give advance notice of their intention to appear so the committee can draw up a schedule of meetings; in some states, they are required to register as lobbyists. They are usually allowed ample time to present their arguments. The committee may take the initiative and request appearances from specialists on the problem. After the hearings, the committee meets in executive session to decide whether it will recommend the bill for passage or defeat, offer amendments, or write a new bill.

As now conducted, committee hearings may not give a balanced discussion of the bill. When the sessions continue for days, the practice of hearing all who favor the measure before those who oppose it are called means that those attending a single session hear only one side of the argument. The method of alternating affirmative and negative speakers would seem preferable for committee members as well. More serious is the possibility that a pressure group will organize a battery of speakers to present its side, while the other side, which may represent the public interest, is presented inadequately if at all.

Typical of the use of public hearings by administrative agencies, are those conducted by the Federal Communication Commission. This Commission has rather broad powers to regulate broadcasting in the public interest. In the process of formulating regulations it has held public hearings on such issues as whether stations should editorialize on current problems and whether the same individuals should own newspapers and broadcasting stations.

Public hearings are also used by committees created to investigate a problem. For example, the President appoints a Committee on Human Rights, or a governor authorizes a committee to study the causes of juvenile delinquency. While the hearings conducted by legislative committees consider the merits of a proposed solution to a problem, those held by investigating committees begin with an analysis of the situation and may, or may not, result in proposals for legislative action.

For the more formal hearings the speaking situation resembles that in the diagram. While the speaker stands with his back to the audience, addressing his remarks to the committee, he is also trying to impress the listeners whose behavior may influence the committee members. The problem is to speak so that members of the audience may hear without seeming to shout at the committee.

The duties of the chairman resemble those of the panel or forum leader. Committee members may question the speaker during his speech, or at its conclusion. They ask for further information, question the value of evidence, or criticize the speaker's conclusions. Depending on the attitude of the committee members towards the bill, the questions may be friendly or hostile. Hearings are no place for a poorly prepared speaker or for one who loses either his head or his temper under cross-examination.

Committee Members

↑
Ⓘ Speaker

———Audience———

READINGS

BAIRD, A. C., *Discussion: Principles and Types* (New York, McGraw-Hill Book Co., Inc., 1943), Chap. 15.

GAISER, H. H., "Using the Panel Discussion Method," *Junior College Journal*, Vol. 18 (December, 1947), pp. 210-4.

GARLAND, J. V., and PHILLIPS, C. F., *Discussion Methods* (New York, H. W. Wilson Co., 1940), pp. 80-101.

LASKER, Bruno, *Democracy Through Discussion* (New York, H. W. Wilson Co., 1949), pp. 89-ff.

McBURNEY, J. H., and HANCE, K. G., *Discussion in Human Affairs* (New York, Harper & Bros., 1950), Chap. 20.

McGOVERN, Elcy, "Principles and Techniques of the Panel Discussion," *Educational Administration and Supervision*, Vol. 32 (February, 1946), pp. 87-100.

NICHOLS, Alan, *Discussion and Debate* (New York, Harcourt, Brace & Co., Inc., 1941), Chap. 8.

O'BRIEN, J. F., "A Definition and Classification of the Forms of Discussion," *Quarterly Journal of Speech*, Vol. 25 (April, 1939), pp. 236-43.

OLSON, O. J., ed., *Education of the Air*, 1948 (Columbus, Ohio State University Press), pp. 67-78, 109-30.

POWERS, J. O., and BLACK, F. M., "Exploring the Panel Method Scientifically," *Progressive Education*, Vol. 12 (February, 1935), pp. 85-88.

ZANDER, Alvin, "The 'Inter-Action-Awareness' Discussion Panel," *Journal of Social Psychology*, Vol. 19 (May, 1944), pp. 369-75.

EXERCISES

1. Make a four-minute speech on one of the suggested readings.
2. Attend a panel discussion, or listen to a broadcast, and note the contributions made by each member.
3. Read a panel discussion and write a report on the amount and quality of evidence.
4. If possible, attend a public hearing and report your observations. If no public hearing is scheduled, read part of the record of a Congressional hearing.
5. Choose the topic, select the members and make a general outline for a panel discussion.
6. Draw up a plan for a colloquy to be held on your campus. Choose a topic and list the authorities you would invite to take part.

CHAPTER 21

Symposiums and Lecture-Forums

THESE TWO TYPES of discussion are treated together because they make the largest use of set speeches. In fact, both the symposium and the lecture may, and often do, provide no opportunity for real discussion. This is true both when the audience members are interested in the topic but feel that they don't know enough about it to ask intelligent questions, and when the listeners know a good deal about the problem but prefer to hear what authorities think about it. We are here concerned, however, with meetings that provide a forum in which audience members are invited to contribute information and state their opinions, as well as to question the speakers.

I. SYMPOSIUM-FORUM

The symposium differs from the panel chiefly in the formality of the opening presentation. The participants are a chairman, or moderator, and from two to four speakers, each of whom speaks on an assigned phase of the topic or problem. After the speeches, the moderator invites audience members to join in the discussion.

Like the panel, the symposium may be used either to give the audience essential information about the topic or to consider the relative merits of various solutions to a controversial problem. The number of speakers depends partly on the number of significant sources of information or points of view essential to a fair presentation of the problem. However, a symposium with more than four speakers is rarely satisfactory; the opening statements must be too brief or too little time is left for the forum period.

The symposium provides more information and, if the speeches are properly related to each other, a more unified consideration of the topic than are easily obtained from the panel discussion. With a definite subject and a fixed time limit, the speakers are more likely to make careful preparation. They know the spotlight will be on them during their speeches. This fact also tends to make the symposium more formal than the panel.

The symposium is essentially a public speaking program; the panel discussion is essentially conversational. For this reason, the symposium is the better method for large audiences.

A. Organizing the Symposium

The preparations for this type of public discussion include:

a. choosing and phrasing the topic to arouse listener interest;
b. deciding the purpose of the discussion;
c. choosing speakers, with the topic and objective in mind;
d. choosing a chairman familiar with this type of meeting;
e. briefing chairman and speakers on the objective of the meeting, the time limits, and the general procedure.

Some of these steps in preparation are self-evident; some are treated generally in the chapters on "Organizing and Leading Discussion" and "Special Discussion Techniques." Here we consider how the general advice contained in those chapters applies to the specific situation.

1. *Preparing an outline.* Before this can be done, the objective of the meeting must be decided. When the problem is new to the prospective audience, the symposium should be designed to supply information about it. Each speaker should present information from a different source or on a different phase of the question. Here is a typical outline.

Topic: "What is our present system of providing medical care?"

		Minutes
Chairman:	Introducing topic and speakers	3
Speaker A:	The private practitioners	8
Speaker B:	State and federal health services	8
Speaker C:	Commercial health and accident insurance . .	8
Speaker D:	Coöperative group health plans	8
Chairman:	Introducing forum period	2
Forum:	Audience questions and comments	30
Summary by *Chairman or recorder:*		3

If, however, the audience is fairly well acquainted with the nature and extent of the problem, the symposium should consider what can be done about it. Here is an abbreviated outline for such a discussion of juvenile delinquency. The first speaker brings the audience up to date on the problem; the other three consider what can be done to solve it.

Topic: What can we do about juvenile delinquency?
Speaker A: What is the problem?
Speaker B: What can be done by home, school, or church?
Speaker C: What can be done by juvenile courts?
Speaker D: What can be done by welfare agencies?

2. *Choosing the symposium speakers.* The choice of symposium speakers often presents difficulties. The qualifications of the ideal speaker would include prestige, knowledge of the topic, familiarity with the discussion method and skill in speaking. It is not easy to secure three or four individuals who excel in all these qualifications for most local meetings; in fact, it is sometimes difficult to get them for the well-established broadcast discussions. However, those who choose the speakers should follow these criteria as closely as they can in making their selections.

The fact that the symposium speakers are usually featured in advance publicity stresses the importance of prestige and knowledge of the problem. Unless they are regarded as thoughtful, well-balanced individuals who can speak with some degree of authority, people will not come to hear them. This does not mean, however, that a speaker must know all about a subject in order to teach us something about it; or that he must be widely accepted as an authority to make his opinions worth while.

The speakers should know, or be willing to learn, something about the discussion method. They should realize that discussion means "thought in process"; that willingness to think about the problem with others should be reflected in their talks. Each talk should be constructed as a phase of the thought process, not as an isolated unit. The speakers should use such phrases as "it seems to me" or "with the information now before us," and avoid, until the time for discussion, those persuasive devices that press for immediate action.

The speakers should be willing to devote some time and thought to the construction of their talks. Those who attend have a right to expect speeches that are well organized and expressed in language familiar to the average listener. At the same time, the speakers should remember that there are distinct limits to what a listener can learn

in eight or ten minutes. "They are as sick who surfeit with too much
as they who starve with nothing."

Excellence in speaking is, of course, desirable, but of less importance than other qualifications. The listeners will excuse lack of skill
in delivery, if they feel the speakers have something they want to say
and are trying to say it effectively.

Those who choose symposium speakers should, to quote Lasswell,
try "to equalize the effect of such factors as skill in the presentation
of a point of view, and the prestige of participants."[1] In a symposium
on the current agricultural program, for example, the Secretary of
Agriculture should be matched with the head of a national farm organization or a well-known agricultural economist. The listeners are
better able to judge the relative worth of arguments if those who
present them have about the same skill in speaking. Moreover, the
different points of view should be represented by individuals who
believe in them. Those who choose symposium speakers should do
their best to equalize these "non-rational factors"—to use Lasswell's
phrase—and thus avoid a discussion that favors one side of a controversy.

B. Conducting the Symposium

The leader's opening statement resembles that of the chairman at
any public meeting. He calls the group to order, states the discussion
topic, comments briefly on its importance, and introduces the speakers. In addition, he should briefly describe the purpose and plan of
the meeting, making sure that the audience members know when
and how they may enter the discussion. This information should be
included in advance publicity and mimeographed for distribution
before the discussion begins.

The leader's introduction of a speaker should begin with a statement of his rôle in the discussion. The purpose is to keep the attention on the process of thinking about the problem rather than on the
individual speakers. For example, "With this statement of the contents of the Taft-Hartley Bill in mind, let's see what organized labor
thinks about it," is better than, "Our next speaker is Mr. John Doe,
representing X Union, who will speak on 'The Taft-Hartley Bill in
Action.'" The introduction should also include the speaker's qualifications as an authority on the discussion topic. Consider, for ex-

[1] Harold D. Lasswell, *Democracy through Public Opinion* (Menasha, Wisconsin, Banta Publishing Co., 1941), p. 93.

ample, how Mr. George V. Denny introduced two speakers on the Town Meeting symposium, December 16, 1947. The question was "How Can We Maintain Prosperity and Avert Depression?"

Moderator Denny: Many of our economists today blame our last crash on the failure of the Federal Reserve System to properly regulate the flow of credit to our economic machines. Mr. Matt S. Szymcyzk has been a member of the Federal Reserve Board since 1933. He has just returned from his job as director of the Economic Division of the American Military Government in Germany, and he is well qualified in the field of economics and finance.

Moderator Denny: Now let's hear another viewpoint. One of the biggest corporations in America, which also operates on a world-wide basis, is the General Electric Company.... Mr. Philip D. Reed, chairman of the Board of Directors of that company, served during the war as a member of the War Production Board and as Chief of the Commission for Economic Affairs in London. He is now chairman of the United States Associates of the International Chamber of Commerce.

Mr. Denny might have said a great deal more about the accomplishments of these speakers. His problem was to select only those items which qualified them to offer opinions on the question under discussion. These statements are about seventy-five words in length, approximately thirty seconds of speaking time.

The leader should be prepared to bridge the gap between the prepared addresses of the symposium speakers and the extemporaneous audience participation in the forum. Mr. Denny sometimes does this by having a period in which the symposium speakers question each other. Another method is to have two or three audience members ready to ask questions or make brief comments. The leader's part in the forum is considered in the chapter on "Special Discussion Techniques."

II. THE DEBATE-FORUM

This is a type of symposium which almost inevitably develops when people with fundamentally different beliefs consider what should be done about an important problem. It differs from debate only in that the lines between affirmative and negative positions are not so sharply drawn. The speakers do not usually function as teams; individuals may favor or oppose a course of action for different reasons. For example, one speaker might oppose the United Nations because he believes it has too little power; another, because he believes it has too much. The speakers may also differ in the intensity of their beliefs or they may base their conclusions on different evidence.

Here is a time schedule for a public debate-forum with four speakers:

		Minutes
Leader: Opening statement about problem and procedure	. .	4
Speaker A: Favoring proposed solution	. . . . . .	8
Speaker B: Opposing it	. . . .	8
Speaker C: Favoring it	. . . .	8
Speaker D: Opposing it	. . . .	8
Forum: Audience participation	. . . .	20-25
Summary by *Speaker B or D:*	. . . .	3
Summary by *Speaker A or C:*	. . . .	3

The Oberlin College Forensic Union uses three speakers in a briefer debate-forum for luncheon clubs and similar organizations. The first speaker says, in effect, "These are the facts"; the second and third speakers, "Here are two ways of looking at them."

Topic: "Should We Outlaw Communist Teachers?"		
Chairman: Timeliness and importance of topic;		Minutes
explaining meeting procedure	. . . . .	3
Speaker A: Analysis of problem	. . . .	8
Speaker B: Favors outlawing Communist teachers	. . . .	8
Speaker C: Opposes outlawing Communist teachers	. . .	8
Forum: Questions and comments from audience	. . . . .	15-20
Summary: One minute for each speaker	. . . .	3

For a number of years, Theodore Granik has served as moderator for the American Forum of the Air, a thirty-minute "dialogue-debate." Granik secures two speakers who differ, sometimes rather violently, on a current issue, introduces them, asks a question, and, in effect, sits back to see what happens. He enters the conversation to ask another question, rap for order if both debaters are talking at the same time, or to clarify a point for the listeners. The debate closes with a one-minute summary by each speaker.

The dialogue-debate has the interest values inherent in spirited extemporaneous conversation. It is most successful when the speakers are about equal in knowledge of the problem and speaking skill and do not interrupt each other too frequently. On February 25, 1950, Arthur Campbell, professor of chemistry at Oberlin College, and Karl Mundt, U. S. Senator from South Dakota, debated whether security regulations on atomic energy matters should be more stringent. Campbell spoke 57 times; Mundt, 55 times; and Granik, 23 times. On six occasions, the debaters spoke at the same time. Of Granik's 23 participations, 13 were such incidental matters as recognition of speakers or transitional phrases; 6 were questions or comments intended to clarify points; and 4 were questions designed to keep the discussion moving.

A common criticism of debate is that it focuses attention on differences in beliefs and thereby increases the difficulty of compromise or reaching a consensus. The criticism is valid only when the debate occurs too early in the process of thinking about the problem or when the speakers are unduly contentious. But debaters do not have a monopoly on this type of behavior; and well-trained debaters avoid it. They believe they have the best answer to the problem, and are anxious to tell others how and why they reached their conclusions.

Discussion is properly open to criticism if it glosses over fundamental differences of opinion and assumes agreement where none exists. The discussion forum, or the debate, is properly used when individuals have studied the evidence and interpret it differently. Because of its competitive nature, the debate-forum has a natural audience appeal. This is an added reason for its frequent use on network broadcasts during campaigns that will terminate in decisions on public policy.

The duties of the leader in arranging and conducting the debate-forum are the same as for the symposium.

III. THE LECTURE-FORUM

This type of public discussion is the most familiar to American audiences. It consists of a talk or lecture, by a speaker who has presumably made a special study of the problem, followed by a forum period for audience participation. An uninterrupted lecture of thirty minutes provides the opportunity for a more orderly and thorough analysis of the problem than is usually possible in the panel discussion or the symposium where speeches are shorter and speakers or audience members may intervene with hostile questions or comments. The lecture-forum is also the easiest type of discussion to arrange since only one specialist is required and the duties of the leader are light. It can be used, with varying degrees of formality, by audiences of all sizes. Though the lecture-forum is widely used, it has serious limitations. A speaker who has studied a problem suffi ciently to talk as an authority usually has formed an opinion as to the proper solution. He finds it difficult, if not impossible, to present other points of view fairly. Thus, the audience is likely to get a one-sided view of the question. Unless the lecturer understands the discussion method and the purpose of the meeting, he may conclude his address with an emotional climax, or a summary that does not encourage audience participation.

Observers of lecture-forums generally agree that it is difficult to get genuine discussion in the forum period. Mary Ely visited seventy-five such meetings and in only six found what she regarded as genuine group thinking. Instead, there was a series of disconnected questions about the lecture. She found that listeners hesitated to challenge the speaker's conclusions, knowing that he usually has the advantage in such interchanges. The lecturer sometimes yielded to the temptation to embarrass the questioner or to make a little speech in response to every question. Miss Ely concluded, however, that the lecture is the most efficient means of presenting new material and that the forum is important "rather more because of its effect upon both speaker and audience throughout the proceedings than for anything that comes out of the discussion period itself." [2] Knowing that his information may be questioned and his opinions challenged, the lecturer adjusts his speech to the needs and reactions of his listeners. Knowing that they will have the opportunity to question or challenge the speaker, the audience members pay active attention to his speech.

These suggestions on arranging and conducting the lecture forum, supplement those in the chapter on "Special Discussion Techniques."

1. Audience participation in the forum period will be improved in quality and quantity if the lecturer ends his speech by raising two or three important questions about the problem in place of the usual summary or appeal for action.

2. If the lecturer does not wish to end his speech in this manner, the leader may ask a series of questions that will direct attention to significant points in the speech.

3. When the lecturer is an advocate of one point of view, that fact should be made clear to the audience. To keep the presentation of the problem from being entirely one-sided, the leader may arrange to have other points of view presented briefly during the forum period. A better procedure would be to have the other side, or sides, presented at another meeting.

[2] Mary Ely, *Why Forums?* (New York, American Association for Adult Education, 1937), pp. 200-13.

4. The panel-forum provides an effective method of making the transition from the lecture to the forum. For this purpose, the panel consists of three or four audience representatives, chosen in advance and briefly instructed on their part in the discussion. At the conclusion of the lecture, the chairman of the meeting leads the panel in a discussion of the speaker's main points and then invites general participation in the forum period. The time allotment for this type of meeting should be about as follows: Leader's opening statement, 3 minutes; lecture, 30 minutes; panel, 15 minutes; and forum, 15 minutes.

There is no magic in method; the goal always is a meeting that serves the needs of the audience and fits the occasion. Those who plan discussion meetings should use their ingenuity in devising variations or combinations of the types described in this section.

READINGS

BAIRD, A. C., *Discussion: Principles and Types* (New York, McGraw-Hill Book Co., Inc., 1943), Chaps. 15-16.

GARLAND, J. V., and PHILLIPS, C. F., *Discussion Methods* (New York, H. W. Wilson Co., 1940), pp. 194-238.

LASKER, Bruno, *Democracy Through Discussion* (New York, H. W. Wilson Co., 1949), Chap. 5.

McBURNEY, J. H., and HANCE, K. G., *Discussion in Human Affairs* (New York, Harper & Bros., 1950), Chap. 20.

MACLATCHEY, Josephine, ed., "Handling Controversial Issues" (A discussion), *Education on the Air, 1940* (Columbus, Ohio State University Press), pp. 49-69.

NICHOLS, Alan, *Discussion and Debate* (New York, Harcourt, Brace & Co., Inc., 1941), Chap. 8.

OVERSTREET, H. A.. and OVERSTREET, Bonaro, *Town Meeting Comes to Town* (New York, Harper & Bros., 1938), Part I.

SCHLESSER, G. E., "Organizing Community Forums," *School and Society*, Vol. 68 (August 21, 1948), pp. 113-8.

SIEGEL, Seymour N., "Handling Controversial Issues," in MacLatchey, Josephine, ed., *Education on the Air, 1939* (Columbus, Ohio State University Press), pp. 45-80.

"Teaching Controversial Issues" (Columbus, Ohio, The Junior Town Meeting League, 1948).

TOZIER, R. B., "A Short Life History of the Chautauqua," *American Journal of Sociology*, Vol. 40 (July, 1934), pp. 69-ff.

EXERCISES

1. Make a short speech on the information contained in one of the suggested readings.

2. Plan a symposium for your home community. Include in your report a description of the situation or problem, the type of symposium you would favor, and the names and qualifications of the speakers you would invite.

3. Attend a symposium, or listen to the Town Meeting of the Air, and comment on the use of evidence.

4. Classify the questions asked by audience members in four or five Town Meeting broadcasts.

5. Make a five-minute speech on one of the following topics:
   a. The American Lyceum
   b. The Chautauqua Movement
   c. New York's Town Hall
   d. The New England Town Meeting
   e. Broadcast Symposia on the Lend-Lease Bill
   f. Discussion at U.N. meetings

CHAPTER 22

Evaluating Discussion

WE ARE HERE concerned with the evaluation of discussion as a method of learning and problem solving and with the criteria for determining the success of a discussion meeting. Writers in such fields as political science, social psychology, and education are practically unanimous in asserting the values of discussion. We turn now to the findings of objective studies to see whether, and to what extent, the evidence supports their opinions.

I. OBJECTIVE STUDIES OF DISCUSSION

The first step in determining the value of discussion is to measure the relative reliability of judgments reached by individuals after discussion and those reached by the same individuals without consultation. Otherwise, effects ascribed to discussion may actually be the result of averaging individual judgments to get a group decision.

Knight asked the subjects in her experiment to judge the intelligence of twelve children by looking at their photographs, to estimate the sales effectiveness of fifteen tested advertisements and to guess the temperature of the room. In estimating intelligence from pictures, the group judgment, obtained by averaging individual scores, was better than the individual decisions of twenty-two of the thirty-five judges. The group average was better than the ratings of thirty of the forty who estimated the effectiveness of the advertisements. The average was better than forty-eight of fifty-six guesses as to the classroom temperature.[1] Gordon found that the accuracy of group judgment, obtained by averaging individual ratings, increased as the

[1] H. C. Knight, "A Comparison of the Reliability of Group and Individual Judgments," unpublished Master's thesis, Columbia University, 1921.

group increased in size.[2] In a study reported later in this chapter Thorndike found that "a small gain in the percentage of correct decisions resulted from simply combining the individual votes into a majority vote for each group."[3]

In matters of this kind at least, several judgments are better than one. There are always some whose decision is better than the group average, but most individual judgments are less accurate. When special knowledge or skill is involved, as in medical diagnoses, we properly leave the decisions to specialists. Otherwise, deciding the question by a majority vote is, in the long run, the most satisfactory method of "government by the people."

Early attempts to measure the effects of discussion on group performance dealt with tasks where an objective measure was possible, or with questions having a correct, or "right" answer. South studied the relative efficiency of committees of three, and of six, in four activities. Over a thousand students took part in the experiment. Each committee had to discuss the problem to reach at least a majority decision. In judging the emotions expressed in photographs, groups of three worked more quickly than groups of six and were equally accurate. The size of the committees made no real difference in solving bridge problems. In grading English compositions, as compared with the judgment of experts, committees of three worked more quickly and were about as accurate as the committees of six. In multiple-choice problems, involving thinking and the acceptance or rejection of hypotheses, there was a good deal of discussion and the groups of six had considerable advantage in both speed and accuracy. South concluded that three heads are better than six when the task is relatively simple and speed is important; that six are better than three when thinking and analyses of alternatives are involved. Six people make more suggestions and the right one is more likely to be found among them.[4]

Watson asked twenty groups, ranging in size from three to ten members, to see how many words they could build from the letters in four key words. The subjects worked alternately alone and in groups. He found the product of group thinking "distinctly superior

[2] K. Gordon, "Group Judgments in the Field of Lifted Weights," *Journal of Experimental Psychology*, Vol. 7 (October, 1924), pp. 398-400.

[3] R. L. Thorndike, "The Effect of Discussion upon the Correctness of Group Decision...," *Journal of Social Psychology*, Vol. 9 (August, 1938), pp. 343-62.

[4] E. B. South, "Some Psychological Aspects of Committee Work," *Journal of Applied Psychology*, Vol. 11 (October, 1927), pp. 348-68; (December, 1927), pp. 437-64.

to that of the average, or even the best, member of the group."
Within the range from three to ten, the number of words produced
increased with the size of the group. In only five of the twenty
groups, however, was the product larger than that obtained by com-
piling a list from the individual efforts of the same persons. This does
not, he says, measure the learning that takes place "when one, as a
part of the coöperating group, helps produce a far larger product
than one could when working alone." [5]

Bechterev and Lange also studied the effects of discussion on group
decisions. Subjects were shown pictures for fifteen seconds. Each
person then listed all the details of the picture he could remember.
After these papers were collected, the group discussed the picture and
reached decisions on all items reported by any individual. Finally,
each member handed in a statement indicating wherein his own
opinion differed from that of the group.

Sixty-six persons who looked at a picture of a locomotive reported
a total of 284 details (including all duplications) of which 29 were
incorrect. After discussion, 118 additional correct details were added
and 17 mistaken ones. The percentage of correct observations before
discussion was 80.9; after discussion it rose to 86.1. Similar results
were obtained when the subjects observed and discussed other
pictures.

Twenty-four teachers, taking a course in child study, were shown
two pictures. In the first, a boy is caught stealing apples and the
owner of the orchard appears with a stick; in the second, the boy is
getting a whipping. Each teacher was asked to write his impression of
the pictures, and his judgment of the situation. Then followed a discussion, after which the teachers wrote their revised opinions. There
were striking changes, due, presumably, to the discussion. Before the
discussion, sixteen said, "Punishment is necessary"; only twelve made
this point afterwards. The sentence, "If he is hungry, he should not be
punished," appeared in three initial statements; eighteen made this
point after discussion. Whereas one individual originally said, "Beat-
ing is barbarous," twenty-two included this idea in their revised
opinions. [6] In commenting on the results of this experiment, Murphy,
Murphy, and Newcomb say, "We have to do here not only with the
alteration of opinions, but with the point, so often emphasized in dis-

[5] Goodwin Watson, "Do Groups Think More Efficiently Than Individuals?"
Journal of Abnormal and Social Psychology, Vol. 23 (October-December,
1928), pp. 328-36.

[6] W. Bechterev and M. Lange, "Ergebnisse des Experiments auf dem Gebiete
der Kollectiven Reflexogie," *Zsch, f. angew. Psychol*, XXIV (1924), pp. 224-254.

cussion of group thinking, that what may be overlooked by the individual may, when pointed out by someone else, be granted by nearly all the members of the group; it may even receive cardinal emphasis."

Thorndike studied the relative efficiency of group work and individual performance, and the effect of discussion on the correctness of group decisions. The first experiment tested "the hypothesis that group superiority in mental work is greater in materials permitting a greater range of response." Fifty-six students at Barnard College worked alternately alone and in groups on: completing sentences, supplying synonyms, completing limericks, solving and, later, constructing crossword puzzles. Results with the first three types of material supported the hypothesis. The groups worked to advantage in solving crossword puzzles, but were less efficient in constructing them.[7]

In Thorndike's second study, almost 1,200 students first recorded their votes on a variety of questions and then discussed them in small groups until they reached a unanimous decision. From this investigation Thorndike drew these conclusions:[8]

1. A small gain in the percentage of correct group decisions followed the discussion.
2. Knowledge of the initial vote of a majority of the group exerted a great deal of influence upon the individual.
3. Individuals tended to hold to the right answer more tenaciously than to the wrong answer when the majority was against them.
4. The tendency to hold to the right answer was in part a function of the greater confidence of those holding the right answers.
5. More shift, and possibly more gain, was found in problems of fact than in problems of value.

Shaw compared the effectiveness of individuals, working alone and in groups of four, in solving problems that "call for real thinking." Here are her conclusions:[9]

1. Groups seem assured of a much larger proportion of correct answers than individuals do.

[7] R. L. Thorndike, "On What Type of Task Will a Group Do Well?" *Journal of Abnormal and Social Psychology*, Vol. 33 (July, 1938), pp. 409-12.
[8] R. L. Thorndike, "The Effect of Discussion upon the Correctness of Group Decisions When the Factor of Majority Influence Is Allowed For," *Journal of Social Psychology*, Vol. 9 (August, 1938), pp. 343-362.
[9] Marjorie E. Shaw, "A Comparison of Individuals and Small Groups in the Rational Solution of Complex Problems," *American Journal of Psychology*, Vol. 44 (July, 1932), pp. 491-504.

2. This seems to be due to the rejection of incorrect solutions and the checking of errors in the group.
3. In groups of the kind here used, more incorrect suggestions are rejected by another member of the group than by the individual who proposed the suggestion.
4. All members do not coöperate or participate equally in the solution of the problems.
5. In erroneous solutions (where it is possible to determine where the error was made) groups do not err so soon as the average member does.

We are especially interested in knowing what changes of attitude result from discussions of current controversial problems. In such cases no "right" answer can be demonstrated. We report here a representative group of experiments whose findings are indicative, though by no means conclusive.

Millson studied the effect of a student symposium on the opinions of audience members. The symposium consisted of speeches supporting four solutions to the problem, and the usual forum period. Listeners indicated their choice of these solutions, or stated that they were undecided, at the beginning and, again, at the end of the meeting. A summary of these ballots appears in the table below.

| | SOLUTION | | | | UNDECIDED | TOTAL |
	A	B	C	D		
Before discussion	28	51	3	9	31	122
After discussion	40	34	10	10	26	122

This table does not reveal the full extent of the shift. An analysis of the individual ballots reveals that 30 per cent of the individuals changed their opinions. About two thirds of the originally undecided made up their minds, and 17 per cent, with an initial preference for one of the solutions, were undecided at the end of the meeting. Comparing these results with shifts of opinion induced by debate, Millson notes that "there appears to be a greater tendency to maintain an undecided group" after discussion, and that the symposium tends to weaken original opinions to a greater degree than does debate. He properly notes that the findings of this study should be regarded as tentative.[10]

[10] William A. D. Millson, "Audience Reaction to Symposium," *Quarterly Journal of Speech*, Vol. 21 (February, 1935), pp. 43-53.

Timmons conducted an extensive investigation "to evaluate the assumption that discussion, in addition to information, is essential for the wise decision on, and the appropriate attitude towards, a controversial social problem." The question was: "What, if anything, should be done about Ohio's system of releasing convicts from prison?" The subjects were 672 juniors and seniors in Ohio high schools.

The students first expressed their attitudes on the question and ranked five proposed solutions in the order of desirability. These responses were compared with the unanimous opinions of experts on prison reform. All students then read a pamphlet containing factual, objective information on the question. The measures of attitude and choice of solutions were repeated and, on the basis of their answers, the students were divided into experimental and control groups. Those in the experimental group were divided into committees of four for a discussion of the problem; members of the control group studied the factual information for the same amount of time. The tests were repeated to measure the relative effects of discussion and reading and, again, a month later to determine the retention of changes.

Here are the findings concerning the ability of the students to rank the five proposed solutions in the order of their merit:

1. Both groups of students made real gains. The students who discussed the merits of the solutions gained significantly more than those who spent their time in reading about the problem.
2. Students with high scores on ranking the solutions before discussion were seldom pulled down by discussing the matter with students who had low scores. Those with low scores gained even after discussion with their fellows, but gained more in a discussion with students having high scores.

There were significant changes towards the desirable attitude in all groups after reading the printed material, but not thereafter. In the author's words: "There was no significant difference between the attitudes of the experimental students after discussion and the control group after study." In interpreting these findings, the fact that no new information was available in the reading or discussion period seems important. Moreover, the students were not skilled in discussion and the problem was far removed from their experiences and interests.[11]

[11] William M. Timmons, *Outcomes of the Discussion of a Social Problem* (New York, Columbia University Press, 1939).

Howell measured the relative effectiveness of the panel and the symposium-forum in providing information and changing attitudes. The subjects were fifty pairs of high-school juniors and seniors, matched as to age and intelligence. One group listened to a panel on the merits of socialized medicine and a symposium-forum on federal aid to education; the other, to the panel on federal aid and the symposium-forum on socialized medicine. The programs were thirty minutes in length and approximately equal in strength of argument and quality of performance. Information and attitude tests were given before the groups listened to the programs, immediately afterwards and, again, five weeks later.

The information tests showed that all programs produced substantial gains in information. Scores made by those listening to the panel were significantly higher than scores made by students listening to the symposium-forum. After five weeks about half of the facts learned from the broadcasts were remembered; the difference in favor of the panel persisted but to a lesser degree.

Since there was no attempt to shift attitudes in any given direction, shifts in either direction were considered as desirable changes. Each program produced significant changes in attitude which persisted practically unchanged, for at least five weeks. The panel and the symposium-forum were equally effective. Forty per cent of the group made significant changes in attitude. The direction of these changes is of interest. Fifty-eight per cent were towards support of the status quo; 37 per cent, towards the proposed change. Obviously, these discussions would be poor tools for the propagandist.[12]

Robinson conducted a series of four experiments to measure the effects of discussing two current social problems on the attitudes of college students. The subjects were 336 sophomores in argumentation courses at Northwestern University; the control groups numbered 225 students. Forty-three discussion groups, ranging in size from eight to twenty members participated in one of the four investigations. For the first experiments, the subjects studied the theory of discussion for a month and engaged in practice discussions once a week. Ten days before the experimental discussions, bibliographies were distributed, and each student was required to hand in an inventory of his reading and thinking on the problems. Each group

12 William S. Howell, "The Relative Effectiveness of the Radio Round Table and the Radio Forum," unpublished Master's thesis, University of Wisconsin, 1938.

participated in a two-hour discussion on each topic. The effects were determined by a battery of attitude tests and personality ratings. The procedure was varied in the other three studies.

Robinson found that significant group changes in attitude on both topics occurred in all forty-three groups. There was practically no correlation between an individual's attitude change and the number of his participations in discussion. Argumentative and dogmatic persons made slightly larger shifts of opinion than coöperative and friendly individuals. Those making very large opinion changes tended to be deficient in emotional control and balance. There was no "very clear relationship between intelligence and attitude changes." [13]

The studies thus far reported have, from lack of funds and research personnel, been classroom or laboratory experiments. This should not minimize their value in developing research methods, or the importance of their conclusions. But they do not tell what happens when a group of adults, freed from the pressures of course assignments and examinations, use the discussion method to analyze a mutual problem. In 1949, the Research Center for Group Dynamics published a report on "action research" that takes an important step in this direction.

This report tells the story of a ten-day workshop designed to "train community leaders to deal effectively with problems of intergroup relations." More specifically, the problems concerned community tensions among racial and religious groups. The project was planned, conducted and evaluated by a team, including: representatives of the Connecticut Interracial Commission and American Jewish Congress; three specialists in discussion methods; and research members who undertook to measure and evaluate the workshop. Each participant was interviewed before, and six months after, the session to determine the effects of the training on his "thinking and performance." These results were compared with the opinions of colleagues. The procedure at each meeting, including the work of the three discussion leaders, was recorded and summarized. Only excerpts from the conclusions can be given here.

The workshop participants spent most of their time in discussion and practice groups of about fifteen members. The leaders occupied about one-third of the time, serving mainly as "coördinators of discussion" and teachers of the method. The members participated

[13] Karl F. Robinson, "The Effects of Group Discussion upon the Social Attitudes of College Students," *Speech Monographs*, Vol. 8 (1941), pp. 34-57.

actively in suggesting problems and day-by-day procedures. Each group devoted some time each day to self-evaluation. The analysis of conflict situations by "rôle-playing" was "a prominent phase of group activity." Each group "went through crises of conflict . . . and resistance to leadership."

The major effects of the workshop, as determined by the interviews six months later, included "a broadened view of the problems of community relations, motivation to become more active in contributing to the solution of these problems, the more effective use of specific skills in stimulating and leading others . . . and personal changes in prejudiced attitudes." [14]

From these studies, and others not here reported, the following general conclusions may be drawn:

1. The average group judgment, without discussion, is superior to the majority of individual judgments; however, some individuals are always better than the group average.
2. Group thinking, after discussion, is superior to individual thinking when these factors are important: "the larger number of ways of looking at a problem; the larger number of suggestions for a solution; the larger number of suggestions for each proposed plan." [15]
3. The group is more likely to accept good suggestions advanced in discussion than to reject them; more likely to reject than to accept bad suggestions.
4. In discussion, individuals tend to retain right answers more tenaciously than wrong answers.
5. Even relatively short discussions may, on problems new to the group, significantly change the attitudes of from thirty to forty percent of the participants.
6. Discussion may significantly change the actions, as well as the opinions, of participants.
7. The contributions of group members differ in quality and quantity.
8. In the discussion of problems involving a number of steps, groups do not err as soon as the average individual.
9. Members of discussion groups are more likely to feel responsibility for decisions than are audience members.[16]
10. Discussion is not a panacea. The enthusiast who expects too much too soon is likely to be disappointed.

[14] Ronald Lippitt, *Training in Community Relations* (New York, Harper & Bros., 1949).
[15] Gardner Murphy, Lois Murphy, and Theodore Newcomb, *Experimental Social Psychology* (New York, Harper & Bros., 1937), p. 738.
[16] Kurt Lewin, "Group Decision and Social Change," in T. M. Newcomb and E. L. Hartley, eds., *Readings in Social Psychology* (New York, Henry Holt & Co., Inc., 1947), pp. 330-44.

II. CRITERIA OF A GOOD DISCUSSION

The methods just described cannot usually be applied in evaluating a single discussion. But leaders should not use this as an excuse for failure to "take stock" after each meeting. For this process, the types of information listed below may serve as criteria of a good discussion.

A. Attendance Records

We have said repeatedly that size may not be an important measure of a meeting. An average attendance of twenty would be plenty for a discussion group; it would indicate failure if the management had planned a series of public forums. Whatever the size, if the attendance steadily decreases, the series can hardly be called a success.

B. Nature and Extent of Participation

The experienced leader, or the trained observer on the discussion team, can judge whether the group members participate freely, keep their contributions relevant, and sustain their interest throughout the meeting. Someone can keep a chart, showing how many members speak, the number of participations for each, and whether there is genuine group discussion or a series of person-to-person dialogues. The observer can analyze group contributions and pass judgment on their quality. He may conduct a self-evaluation period at the close of the discussion.[17]

C. Changes of Attitudes

One criterion of a good discussion is the behavior of group members towards those holding other hostile opinions. Is there an increased willingness to listen to the other fellow's point of view? Is there a decreasing tendency to indulge in personalities and name calling? Is there less inclination to be dogmatic? Is there increased skill in making relevant contributions to the discussion?

The leader may also seek information on change of attitudes towards the problem. For his purpose, this need not be done with scientific precision. He may ask members to indicate on an unsigned ballot whether they have formed new attitudes, shifted attitudes previously held, or strengthened their individual beliefs.

[17] See pp. 293-4, exercise 5, for procedures in charting individual participations and group patterns of discussion.

D. Individual or Group Action

The test is whether the discussion has changed individual behavior, or culminated in group action. The results, in either case, may not be immediately apparent. If the group discusses the advantage of home ownership, it may be months or years before a convinced member may be able to buy a home. On the other hand, a discussion of the values of church membership may result in immediate action. A committee or business meeting usually deals with questions requiring group decisions. Here the leader may inquire whether the discussion provided needed information or was otherwise helpful in formulating a solution to the problem.

E. Post-Meeting Conversations

Participants report that the best discussion often takes place after the meeting has adjourned, when people gather in small groups and continue talking until the janitor turns out the lights. If the topic still is talked about weeks or months later, the meeting was a success. If, when the meeting adjourns, the members seem only interested in getting home and speak only of matters unrelated to the topic, the attendance will likely be smaller next time.

To get the full value of these post-meeting conversations, the leader may, before adjournment, ask those present to evaluate the discussion and suggest topics for future meetings. For this purpose, he may use part, or all, of the questionnaire on page 368.

F. Expressions of Outside Interest

A meeting attended by a small group may set off a whole chain of events. Other groups may discuss the problem; it may be the subject of newspaper editorials or letters to the editor; a minister may preach a sermon on it; or students may choose it for class debates. Such developments would indicate the success of the original meeting.

G. Evidence of Reader Interest

When their interest is aroused, members of discussion groups are likely to want further information about the problem. Evidence of this interest may be obtained from libraries and book stores. The directors of America's Town Meeting of the Air, the Chicago Round Table, and the Northwestern Reviewing Stand regard the sale of transcripts of the broadcasts as evidence of their effectiveness.

Your answers to these questions will be helpful to those in charge of planning these discussion meetings. Please be frank. Check the answers which most nearly fit your reaction.

1. Was the subject of interest to you?
   _____ very interesting.
   _____ mildly interesting.
   _____ not at all interesting.

2. Did you learn something new about the subject?
   _____ a good deal.
   _____ a little.
   _____ nothing at all.

3. Do you now have a better understanding of the subject?
   _____ much better.
   _____ somewhat better.
   _____ no better.

4. Was the meeting an interesting experience?
   _____ very interesting.
   _____ moderately interesting.
   _____ not at all interesting.

5. Did the leader (or speakers) talk...
   _____ too long?
   _____ just long enough?
   _____ not long enough?

6. Did you take part in the discussion (or forum period)?
   _____ more than once.
   _____ only once.
   _____ not at all.

7. Will you come again?
   _____ yes.
   _____ perhaps.
   _____ no.

8. What suggestions would you make for improving these meetings?
   _____

9. What subjects would you suggest for future meetings?
   _____
   _____

III. OBJECTIVE MEASURES OF DISCUSSION

In addition to the general objective of arousing interest in the problem, discussion has one of these purposes: to supply background information, to form or change attitudes, or to secure action. When differences of opinion persist, debate should precede action.

When the purpose is to provide a factual basis for further discussion, an information test is used to measure the meeting's effectiveness. To differentiate what was learned from what was already known, the test is given before and after the discussion.

These techniques are commonly used to measure the effectiveness of discussions and debates in forming or changing attitudes.

A. The Simple Ballot

In its simplest form, the ballot consists of a single question or statement; for example, "Do you support the proposed bond issue for a new high school?" or, "Every able bodied young man should spend a year in military service." Audience members are asked to write "Yes" or "No" on slips of paper, but not to sign their names. This provision is important; individuals feel free to indicate what they really believe and can change their opinions without letting their neighbors know about it. The simple ballot is the easiest way of surveying the opinions of large groups. However, it is not a very accurate method of measuring the effects of a single discussion, because it does not give the voter a chance to register a weakening or strengthening of his original opinion that falls short of changing his vote.

B. The Shift-of-Opinion Ballot

Developed by the late Professor H. S. Woodward of Western Reserve University, this ballot permits the voter to record opinion changes smaller than a shift from one side of the question to the other. On the next page is a sample ballot used in one of a series of discussions on "How can the buyer get his money's worth?"

Though this type of ballot does not give the listener an opportunity to express his reactions to various arguments advanced in support of the central question, it does provide some basis for evaluating the effect of the discussion in shifting individual opinions. The ballot should be distributed at the beginning of the meeting and the group members should check it before and after the discussion, at neither time signing their names.

QUESTION: WHAT SHOULD BE MY ATTITUDE TOWARD
CONSUMERS' COÖPERATIVES?

Before Discussion   After Discussion
(check one)   (check one)

                                      _____ I am more strongly in
                                          favor of consumers' co-
_____ I am in favor of con-   operatives.
         sumers' coöperatives.   _____ I am in favor of them.
_____ I am undecided.   _____ I am undecided.
_____ I am opposed to them.   _____ I am opposed to them.
                                        _____ I am more strongly op-
                                        posed to them.

C. The Rating Scale

The use of a rating scale enables participants to rank proposed solutions to the problem in the order of preference. When members of the group are fairly familiar with the arguments for and against various alternatives, the rating scale can be used at the beginning and the end of the discussion to indicate shifts of opinion as to the merits of the different solutions. Here is a sample rating scale, used for a discussion on "the right to strike."

QUESTION: WHAT ABOUT THE "RIGHT TO STRIKE"?

Below are five possible solutions to this problem. Place a "1" before the solution you believe best, a "2" before the second best, etc.

_____ The right to strike is the union's only effective weapon.
_____ The right to strike should be limited only by making unions legally liable for losses to employers through unauthorized strikes.
_____ The right to strike should continue as at present.
_____ There is no right to strike when the public would be harmed thereby.
_____ Strikes should be forbidden by law.

D. The Linear Scale

This is a simple, and fairly accurate device for measuring attitudes. It consists of a line that supposedly represents the range of attitude, from extreme hostility to the proposal in question to complete belief in it. The individual marks the point on the line that represents his attitude on the issue. Here is such a scale on the state medicine question.

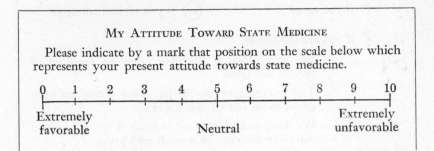

MY ATTITUDE TOWARD STATE MEDICINE

Please indicate by a mark that position on the scale below which represents your present attitude towards state medicine.

0   1   2   3   4   5   6   7   8   9   10

Extremely   Extremely
favorable   Neutral   unfavorable

The obvious advantages of such a scale are the ease with which it can be constructed, and the fact that the individual is free to indicate his position at any point on the line, instead of being limited to certain expressed alternatives. But such scales are of little value in stimulating discussion; moreover, they seem more artificial to the members of the average audience than the other methods.

E. The Attitude Test

Attitude tests are the most precise methods of measuring changes of opinion, but they are also the most difficult to construct. They consist of statements, carefully chosen to reflect opinions on different aspects of the question. The individual records his degree of agreement or disagreement. Each answer is assigned a numerical value; the total score reflects the individual's central attitude toward the issue. A sample test is shown on the next page.

We have not included the interview method used in the study reported by Lippitt in *Training in Community Relations*. This method is valuable when trained interviewers are available, but cannot usually be undertaken by classes or single research workers.

OPINION SURVEY OF FREEDOM OF SPEECH AND PRESS.[18]

We want to know what you really believe about this important problem. Here are some statements which high school and college students have made. Please indicate how much you agree or disagree with them by placing one of the following marks in the blank space before each statement:

⊕ if you strongly agree   — if you disagree

➕ if you agree   ⊖ if you strongly disagree

❓ if you are undecided

1. _____ We are foolish if we give everyone freedom of speech and press.

2. _____ The government should have the power to keep crime news out of the papers.

3. _____ We have reason to fear radicals if we give them complete freedom of speech and press.

4. _____ One of the best things we can do is to keep fascists and communists from saying what they like.

5. _____ Nazis and communists have as much right to freedom of speech and press as we have.

6. _____ Newspapers should be free to print whatever they wish.

7. _____ We should permit people to speak for communism.

8. _____ Complete freedom gives too much power to those opposed to our form of government.

9. _____ There should be unlimited freedom of speech and press.

10. _____ These freedoms should be given even to those who do not give them to others.

It is important that we know what can reasonably be expected of a discussion, that we become intelligent critics as well as skilled participants. The Readings suggest sources of further information; the Exercises give practice in evaluating the work of others.

[18] This sample includes the directions and ten of the thirty statements from an attitude test constructed by Edgar E. Willis.

READINGS

ANGELL, Ernest, "Some Experiments in Group Persuasion," *Journal of Educational Sociology*, Vol. 19 (September, 1945), pp. 57-8.

BANE, C. L., "The Lecture Versus the Class Discussion Method of College Teaching," *School and Society*, Vol. 21 (March, 1925), pp. 300-02.

EWING, W. H., "An Evaluation of the Individual vs. the Group Speaking Methods of Teaching the College Speech Course," *Speech Monographs*, Vol. 11 (1944), pp. 80-7.

JACQUES, Elliott, "Interpretative Discussion as a Means of Facilitating Social Change," *Human Relations*, Vol. 1 (June, 1948), pp. 533-49.

JOHNSON, Alma, "Teaching the Fundamentals of Speech Through Group Discussion," *Quarterly Journal of Speech*, Vol. 25 (October, 1939), pp. 440-7.

KLUGMAN, S. F., "Group and Individual Judgments for Anticipated Events," *Journal of Social Psychology*, Vol. 26 (August, 1947), pp. 21-8.

LIPPITT, Ronald, *Training in Community Relations* (New York, Harper & Bros., 1949), Chap. 12.

MILLER, D. C., "An Experiment in the Measurement of Social Interaction Through Group Discussion," *American Sociological Review*, Vol. 4 (June, 1939), pp. 341-51.

RYDER, Walter and CHENOWETH, Eugene, "Community Discovery Through Survey and Discussion," *Journal of Educational Sociology*, Vol. 19 (March, 1946), pp. 436-44.

SCHONBAR, R. A., "The Modification of Judgments in a Group Situation," *Journal of Experimental Psychology*, Vol. 37 (February, 1947), pp. 69-80.

SIMPSON, Ray H., *A Study of Those Who Influence and of Those Who Are Influenced by Discussion* (New York, Columbia University Press, 1938).

TIMMONS, William M., "Sex Differences in Discussion," *Speech Monographs*, Vol. 8 (1941), pp. 68-75.

UTTERBACK, W. E., "The Influence of Conference on Opinion," *Quarterly Journal of Speech*, Vol. 36 (October, 1950), pp. 365-70.

EXERCISES

1. Give a four-minute expository speech on one of the suggested readings. Compare the information with that in this chapter.

2. Attend a discussion and prepare a written evaluation.

3. Form an evaluation team and bring in a composite report on one of the class discussions.

4. Study the public opinion polls for evidence of possible effects of nation-wide discussion on public opinion.

5. Compare changes of opinion resulting from discussion with those resulting from persuasion.

6. Lead a self-evaluation period at the conclusion of your class discussion.

Part V

DEBATE

CHAPTER 23

The Nature, Purposes, and Limitations of Debate

THE FOURTH STEP in the consideration of a problem requiring group action is to choose from the proposed solutions the one best suited to the immediate situation. When this stage is reached discussion has served its proper function and the opportunity for debate should always be provided. The more enthusiastic advocates of the discussion process seem to assume that if intelligent men and women think together in an atmosphere free from strife or disputation they will all arrive at the same conclusion or make reciprocal concessions until substantial agreement is reached. True, this sometimes happens; but often there are fundamental points of difference which no amount of discussion will obliterate. When this situation exists, the democratic procedure gives each member, or each side, an equal opportunity in debate after which a vote is taken and the will of the majority prevails.

Majority rule in a milieu of free speech is one of the most basic ideas of democracy. Our legislative procedure provides a series of opportunities for discussion and debate and takes especial care to guard the rights of minorities. Americans believe that no one should be adjudged guilty in our courts without a trial in which a properly qualified advocate presents his case and pleads in his behalf. Our system of parliamentary law requires the chairman to call for debate on all motions or resolutions. We believe that properly conducted debate is prerequisite to an intelligent decision.

I. THE GENERAL NATURE OF DEBATE

Debate, whether in a school exercise or in the deliberations of a judicial or legislative body, has these essential characteristics:

1. Whereas the discussion process begins with the analysis of a problem and works towards a solution, the debater begins with a solution which he urges others to accept or to reject. It is assumed that the debater has reached his position on the question after due consideration of other alternatives. The member of a discussion group is thinking his way through to a conclusion; after he has reached it he may uphold it in debate.

2. The conclusion must be so stated, in the form of a motion, resolution, bill, proposition, or indictment, as to give the voter a choice between two alternatives. The member of a jury must vote, "Guilty" or "Not Guilty." The member of a legislative assembly may attempt to change a bill by the process of amendment but, when the moment for final action arrives, he can only avoid voting "Yes" or "No" by absenting himself or voting "Present." The same situation prevails in the ordinary business meeting.

3. After the proposition is properly worded and presented to the group whose judgment is desired, care is taken to see that both sides have an equal opportunity to present their arguments. In a trial or hearing, the judge and the attorneys reach an agreement on the amounts of time allotted to each side. When a legislative assembly is debating an important measure, leaders of each party decide who shall speak for them. School debates follow a schedule which alternates arguments for and against the motion and allows each side the same number of minutes.

4. When all who desire to participate in the debate have done so, or when the allotted time has expired, a vote is taken and the will of the majority becomes, until the matter is again up for consideration, the decision of the organization. The minority must abide by this decision as long as it stands but, on proper occasions, may continue to argue for a reversal of judgment.

Debate, then, is a parliamentary procedure designed to give proponents and opponents of a measure as nearly equal opportunities as possible to present their evidence and to argue their conclusions before the voters make their decisions. Debate is usually oral, although written controversies do take place. Advocates and opponents of a measure usually speak alternately so that the attention of the listeners may not remain focused on one line of argument to the exclusion of the other.

II. PURPOSES OF DEBATE

Through our consideration of the characteristics of debate, we have gained an understanding of its general purposes. The next step is to inquire how debate functions in certain broad areas of American life. We shall discuss debate as an *educational method*, as a *legislative procedure*, and as a *judicial process*.

A. Debate as an Educational Method

Debate and its predecessor, the disputation, are among the oldest of teaching devices. Diogenes believed that Protagoras of Abdera, who did his teaching about 2,400 years ago, was the first to institute debates between his pupils on questions akin to those facing their elders. Whether this is true or not, we know that Aristotle, the famous Greek philosopher who taught a century later, complained because the subjects chosen for debate in the school exercises of his day were not sufficiently true to life. He was familiar, too, with the problems arising from the practice of having decisions at the conclusion of these debates. "Victory also is pleasant," he said in *De Rhetorica* (1370b-1371a), "and not merely to bad losers but to everyone; the winner sees himself in the light of a champion and everybody has more or less of an appetite for that. . . . That is why forensic pleading and debating contests are pleasant to those who are accustomed to them and have the capacity for them."

Aristotle's advice that the subjects for debate be problems arising in everyday life was not followed during the Middle Ages. Perhaps it was because of the risks involved in arguing against the positions taken by those in power. During that period debate most often took the form of the disputation, an exercise designed to cultivate ability in abstract reasoning. William Fitz-Stephen, writing before 1190, tells of grammar school disputations in the London Schools. "There," he wrote, "the scholars dispute; some use demonstrations, others topical and probable arguments. Some practice enthymemes; others are better at perfect syllogisms. Some for a show dispute and for exercising themselves, and strive like adversaries; others for truth, which is the grace of perfection." [1]

[1] Quoted by Foster Watson, *The English Grammar Schools to 1660* (London, Cambridge University Press, 1938), p. 92.

In the lower schools, the questions chosen for disputation dealt largely with points in grammar and rhetoric; in the universities the subjects were drawn from logic and philosophy. Many of the universities held a weekly disputation or debate, attended by the entire faculty and student body. On these occasions the presiding officer proposed theses which were attacked in turn by various masters. The students defended the positions taken by their masters. One of the main advantages claimed for the University of Toulouse in a circular issued in 1229 was that disputations were held there twice as often as at the University of Paris.

The term *disputation* was also applied to public debates, especially those on religious issues. In 150 B.C. such a debate was held in Alexandria on the comparative merits of the Jewish and Samaritan texts of the Old Testament. A famous debate took place in Barcelona, June 20, 1263, on the question whether the Messiah had appeared or not. This was held in the royal palace in the presence of James I of Aragon and his court.

Thomas Fuller tells of disputations between Cambridge and Oxford in 1531 and 1533. For the latter, Cambridge paid 6s. 8d. to entertain the speakers and 13d. to pay the carpenter "who repaired the doors of the schools broken in the disputation of the Oxford men." [2]

Current procedures in British debating societies are described by Norman J. Temple and Edward P. Dunn,[3] members of the Bates College team that toured England in 1946. The older universities have debating halls modeled after the House of Commons. Members are seated according to political affiliation; conservatives on the right, facing the liberals on the left; other minority groups on the back benches. A different motion, dealing with an issue facing the government, is debated each week. Any member may interrupt the speaker at any time with a point of information or a point of order.

The Bates debaters tell of their visit to the University of Glasgow. Handbills were distributed to society members the evening before the debate stating the motion, assigning government offices to members of the Student Labor Party and naming the leader of the opposition. The handbill also contained a statement of the Labor government's policy on various matters. The debate began at 1:15 the next

[2] Thomas Fuller, *History of the University of Cambridge* (London, T. Tegg, 1840), p. 64.

[3] "British Debating Is Parliamentary," *Quarterly Journal of Speech*, Vol. 34 (February, 1948), pp. 50-53.

afternoon with the formal entry of the Speaker of the House, accompanied by a uniformed Sergeant-at-arms carrying the Mace, symbol of the Speaker's authority. The Labor Party spokesman presented the motion and the opposition leader replied in ten-minute speeches. A seconder for each side spoke for five minutes. There were frequent interchanges with members. At 2:15 the meeting adjourned to convene at 7:15, and members went off to prepare for the evening session.

The evening debate combined the serious and the frivolous. An opposition member would attack some government policy. The appropriate Labor spokesman defended his party's actions with frequent interruptions for cross-examination.

"Diversion came when a member delivered a lengthy speech in faultless German, with frequent 'Heil Hitler's' interspersed. At one time, the debate on national issues was forgotten in favor of a lively and witty discussion on the correct name for the rostrum used by the speakers. The debate thus alternated between serious and hilarious topics until almost four in the morning."

The British societies also have debates that more nearly resemble ours. Two speakers for each side of the motion are seated on a platform facing the audience. After the four opening addresses any audience member may speak for five minutes. All speakers may be, and usually are, interrupted on points of information and points of order. This procedure is usually followed in the "rag debates" on such topics as: That Monogamy Is Monotonous, That the Old Should Be Seen and Not Heard, That Humor Is No Longer Funny. These occasions call for such wit and humor as the speakers can summon to their assistance.

The members of the Cambridge Union Team that toured this country were surprised at the lack of "formal interruptions," that speakers of distinction did not debate with student speakers and that audience members were just that. They thought our time limits too rigid, found "the rebuttals a most enjoyable feature" and felt that debating the same question repeatedly would result in boredom. The only question debated more than once a year at Cambridge is, "That this House Has No Confidence in His Majesty's Government." [4]

Professor Brooks Quimby of Bates College believes that American debaters "excel at careful preparation"; the British, at securing audi-

---

[4] I. S. Lloyd and W. H. L. Richmond, "The 1947 Cambridge Union Tour," *Quarterly Journal of Speech*, Vol. 34 (February, 1948), pp. 46-9.

ence participation and at "coming closer to life situations." The
British "try so hard to avoid boring the audience that they sometimes mislead; often they are merely entertaining." [5]

The early history of debating in our colleges reflects the differences in social and economic backgrounds of the student debaters.
The American colonists were men of intense political and religious
convictions, engaged in the dual task of conquering the wilderness
and establishing a government "of, for and by the people." The
colonial colleges were established to train ministers and leaders for
the new government. They were attended by young men for whom
life was real, earnest and strenuous, who had little time or inclination
for the "merely entertaining."

The colonial literary societies often held "forensic disputations"
on religious and moral questions. In the 1720's, the Spy Club at Harvard debated: "Whether Sins of Ignorance will be Imputed";
"Whether there be Any Standards of Truth"; and "When May a
Man be Said to Lie?" [6] A student at Yale, in 1747, recorded these
topics for forensic disputation: "Whether a Volition or Determination to do an evil Action be sinful"; and "Whether any can be Saved
without a Divine Revelation." [7]

At the same time current political questions and topics of a more
general nature were disputed. The program of Brown University's
first commencement, in 1769, included a debate on this statement:
"The Americans, in their present Circumstances, cannot, with good
Policy, affect to become an Independent State." In 1772, the Linonia
Society at Yale argued whether "it is right to Enslave Africans."
Princeton's commencement exercises included debates on such topics
as "Civil Liberty is necessary to give Birth to the Arts and Sciences"
(1766); "To play at Cards or Dice is neither expedient or lawful"
(1765); and "The Non-importation agreement Reflects a glory on
the American Merchants."

In 1858, a Northwestern University literary society debated:
"That the signs of the times indicate a dissolution of the Union" and
"That S. A. Douglas is more worthy of a seat in the United States
Senate than the Honorable A. Lincoln." In that year, the Athena So-

5 "Can We Learn from Debating with the British?" *Quarterly Journal of
Speech*, Vol. 33 (April, 1947), pp. 159-61.

6 *Publications of the Colonial Society of Massachusetts*, Vol. 12, pp. 220-31.

7 Quoted by David Potter in *Debating in the Colonial Chartered Colleges*
(New York, Columbia University Press, 1944), p. 44.

ciety at the University of Wisconsin replaced candles with two lamps "using a burning fluid" and argued whether "four years at the university is of more value to a young man than $2,000 at 12%." But these young Athenians also debated: "That the signs of the times predict a downfall of American liberty," and "That the greatest good of the North requires a dissolution of the American Union."

Intercollegiate debating is primarily an American institution. The first intercollegiate debate seems to have taken place in 1883 between Knox College and the Rockford Female Seminary on the "Social benefits and evils of the lavish expenditure of wealth by the rich." Ten years later Harvard and Yale had their first intercollegiate debate; Michigan and Wisconsin followed in 1894. Within a year or two, a number of other colleges and universities adopted the practice which soon became almost universal.

This is not a complete history of debating. The point is simply that debating and forensic contests are not new. In one form or another, they have existed almost since the beginning of schools and colleges. Although we have not made the point, debating societies were formed in many American communities where schools, beyond those teaching the three R's, did not exist. When freedom of speech did not prevail, and when the citizen had little voice in his government, debates, often on non-controversial topics, were justified because they stimulated students to greater efforts than they otherwise would have made. For students who live in democracies, school debates provide direct training for citizenship. For the teachers in such fields as social studies, discussion and debate provide an excellent method of dealing with controversial topics.

B. Debate as a Legislative Procedure

In dictatorships and absolute monarchies, laws originate in the mind of the ruler or of his advisers and are promulgated by decree. Sometimes, the pretense of consulting the people is maintained by giving them the chance to vote "Yes" under circumstances which make it unlikely that they will vote "No." Whenever the people have a real voice in the affairs of government, it has become necessary for them to devise some plan for using this power effectively. If the voice of the people is even faintly to resemble the voice of God, mob psychology and mob action must be avoided. It has been said that the excesses of the French Revolution were attributable to the fact that the people had no system of parliamentary law and were free to follow immediately the suggestions of the orators who were themselves intoxicated by the phrases they shouted.

The first steps in the evolution of parliamentary practice undoubtedly dealt with maintaining order and compelling the attendance of members at business meetings. Complete freedom of the individual would mean chaos. Of especial interest are the rules for the conduct of members adopted by our Continental Congress. They provided that "no member shall read any printed paper in the house during the sitting thereof without leave of the Congress; no member shall speak to another or otherwise interrupt the business of the house while the journals or public papers are read for the benefit of Congress, or when any member is speaking in any debate; every member, when he speaks, shall rise from his seat and address himself to the chair, and, when he is finished, shall sit down again; no member shall speak more than twice in any one debate, on the same day, without leave of the house." [8]

But the maintenance of order was only the first step. It soon became evident that the business of investigating a problem and proposing a solution in a carefully drawn bill or resolution could not be accomplished efficiently by large groups. This led to the committee system. To guard against hasty action, no measure could be brought to final vote on the day on which it was originally presented.

Our present rather complicated system of parliamentary law for all public meetings is based on these fundamental principles:

1. Only one subject can be before the house at any one time.
2. This must be stated in the form of a motion, bill, or resolution to give the member the choice of voting "Yes" or "No" on a single proposition.
3. Each proposition is entitled to full and free debate.
4. Each member has rights equal to those of each other member.
5. The will of the majority must be carried out but the rights of the minority to be heard and to reopen the question at the next session must be preserved.

While every legislative body adopts its own rules, the usual procedure is about as follows: A bill is introduced and referred to the proper committee. This committee considers all bills dealing with the same subject. Public hearings are usually held at which interested citizens and representatives of organizations may present their arguments. If a number of bills on the same subject are presented, the

[8] *Journals*, July 10, 1776; May 26, 1778, Rules 3, 4, 5, 6.

committee may choose the one it believes best or write a bill of its own. The bill is reported out to the assembly with a recommendation for or against its adoption. It may be given a place on the calendar and come up for final vote. Members of the assembly may move to amend the bill, may attempt to influence the votes of others in debate, and finally vote on the adoption of the amended measure. In a bicameral legislature such bills as are passed are referred to the other house where they go through the same process.

This rather involved process, irritating to the individual who wants to get a bill passed in a hurry, was created in the belief that hasty action is often unwise action and that as many people as possible should consider a measure before it is enacted into law. It provides a number of opportunities for debate. Citizens may argue for and against the bill at public hearings. Members may debate the merits of the measure outside of legislative sessions and join in more formal debate when it is before the house for final action.

This system has always had its faults and its critics to point them out. John Adams complained in his *Diary* that "the business of the Congress is tedious beyond expression. . . . Every man in it is a great man, an orator, a critic, a statesman: and therefore, every man, upon every question, must show his oratory, his criticism, and his political abilities. The consequence of this is that business is drawn and spun out to an immeasurable length." Bohman, who examined the contemporary writings on the early American Congress, found three objections to the debates: (1) noisiness and lack of proper order; (2) tedium and wastefulness of time; and (3) contentiousness and bickering among members.[9]

Some of these faults are inherent not so much in the legislative system as in human nature. Others can be corrected by experience. The delays that seem like a weakness to members whose opinions are already formed, are justified when they serve to instruct members who have not considered the problem and when they bring to light new evidence which those who entered the debate with an opinion already formed had not considered. With all its slowness and seeming inefficiency, the legislative procedure of the democracy is, in the opinion of most of us, vastly superior to legislation by executive decree.

We hear and speak much about freedom of speech, often putting

[9] George V. Bohman, "Debates in the American Congress, 1774-1789," an unpublished paper.

the emphasis on the right to speak. Walter Lippmann believes that freedom of speech "achieves its essential purpose only when different opinions are expounded in the same hall to the same audience. . . . For, while the right to talk may be the beginning of freedom, the necessity of listening is what makes that right important. . . ." Freedom of speech is best conceived, he believes, "by having in mind the picture of a place like the American Congress, an assembly where opposing views are presented, where ideas are not merely uttered but debated, or the British Parliament, where men who are free to speak are also compelled to answer." [10] He believes that the democratic system cannot be operated long without effective opposition. Effective opposition provides speakers for the negative in debates on important issues. Without these opposing speakers there can be no real debate and legislation is likely to be hasty, ill-considered, and arbitrary.

C. Debate as a Judicial Process

The right to have one's guilt or innocence determined by a jury of neighbors, instead of by a representative of the central government, was a considerable victory in the long battle for human liberty. But this right could not be properly exercised until a procedure, based on many of the same principles that underlie the legislative process, was established.

A grand jury listens to a preliminary statement of the charge and the evidence to determine whether there is sufficient probability of the individual's guilt to warrant holding him for trial. If the individual is held for trial, he must know of what he is accused and must have an opportunity to prepare his defense. If he is too poor to employ an attorney, the government assigns counsel to see that his legal rights are protected and that his defense is heard.

The trial follows the general procedure of debate. Attorneys for the state, or the complainant, charge that the accused violated certain criminal or civil statutes; those for the defense argue that he is not guilty, or conceding guilt, present extenuating circumstances and plead for leniency. Each side presents evidence under rules that are intended to exclude that which is irrelevant or immaterial. Witnesses are cross-examined by attorneys for the other side in an attempt to discredit their testimony or to lessen its importance.

After the evidence has been presented, the counsel on each side at-

[10] Walter Lippmann, "The Indispensable Opposition," *Atlantic Monthly*, Vol. 164 (August, 1939), pp. 186-190.

tempt to minimize evidence that is unfavorable to their client and to attach weight to that given by their own witnesses. During this process, in the words of A. Lawrence Lowell, who believes our judicial system is the best yet devised for the determination of guilt or innocence, ". . . the attention of the jury is directed, first by one side and then by the other, to every material point in the case, thereby avoiding the danger of having the verdict result from fixing the attention on facts bearing one way to the comparative neglect of those on the other side." [11]

So accustomed are we to the provision that the judge and the jury must hear the whole evidence and the arguments on both sides before making their decision, that we often fail to sense its importance. It is this requirement that Lippmann believes to be the essence of freedom. "We may picture the true spirit of freedom," he says, "as existing in a place like a court of law, where witnesses testify and are cross-examined, where the lawyer argues against the opposing lawyer before the same judge and in the presence of one jury." [12]

Debate has suffered alike from over-zealous friends and misinformed critics. It is not the one sure cure for whatever is wrong with the student speaker, or the best method of presenting every problem; nor, on the other hand does it inevitably harm the debater and befog the listeners. There are occasions listed below when debate should not be used; but there are oft repeated criticisms which properly apply only to bad debating and others that arise from a misunderstanding of its nature and purposes.

1. Debate should not be used when the listeners are just beginning to learn about the problem. Such situations call for exposition and analysis, not argument.

2. Debate should not be used when the group, or audience, is beginning to consider alternative solutions to the problems. The debate focuses attention on the affirmative proposal, with the possibility that a second may be advanced by the negative. But, at this point, all practical solutions should be considered.

3. Debate on the wisdom of existing policies should generally be avoided during crises involving those policies. When we were attacked we stopped debating whether we should be in World War II and devoted our attention to methods of winning as quickly as possible.

4. Public debate should not be used to deepen disagreements or heighten emotional tensions. When emotions run high and tempers are

[11] A. Lawrence Lowell, *Public Opinion in War and Peace* (Harvard University Press, 1923), p. 68.
[12] Lippmann, *op. cit.*, p. 188.

near the boiling point, public debate, unless the speakers are calm and deliberate, is likely to result in confusion rather than enlightenment. We are aware that this may serve as an excuse for closed meetings and executive sessions. We often underestimate the ability of the public to separate the logical grain from the emotional or irrelevant chaff.

III. COMMON CRITICISMS OF DEBATE

Perhaps the most frequent criticism is that debaters become more interested in winning than in finding "the truth." Individuals making this charge often seem to believe that "truth" will be found in one easily identifiable package. On really debatable questions, this is not so. The audience, it is hoped, is searching for the best course of action; the opposing debaters think they have found it. The more certain they are of this, the more interested they are in winning. And rightly so. There is nothing blameworthy, in these circumstances, about wanting to win.

The critics often seem not to understand the purposes and procedures in school debates. Members of opposing teams are not usually trying to convince each other. The affirmative speakers are charged with the responsibility of presenting the evidence and arguments for passing the motion; the negative speakers have the same responsibility for its defeat. The critic judges decide which team did the better debating; the audience members may be asked to record their beliefs on the question.

A second charge is that, in their desire to win, debaters present arguments in which they do not believe. Those who make this charge assume that they can tell when a debater believes what he says, but that audience members, and judges, cannot. This criticism is usually directed at opponents by those who are so sure of their position that they cannot see how an intelligent, honest person can believe otherwise.

We are not, for a moment, condoning dishonesty and sharp practice in debate or anywhere else. But dishonesty and sharp practice are not common in debate, if for no higher reason than that such things will almost inevitably be exposed by the opposing speakers, or the judge, to the discomfiture of the culprit. Indeed, the temptation to unfairness is stronger in other types of meetings where opponents with equal skill and advance preparation are not given equal opportunity to reply.

Other critics of school debates claim that speakers are often forced to debate on what they believe to be the wrong side of the question. The burden of proof should be on those making the charge, both to prove that the practice is prevalent and that it is harmful. The fact that schools usually debate both sides of the question makes it possible to place speakers on the side they prefer. When the coach comes to choose his teams, he usually finds that part of the squad have strong arguments on both sides. There seems no good reason for assuming that debaters are commonly forced to debate against their convictions.

Even if debaters are assigned to the side of the question in which they do not believe, it does not necessarily follow that the experience is harmful; on the contrary, they are almost sure to get a more thorough understanding of the problem. If it is understood that the debaters are advocates, presenting arguments for and against the motion so that the audience may get a fair view of the question, there is no basis for criticism on the ground that the debaters are hiding their real beliefs. In his essay on "Debating Societies" Robert Louis Stevenson praised

that wholesome rule which some folks are most inclined to condemn—I mean the law of obliged speeches. Your senior member commands; and you must take the affirmative or negative, just as best suits his convenience.... You are forced, by regards for your own fame, to argue out, to feel with, to elaborate completely, the case as it stands against yourself; and what a fund of wisdom do you not turn up in this idle digging of the vineyard! How many new difficulties take form before your eyes! How many superannuated arguments cripple finally into limbo, under the glance of your enforced eclecticism.

Another criticism is that the wise solution lies somewhere between the positions taken by the two teams but that neither will admit it. In legislative debate, the bill may be strengthened or weakened by amendments. We should remember, however that school debates often concern the acceptance or rejection of a policy. We either have a state income tax or we do not. We either have compulsory attendance at elementary schools or we do not. In such debates there can be no middle ground, but speakers can properly be criticized if they overstate the benefits or the evils that will follow adoption or rejection of the policy.

The weaknesses of debate grow out of the weaknesses of human nature. Sometimes debaters are uninteresting or overly contentious; sometimes they give more information than the listener can absorb and use terms that he cannot understand. Critics often compare a poor debate with a good discussion, and come to the conclusion that debate is a survival of the horse-and-buggy days. In our opinion, this is a mistaken conclusion. When the time for taking action on a question has arrived, some form of debate is the best method yet devised for securing a wise and workable decision. The remedy for poor debate is reform, not capital punishment.

READINGS

BAIRD, A. C., *Public Discussion and Debate* (New York, Ginn and Co., 1937), Chap. 1.

CASTEEL, J., "Debate and Scientific Attitude," *Quarterly Journal of Speech*, Vol. 19 (April, 1933), pp. 186-92.

CHESTER, Giraud, "Contemporary Senate Debate," *Quarterly Journal of Speech*, Vol. 31 (December, 1945), pp. 407-11.

EMERSON, J. G., "The Old Debating Society," *Quarterly Journal of Speech*, Vol. 17 (July, 1931), pp. 362-75.

FEST, Thorrel, "A Survey of College Forensics," *Quarterly Journal of Speech*, Vol. 34 (April, 1948), pp. 168-73.

HANCE, Kenneth, "Adapting the 'Teaching Cycle' to Debate," *Quarterly Journal of Speech*, Vol. 30 (December, 1944), pp. 444-50.

LAHMAN, C. P., *Debate Coaching* (New York, H. W. Wilson Co., 1936), Chap. 1.

LOWELL, A. L., *Public Opinion in War and Peace* (Cambridge, Harvard University Press, 1923), Chap. 3.

NICHOLS, E. R., and BACCUS, J. H., *Modern Debating* (New York, W. W. Norton & Co., Inc., 1936), Part 1.

O'NEILL, J. M., and McBURNEY, J. H., *The Working Principles of Argument* (New York, The Macmillan Co., 1932), Chap. 1.

POTTER, David, *Debating in the Colonial Chartered Colleges* (New York, Columbia University Press, 1944).

RADIN, Max, *The Law and You* (New York, New American Library, 1948), Chap. 5.

RUBENSTEIN, Ronald, *John Citizen and the Law* (Middlesex, England, Penguin Books, Ltd., 1947), Chap. 29.

SMITH, Bromley, "Extra-curricular Disputations; 1400-1560," *Quarterly Journal of Speech*, Vol. 34 (December, 1948), pp. 473-6.

EXERCISES

1. Make a five-minute informative speech based on one of the above references. Give information not contained in this chapter and comment on any differences of opinion you may find.

2. Make a four-minute argumentative speech stating and defending your opinion on the position taken in one of the following quotations:

a. "The one thing essential is a deep personal sense of the problem to be dealt with. Training for public debating often ignores this fact; the result is that mere debating is confused with argumentation— a confusion which to my mind is the heart of what the old Greek philosophers meant by sophistry. For debate as it has come to be conceived is associated with winning in a controversy." (John Dewey)

b. "We have emphasized the social utility of public discussion rather than its personal value. For that reason we have raised certain questions concerning the educational value of debate and have recommended the symposium discussion.... We have felt that what we need today is not training in winning an argument but skill in working through the complexities of a given social question." (Pellegrini and Stirling, *Argumentation and Public Discussion*, pp. vii-ix)

c. "Complete liberty of contradiction and refuting our opinion is the very condition which justifies us in assuming its truth for purposes of action; and on no other terms can a being with human faculties have any rational assurance of being right." (John Stuart Mill, *On Liberty*)

d. "In proportion as we love truth more and victory less, we shall become anxious to know what it is that leads our opponents to think as they do. And we shall aim to supplement the truth we have found with the truth found by them. (Herbert Spencer, *First Principles*)

e. "Men may read on both sides but it seldom happens that men who are impressed by one side care to read the other. In discussions (debates) they are obliged to hear both sides. If men do read both sides, unless they read a discussion, they do not find all the facts stated by one side especially considered by the other." (G. J. Holyoake)

f. "Debate is deeply in conflict with the scientific spirit of our age.... By teaching young minds to start with their conclusions and then find the facts to justify them, it is the great aider and abettor of the noble art of rationalizing." (H. A. Overstreet, *Influencing Human Behavior*)

3. Make a short informative speech on one of the following topics:

a. The distinction between discussion and debate

b. Debating societies in Great Britain

c. Debate and freedom of speech

d. Common criticisms of Congressional debate

e. A comparison of dialectic and debate

f. Debates in the Continental Congresses

g. A comparison of legislative and judicial debating

4. Read three or four pages of debates on a current problem in the Congressional Record and report your observations in a 1,000-word paper.

5. Listen to a debate on the Town Meeting of the Air and report as above.

CHAPTER 24
Forms of Debate

HAVING CONSIDERED the general purposes and characteristics of debate, we here describe the forms commonly used in inter-school contests and conferences, and in presenting controversial subjects to public audiences.

I. FORMAL DEBATE

This term designates the traditional procedure in American schools and in many public debates. The issue is stated in one of these forms:

a. As a question: Should the Taft-Hartley Law be repealed?

b. As the last part of a formal resolution: Resolved, that the Taft-Hartley Law should be repealed.

c. As a simple motion: I move that the X plan of hospital insurance be adopted.

d. As a motion on a committee report: I move the adoption of the committee report on hospital insurance.

Affirmative speakers urge that the question be answered "Yes"; that the resolution or motion be adopted. *Negative* speakers take the opposite position. Each debater usually makes two speeches: a *constructive* argument in which he presents and supports part of the case, and a *rebuttal* in which he seeks to answer opposing arguments and to reënforce his own. The current practice is to have two speakers on a team in school debates. There is, of course, no magic in that number. Debates may take place between two individuals; in legislative debates there may be as many speeches on each side as time permits.

A typical schedule for two-speaker teams follows:

Constructive Speeches (*10 minutes*)	Rebuttals (*5 minutes*)
First affirmative	First negative
First negative	First affirmative
Second affirmative	Second negative
Second negative	Second affirmative

Occasionally this arrangement is varied by having the second speakers combine constructive and rebuttal arguments into one speech or by having only one rebuttal on each side. The affirmative has the last rebuttal to compensate for the supposed disadvantage of having to devote part of the first speech to an exposition of the question. There may be a forum period in which audience members question the debaters or join briefly in the debate.

The debate tournament developed in the early 1930's. Teams from a number of schools assemble for a series of debates. Some of these events bring two or three hundred debaters together; there may, or may not, be an elimination series from which one school emerges as champion. The current trend is to omit the elimination series and arrange a program including various forms of discussion and debate.

The tournaments were originated as an economy measure and continued for other reasons. Debaters meet and form acquaintances with fellow debaters from different parts of the country. Some tournaments include a series for inexperienced debaters; some provide that a school may enter as many teams as it wishes. It is not uncommon for thirty students to represent an institution in intercollegiate debate in the course of a year, compared with the six or eight that gained this experience in the "good old days." The chief disadvantage is that, since most tournament debates are held without audiences, they do not provide experience in *public* speaking. But many debates in life situations are held before judges, boards, or commissions, without audiences. For training in logical presentation a large audience is not essential. Tournament debating constitutes valuable training for this type of occasion. Moreover, these debates may properly be regarded as practice sessions, preparing the students for appearances before audiences. When this is the objective, the judges should be so instructed.

Public debates follow a variety of patterns. In the famous Lincoln-Douglas series, the first speaker spoke for an hour; the second, for an hour and a half; and the first closed the debate with a half hour rebuttal. Our presidential campaigns are often running debates, though the candidates do not speak from the same platform, or into the same microphone. The nation-wide isolationist-interventionist debate preceding our entry into World War II, included hundreds of speakers and scores of mass meetings and network broadcasts. Many Town Meeting of the Air programs are essentially debates between well-known advocates of opposed points of view or courses of action.

The formal debate gives listeners an orderly and uninterrupted statement of the arguments on both sides of the question. It gives the debater training in thorough analysis, in the construction and delivery of argumentative speeches, and in defending his position against equally prepared opponents. As a school exercise, the formal debate gives the student the basic training in thinking and speaking he should have before he undertakes other forms requiring greater adaptability and more skill in extemporaneous utterance.

II. CROSS-EXAMINATION DEBATE

One of the criticisms of the formal debate grows out of its formality. If a speaker has carefully prepared his constructive speech, he may find it difficult to adapt it to what his opponent has just said. Or he may choose to ignore the arguments of the other side and to proceed with the development of his own. It is possible for a formal debate to continue as far as the rebuttals with little direct clash of argument and a consequent lack of interest and logical values.

To find a method that would hold the attention of the average listener more easily and, in addition, come closer to the situation confronting legislative assemblies, the Cross-Examination Debate was developed at the University of Oregon.[1] The schedule for a debate between two-speaker teams in which each speaker joins the cross-examination follows:

Minutes

1. First affirmative speech 10
   Cross-examination by second negative 5
2. First negative speech 10
   Cross-examination by first affirmative 5
3. Second affirmative speech 10
   Cross-examination by first negative 5
4. Second negative speech 10
   Cross-examination by second affirmative 5
5. Refutation and summary for negative 5
6. Refutation and summary for affirmative 5

Total time 70

The advantages of this form are that it places a premium on ability to answer questions about the prepared argument, insures a direct clash of opinions and points of view, and maintains a high degree of

[1] Stanley J. Gray, "The Oregon Plan of Debating," *Quarterly Journal of Speech*, Vol. 12 (April, 1926), pp. 176-180.

spontaneity. The interest of the audience is held by the four struggles for supremacy between questioners and answerers in the cross-examination periods.

But there are also disadvantages. Wellman points out in his book, *The Art of Cross Examination*, that relatively few lawyers become expert in cross-examination. To frame a series of concise, pointed questions which strike at important arguments in the opponent's case, or which require the opponent to admit the validity of one of the questioner's main arguments, is a difficult task for the beginning debater. Aside from this inherent difficulty, the tendencies to quibble over terms, to ask irrelevant questions, and to adopt the methods of the stage attorney who browbeats the witness, constitute disadvantages to be guarded against.

The following rules have been found helpful in guiding the work of questioners and answerers in the cross-examination process:

1. The questioner and answerer should stand well toward the front of the platform and, while addressing their remarks to each other, must speak loudly enough so members of the audience will feel included in the conversation.

2. Questions and answers must be brief, lest the cross-examination be a series of speeches. While some questions can be answered by a simple "Yes" or "No," others properly require a sentence or two for a reply that makes the speaker's position clear to the audience.

3. While the questioner is in direct charge during the cross-examination, there may be occasional matters dealing with the relevancy of questions or the propriety of the procedure that should be referred to the chairman.

4. Questions may deal either with arguments of the opponent or those of the questioner.

5. Questions dealing with the opponent's arguments may be designed to reveal (a) lack of evidence, (b) weaknesses in the evidence, or (c) weaknesses in the reasoning process. Those dealing with the questioner's own arguments will be designed to force the opponent to admit the strength of the questioner's evidence or reasoning.

6. Questions should often be arranged in series, beginning with admitted matter and working towards the alleged weakness or inconsistency of the opponent's argument.

7. The questioner may find it advantageous to ask questions that seem irrelevant but which deal with situations familiar to the audience. If he secures favorable answers, he should point out the analogy between the seemingly irrelevant matter and the issue before the group.

8. The questioner should be careful to show the significance of the respondent's answers, remembering that implications clear to him may not be clear to others.

9. The questioner should show that silence, or evasiveness in answering important questions, may be an admission that the opponent's argument is weak at this point.

III. LEGISLATIVE SESSION

Designed to provide training in the types of discussion and debate used at different stages in the legislative process, the legislative session is a valuable addition to the forensic program. Sessions extend over two or three days to allow time for a series of meetings to exemplify, in simplified form, the main steps in enacting legislation.

The schedule followed at the 1949 National Student Congress of Delta Sigma Rho is a typical example. The problem, announced some weeks in advance, was: "What federal legislation should be enacted regarding civil rights?" There were four committees, each to consider legislation dealing with one of the following basic rights considered by the President's Committee on Civil Rights:

1. The right to safety and security of the person.
2. The right to citizenship and its privileges.
3. The right to freedom of conscience and expression.
4. The right to equality of opportunity.

Each school was allowed four "congressmen," one for each committee. The legislators joined one of three parties: Center, Right of Center, and Left of Center. Delegates were urged to prepare bills in advance and to furnish copies for distribution at the first committee meeting. The faculty committee on arrangements prepared a pamphlet outlining objectives and procedure for each meeting and stating the parliamentary rules for assembly sessions. Faculty observers were provided for each committee to help the groups function more effectively.

THE SESSION CALENDAR

Thursday

5:00- 8:00 P.M.   Registration, committee assignments, etc.

8:00- 8:30 P.M.   *Preliminary Assembly.* Statement of objectives and procedures governing elections

8:30-10:00 P.M.   *Party Caucuses.* Each party elected party chairman and secretary, chose candidates for assembly and committee offices, elected members to make nominating speeches, and discussed party attitude on proposed legislation.

Friday

8:30-10:00 A.M.   *General Assembly.* Election of speaker and secretary. The procedure included nominating speeches, speeches by the candidates, and voting by roll call of delegations. Statement of committee procedures.

10:15-12:00 A.M.   *First Committee Meetings.* Election of committee chairman and secretary. Reading and brief explanations of advance bills by delegates introducing them. Discussion of committee procedures.

1:30- 5:00 P.M.   *Second Committee Meetings.* Decision whether committee will recommend one of the advance bills, with or without amendment, or write one of its own. Discussion of bills, based on this decision. Arrangement for minority report if committee is unable to agree on a measure.

6:00- 8:00 P.M.   *Banquet.*

8:15-10:15 P.M.   *Joint Conference Committee Meetings.* Consideration of problems confronting committees. Agreement on calendar for the plenary session.

Saturday

8:30 A.M.- 1:00 P.M.   *Plenary Session.* Consideration of bills recommended for passage by the committees. Debate and action on proposed amendments; debate and roll call vote on the bills.

2:00 P.M.   *Adjournment.* Meeting of steering, evaluating and legislative committees to prepare a report on this Legislative Session, and make recommendations for the next.

There were also unscheduled meetings of the party caucuses to discuss strategy; of sub-committees, to draft bills and resolutions; of minority members of committees, to prepare amendments.

The legislative session provides training in various types of speaking, ranging from informal talk and committee discussion to nominating speeches and parliamentary debate. The almost unanimous opinion of observers is that it is excellent experience for students with some skill in public speaking and debate who have studied the topic and acquired a fair knowledge of parliamentary procedures.

The most commonly noted weakness are (1) the tendency of a few individuals to dominate the meetings, (2) the possibility that timid members may remain silent through the entire session, (3) the

difficulty in securing skilled committee chairmen, (4) the temptation
to spend too much time in party or parliamentary maneuvers, (5)
the usual lack of a method of evaluation that recognizes skilled performance at the conclusion of each session.

IV. INTERCOLLEGIATE CONFERENCE

Closely related to the legislative session, the intercollegiate conference brings together delegates from a number of schools for a
week-end of public speaking, discussion and debate on current national or international questions.

The Intercollegiate Conference on World Problems, developed at
the State University of Iowa, is an example. The objective is to combine training in varied types of speaking with study of important
public issues. The schedule for the 1949 Conference, covering two
days, includes:

1. A series of discussions on "Problems of the Far East," culminating
   in a parliamentary session which seeks to formulate a single resolution embodying the conclusions of the Conference.
2. A series of four debates on the nationalization of basic industries.
3. Extemporaneous speeches on national or international problems
   other than those considered in discussion and debate.
4. Public speeches (previously prepared) on topics of current
   significance other than those considered in discussion and debate.
5. After-dinner speeches on "Should Congress investigate Congressional investigations?"

It is not expected that a delegate will participate in more than two
events. Critics rate each speaker and each team, on a five-point scale
from (1) below average to (5) superior, and give such oral comments as time permits.

The Ohio State University sponsors an Annual Conference on
Public Affairs. The 1950 topic was "Major Problems of United
States Foreign Policy in Western Europe," based on a study guide
prepared by the Brookings Institution. To make sure that the conference delegates have basic information on the issues, specialists on
the major problems appear at open hearings and, on request, at committee meetings.

Each participating school may send six delegates, and any number
of alternates. The delegates form three parties: Center, Right of

Center, and Left of Center. Each delegation may submit three resolutions. The sponsoring committee issues a handbook, describing in detail the procedure at each meeting and the official parliamentary procedures.

THE SCHEDULE OF EVENTS

Thursday

10:00 A.M.- 1:30 P.M.	Registration of Delegates
1:30- 2:00 P.M.	Announcement of Committee Assignments
2:00- 3:30 P.M.	Committee Meetings
4:00- 5:00 P.M.	Committee Meetings
7:00-10:00 P.M.	Open Hearings

Friday

9:30 A.M.-12:00 N.	Committee Meetings
1:30- 2:30 P.M.	Party Caucuses
2:45- 4:00 P.M.	Nominating Assembly
4:15 P.M.	Meeting of Steering Committee
7:00-10:30 P.M.	General Assembly

Saturday

8:30 A.M.-12:00 N.	General Assembly
12:15 P.M.	Conference Luncheon and Address
2:30 P.M.	Meeting of Evaluation Committee

The distinctive features of this Conference are the provision of subject-matter specialists, and the allotment of seven hours each for discussion in committee and for debate in the General Assembly.

V. "PROBLEM-SOLVING" DEBATE

A combination of discussion and debate, this form was developed at the University of Washington about 1935. It grew out of a conviction that debaters often take sides too early and that coöperative efforts to solve the problem should continue until it is clear that a real difference of opinion exists.

The topic is stated as an open question: for example, "How can we most effectively provide an adequate standard of living?" The first speaker on each team of three analyzes the problem; the second presents the solution that logically follows his colleague's analysis; the third compares the solutions advanced by the second speaker on each team.

A program for the problem-solving debate follows:

Minutes

Analysis of the problem, by first speaker of team X 10
A second analysis, by the first speaker of team Y 10
Presentation of proposed solution, by second speaker of team X 12
Presentation of second proposed solution, by second speaker of
team Y 12
Evaluation and comparison of the two solutions, by third
speaker of team X 8
A second evaluation and comparison, by the third speaker of
team Y 8
Total time 60

To clarify the issue, the third speaker on each team may question any preceding speaker. His conclusion may disagree with that of his colleagues. His chief aim should be to discover the best solution regardless of his past beliefs.

This procedure meets the needs of audiences who are not familiar with the problem and require more background information and analysis than can be included in the formal debate. It is adapted for use early in the forensic season before the debaters develop considered differences of opinion on the issue. But the expenditure of more time on information and analysis leaves less time to argue the strengths and weaknesses of the proposed solutions. If possible, the audience should hear a problem-solving debate and, later, a formal debate on the solution preferred at the first meeting.

This type has one real disadvantage for intercollegiate events. Both teams might propose the same course of action. Opinion would then be formed without the opportunity to evaluate the strength and weaknesses of other solutions. This could be avoided by advance arrangements between the schools.

VI. DIRECT-CLASH DEBATE

This form was originated by E. H. Paget [2] in 1931. It differs from the formal debate by shortening the speeches and dividing the event into a series of clashes on individual arguments. Teams consist of from two to five members. The procedure follows.

1. *Definition and Analysis.* The affirmative has five minutes to define terms and outline the case. The negative, in five minutes, accepts or rejects the affirmative analysis and states its position on the issue.

[2] E. H. Paget, "The Direct-Clash Debate Plan," *Quarterly Journal of Speech*, Vol. 27 (February, 1941), pp. 125-8.

2. *The First Clash.* An affirmative speaker, in three minutes, states an important argument. A negative speaker replies in two minutes. A second affirmative debater makes a rejoinder and so on until each side has spoken three times. The judge then decides which team has won the clash. (He may declare a winner earlier if a speaker has evaded the issue or replied ineffectively.)

3. *Succeeding Clashes.* Affirmative and negative speakers alternate in initiating arguments and the procedure is repeated until one side has won three clashes.

This procedure adds variety to the forensic program and puts a premium on quick thinking and extemporaneous speaking. The disadvantage is that the different arguments may not be properly related to each other or to the main question, making it difficult for the listeners to get a unified view of the issues.

VII. THE DOCUMENTARY DEBATE

The essential feature of the documentary debate is that the participants dramatize actual situations for use as evidence or impersonate authorities on the question. In the latter instance, the debaters present statements of opinion or selections from speeches prepared by the authorities they represent.

This method has taken a variety of forms. At Syracuse University, Milton Dickens [3] produced, in 1937, a series of dramatized radio debates. The debaters, in conference with the coach, select three or four issues, and the strongest pro and con arguments on each. They prepare a script which may include a rather large number of speaking parts and rehearse the debate before it is broadcast.[4]

At Western Reserve University, Warren Guthrie [5] developed a dramatized debate, based on courtroom procedure. Three debaters carry the leading rôles, as judge and attorneys. Each attorney may call three witnesses. Each witness represents a prominent authority on the question and must confine his testimony to statements of historical fact or the published statements of the person he represents. This same procedure has been followed in television broadcasts.

[3] Milton Dickens, "Adapting Debate to the Air," *Quarterly Journal of Speech*, Vol. 27 (April, 1941), pp. 255-61.

[4] For a specimen script, see Sherman P. Lawton, *Radio Continuity Types* (Boston, Expression Company, 1938), pp. 412-24.

[5] Warren Guthrie, "The Reserve Plan for Intercollegiate Discussion," *Quarterly Journal of Speech*, Vol. 25 (October, 1939), pp. 392-6.

The "Following Congress" series, broadcast for some years by Station WHA, at the University of Wisconsin, is yet another type of documentary debate. Each program is a thirty-minute condensation of a current congressional debate, prepared by Mrs. Jennie M. Turner, of the State Board of Vocational and Adult Education. All speeches are direct quotation from the *Congressional Record*. Students and members of the WHA staff take the parts of the senators or representatives.

VIII. PARLIAMENTARY DEBATE

In the preceding chapter, we described the procedure followed in British debating societies. The Oberlin Forensic Union uses a modification of the British method. Here is the outline for a parliamentary debate on the resolution, "That this house favors the nationalization of our basic industries."

1. Seven-minute speech supporting the motion.
2. Seven-minute speech opposing the motion.
3. Three-minute seconding speech supporting the motion.
4. Three-minute seconding speech opposing the motion.
5. The floor is then open to members who may speak not more than three minutes. The chairman recognizes speakers alternately for and against the motion.
6. Any speaker except the maker of the motion may be interrupted at any time if a member wishes to call attention to a violation of the rules by "rising to a point of order" or if he wishes to question the speaker "on a point of information." The speaker may refuse to answer the question or even to give the member the chance to ask it. He cannot refuse to yield for points of order. The time involved in stating the point of information is not charged against the speaker; the time consumed in giving the information is.
7. The debate proceeds in this manner for not more than ninety minutes. The chairman then recognizes speakers to summarize the arguments, first against and then for the motion.
8. The chairman calls for a division of the house and announces the result.
9. Only these points of order will be considered: objections to unsuitable language by a speaker; objections to the behavior of an audience member; objections that a speaker's remarks are irrelevant.
10. Members favoring the motion at the beginning of the debate seat themselves to the chairman's right; those opposing it, to his left.

The parliamentary debate is better adapted to forensic groups and literary societies than to inter-school debates. Its advantages are that any member of the group may take part and that, like the direct clash debate, it puts a premium on quick thinking and extemporaneous speaking. Unless the members have some knowledge of the issue, it may cultivate fluency at the expense of thorough analysis.

IX. WHICH FORM?

None of these forms, or of others that may be devised, is inherently superior to all others. When the debater has learned how to analyze a question, brief an argument, and make a speech, he should have the opportunity to participate in as many forms of debate on as many types of occasion as can be arranged. The debater who must always follow a set routine—with speeches of a certain length and a pitcher of water for each team—may be unable to adapt himself to out-of-school situations. Variety here is more than the spice of life; it is preparation for life.

READINGS

BAIRD, A. C., "How Can We Improve International Debating?" *Quarterly Journal of Speech*, Vol. 34 (April, 1949), pp. 228-30.

BAKER, G. P., "Debating at Harvard," *Harvard Graduates' Magazine*, Vol. 7 (March, 1899), pp. 363-72.

CHESTER, Giraud, "Contemporary Senate Debate," *Quarterly Journal of Speech*, Vol. 31 (December, 1945), pp. 407-11.

DICKENS, Milton, "Intercollegiate Convention Debating," *Quarterly Journal of Speech*, Vol. 20 (February, 1934), pp. 30-7.

———, "Adapting Debate to the Air," *Quarterly Journal of Speech*, Vol. 27 (April, 1941), pp. 255-61.

FITZPATRICK, J. R., "Congressional Debating," *Quarterly Journal of Speech*, Vol. 27 (April, 1941), pp. 251-5.

GUTHRIE, Warren, "The Reserve Plan for Intercollegiate Discussion," *Quarterly Journal of Speech*, Vol. 25 (October, 1939), pp. 392-6.

HANCE, Kenneth, "The Dialectic Method in Debate," *Quarterly Journal of Speech*, Vol. 25 (April, 1939), pp. 243-8.

McKEAN, Dayton, "Debate or Conference?" *Quarterly Journal of Speech*, Vol. 20 (April, 1934), pp. 223-36.

McPHERSON, E. G., "Reports of the Debates of the House of Representatives during the First Congress," *Quarterly Journal of Speech*, Vol. 30 (February, 1944), pp. 64-71.

MORRIS, D. W., "The Intercollegiate Forum," *Quarterly Journal of Speech*, Vol. 24 (April, 1938), pp. 212-20.

NICHOLS, E. R., "Historical Sketch of Intercollegiate Debating," *Quarterly Journal of Speech*, Vol. 22 (April, 1936), pp. 213-20; (December, 1936), pp. 591-602; Vol. 23 (April, 1937), pp. 259-78.
PAGET, E. H., "Direct Clash Debating," *Quarterly Journal of Speech*, Vol. 27 (February, 1941), pp. 125-8.
RINGWALT, R. C., "Intercollegiate Debating," *Forum*, Vol. 22 (January, 1897), pp. 633-40.

EXERCISES

1. Prepare a four-minute speech, based on one of the above readings.
2. If you were in charge of your institution's debate program, which forms would you use? In what order?
3. Make a four-minute argumentative speech supporting your views on a question such as these:
   a. Should formal debating be replaced by discussion?
   b. Should the cross-examination form be used in high schools?
   c. Should we adopt the British style of debating?
   d. What are the advantages of the legislative session?
4. Write a report on a current legislative debate, from the *Congressional Record*. Note especially the parliamentary procedures.
5. Write a similar report describing a debate on America's Town Meeting of the Air.
6. Prepare and present to the class, with the assistance of others, a thirty-minute condensation of a legislative debate as reported in the *Congressional Record*. Be sure that both sides are fairly represented.
7. Prepare a debate that presents the problem in dramatized form, followed by affirmative and negative arguments.

CHAPTER 25

Building the Case

THE PROCESS OF building the case properly begins after the debaters have studied the question and made a brief. Teams of speakers have been chosen and the members are ready to begin final preparations for the debates. The first step is to make as complete an analysis of the prospective audience as is possible. The next is for the members of each team to agree upon the case to be advanced in support of the desired conclusion.

I. WHAT IS MEANT BY THE "CASE"?

The case is a series of statements which, if supported to the satisfaction of the listeners, should logically lead them to the desired conclusion on the main proposition. The statements should present the strongest arguments found in constructing the brief. The wording of the arguments and the order in which they are presented may differ from those of the brief. Indeed, this is one of the main differences between the two forms. While the brief is an impersonal record of the evidence and arguments, the case represents an adaptation of this material to the information, prejudices, and interests of the prospective audience. In constructing the brief, the requirements of logical arrangement are uppermost; in building the case, the psychological order should sometimes be used. If the listeners are comparatively neutral on the topic, the logical order should be followed in presenting the arguments, but they should be so worded as to be interesting and meaningful to that particular group.

While each debater may prepare his own brief, it is necessary for the members of a team to agree upon the case. The process of choosing and framing the strongest and most convincing series of propositions often requires considerable time, but it is time well spent. A loosely constructed and carelessly worded case gives the impression of loose thinking; a case composed of carefully worded statements, connected by the proper conjunctions, is accepted by the audience as an indication that the debaters have thought their way through to the basic issues underlying the controversy.

Here are the main headings in cases drawn by affirmative and negative teams on the proposition: "Resolved, that a judge or commission should be substituted for the jury in our judicial system."

THE CASE FOR THE AFFIRMATIVE

I. The jury is an outworn relic of the past; *moreover,*
II. The jury system is inherently defective; *and*
III. Judges or commissions are better equipped to render decisions on the complicated questions that come before modern courts.

THE CASE FOR THE NEGATIVE

I. The jury has been made the scapegoat for the sins of our whole judicial system; *moreover,*
II. The jury gives the best judgment on many types of cases; *and.*
III. The right to trial by jury is basic to the preservation of democracy.

In 1945, Mrs. Glenn Frank, a graduate of the University of Missouri and wife of a former president of the University of Wisconsin, published an article in *Woman's Home Companion,* attacking fraternities and sororities. The two universities held a debate on the question, "Resolved, that this house approves Mrs. Glenn Frank's objections to social fraternities and sororities." The cases of the two teams are here stated in some detail.

THE CASE FOR THE AFFIRMATIVE

I. The following weaknesses, stressed by Mrs. Frank, are apparent:
A. The rushing system is bad.
B. The system encourages race prejudice and religious bigotry.
C. The system fosters class consciousness by prohibitive membership fees; *moreover,*

II. The following weaknesses, not stressed by Mrs. Frank, are equally serious:
A. Fraternities and sororities are a controlling minority in campus society.
B. They breed a narrow, isolationist spirit; *and*

III. The weaknesses are inherent in the fraternity-sorority system.
A. The evils of the rushing system are inherent.
B. Class consciousness is inherent.
C. Discrimination because of race and creed is inherent.
D. Narrowness and isolationism are inherent.

THE CASE FOR THE NEGATIVE

I. Fraternities and sororities contribute a great deal to the college student:
A. Scholarship is stressed.
B. Participation in extra-curricular activities is encouraged.
C. Fraternities are helping veterans adjust to civilian life, *and*

II. Fraternities and sororities contribute to life after college.
A. Members gain poise and social ease.
B. Members learn to shoulder responsibility.
C. Members learn the value of coöperation, *moreover*,

III. Fraternities and sororities make valuable contribution to society.
A. They played an active part in war work.
B. Members become good citizens in peace or war.

The reader should judge these cases according to the general rules which follow.

II. GENERAL RULES FOR BUILDING THE CASE

Affirmative and negative cases differ in ways that will be considered later. However, these rules apply to both.

A. The Statements Should Be Arranged to Show a Progression of Ideas

The listeners should feel that the first argument is the proper place to begin, and that the others follow in their natural order. This does not mean that there is one inevitable sequence to be followed in all debates on a question. Of course, the affirmative must prove the existence of a problem before presenting the merits of their solution, but, within this general framework of the argument, variations may be made for different audiences. Let us suppose that a speaker is supporting government ownership of the railroads. The first point in proving to an audience of shippers that a problem exists might be the argument that freight rates are too high; for an audience of bond-holders, the first point might be that the financial structure of the railroads is unsound. Similarly, the negative team may vary the order of their objections to the affirmative proposal placing first the one that touches the interests of their listeners the most closely.

The traditional arrangement is to put the strongest argument last. Recent experiments, showing that listeners remember the first part of a speech better than the rest and are influenced more by whichever side of an argument is presented first, cast doubt on the wisdom of this arrangement. If the strongest argument is not announced until the last speech the audience will have little time to come to a full realization of its importance. Whenever possible, therefore, the strongest arguments should be presented early in the debate. They are more difficult to refute and more likely to be remembered.

B. The Main Points Should Be Few in Number

A case consisting of three or four fundamental propositions, well supported by evidence and skillfully reiterated, is more likely to be remembered than one which attempts to establish a larger number of contentions. The intelligent listener is not influenced by the quantity of arguments alone; their quality also counts.

C. The Relations between Statements Should Be Clearly Indicated

Mentioned earlier, this rule is so important as to merit amplification. If the successive statements are links in a chain of reasoning, that fact should not be left for the listener to discover for himself. If the negative is presenting three indictments of the affirmative proposal, the fact that the failure to prove one indictment does not invalidate the others should be clearly stated. In the case outline, these connections may be shown by conjunctions or phrases; in the speech, they require fuller treatment so the unity of the arguments will be apparent to the listener.

D. The Phrasing of the Statements Should Have "Headline Value"

Headlines attract our attention because they are short; because they use familiar words; because they tell a story in a sentence or express an argument in a phrase. Did you ever see a headline reading, "Present administration produces significant increase in employment"? Wouldn't it be more like "Fair Deal brings jobs"? The case phrased in short sentences and everyday words is likely to be remembered. Arguments expressed in technical language are likely to be forgotten.

E. The Case Should Not Attempt to Prove Too Much

In their eagerness to win votes, debaters often make extravagant claims. Reformers argue that their remedy will cure most of the things wrong with society at the moment; opponents prophesy that grass will grow in the streets if the proposal is adopted. So pronounced is this tendency in political debate that the phrase "campaign promises" has come to stand for arguments that are forgotten after election day.

But the habit of overstatement is not confined to candidates for office. Advocates of the public ownership of utilities picture private owners as robber barons and promise increased service at decreased cost, with enough money left over to make possible a decrease in taxes. Opponents often make blanket charges of bureaucracy, governmental inefficiency, socialism, and dictatorship.

Debate should be an exercise in restraint and discrimination. Affirmative debaters need not argue that the present situation is entirely bad, or that their proposal is entirely good. Negative speakers need not picture the present situation as pure white; the proposed solution as black or red. The affirmative team which limits its attack on the existing situation to the establishment of certain specific weaknesses, and shows that their proposal would bring about sufficient improvement to make its adoption worthwhile, is doing all that is necessary to justify an affirmative vote. Negative debaters need only convince the audience that the weaknesses in the proposal outweigh its good points. Cases that do not attempt to prove too much have two decided advantages; they limit the debate to real issues on which there is conflicting evidence, and they are the most difficult for the other side to attack.

III. THE AFFIRMATIVE CASE

One of the best-known axioms of debate is that the burden of proof rests upon the affirmative. This means that the responsibility for presenting the evidence and arguments in support of the resolution rests with those who present the resolution and argue for its adoption. Unless members of the group are already dissatisfied with the existing situation, they will say to the affirmative, "You've made this motion. Now let's see what you have to say for it. Unless you can give us some good reason for making this change, or taking this action, we will vote against you."

The first step in drawing up the affirmative case is to decide what constitutes a reasonable burden of proof. We have already cautioned both teams against attempting to prove too much; it is equally important that the affirmative avoid the other extreme. While the decision as to what constitutes this reasonable burden of proof depends on the nature and extent of the proposed action, the audience should require affirmative answers to most of the following questions:

1. Are there serious weaknesses in the present system?
2. Are these weaknesses inherent in the system?
3. Will the proposed change remedy these weaknesses?
4. Will it do this without introducing other equally serious, or even more serious, evils?
5. Does the proposed plan have advantages, in addition to remedying the existing weaknesses?
6. Is the proposed plan the best one available?

These "stock issues" are helpful in deciding what the affirmative must prove. Indeed, the affirmative case may consist of statements answering the questions applicable to the current controversy. The "stock" wording should not usually be employed. The phrases are too general and too trite to be valuable as captions.

A. Types of Propositions of Policy

The stock issues do not apply equally to every question. Most debates before legislative bodies, and most school debates, are on what we have classified as questions of policy. But there are at least three kinds of these propositions: (1) resolutions advocating the adoption of a general policy; (2) resolutions urging the adoption of a specific measure or plan; and (3) resolutions asking a vote of confidence. Let us consider the task of the affirmative with each of these types of question.

1. *Resolutions advocating a general policy*. Every organization, from a local club to our national government, is founded on certain general principles that guide its actions on specific questions. Some of these principles, or ideals, are written down in laws and in constitutions; others are unwritten traditions. In debates advocating the adoption of a general policy, the affirmative urges an organization to alter, in some significant manner, one of these basic principles. The

purpose is to effect a change of attitude that will make possible the later enactment of specific legislation. Questions of this type have been widely debated: "Resolved, that wealth should be conscripted in time of war," "Resolved, that the powers of the federal government should be increased."

Should the affirmative present a plan for activating the proposed policy? Only, we believe, when they think it will help convince the audience of the value of their proposal. Usually, only the broad outlines of the plan should be presented. Otherwise, the negative may shift attention from the merits of the general idea, by attacking one detail after another. If the negative insist on a detailed plan, the affirmative may properly reply that the purpose of the debate is to secure acceptance of the general idea and that a plan, drawn by experts, should be debated later. If the negative argue that the proposed idea is wholly impractical, the affirmative may refute this contention by showing, if they can, that different workable plans are already in existence.

In debates on propositions of policy, the question of constitutionality is usually waived. However, the practicability of the measure is properly an issue. Debaters should be concerned with reality. The affirmative speakers should do more than picture the advantages of their plan; they should consider whether there is any likelihood of securing its adoption within a reasonable time. For example, outlawing the atomic bomb is certainly an attractive ideal, but there is little point in urging the adoption of such a policy at present. The opposition debaters should insist that questions of policy be debated in the light of existing conditions.

2. *Resolutions advocating a specific plan.* Once the organization accepts a general principle, there still remains the task of embodying it in specific legislation. There are differences of opinion as to the extent to which the principle should be applied, or on the relative merits of different methods of attaining the same result. In debates of this type, the question is on the adoption of a certain bill, motion, or report. Questions of general policy were debated in the convention that framed our Federal Constitution; when the document was submitted to the colonies, matters of policy were still discussed but the central question was on the adoption of the proposed Constitution. In legislative assemblies, the debate is on the merits of a bill or resolution; in business meetings of any group, debate deals with a specific motion. Questions of this sort may also be used in school de-

bates. They usually read, "Resolved, that the————bill should be adopted."

The affirmative debaters on such propositions must support both the principles on which the measure is based, and the specific provisions of the bill. They may admit that the bill is not perfect but argue that it is the best that can be obtained at the moment, that its merits outweigh its weaknesses which can be remedied in the light of experience. Should the negative advocate another measure, the affirmative must attempt to show the superiority of the bill they are defending. The stock issue, "Is the proposed plan the best one available?" is especially important in these debates.

3. *Resolutions asking a vote of confidence.* This type of question is commonly associated in our minds with the British Parliament, where the Prime Minister may ask for a general vote of confidence. If he fails to get it, he resigns and a general election is called. This is the broadest and most inclusive of the three types of questions of policy. Affirmative speakers may be called upon to defend, in the same debate, administration policies on such questions as national defense, foreign trade, treatment of minority groups, conservation of natural resources, and unemployment. For example, when a president is a candidate for re-election, the voters of the United States are considering the question, "Resolved, that this house lacks confidence in the present administration." The specific question, of course, is whether the administration should be continued in power.

The affirmative speakers need not defend every action of the party in power. They must argue, however, that the balance is on the favorable side of the ledger, that on most important questions the right policies have been applied. Such debates generally consider several problems, rather than a single issue.

B. General Outline of Affirmative Speeches

The next step is to divide the case between the debaters. On this point the stock outline below should be helpful.

FIRST AFFIRMATIVE SPEECH

I. *Introduction*
  A. Show why the question is of interest and importance to the listener.
  B. Give such explanation and historical background as may be necessary for an understanding of the question.

C. Give careful definitions of any terms not already familiar to the listeners.

D. State the main issues and give the main points in your case, containing your answers to these issues.

II. *Discussion*

A. State your first main point and show its significance. (In many instances this will be to prove the existence of a problem on which action is needed.)
   1. Support this point with the best evidence available.
   2. Summarize your argument, restating your point or contention.

B. If your speech has a second main point, follow the same procedure in presenting it. Be sure that the relation of each point to the main proposition is clearly indicated.

III. *Conclusion*

A. Summarize your argument.

B. Show what progress you have made towards proving the affirmative case.

SECOND AFFIRMATIVE SPEECH

I. *Introduction*

A. Devote a minute or two to an analysis of the first negative speech.

B. Restate the main contentions in the affirmative case.

C. Summarize what has been done by the first speaker.

II. *Discussion*

A. Present your first main contention and explain its significance.
   1. Support this point and summarize, as in the first speech.

B. If there is a second main point, develop it in the same manner. Be sure that the relations of these points to each other, and to the case, are clearly indicated.

III. *Conclusion*

A. Summarize your own argument.

B. Show what progress you and your colleague have made toward proving the affirmative case.

If the team consist of two speakers, this concluding summary will, of course, include the entire affirmative case. The last speaker should try to show that the evidence justifies an affirmative vote on the resolution.

C. Meeting the Specific Situation

In adapting this general outline to the needs of a specific situation, these three factors should be considered: (1) the amount of information the audience already has; (2) whether the audience is likely to favor or oppose the motion; (3) whether the negative will probably admit the existence of a problem and argue for another solution.

The first of these factors applies especially to the first affirmative speech. If this speaker is well prepared, he has much more historical and background information than he can possibly use. He must decide how much of it is probably familiar to his listeners, and how much of what is unfamiliar is essential to an understanding of the points at issue. Listeners are properly critical when a speaker underestimates their grasp of the question; they are confused if the debate proceeds before they understand the proposition. When the audience has a very limited, or an inaccurate, knowledge of the problem, a large part of the first speech may properly be devoted to what might be classed as exposition. But, in these circumstances, exposition may have great value as argument. The listener who understands a proposal of real merit has come a long way towards accepting it.

As Raymond Clapper said, "Never underestimate the intelligence of your audience and never overestimate its knowledge."

The second factor, i.e., the attitude of the audience towards the proposition, is important in deciding the order in which arguments should be presented and the amount of evidence that will be required to have them accepted. Listeners who are already favorably inclined offer the least difficulty. They are not likely to be critical of the amount or quality of the evidence. The best order is that which enables the speakers to arouse enthusiasm so the listeners will feel they are supporting a great cause. The hostile audience offers quite another problem: the members are ready, not to believe, but to condemn. They will be on the lookout for flaws in the evidence and overstatements in the arguments. The affirmative case presented to a hostile audience should begin by stressing points of agreement; the first argument should be the one most likely to be accepted; the point on which there is the greatest disagreement should come last. Between these two extremes, there is the audience composed of persons who have not made up their minds. They demand more evidence than would be needed to satisfy the favorable audience, but are more ready than members of a hostile audience to accept conclusions based on satisfactory evidence and sound reasoning. Here arguments should be presented in their logical order. When the audience contains representatives of all three groups, the speakers face the difficult task of pleasing the greatest number without offending the minority.

The probable attitude of the negative on the seriousness of the problem should also be considered. The affirmative team is sometimes confronted with a dilemma. If the first speaker, in addition to presenting the introductory analysis of the question, spends the rest of his time proving the existence of serious inherent weaknesses in the present system, the first negative speaker may admit the whole speech and argue that the affirmative is advocating the wrong remedy. If, on the other hand, the first affirmative assumes that the negative will admit the existence of a problem and proceeds to show the merits of the proposed solution, the negative speaker may criticize his opponent for failure to prove the existence of a serious problem. Usually, the first affirmative should follow a middle course, presenting some evidence that a real problem exists and some of the merits of the proposed solution. The negative cannot then admit the entire first affirmative speech. If the negative argues that no serious problem exists requiring the adoption of a new plan, the second affirmative speaker must be prepared to present further evidence on this point.

Should the first affirmative speaker outline the team's case? We believe so. The objection is that this procedure gives the whole case to the opposition, allowing them more time to prepare their refutation. The advantage is that it also gives the whole case to the audience, making it easier for them to follow the argument. The listeners will usually be more impressed by a strategy of fairness and frankness than by one of concealment.

IV. THE NEGATIVE CASE

Much of what we have said about organizing the affirmative case applies here. Negative debaters are also interested in determining what constitutes a reasonable burden of proof, but with a different motive. They will argue that the affirmative speakers have failed to establish their case. The negative team also wants to find out what the listeners know about the question and their attitude towards the existing situation and the affirmative proposal.

A. Possible Negative Positions

In preparing their case, members of negative teams must first decide which of the four possible positions on the question they wish to uphold:

1. *The negative may stand for the status quo.* This may be done

by presenting the merits of the present plan, or by attacking the affirmative argument that a change is necessary or desirable. The negative team that takes this stand need not greatly concern themselves with the affirmative plan. Their position is: Since we have shown there is no reason for altering the present method of doing things, why bother to consider the alleged merits of suggested remedies?

This position is more often taken by the opponents of proposed legislation than in school debates. Seldom is a question chosen for interschool contests unless there is considerable dissatisfaction with the existing situation. However, it may happen that this dissatisfaction is not shared by the audience to which a debate is addressed. For example, one can imagine audiences that believe there is nothing wrong with the present workings of the National Labor Relations Board, or the plan for compulsory military training. In such instances, the negative may stand on the record and argue that complaints would be just as great, or greater, under any other plan.

2. *The negative may admit weaknesses but argue that they are not inherent in the existing system, and can be remedied without changing the system.* Thus, opponents of government ownership of public utilities stand for the method of government regulation and argue that when weaknesses develop they may be remedied by amending the regulatory legislation, or by changing the personnel of regulatory bodies. A great many reforms are brought about by advocates of the existing order to offset demands for more radical changes. In this way, minority groups may, over a period of time, greatly modify legislation without ever having sufficient votes to pass a bill of their own.

This stand is often taken by negative teams in school debates. It has the advantage of a seeming fairness and a willingness to concede that there is some cause for dissatisfaction. The team taking this position cannot be attacked as "stand-patters" or "die-hard conservatives." They are willing to progress, but within the existing order.

3. *The negative may admit the existence of a serious problem, but argue that the affirmative is advocating the wrong solution.* This position is often taken by the opposition in legislative and political debates. For example, both major parties believe something should be done for the farmer; but each has its own farm program and each fears the worst should the opposition's plan be adopted.

Negative speakers in school debates often take this stand when the existence of a problem is generally recognized. They either argue that the affirmative plan should be defeated because it would not improve the admittedly bad situation, or that it is inferior to their own proposal. If negative debaters take the first alternative, they may be charged with being purely destructive in their attitude. An affirmative debater may say, "We've done our best to find a way out of a bad situation and all you do is criticize. Why don't you produce something better?" The negative may advocate a counterplan both to avoid this criticism and to give the audience the chance to choose the relative merits of the two solutions. The debate then becomes in effect, a contest between two affirmative teams, each presenting the merits of its own proposal and the defects in that of the opposition.

4. *The negative may take this stand that combines the second and third alternatives:*

First: The present situation is not nearly as black as the affirmative has painted it;

Second: *But even if* the situation were serious, we would oppose the affirmative solution because it would not remedy the alleged evils, or because we believe there are better solutions.

This double stand forces the affirmative to argue both issues; it also provides a second line of defense if the audience is convinced that a serious problem exists. The team using this case must be sure the audience understands the "even if" connection between the two propositions. It should suggest other solutions but will not usually advocate one of them as a counter-plan.

When the negative team chooses one of these four positions, the next step is to phrase the reasons for asking the defeat of the motion. Usually these may be presented as separate objections or indictments. They do not constitute a chain of reasoning in which the case is overthrown if one link is broken, but different arguments any one of which if established, may defeat the motion.

B. General Outline of Negative Speeches

Here is a general outline of the duties of the negative speakers:

First Negative Speech

I. *Introduction* (These steps are not necessarily taken in this order.)
   A. Accept or reject the affirmative analysis and definitions.
   B. Refute some point made by the first affirmative speaker.

    C. State what, in your opinion, the affirmative must prove.
    D. State the position of your team on the question.
       Show wherein you agree with the affirmative.
    E. Give the main propositions in your case.

II. *Discussion*
    A. Present your first contention and explain its importance.
      1. Support it by the best evidence available.
      2. Make a summary, including a restatement of this point.
    B. Present and support any other propositions in the same
       fashion.

III. *Conclusion*
    A. Summarize your argument.
    B. Show what progress you have made towards defeating the
       motion.

Second Negative Speech

I. *Introduction*
    A. Refute some argument made by the preceding affirmative
       speaker.
    B. Recall the burden of proof that rests upon the affirmative.
    C. Summarize the argument made by your colleague.

II. *Discussion*
    A. State your first proposition, define it if necessary, and explain
       its importance.
      1. Support it with the best evidence available.
      2. Summarize, including a restatement of your point.
    B. Present and support any other arguments in the same fashion.

III. *Conclusion*
    A. Summarize your own arguments and those of your colleague.
    B. Show what progress you have made towards defeating the
       motion.

If there are three speakers, the third speech will follow the same general pattern as the second. The conclusion should contain as effective a summary of the whole argument as the speaker can devise, ending with an appeal that the audience vote "No," on the resolution. Even when there is no formal audience vote, the debaters should remember that they are attempting to influence all the listeners, not just the official judge or judges.

In the section on the affirmative case, we advised the first speaker to outline the entire argument. The same advice applies here, and for the same reason.

Some may feel that we have made the process of building the case too complex and difficult. However we believe that, until the debater has thought his way through the question in some such fashion as this, he is in no position to face an audience of intelligent and thoughtful listeners, or to defend his arguments against the attacks of well-prepared opponents. Others may object that a case, built according to these directions, is likely to result in formalized speeches that lack ease of style and freedom of expression. Our first answer is that it is better to have an outline that is too evident than a series of speeches that lack plan and sense of direction. More debate speeches suffer from lack of outline and method than from too much attention to the framework on which they are built. The listener who is hearing about a question for the first time welcomes the assistance of topic sentences, transitions, and summaries that seem overly obvious to the debater to whom the evidence and the argument are familiar. The next answer is that, as the debater acquires skill in constructing his speeches, he learns to vary his transition devices and his methods of restating arguments. His speeches are clear but the devices making them clear are not so obvious. This is the goal toward which all debaters strive. The old proverb is irritating, but true: There is no excellence without great labor. The student learns to build strong cases by practice in building them and by observing the work of skilled debaters.

READINGS

BROOKS, G. E., "A Revised Method of Case Analysis," *Quarterly Journal of Speech*, Vol. 27 (February, 1941), pp. 46-51.

COURTNEY, L. W., and CAPP, G. R., *Practical Debating* (New York, J. B. Lippincott Co., 1949), Chap. 2.

CROCKER, Lionel, *Argumentation and Debate* (New York, American Book Co., 1944), Chaps. 4, 13.

EMERSON, J. G., "The Case Method in Argumentation," *Quarterly Journal of Speech*, Vol. 31 (February and October, 1945), pp. 8-15, 282-91.

GRAVES, H. F., *Argument* (New York, The Cordon Co., 1938), Chap. 8.

KNOLL, P. X., "Presumption in the Introduction to the Argumentative Speech," *Quarterly Journal of Speech*, Vol. 18 (November, 1932), pp. 637-42.

NICHOLS, Alan, *Discussion and Debate* (New York, Harcourt, Brace & Co., Inc., 1941), Part 2, Chap. 3.

NICHOLS, E. R., and BACCUS, J. H., *Modern Debating* (New York, W. W. Norton & Co., Inc., 1936), Chap. 9.

O'NEILL, J. M., and McBURNEY, J. H., *The Working Principles of Argument* (New York, The Macmillan Co., 1932), Chap. 6.

EXERCISES

1. Make a four-minute speech comparing the material in one of the above references to that in this chapter.

2. In coöperation with your teammate, prepare the case you will use in a debate. Comment on any difficulties you encounter in following the directions in this chapter.

3. Attend a debate and report, with comments on their effectiveness, the cases used by the opposing debaters.

4. Analyze the cases used in a debate reported in the *University Debaters' Annual* or similar publication.

5. Analyze, with comments, the cases used in a legislative debate reported in the *Congressional Record*.

6. Analyze the cases advanced in one of the Lincoln-Douglas debates.

7. Analyze the case presented by a lawyer as recorded in *Famous American Jury Speeches* (Frederick Hicks, ed.) or similar publications.

CHAPTER 26

The Debate Speech

THE JUDGE WAS giving his decision after an intercollegiate debate. "The second affirmative speaker," he said, "obviously did not know enough about the question. I didn't get much out of his speech. Because he failed to establish his part of the case, my decision goes to the negative." The judge was probably right about the decision, but certainly wrong in his judgment of the speaker. This debater knew a great deal about the question. But that night he learned that mastery of subject matter is not enough. He failed because he lacked skill in conveying his knowledge to others; he did not know how to make an effective speech.

I. QUALITIES OF THE GOOD DEBATE SPEECH

One of the first lessons the speaker learns is that every speech should have a specific purpose. The debater's purpose is clear; he wants the listeners to support his position on the question. He cannot, of course, expect to win every vote on a controversial issue. The debater often attacks ideas that have been believed for a long time. It took years and thousands of good speeches to convince even a majority of men that women should have the right to vote. When an idea is relatively new, however, a single speech may significantly influence the attitudes of 20 or 30 per cent of the listeners. A debate speech is successful to the degree that it wins approval from those without strong conviction on the subject and weakens the beliefs of those who oppose the speaker's stand on the question.

What kind of speech is likely to have this success? We can make only a general answer: a good debate speech has the following qualities.

A. A Definite Plan

The debate speech, like all others, should have a definite plan, as well as a specific purpose. It should fit the time limits. The speaker should discover the number of words he can speak meaningfully in the allotted time. The average is from 140 to 160 words a minute. The speaker's next step is to select the best evidence and the strongest arguments to support his contentions. This may mean discarding much the speaker would like to say. He should phrase these supporting arguments in topic sentences and arrange them in the most effective order. This done, the speaker decides how much time he will devote to each point.

The time outline for a ten-minute speech follows:

I. Introduction and refutation of preceding speaker	1½ min.	225 words
II. Restatement of case and introduction of main argument	1 min.	150 words
III. Development of first supporting argument	3 min.	450 words
IV. Development of second supporting argument	1½ min.	225 words
V. Development of third supporting argument	2 min.	300 words
VI. Summary and conclusion	1 min.	150 words
		1500 words

Except when the speech is prepared for a hostile audience, the outline should be stated in the introduction so the listeners can easily follow the argument. The transitions, including a brief statement of the argument just completed, should be clearly indicated. Speakers inclined to neglect this step in speech construction should study the work of great debaters.

Lincoln's address at Cooper Institute, February 27, 1860, is rightly regarded as a masterpiece. Note the precision with which the outline of the argument is indicated in the introduction.

Mr. President and Fellow Citizens of New York: The facts with which I shall deal this evening are mainly old and familiar; nor is there anything new in the general use I shall make of them. If there shall be any novelty, it will be in the mode of presenting the facts, and the inferences and observations following that presentation. In his speech last autumn at Columbus, Ohio, as reported in the New York *Times*, Senator Douglas said:

'Our fathers, when they framed the government under which we live, understood this question just as well, and even better, than we do now.'

I fully endorse this and adopt it as a text for this discourse. I so adopt it because it furnishes a precise and an agreed starting point for a discussion between Republicans and that wing of the Democracy headed by Senator Douglas. It simply leaves the inquiry: What was the understanding those fathers had of the question mentioned?

What is the frame of government under which we live? The answer must be, "The Constitution of the United States." That Constitution consists of the original, framed in 1787, and under which the present government first went into operation, and twelve subsequently framed amendments, the first ten of which were framed in 1789.

Who were the fathers that framed the Constitution? I suppose the thirty-nine who signed the original instrument may be fairly called our fathers who framed that part of the present government. It is almost exactly true to say that they framed it, and it is altogether true to say they fairly represented the opinion and sentiment of the whole nation at that time. The names, being familiar to nearly all, and accessible to quite all, need not now be repeated.

I take these thirty-nine, for the present, as being "our fathers who framed the government under which we live." What is the question which, according to the text, those fathers understood "just as well, and even better than we do now?"

It is this: Does the proper division of local from Federal authority, or anything in the Constitution, forbid our Federal Government to control as to slavery in our Federal Territories?

Upon this, Senator Douglas holds the affirmative, and Republicans the negative. This affirmation and denial form an issue; and this issue—this question is precisely what the text declares our fathers understood better than we. Let us now inquire whether the thirty-nine, or any of them ever acted on this question....

In the chapter on "Building the Case" we noted that the inexperienced debater is often afraid of making his outline too obvious. Consequently, he plunges into his speech without a clear statement of the point he seeks to establish and its bearing on the main proposition; he moves from one argument to another without specific summary and transition sentences and stops without an adequate conclusion.

B. Clear Language

Remember what happened when you tried to explain football to someone who knew nothing about the game? You found that terms like *punt*, *T formation*, and *naked reverse* had to be explained. You discovered that words clear to you meant something quite different, or nothing at all, to someone else. Experiences such as this bring us face to face with the difficulties of communication. Words do not necessarily mean what we intend them to mean; they have meaning for the listener only as they are connected with his past experiences.

The more deeply a debater studies a question, the more likely he is to talk about it in terms that have precise meanings for students of the subject, but only vague meanings for others. He reads articles, written by specialists for other specialists, and learns to use, if not fully to understand, their vocabulary and their generalizations. The way out of this difficulty is certainly not for the debater to avoid the writings of authorities on the subject. His task is, rather, to translate their technical language into words that his listener uses and understands. He can usually assume that his audience knows about as much, or as little, about the question as he did when he began preparations for the debate.

C. Appeal to the Listeners' Interests and Desires

If the average listener is to be interested, he must see how the subject touches his job, the welfare of his family and friends, or his basic beliefs. This does not mean that the appeal is always to selfish motives. Most individuals will make great personal and material sacrifices if they believe their ideals and principles are at stake.

Many accept as a truism the statement that statistics are bound to be uninteresting. A student was overheard to remark, "This course is going to be plenty dull. It has lots of statistics in it." He had looked at tables showing population trends, indices of employment, carloadings, and bank clearings, and felt no interest in them. But that evening he listened with close attention to a statistical summary of the day's football games; he had even worked out a complicated formula for predicting the winners. Statistics are neither inherently interesting, nor inevitably dull; the speaker's task is to make them interesting.

D. Appeal to Authority

If the speech is to be convincing, the listener must feel that the speaker knows what he is talking about. Here the person who is recognized as an authority has a decided advantage. His listeners are inclined to accept his conclusions, thereby avoiding the work involved in testing the quality of his evidence and the validity of his reasoning. The authority's prestige is so generally admitted that chairmen often introduce a speaker with the vague statement that "Mr. X is a recognized authority in his field."

The college debater rarely gets such an introduction. If he is well prepared, he knows more about the question than most of his listeners, but usually not as the result of original research. He reports the investigations made by authorities; and draws conclusions from them. While he is not an authority on the question, he can make an authoritative speech if he does these things:

1. He can analyze the question and state his team's case with clarity and precision. If he does this, and avoids vague generalities throughout his speech, his listeners will decide he knows what he is talking about. The introduction to Lincoln's Cooper Institute speech should be re-read with this advice in mind. Lincoln was not regarded as an authority by most of his audience when he began to speak. Many came merely to see this "uneducated" man who had so effectively opposed the distinguished Senator Douglas in debate.

2. He can state the evidence supporting his contentions with accuracy and sufficient detail to indicate that he really understands its meaning and importance. This does not mean that the speaker should tell all he knows about a piece of evidence. Too much detail impedes the movement of the argument. The problem is to give those items of information that clarify the evidence and that could only be given by someone who has really studied the problem. Note how Lincoln included those significant details early in the Cooper Union speech:

> In 1784, three years before the Constitution, the United States then owning the Northwestern Territory and no other, the Congress of the Confederation had before them this question of prohibiting slavery in the territory, and four of the thirty-nine who afterwards framed the Constitution were in that Congress, and voted on the question. Of these Roger Sherman, Thomas Mifflin, and Hugh Williamson voted for the prohibition, this showing that in their understanding, no line dividing local from Federal authority, nor anything else, properly forbade the Federal Government to control as to slavery in Federal territory. The other of the four, James McHenry, voted against the prohibition, showing that for some reason he thought it improper to vote for it.

3. The debater should give enough information about the individuals whose opinions he cites to make it clear that he knows who these authorities are, and so his listeners will be able to estimate the importance of their opinions. The phrase "enough information" must

be interpreted in the light of what the audience already knows about the individual. It might not be necessary to inform listeners that Harold E. Stassen was governor of Minnesota and is president of the University of Pennsylvania. However, his opinion of the United Nations should be prefaced by the information that he was a member of the United States delegation at the San Francisco Conference which created the United Nations. Such vague references as "that great scholar," "distinguished economist," or "noted student of the subject" give the impression that the speaker doesn't know much about the individual whose opinion he quotes. Nor is it enough to quote *Vital Speeches*, the *Reader's Digest*, or the *Congressional Record*. Cite the person who said it. It is not the number of items about the authority, but their relation to the question under discussion that is significant. Note how effectively this debater indirectly shows his knowledge of Joseph B. Eastman while stating his qualifications as an authority on public ownership:

Mr. Eastman's position as Federal Coördinator of Transportation was not a political appointment. He had unusual training and experience in utility regulation. From 1906 to 1913, he was secretary of the Public Franchise League of Boston. In the next two years he was counsel for various street-railway companies in wage-arbitration cases. Then for four years he was a member of the Massachusetts Public Service Commission. Since 1919 he has been a member of the Interstate Commerce Commission. It is from this background of knowledge and experience that he says. . . .

E. Adaptation to the Average Listener

The speech may have the four qualities just presented and yet fail because the speaker sets too rapid a pace for his audience. Ten minutes of solid facts, opinion and argument, delivered at machine-gun rate, are more likely to tire and confuse the listener than to convince him. If the debate is intended for the average listener, the amount of information, and the language, should be adjusted to what he can be expected to comprehend and absorb. If it is intended for an audience of experts, the general public should not be invited. Few citizens would care to attend even the most important debates before the Supreme Court. However, they flock to criminal trials where the issues are simpler and more directly rooted in primitive emotions.

II. PREPARING FOR DELIVERY

At this point, the student debater is confronted with a seeming dilemma. Should he write out and perhaps memorize his speech, or prepare an outline and compose his speech under the stimulus of the occasion? The first method assures a more concise style with greater accuracy of statement; the second has both the strengths and the weaknesses of conversation. The debater often has difficulty in adapting a written speech to needs of the moment; the extemporaneous speaker may say things he didn't intend to say and is often guilty of using trite phrases and bad grammar.

Perhaps we can get some advice from studying the methods used by successful debaters. Early in his speaking career, William Jennings Bryan wrote out and memorized his speeches; later he spoke from notes. Patrick Henry, who usually spoke extemporaneously, spent three days preparing detailed notes and writing out parts of his argument on an important case. Robert M. LaFollette, Sr., wrote out most of his speeches in longhand. "He was," says his biographer, "a slow writer, taking great pains to find the right word." Samuel Gompers seldom prepared written outlines, and rarely wrote out a speech; but observers noted that his introductions were often clumsy and that his speeches "rambled about a good deal."

Henry Ward Beecher wrote his special lectures, sometimes in longhand, sometimes dictating to a secretary as he paced up and down the room. Late in his career he said, "I never dare nowadays to write out a sermon during the week; that would be sure to kill it." Wendell Phillips was a master of the art of extemporaneous speaking but he frequently wrote and memorized his public lectures. Henry W. Grady, also a successful journalist, prepared written drafts of all important addresses, but often departed widely from them under the stimulus of the occasion. Booker T. Washington prepared an outline with "headlines" for topic sentences. He then dictated his speech, but spoke with only the outline before him. Woodrow Wilson told Ida M. Tarbell that for important occasions he began with a list of topics, "arranging them in my mind in their natural relations." Then he wrote a first draft in shorthand. "This done, I copy it on my own typewriter, changing phrases, correcting sentences and adding new material as I go along." [1]

[1] Ida M. Tarbell, "A Talk with the President," *Collier's*, Vol. 58 (October 28, 1916), p. 5.

Norman Thomas, an intercollegiate debater during his under-graduate days at Princeton, and one of our best contemporary de-baters writes: [2]

Except for radio speeches and a few exceedingly formal addresses, I do not write out and read my speeches. ... Long ago I came to the conclusion that for me, at least, to read speeches raised a certain barrier between me and the audience. To try to remember carefully written speeches also raised a barrier. I found myself turning myself inward toward my own memory instead of outward to the audience. Therefore I adopted the method of making rather careful outlines instead of writing out whole speeches. ... The result of this, and of the col-loquialisms, the "wisecracks," and, so to speak, the change of pace and style which I frequently use, is, when stenographically reported, a document which I sometimes shudder to read. ... Indeed, I am prepared to argue that many a good speech, resting as it does upon some give-and-take between speaker and audience, is bad reading, and that often one is justified in making speeches that are bad reading in preference to speeches which would be better reading. ...

The methods I use I do not recommend to young speakers as necessarily the best. They are best for me. One's own temperament, the nature of one's memory, the kind and degree of inspiration one draws from the audience—all these legitimately affect the style one uses and the methods one employs.

The Reverend Bernard C. Clausen refers to his debating experi-ences at Colgate in describing his procedure in preparing a sermon for delivery: [3]

I arrange a typical debater's outline for each sermon, charting the course of the general argument in graphic form, under heads and sub-heads, writing in the outlines of evidence and illustrations under these heads and subheads, and using the opposite side of the sermon outline paper for quotations, statistics, and poetic references—all written out in longhand. ...

I never refer to these sermon outlines when preaching but do my best to achieve a photographic memory of them before the service begins.

The method of preparation used in a given instance depends on such factors as the nature and importance of the occasion, the speak-er's knowledge of the topic, the time available for preparation, and the way his mind works under fire. The give-and-take of the court-

[2] Norman Thomas, letter quoted in *Representative American Speeches: 1939-40*, A. Craig Baird, ed. (New York, 1940), pp. 276-7. By permission of The H. W. Wilson Company, publishers.

[3] Edgar DeWitt Jones, *American Preachers of Today* (Indianapolis, Ind., The Bobbs-Merrill Company, 1933), p. 137. Used by special permission of the publishers.

room and the legislative assembly require competence in extemporaneous speaking; the pulpit and the lecture platform do not.

For many student debaters, the best method is to write the speech in "talking sentences," then to discard the manuscript and speak from a memorized outline. The speaker will usually follow the manuscript, but since he has not attempted *verbatim* memory, he is free to adapt what he has written to the occasion. Recording equipment can be used to advantage in preparing for a debate. Listening to a "play-back" of one's extemporaneous speech may be a painful but rewarding experience.

III. THE STYLE OF THE DEBATE SPEECH

We are here concerned with the speaker's choice of words and their arrangement, first into sentences, then into larger units of argument. The real test is the effect of the speech on the audience; not its effect on the critic who wasn't there; or how it would look in print.

A. Basic Facts About Listening

The reader can go back and forth over a difficult passage until its meaning is clear or he gives up in disgust; the listener can rarely ask the public speaker to repeat or explain. It is important, then, that we understand the basic facts about the listening process and their effect on speech style.

1. *Listeners cannot give continuous attention.* Even when the listener is trying to pay attention, he does not hear everything. Attention is not a continuous process; rather, it comes in spurts. Pillsbury estimates that the length of an attention unit is from five to eight seconds; other psychologists believe that it is even less. The length varies with individuals and, for any individual, with his interest and his degree of fatigue. In sustained attention, the rest periods are short and the listener is usually unaware of their existence.

Knowledge of these attention fluctuations should influence the length and complexity of the spoken sentence. In a speech delivered at the rate of 150 words a minute, the average listener may hear twelve or fifteen words in one unit of attention.

This is one reason for the advice that the speaker use more short sentences than long ones; more simple sentences than complex or compound; more loose sentences than periodic. However, this advice should not be taken too literally. A speech composed of nothing but short, simple sentences may become monotonous; but there is considerable evidence to support the rule that spoken sentences should seldom be long and rarely be complicated.

Note the variety of sentence length in this paragraph from William Jennings Bryan's famous "Cross of Gold" speech at the Democratic National Convention in 1896:

They tell us that this platform was made to catch votes. We tell them that changing conditions make new issues; that the principles on which the Democratic party are based are as everlasting as the hills, but that they must be applied to new conditions as they arise. Conditions have arisen, and we are here to meet those conditions. They tell us that the income tax ought not be brought in here; that it is a new idea. They criticize us for our criticism of the Supreme Court of the United States. My friends, we have not criticized; we have simply called attention to what you already know. If you want criticisms, read the dissenting opinions of the court. There you will find criticisms. They say that we passed an unconstitutional law; we deny it. The income tax was not unconstitutional when it was passed; it was not unconstitutional when it went before the Supreme Court for the first time; it did not become unconstitutional until one of the judges changed his mind, and we cannot be expected to know when a judge will change his mind. The income tax is just. It simply intends to put the burden of government justly upon the backs of the people. I am in favor of an income tax. When I find a man who is not willing to bear his share of the burdens of the government which protects him, I find a man who is unworthy to enjoy the blessings of a government like ours.

These attention fluctuations also indicate the need for more repetition of important facts and ideas than may be desirable in writing. A statement made once during a speech may not be heard at all by some listeners. To assure recall by everyone requires several repetitions.

Jersild,[4] in 1928, and Ehrensberger, in 1945, reported studies showing the effects of varying repetition on the listeners' retention and recall of information in speeches especially designed for their experiments. Using a score of 100 to represent the recall value of a statement made once, Jersild found these comparative scores:

Score

5 distributed repetitions	315
4 distributed repetitions	246
3 distributed repetitions	197
2 distributed repetitions	167
2 successive repetitions	139

[4] A. T. Jersild, "Modes of Emphasis in Public Speaking," *Journal of Applied Psychology*, Vol. 12 (December, 1928), pp. 611-20.

Ehrensberger[5] found two successive repetitions more effective than two distributed restatements and four repetitions at close intervals less effective than three. Both agree, however, that repetition must be used to insure retention, and that increasing the number of restatements beyond three or four does not produce a proportional increase in scores. This seems reasonable enough. If nearly everyone recalled the item after three repetitions, further statements could produce little except boredom.

To avoid this negative reaction, the speaker should use: (1) reiteration of key words and phrases; (2) restatement of important sentences in the same words; and (3) repetition of the same idea in different words. Vice-president Alben W. Barkley used the first and second types in a speech, delivered while he was a Senator to prove "that there is nothing satanic about the word 'revolution.'" Here are the beginnings of some of his sentences: "Washington ... was a revolutionary. ... Jefferson was a revolutionary. ... Andrew Jackson was somewhat of a revolutionist. ... Abraham Lincoln was a revolutionary. ... Theodore Roosevelt was a revolutionist. ..."

Repeating the idea in different words is illustrated in the paragraph from Webster's speech in his debate with Hayne. Webster began by asking that the clerk read the resolution which was before the Senate. Then he said:

We have thus heard, sir, what the resolution is which is actually before us for consideration; and it will readily occur to everyone that it is almost the only subject about which something has not been said in the speech, running through two days, by which the Senate has been entertained by the gentleman from South Carolina. Every topic in the wide range of our public affairs, whether past or present—everything general or local, whether belonging to national politics or party politics —seems to have attracted more or less of the honorable member's attention, save only the resolution before the Senate. He has spoken of everything but the public lands; they have escaped his notice. To that subject, in all his excursions, he has not paid even the cold respect of a passing glance.

The speaker should repeat only the key ideas and his most important pieces of evidence; otherwise, his listeners will get the impression that "he is simply saying the same thing over and over." But the skilled speaker, by varying the type of repetition, can say the

[5] Ray Ehrensberger, "The Relative Effectiveness of Certain Forms of Emphasis in Public Speaking," *Speech Monographs,* Vol. 12 (1945), pp. 94-111.

same thing a good many times without the audience being aware of it. When rightly used, repetition serves to emphasize the material as well as to make sure that all members of the audience hear it.

2. *To hold attention, the style of the speech must be varied.* Eisenson says, "Change or variety is probably the most fundamental and important attention value. To maintain attention we must have diversification of stimuli." [6] We have urged variety of sentence length and have noted the value of reiteration. The speaker can also provide variety by frequent changes from abstract to concrete material and vice versa, by using narrative illustrations and by employing verbs of action in the active voice. The speech has this quality of variety when the style changes to suit the different types of material, when the same rhythm pattern is not used throughout, when the old idea is expressed in slightly different ways. Variety is the difference between a speech that keeps the listeners alert and one that puts their minds, if not their bodies, to sleep.

3. *We attach meanings more easily to concrete and specific symbols.* Words, we have said, are symbols which we must interpret in terms of our experiences. These experiences exist as memories of specific stimuli to one or more of our physical senses. Abstract words apply to whole classes of objects, groups of ideas, or series of events and depend for their meaning on our ability to translate them into memories of specific events. This process may take time that the listener does not have and energy he does not care to expend.

Abstract words offer another difficulty; they are subject to a wide variety of interpretations by listeners with varying backgrounds. On this point Hollingworth says, [7]

Men are more alike in their ability to hear sounds and merely to see words than in their capacity to treat such sounds and shapes as symbols. The more subtle the sign and the more abstract the meaning, the greater will be the diversities in understanding among the members of an audience.

There is a good psychological basis for the advice of Sir Arthur Quiller-Couch: "Almost always prefer the concrete word to the abstract." Note how Henry Grady, speaking before the Bay State Club in Boston, 1889, used concrete words in developing the idea that,

[6] Jon Eisenson, *The Psychology of Speech* (New York, Appleton-Century-Crofts, Inc., 1938), p. 214.

[7] H. L. Hollingworth, *The Psychology of the Audience* (New York, American Book Co., 1935), pp. 76-77.

until recently, the South had failed to take advantage of her natural resources:

I attended a funeral once in Pickens county in my state.... It was a poor "one gallus" fellow whose breeches struck him under the armpits and hit him at the other end about the knee. They buried him in the midst of a marble quarry—they cut through solid marble to make his grave—and yet a little tombstone they put above him was from Vermont. They buried him in the heart of a pine forest, and yet the pine coffin was imported from Cincinnati. They buried him within touch of an iron mine and yet the nails in his coffin, and the iron in the shovel that dug his grave, were imported from Pittsburgh. They buried him by the side of the best sheep-grazing country on the earth, and yet the wool in the coffin bands, and the coffin bands themselves, were brought from the North. The South didn't furnish a thing for that funeral but the corpse and the hole in the ground.

"Logicians may reason about abstractions," said Macaulay, "but the great mass of men must have images." The debater whose speech consists largely of abstract statements supported by equally abstract statistics, should not be surprised if his listeners are bored and unmoved.

B. Effective Rhetorical Devices

In addition to a general knowledge of speech style, the debater should be acquainted with these rhetorical devices which are frequently used by successful speakers:

1. *Questions*. The idea that a speech is really one side of a conversation with the listener is heightened by frequent questions. Three types are: (*a*) questions to be answered by the opposition; (*b*) questions which serve as topic sentences; and (*c*) rhetorical questions that suggest the answer and are really persuasive in purpose.

2. *Illustrations*. An illustration shows how a plan would work in a typical, but imagined situation. Thus the debater might show how hospital insurance would serve the needs of a typical family.

3. *Examples*. The example is an actual, not an imagined instance. The use of examples is effective in clarifying abstract plans or principles.

4. *Figurative language*. The speaker can supplement illustrations and examples by such figures of speech as similes, metaphors, and analogies that suggest comparisons with familiar ideas or objects.

5. *Loaded words*. In the chapter on persuasion we learned that many words have strong affirmative or negative connotations. We

favor *justice, liberty, freedom of speech, democracy;* we oppose *injustice, tyranny, liars* and *traitors.*

6. *Humor.* Touches of humor, unexpected comparisons and turns of phrase, are good when they do not distract attention from the central idea. Relevant humor is an excellent means of providing relaxation, but the debater should remember that he is trying to convince his listeners, not to entertain them.

These devices are good when used in moderation. The speaker should not introduce every point with a story; questions are good but more questions are not necessarily better. The listener may be dazzled by the figurative language and miss its bearing on the argument. Skilled speakers often combine several of these devices in the same paragraph. Note, for example, this quotation from Robert Ingersoll's plea in the Davis Will case. He is arguing that Job Davis did not write the disputed will.

Now, the next question is, was Job Davis a good speller? Let us be honest about it. How delighted they would have been to show that he was an ignorant booby. But their witnesses and our witnesses both swear that he was the best speller in the neighborhood; and when they brought men from other communities to a spelling match, after all had fallen on the field, after the floor was covered with dead and wounded, Job Davis stood proudly up, not having missed a word. He was the best speller in the county, and not only so, but at sixteen years of age he wasn't simply studying arithmetic, he was in algebra; and not only so, after he had finished this common school education in Salt Creek Township, he went to the Normal School in Iowa and prepared himself to be a teacher, and came back and taught school.

Did Job Davis write his will? Senator Saunders [of the opposing counsel] says there are three or four misspelled words in this document, while the fact is there are twenty words in this document that are clearly and absolutely misspelled. And what kind of words are misspelled? Some of the easiest and most common words in the English language. Will you say upon your oaths that Job Davis, having the reputation of the champion speller of the neighborhood . . . spelled shall "shal" every time it occurs in this will? Will you say that this champion speller spelled the word whether with two "r"s and made it "wherther". . . .? Will you say that this champion speller could not spell the word dispose, but wrote it "depose"? And will you say that the ordinary word give was spelled by this educated young man "guive"? . . .

Here is another example taken from President Franklin D. Roosevelt's campaign speech at Worcester, Mass., October 21, 1936. His thesis was: "In 1776 the fight was for democracy in taxation; in 1936, that is still the fight."

In 1933, when we came into office, fifty-eight cents out of every dollar of Federal revenue came from hidden taxes. Leaving out of account the liquor tax—for liquor was illegal in 1933—we have reduced these indirect taxes to thirty-eight cents out of every dollar.

How else have we improved and Americanized the tax structure?

First, we have a credit to earned income—that is, income from personal work or service—thus substantially reducing taxes paid by the working citizen. Wasn't that the American thing to do?

Second, we decreased the tax rates on small corporations. Wasn't that the American thing to do?

Third, we increased the taxes paid by individuals in the higher brackets —those of incomes over $50,000 a year. Wasn't that the American thing to do?

Fourth, we increased still further the taxes paid by individuals in the highest brackets—those with incomes over one million dollars a year. Wasn't that the American thing to do?

Finally, this year we had to find new revenues to meet the immediate bonus payments and to take the place of the processing taxes. This new tax, called the undistributed profits tax, is merely an extension of the individual income tax and a plugging up of the loopholes in it, loopholes which could be used only by men with very large incomes.

IV. PRESENTING STATISTICAL EVIDENCE

The advantage of statistical evidence is that it summarizes hundreds or thousands of instances in a phrase or sentence; the disadvantage, that it is often so complex as to to be meaningless to a public audience. For this reason, speakers who announce that they will "avoid statistics and just appeal to your reason" are often greeted with applause. But this is one of the sillier remarks about argumentation; reasoning is no substitute for evidence. The debater's task is not to shun statistics, but to *make them meaningful*. For that purpose, these suggestions may be helpful.

1. When possible, combine statistics with examples. Describe an automobile accident, and follow with the number of such accidents during the year.

2. Before giving the statistics, show why they are important, how the information affects the listener. After giving them, show their significance.

3. Shun the temptation to use statistical terminology. Terms like *standard error, critical ratio,* or *method of variance,* may satisfy your ego, but they do little for the general listener.

4. Large amounts should be stated in round numbers. Unless absolute precision is required, say "nearly four million" instead of

"three million, nine hundred and ninety six thousand, nine hundred and nineteen dollars and eighteen cents." The listener may remember only the eighteen cents! The exact figures should be available, if needed.

5. Large amounts can often be made more meaningful by breaking them into smaller units. For example, if an individual earned a dollar a minute, it would take him about 5,100 years to earn a billion dollars, if he worked eight hours a day including Sundays and holidays.

6. Compare your statistics with familiar ideas or information. A student orator used this method to impress his audience with the number of murders in this country: "The American Bar Association reports that four times as many people are murdered in the United States each year as were killed in the battle of Gettysburg. And the rate is increasing by 1,000 murders a year."

7. Charts and other visual devices are often effective in clarifying statistical evidence. Line charts may be quite as abstract as the statistics they seek to clarify. At times, pictographs of various sorts can be used to advantage. (See, also, the section on the use of visual aids in the chapter on evidence.)

8. Like other important evidence, statistics must be repeated if they are to be remembered.

V. DELIVERING THE SPEECH

It is not enough that the speaker have a message. If he wants us to listen, we ask that he be at least reasonably proficient in the art of oral communication.

The ability to speak well cannot be gained, in the privacy of one's study, in ten easy lessons. There is no magic formula that will enable the speaker suddenly to master his voice, his hands, and his fears. Skill in speaking comes from continued study and practice, just as in singing, acting, or playing the piano. All that can be done in this chapter is to call attention to the importance of delivery, to state a few of the basic principles, and to list some of the faults that often occur in debate speeches.

The first essential of effective delivery is that the speaker talk *with* his listeners, not *at* them. But the advice to converse with the audience does not mean that the speaker should talk as he does in ordinary conversation. Perhaps his conversation is uninteresting, lacking in animation, common-place; if so, he certainly should not use it as a model for his public speaking. Good speaking is good conversation—not ordinary talk—spoken loudly enough so that all may easily hear, and with the accompanying facial expressions and gestures magnified so that all may see them.

Another important characteristic of good delivery is variety in the use of voice and action. It is impossible for the listener to pay attention very long to a uniform series of stimuli. If you don't believe this try listening to the ticking of a clock or watching the facial expression of a wooden Indian. Uniformity of stimuli produces monotony; even a uniformly pleasant voice may soon produce a mood in which the listener is aware only of a pleasing succession of sounds. The speaker may avoid vocal monotony by modulating the pitch, by changing the rate at which he speaks, by varying the degree of force or loudness, and by shifting his vocal quality. These changes should adapt the voice to the idea that is being uttered.

The speaker who stands as though fastened to one spot, with a fixed facial expression, and repeats a few standard gestures at uniform intervals, also achieves monotony. Monotony of voice and of action are closely related. The speaker whose muscles are continuously tense is likely to have a monotonous, high-pitched voice; the speaker who slouches, whose manner gives the impression that he is tired or bored, usually has a voice lacking in animation. The listener tends to assume the muscle tensions of the speaker. If the speaker is tense, the listener feels uncomfortable; the speaker who "suits the action to the word" is making it easy for the members of the audience to stay interested.

Perhaps the most frequent fault in the delivery of debate speeches is a belligerent, overbearing manner. Debaters who challenge the information and honesty of their opponents, and who make frequent use of sarcasm and name-calling, are seldom successful at making friends or influencing people. Every speaker should profit by the experience which Benjamin Franklin relates in his *Autobiography:*

A Quaker friend informed me I was not content with being in the right when discussing my point, but had to be overbearing and insolent about it—of which he convinced me by witnessing several instances. Endeavoring to cure myself of this fault, which I now realized had lost me many an argument, I made the following rule: to forbear all direct contradictions of the sentiments of others and all over-positive assertions of my own. Therefore, when another asserted something I thought an error, I denied myself the pleasure of contradicting him abruptly and showing immediately some absurdity in his proposition. Instead I began by observing that in certain cases or circumstances his opinion would be right, but in the present case there appeared or seemed to me some difference, etc.

I soon found the advantage of the change in my manner. The conversations I engaged in went more pleasantly. The modest way in which I proposed my opinions procured them a readier reception and less contradiction. I had less mortification when I was found in the wrong, and I more easily prevailed upon others to give up their mistakes and join me when I happened to be right. To my new tactics, I think it principally owing that I had such early weight with my fellow citizens when I proposed new institutions, or alterations in the old, and so much influence in public councils when I became a member. For I was but a bad speaker, never eloquent, subject to much hesitation and my choice of words hardly correct in language—and yet I carried my points.

The speaker who follows Franklin's advice will speak as quietly as is consistent with the size of the audience. He will avoid the loud tones that indicate anger or undue excitement and modulate the volume of his voice to accord with the importance of what he is saying. One of William Jennings Bryan's greatest assets was his ability to speak to large audiences without seeming to shout at them. His listeners felt that he was using the tones they associated with conversation between equals. The debater must be audible and animated, but he should not confuse volume of voice with weight of argument. Indeed, we commonly regard the "loud-mouthed" individual as an empty-headed fellow who attempts to make up in noise what he lacks in knowledge.

The excitement of debate often causes speakers to "tighten up" in much the same way that athletes do in a championship game. Too much muscle tension adversely affects the speaker's voice, raising the pitch and preventing the production of full, resonant tones. As the debater acquires confidence in his ability, these tensions are reduced and the quality of his voice is likely to improve. He can hasten this improvement by learning to control the tension in the muscles of his throat, thus regulating the pitch of his voice, and by consciously cultivating the use of full, pleasant tones.

Stimulated both by excitement and the desire to say as much as they can in the allotted time, debaters often talk too fast. The voice can utter sounds faster than the average listener can attach meanings to them. The experienced speaker varies his rate of utterance and uses pauses, both to avoid monotony and to indicate the relative importance of different parts of the speech.

The debater should take advantage of every opportunity to improve the quality of his speaking voice. However, individuals with average voices should not conclude that they are doomed to be average speakers. Some of our country's great debaters have had ordinary voices. They succeeded, in spite of their voices, because they were great thinkers, and because they excelled in other aspects of effective speaking.

The usual practice is for the debater to be seated on the platform, in full view of the audience. He is judged by his behavior when others are talking as well as by the effectiveness of his own speech. When not speaking, he should do nothing to attract attention to himself; but should listen courteously to the other speakers. If an opponent uses an argument he thinks he can refute easily, he should not show his pleasure; if the opposition presents a case that he does not know how to meet, he should not register his consternation. The debaters should give the audience an experience in vigorous but courteous debate where the attention is focused on the evidence and its implications, rather than on the elements of personal conflict.

READINGS

BAIRD, A. C., ed., *Representative American Speeches* (New York, H. W. Wilson Co., published annually).

BEHL, W. A., "Thomas E. Dewey," *Quarterly Journal of Speech*, Vol. 34 (December, 1948), pp. 425-31.

BRIGANCE, W. N., "What Is a Successful Speech?" *Quarterly Journal of Speech*, Vol. 11 (November, 1925), pp. 372-7.

CLARK, Robert D., "Lesson in Persuasion," *Quarterly Journal of Speech*, Vol. 33 (October, 1947), pp. 265-73.

CROCKER, Lionel, *Argumentation and Debate* (New York, American Book Co., 1944), Chaps. 16-17.

FOSTER, W. T., *Argumentation and Debating* (Boston, Houghton Mifflin Co., 2nd rev. ed., 1930), Chaps. 10-11.

FRITZ, Charles A., *The Method of Argument* (New York, Prentice-Hall, Inc., 1931), Chaps. 9, 14.

GULLEY, H. F., "Churchill's Speech on the Munich Agreement," *Quarterly Journal of Speech*, Vol. 33 (October, 1947), pp. 284-91.

MALONEY, Martin, "The Forensic Speaking of Clarence Darrow," *Speech Monographs*, Vol. 14 (1947), pp. 111-26.

NICHOLS, Alan, *Discussion and Debate* (New York, Harcourt, Brace & Co., Inc., 1941), Part 2, Chaps. 4, 5.

RANDOLPH, Jennings, "Truman: A Winning Speaker," *Quarterly Journal of Speech*, Vol. 34 (December, 1948), pp. 421-4.

VOORHIS, Jerry, "Effective Speaking in Congress," *Quarterly Journal of Speech*, Vol. 34 (December, 1948), pp. 462-4.

EXERCISES

1. Make a four-minute speech on one of the above readings. Your purpose is to supplement the information in this chapter and to comment on any differences of opinion.

2. Read the transcript of an intercollegiate debate. Write a report applying the advice given in part I of this chapter to the first speech on each side.

3. Attend a debate and pay special attention to the delivery. Choose the best speaker and, in a written report, analyze the reasons for his superiority.

4. Give a two-minute speech on the methods of speech preparation used by some great argumentative speaker.

5. Read a debate speech in the *Congressional Record*. Compare, or contrast, the style and method with that found in intercollegiate debates.

6. Compare speeches made by the same speaker in a political campaign and on a quite different occasion.

7. Read to the class a 500-600 word selection from an outstanding argumentative speech. Preface the reading with the essential information about the speaker and the occasion, and follow it with your reasons for regarding the selection as an example of good debate style.

8. Hand in the manuscript of your speech prepared for a class debate.

CHAPTER 27

Refutation and Rebuttal

EACH DEBATER USUALLY makes two speeches: In the first, commonly called a *constructive speech* (although its purpose may be to destroy an opponent's argument or a belief held by the audience), he presents the evidence and the argument supporting one part of his team's case. While this speech is carefully prepared in advance, some time is properly reserved for extemporaneous adaptation to what has been said by the preceding speaker. The second or *rebuttal speech* should not contain new arguments. The debater shows weaknesses in his opponents' evidence and reasoning, presents evidence tending to disprove their contentions, and further defends the case advanced by his own team.

Skill in refutation often means the difference between success and failure, both in school debates and in arguments after school-days. The legislator who cannot answer objections to his bill in the running fire of extemporaneous debate is greatly handicapped. The lawyer cannot hope to win many cases unless he can refute the evidence produced by opposing counsel. The salesman cannot rely on his constructive speech. He must be prepared to adapt his argument to the needs and interests of his prospective customer and to answer all manner of objections. The candidate for office must answer attacks made by his opponents and questions, relevant and irrelevant, put to him by those who attend his meetings. The citizen who is unable to deliver an effective attack on what he believes to be a dangerous proposal or to defend his own committee reports and motions against the opposition of others, cannot be an effective leader.

Skill in refutation comes largely, but not entirely, from practice. Practice may not always make *perfect;* it may only make *permanent* errors arising from failure to understand what one is trying to do.

This chapter analyzes the nature and function of refutation, gives the methods of refuting opposing arguments, lists common errors in refutation and rebuttal and concludes with advice on the preparation of rebuttal speeches.

I. REFUTATION OR REBUTTAL?

We apply the term *refutation* to the process of answering or disproving opposing arguments, whether in constructive or *rebuttal* speeches. Rebuttal speeches should include restatement and amplification of strong arguments that may not have been attacked, as well as attempts to disprove arguments advanced by the opposition. The debater uses refutation for these purposes: (1) to deal with hostile audience attitudes; (2) to anticipate arguments that will almost certainly be advanced by his opponents; and (3) to answer arguments made by opposing speakers.

Whatever the situation, the function of refutation is essentially the same. The affirmative speaker must repeatedly focus his listeners' attention on the merits of his case. He must convince them that their doubts, while natural enough, are exaggerated, or based on misunderstanding, and that the opposition's objections are not of sufficient importance to outweigh the merits of his proposal. The negative debater reënforces the listener's doubts as to the merits of the affirmative proposal, presents evidence of its weaknesses or of new problems that would result from its adoption.

The rebuttal speeches should help to give the listener the basis for a more intelligent decision on the questions. He sees which arguments stand up under fire. He learns that "there is much to be said for both sides" and is less inclined to expect the impossible if his pet reform is adopted or to fear the worst if it is defeated.

At what points in the debate should refutation occur? When the audience has formed opinions on the issue, refutation of these beliefs may well begin with the first affirmative speech. Every speaker thereafter should devote some time to refuting arguments made by his opponents.

The refutation may constitute the first section of the speech, or it may be inserted at appropriate places throughout the argument. The first method is the easiest; the second is often the more effective. When skillfully done, it gives the impression that the speech has grown out of the one just made by the opposing speaker. If all the refutation comes at the beginning, care must be taken to make a smooth transition to the "constructive" argument.

Refutation of a point before it is made by the opposition is usually found in the opening speech on either side. The advantage of such anticipatory refutation is that, when successful, it destroys much of the effect of the opposing argument. The disadvantage is that the speaker may suggest arguments that the opponents had not planned to use, thus leaving the way open for an effective rejoinder. Again, the speaker may present the opposing argument more effectively than he refutes it. Anticipatory refutation should be confined to points or arguments that will almost certainly be advanced. In introducing it, such expressions as "Our opponents will undoubtedly attempt to prove..." or "Some misinformed persons believe..." should be avoided. The first introduction tempts your opponents to reply that they will do no such thing; the second will arouse the indignation, both of the opposition and of those listeners who believe the argument that is attacked. It is more effective to begin in some fashion as "The objection most frequently advanced by opponents of this measure is..." or "Perhaps the strongest argument against us is...." These introductions avoid name-calling and indicate that the debater is considering basic arguments.

II. GENERAL METHODS OF REFUTATION

The debater should be familiar with the tests of evidence and reasoning; his task in refutation is to apply them to the arguments of his opponents.

In refuting an argument, you will use one or more of the following methods:

1. You may show that a conclusion is based on insufficient evidence, or on evidence drawn from doubtful sources.

2. You may admit the accuracy of the evidence but argue that the opposition has drawn the wrong conclusion from it.

3. You may show that the weight of evidence favors your side. This may or may not be coupled with an attack on the value of opposing evidence.

4. You may argue that the opposing argument is based on an incomplete or faulty analysis of the question.

5. You may show that the opposition has fallen into other errors in reasoning, described in the chapter on fallacies.

To give specimens of all these types of refutation would require more space than is here available. Examine such classics as the Lincoln-Douglas and Webster-Hayne debates, or great jury speeches, for examples of refutation on which to pattern your efforts.

A. Selecting Points to Be Refuted

Obviously, it is impossible for an affirmative speaker both to present his case and to answer all objections that may be raised by a skilled and versatile opponent. An attempt to do so usually results in refutation which is little more than a series of contradictory statements, i.e., "They say . . . But we deny it." But the audience does not require the impossible. As the debate progresses, the attention of the listeners is focused on a few points; their decision depends on the manner in which these arguments are presented and answered.

The problem, therefore, is to select the points in which the listeners are interested. To do this, the debater should watch the audience as closely as possible. Beginners are likely to spend their time looking up material in the card files or watching their opponents instead of noting the effect of their own and their opponents' arguments on their listeners. If the audience wants to know the answer to a question or objection raised by the opposition, an answer should be given even though the point seems intrinsically unimportant. Furthermore, these answers should be made at the beginning of your speech; otherwise, the audience will not really listen to the points you are making.

The debater can also get assistance in choosing the points to be refuted by noting the relationship of the opponents' case to that of his own team. This device is helpful. Record on the left half of a full sheet of paper, an outline of the case presented by your team. As the debate progresses, record the attacks made by opposing speakers on the right half of the paper opposite the point attacked. This done, you can see at a glance where the two teams clash. These points should be stressed in refutation. It is also important to note any points that your opponents have not contested. If a section of your case is admitted, there is no need of spending time in expanding or reinforcing it; all that is necessary is to show your listeners the significance of this admission.

B. Steps in Effective Refutation

Refutation is ineffective when the listener sees neither the relation of the argument refuted to the proposition nor the significance of the answer. In his desire to cover as many arguments as possible, the debater is likely to omit the introductory, explanatory, and concluding sentences that make the refutation meaningful. Four steps are involved in effective refutation.

1. *State accurately and concisely the argument you propose to refute.* Whenever possible state the argument in the words used by your opponent. This requires careful listening and accurate note-taking but it relieves you from any charges of misstatement. If you are prepared to meet certain arguments, it may be easy to convince yourself that your opponent made them. Avoid such trite and general introductory statements as, "They have said something about ..." "They would have you believe..." "Our opponents have pointed out that..." or "They have spent a great deal of time trying to convince you...."

2. *State the importance of this argument and its bearing on your opponent's case.* If it is a basic contention do not be afraid to say so. Remember that you get more credit for casting doubt on the validity of a fundamental argument than for destroying an unimportant point or for knocking down a "straw man" you have set up.

3. *Refute the argument.* It is generally not sufficient to offset one piece of statistical information with another, or to counter an opposing authority with someone who favors your side. You may be able to show that the weight of evidence is in your favor, to raise questions about the qualifications of "authorities" cited by your opponents, or to establish the greater reasonableness of your position. If the argument is very important you will attempt to attack your opponent's contention from various angles, and to support your own with all available types of proof.

4. *Conclude by showing the effect on your opponent's case.* This may require no more than a sentence but that sentence is important. Your listeners may be thinking about the problem for the first time; they must listen to a number of conflicting arguments in a few minutes and cannot be expected to make applications and draw conclusions that seem obvious to you.

III. SPECIAL METHODS OF REFUTATION

These rebuttal methods or techniques are used with sufficient frequency and success, both in the speeches of great lawyers and statesmen and by college debaters, to warrant special consideration.

A. Asking Questions

We do not here refer to rhetorical questions intended to be answered silently by the audience; we are thinking of direct questions intended to expose a weakness in the opponent's argument or to place him in a dilemma. A classic example of the dilemma is the question Lincoln asked Douglas in their Freeport debate. Douglas' doctrine of popular sovereignty meant that the slavery question should be settled by the citizens of a territory. But the Supreme Court ruled, in the Dred Scott Case, that a slave did not win his freedom if taken into free territory. This was in conflict with the doctrine of popular sovereignty. Directing his question at this conflict, Lincoln asked, "Can the people of a United States territory, in any lawful way, ... exclude slavery from its limits....?" If Douglas answered "Yes," he would displease the Southern Democrats; if he said "No," he would, in effect, abandon popular sovereignty and alienate many of his Illinois constituents. He attempted a compromise which temporarily satisfied the Illinois legislators who returned him to the Senate, but lost the support of Southern Democrats who left the party and nominated their own candidate for the presidency in 1860. Lincoln's question did much to split the Democratic party and insure his own election.

This, of course, was an unusual situation. Rarely can a single question, or any other method of refutation, have such far-reaching results. Questions of this type should be used when your opponent avoids a difficult issue or fails to give information you believe essential to an intelligent decision. The practice of asking various questions, some of which are unimportant, should be discouraged. These questions may confuse the opponent, but they are just as likely to confuse the audience.

Generally, not more than one or two questions should be used. They should be asked early in the debate and so phrased that the audience will see their significance and want to know the answers. Debaters often put questions in this fashion: "We would like to have our opponents answer this question in their next speech." Unless the listeners happen to think the information important, questions asked in this manner are ineffective. Questions should not be used unless the debaters are prepared to show the significance of whatever answer may be made, or of the opposition's failure to answer them.

It is equally important to know how to deal with questions. On this point Lahman says: [1]

One hard and fast rule can be laid down. Don't ignore questions your opponents ask. If they are trivial or irrelevant or ulterior in motive, tactfully point that out. If they are *bona fide*, meet them straight-forwardly. . . . You can be sure that your opponents intend to capitalize on your answers if you give them the chance. Categorical "yes" and "no" answers are the most vulnerable.

Do not say, "This question will be answered by my colleague." This usually gives the impression that you do not know how to deal with it and are shifting the responsibility to your teammate. Answers to relevant questions should never be deferred until the last rebuttal speech.

B. Exposing Inconsistencies

One of the basic tests of an argument is that of internal consistency. Logically, we ask that the different parts of the case rest on the same general assumptions; psychologically, we are capable of accepting contradictory reasons for believing what we want to believe. For example, when the repeal of the Eighteenth Amendment was before the country, advocates of repeal claimed that it would both eliminate bootlegging and other forms of tax evasion and that liquor taxes would help balance the nation's budget. These two arguments are at least partially inconsistent. High liquor taxes would not remove the incentives to tax evasion; low taxes would, but the revenue would be insignificant.

A series of debates, a political campaign for example, may contain inconsistencies of another kind. Thus, a candidate for office, in agri-cultural areas, may favor higher prices for farm products; in the cities, he may argue that food prices are too high. Each speech may be consistent; the inconsistency is between speeches delivered before audiences with different interests and desires.

The debater who charges his opponent with an inconsistency must do more than make the charge. He must convince the audience that

[1] C. P. Lahman, *Debate Coaching* (New York, H. W. Wilson Co., 1936), p. 173.

the two arguments, or positions, really contradict each other. This done, he can properly ask his opponent where he stands. In their eagerness to use this method of refutation, debaters sometimes seize upon inconsistencies that are verbal rather than real.

The only adequate defense against the charge of inconsistency is an argument that does not contain one. When the alleged contradictions are unimportant or the result of bringing together statements without full regard for their context, that fact should be immediately made clear to the audience.

C. Showing Trend of Opposing Argument

Debaters frequently argue that the opposition's proposal is a significant step toward an undesirable goal. Thus, Douglas repeatedly charged that Lincoln's stand against the extension of slavery was based on a desire for racial equality, including intermarriage. Some people fear that each measure giving the federal government more power is a step towards ultimate dictatorship. Liberals charge that bills sponsored by conservatives are part of a plan to put Wall Street and the reactionaries into power. The attempt is to shift attention from the current proposal to what might happen if a series of more extreme measures were adopted.

This method of refutation is based on the assumption that, if we favor the application of a principle to one situation, we must logically favor its application to many other situations. For example, it might be argued that, because we favor municipal ownership of one utility, we must secretly favor public ownership of all utilities. Actually, we might, without any loss of logic, favor municipal ownership of the waterworks in one city and private ownership in another. The explanation would lie in differences between the two situations.

It should not be assumed that showing the ultimate trend of an opposing argument is always a stratagem intended to confuse the issue. Quite the contrary. Many measures are proposed by individuals or organizations with far-reaching plans and motives that are not easily apparent. For example, any evidence that the specific bill, or motion, is really one step in a series of actions that would deliberately lead us into war, or in the direction of communism, or fascism, is pertinent and should be fully considered.

The answer to the charge that a measure is a step towards an undesirable goal, of course, depends on the situation. Usually, the best course is to insist that the question be debated on its own merits. One might favor one step but oppose going all the way: Lincoln was not bound to favor intermarriage between Negroes and whites because he opposed slavery! Discriminating voters can be trusted to decide how far, and in what instances, they wish to apply a given principle.

D. Adopting Opposing Arguments

Occasionally a debater finds it possible to take over an argument, or a section of his opponent's case, and show that it supports his own position. In one debate on government ownership of the railroads, the affirmative presented data showing the number of roads in serious financial difficulty, as evidence of need for government ownership. The negative accepted the evidence but argued that it showed the railroads would be a bad financial risk, that the government should certainly not take over every business that gets into financial difficulty. Another affirmative debater on the same question presented the success of the government in regulating the railroads as proof that the government could operate them effectively. His opponent accepted the evidence of the success of government regulation and argued that this proved there was no need for government ownership.

The effectiveness of this type of refutation depends on the debater's ability to convince his listeners that this interpretation of the evidence or argument is more nearly correct than his opponent's.

E. Using Evidence of Silence

The debater should note whether the opposition avoids points that it would be to their advantage to establish. In such cases, silence is significant. In calling this to the attention of the audience, the debater should stress his opponent's knowledge of the question: "Our opponents have made a thorough study of this matter. If such evidence existed they would have presented it to you. Their silence is proof that this argument cannot be substantiated."

Other special methods that can be used occasionally deserve brief mention. Sometimes the debater discovers that his opponent is making a good impression on the audience with a speech that contains very little evidence. Instead of pointing this fact out directly, he should repeat a number of the assertions, asking after each what proof was given. If all the opposing evidence is drawn from one source, or supported by very few authorities, or if the same authority is quoted by both sides, this fact should be noted. A rather common tendency of affirmative teams is to give plenty of evidence showing the existence of a problem and to pass hurriedly over proof that their proposal would remedy the situation. As one negative debater put it: "Our opponents have proved that a good many of us are ill-fed, ill-housed, and ill-clothed. From that they jump to the conclusion that giving the federal government more power would insure more food, warmer clothing, and better houses." In such situations, the negative speakers should persistently ask the affirmative to show how their proposal would better the situation sufficiently to warrant its adoption.

IV. PREPARATION FOR REBUTTAL

Here we are concerned with the advance preparations for refutation and rebuttal. There are three phases to this preparation: (1) building a strong case that will be difficult to attack; (2) gathering supplementary evidence to reinforce the points that are attacked; and (3) discovering the weak points in the opposing case and gathering evidence to weaken whatever arguments the other side may advance.

Cases are relatively easy to attack when they attempt to prove too much. Reformers often succumb to two temptations in presenting their arguments: they picture the existing situation as worse than it is, and they claim too much for their reform. A more discriminating analysis of the problem, coupled with more modest claims for the remedy would be more accurate and much more difficult to refute. Negative debaters often fall into the same type of error. They see no good at all in the proposal, or they criticize it for not doing things it was never designed to do. Few proposals are entirely bad. The negative is on stronger ground when it argues that there is not enough good in the affirmative plan to outweigh its weaknesses.

Preparation for refutation involves the gathering and filing of evidence in a form that makes it readily accessible during the debate. Witnesses at important hearings often have filing cases filled with materials that may be needed in answering a question, and secretaries to locate the needed document. The debater must usually content himself with a card file and a supply of cards on which the evidence is recorded. After the evidence is gathered, the next step is to prepare a rebuttal card for each main point or argument that may be advanced by the opposition. At the top of the card record the argument to be refuted; then list briefly all of the evidence and arguments that may be used in answering it. These cards should be prepared by members of the team in conference, so that each may benefit from the suggestions of others. Whether all of the material listed should be used in refuting an argument will depend on its importance in the debate. While each debater should be especially prepared to answer attacks on his constructive speech, he must also be ready to make some answer to any argument made by the preceding speaker.

Before an important debate, participants usually engage in a number of practice contests. From these sessions, the team should develop a general plan or strategy for the refutation and rebuttal. The affirmative team may decide to insist that the negative meet them on two or three basic points; the negative may plan to keep hammering at one or two fundamental weaknesses in the affirmative case. Both teams will have some plan to prevent getting on the defensive. Because even experienced debaters are likely to forget some parts of this plan in the excitement of the debate, it is a good idea for each speaker to have before him a list of points to be stressed, things to be done, and other things to be avoided. Lahman gives us the specimen cards, used by his students in a series of debates on the proposition, "Resolved, that Congress should be given power to override decisions of the Supreme Court declaring acts of Congress unconstitutional." [2]

Affirmative Suggestions

1. Stress issues & contentions; make opps. meet us.
2. Insist that disc. be common-sense consid. of live public question; not mere academic debate.
   a. Ridicule overuse of authorities.
3. Don't let neg. overdo flag-waving; we are real protectors of Constitution.
4. Don't let them say we haven't est. need and show how plan meets need.
   a. Quote Court's own words on judicial legis.
5. Drive home demand for list of foolish or vicious laws passed by Congress.
6. Don't let neg. put us on defensive.
7. Rebuttal.
   a. Organize around actual issues & make opps. meet us.
   b. Watch for our constructive args. ignored by opps.

---

[2] C. P. Lahman, *Debate Coaching* (New York, 1936), pp. 209-10. By permission of the H. W. Wilson Company, publishers.

NEGATIVE SUGGESTIONS

1. Keep constantly attacking; don't let them ever put us on defensive.
2. Adapt to case of opps. but hold to our own contentions if at all possible.
3. Press home questions.
    a. Parliamentary govt.
    b. List authorities.
4. Stress
    a. Congress would be supreme; able to pass law depriving Court of review power.
    b. Judicial power given Congress; final judge of constitutionality.
5. Rebuttal
    a. Reëmphasize const. arguments; watch for those ignored.
    b. Support one another's arguments.

V. THE REBUTTAL SPEECHES

The rebuttals should be speeches, organized with a central purpose, not a series of disconnected remarks. While answers to individual arguments can be prepared in advance, the speeches must be organized during the debate. Sometimes, indeed, the outline must be changed at the last moment to reply to an argument made near the end of the preceding speech. "Canned" rebuttals, memorized in advance, may have excellent organization and sentence structure but rarely can they be made to sound like extemporaneous conversation or be closely adapted to what has just been said. In this situation, the listener prefers extemporaneous thinking and speaking to a more polished style.

There is an important difference between the functions of affirmative and negative rebuttal speeches. The negative speakers are constantly attacking, arguing that the affirmative have failed to make a case for the adoption of the motion. Naturally enough, these attacks will be directed at the weakest points in the affirmative argument; the strong points will be admitted, attacked lightly or, sometimes, ignored. The affirmative rebuttal speakers must do more than answer these attacks; they must restate and amplify their strongest contentions. Otherwise the effect will be to ask for adoption of the motion because the proposal is not as bad as the negative contend. Failure to keep the strongest arguments before the audience is one of the common weaknesses in affirmative rebuttals.

Rebuttals often lack the topic sentences and the transitional devices that would knit the separate arguments into a unified speech. Sometimes the debater comes to a full stop at the conclusion of one bit of refutation while he consults his notes; then he looks up and begins with, "Then, too . . .," "They say," or "So far in this debate. . . ." Transitions of this sort neither show the relationship between the arguments nor do they give the listener the impression of progress towards a central goal. The rebuttal needs organization as much as any speech; the debater should make special preparations to provide it.

A. Organizing Rebuttal Speeches

The organization of rebuttal speeches will be improved if the debater follows these suggestions:

1. Avoid such trite opening phrases as "The gentleman who has just left the floor" or "My worthy opponent spent nearly all of his time. . . ." Remember that, in a five-minute speech you have time for only about 750 words; try to make all of them count. Here are some effective sentences used by college debaters in beginning their rebuttal speeches:

"Frankly, I am astounded. The gentlemen have come all the way up here from Boston to rebel against the realities of life."
"I should like to read to you the resolution which we are debating tonight."
"May I ask you to go back with me to the beginning of this debate and consider the first argument for government ownership advanced by Mr. Miller?"
"The process of debate is a limited one. For that reason it is necessary that we choose the vital issues and confine ourselves to them."

2. To show that you are following the course of the debate, it is often wise to take up first some point made by the preceding speaker. Sometimes, indeed, you can begin by referring to his concluding argument.

3. If your opponent has raised a large number of questions see if they cannot be grouped under two or three headings. Outline your speech so that you have a strong point near the beginning and another at the end. Just before this strong concluding point put others that you will take up if there is time. Get clearly in mind a picture

of your speech as a whole and plan transition sentences that will both introduce the next argument and indicate its importance.

4. Remember that the closing sentences of your rebuttal are your last chance to make a good impression, both for yourself and for your side of the argument. Watch the time signals closely; if something must be omitted, be sure that it isn't the strong argument you have left for the conclusion. The last sentences should be a summary or a conclusion in which, on the basis of the evidence, you ask the audience to join you in your stand on the question. Too many rebuttals end without finishing; the speaker stops wherever he may be and remarks, with an air of surprise or complaint, "Well, I see my time is up." When asked why he did not answer the most important argument, he replies that he intended to but there simply wasn't time. The debater can be excused for failure to recognize the importance that the audience or judge is attaching to an argument; but, having recognized it, he can have no adequate excuse for failure to find time for it in his speech.

B. Special Problems in Rebuttal Speeches

Let us consider the special problems that confront the speakers who make the opening and closing rebuttals for each side.

1. The *first negative rebuttal* usually follows the last negative constructive speech. This gives the negative the longest period of time for the uninterrupted presentation of one side of the argument and compensates for the advantage the affirmative gains from the last rebuttal. The first negative rebuttal may be regarded as the last section of the final constructive speech. If these two speeches effectively supplement each other, the affirmative will have difficulty in overcoming the impression they have made.

How, then, can the two speeches be made to supplement each other? Since the presentation of the main arguments must be completed in the constructive speeches, the first negative rebuttal speaker must either reinforce these arguments or continue the attack on the affirmative. Usually he does both. If his colleague does not conclude with a summary of his team's case, he may begin with such a summary and then proceed to attack affirmative contentions, arguing that they cannot be substantiated in the light of the counterevidence his team has presented. If his colleague has summarized the negative case, he should attack any affirmative arguments that have not been refuted, supplement the attacks on others, and continue the process of pointing out weaknesses and dangers in the affirmative proposal. The introductory sentences should be planned in advance to make sure that his speech starts off effectively; otherwise the rebuttal may impair the impression made by the conclusion of the preceding speech.

2. The *first affirmative rebuttal* speaker faces the difficult task of erasing the impression made by two negative speeches. If the opponents are effective debaters, the attention of the audience will be focused on weaknesses in the affirmative argument. If this rebuttal speaker begins immediately to deal with the strongest negative attacks, he will be at a disadvantage. It is at this point that affirmative teams often go onto the defensive. What, then, should the speaker do? After a sentence or two of reply to some minor point, he should briefly, but vigorously, restate the affirmative case. This summary should serve to recall to the listeners the effectiveness of the original presentation of those arguments.

Here are the opening sentences of a first affirmative rebuttal that kept from getting on the defensive:

I hope you will pardon me if, after these fifteen minutes of objections to a union of the nations of the Western Hemisphere, we restate our reasons for favoring such a union. [Then follows the summary of the affirmative case.] Now, in the light of these reasons and arguments, let's consider some of the objections raised by our opponents.

Each negative objection should be analyzed in the light of its bearing on the affirmative argument. While this speech seeks to reëstablish the affirmative case, it should be more than a restatement of the materials contained in the constructive speeches; new evidence should be introduced, and at least half of the time should be devoted to direct refutation.

3. The *last negative rebuttal* speaker must resist the temptation to talk about minor points and make a comprehensive analysis of the debate from his point of view. This does not mean that his speech should be all summary and restatement. There should be new evidence and further analysis of important affirmative contentions. The audience should be reminded of points that the affirmative have evaded or ignored. When it seems advisable, the speaker may predict, and answer in advance, the arguments that will be made in the final affirmative rebuttal.

The last part of this speech should be a restatement of the negative case, stressing the strongest arguments against the proposal and

casting doubt on affirmative claims. Debaters sometimes undertake
to do this by using a balanced summary of the two cases. One difficulty of the balanced summary is that it may summarize the opposing
argument more effectively than one's own. Especially is this true if
the opposing case is stated in its entirety before the comparison begins. Another common practice is to close with a statement of the
things the affirmative speakers have not done but must do before
they can reasonably expect the audience to vote for their proposal.
This device is effective if not overdone and if the speaker assumes
that the affirmative's failure is due to weakness in that side of the
question rather than to lack of preparation or ability.

4. The *last affirmative rebuttal* speaker in a close debate occupies
a position of strategic importance. He must be able to pick out the
essential issues and to concentrate his efforts on them. If the preceding speaker has made an impressive summary, he must attack certain
of the negative arguments so vigorously that the summary is forgotten. He must answer any suggestion that he is using the last speech
to make points that would not stand the fire of negative rebuttal, and
be careful to take no unfair advantage of his opponents. He must
avoid getting on the defensive, both by an assured manner of delivery and by refusing to be diverted from his main purpose by last-
minute questions or challenges.

The last section of the speech should take up, one by one, the arguments that constitute the affirmative case and show that the opposition has not successfully answered them. Admitting that no affirmative team can answer all the questions that can be raised, or tell just
how a plan that has not been put into operation would work in every
instance, the closing speaker should argue that his team has demonstrated a strong probability that their proposal would improve the
existing situation.

VI. COMMON FAULTS IN REBUTTALS

This list of faults, and the explanatory comments, are from notes
taken by judges while listening to a series of debates.

1. *Poor organization.* Rebuttals were not really speeches; rather,
a series of disconnected items. Instead of throwing more light on the
question, the rebuttals were confused and wandering. Some began
well but got worse instead of better.

2. *Lack of summaries.* Time was called when speaker was beginning a minor point; he closed by saying, "Therefore, we believe that

the powers of the Federal Government should be increased." Nothing to connect the speech with the proposition.

3. *Lack of new evidence.* Rebuttals were simply five-minute condensations of first speeches. Give us some additional evidence, some further analysis.

4. *Overstatement.* "They have utterly ignored...," "We have absolutely proved...." One debater said, "I dcfy the affirmative to name a single authority." The next speaker named one!

5. *Failure to apply evidence to question.* Show why authorities believe what they believe. Let us see what your facts and statistics mean. You have more evidence than you know what to do with.

6. *Too much assertion.* The lack of evidence was excused by saying, "Oh well, you can get authorities (or statistics) on both sides; let's just reason this out together." But reasoning should be based on evidence; otherwise there would be no real debate.

7. *Confusing authorities and persons named as sources of information.* Both sides can properly quote the same sources of information, but this does not make the person "our authority." An authority might be quoted by both sides in supporting subordinate arguments; but certainly no real authority would be on both sides of the main question!

8. *Failure to distinguish between functions of affirmative and negative rebuttals.* The negative seemed to accept the burden of proof, instead of attacking the affirmative. The affirmative attempted to refute the negative arguments but failed to reëstablish their own.

VII. DEPARTURES FROM THE CODE OF FAIR PLAY

The judges mentioned above also found these occasional, but regrettable, departures from the code of good manners and fair play.

1. *Misquoting an opponent.* This was unintentional, no doubt, but none the less unfair. The speaker evidently wanted his opponent to make that argument because he had an answer ready. Another speaker misquoted because he was so busy talking with his colleague that he did not listen carefully.

2. *Attacking the opponent instead of the argument.* "They have deliberately misquoted us...." How do you know? Why not assume that they are as honest as you are? "If they had studied the question thoroughly...." People who live in glass houses.... Why not let the audience be the judge?

3. *Misquoting an authority.* Giving only the part of a quotation that favors your side was probably due to carelessness in checking the authority's statement. Fortunately the other side corrected the omission and administered the deserved rebuke; otherwise the listeners would have been misinformed.

Refutation is an important part of every argument, whether about the conference table, or in the deliberations of legislative assemblies. Poorly done, it may divert attention from the central issues to personal attacks and recriminations, and serve only to confuse participants and listeners. Properly conducted refutation and rebuttal subject each important argument to searching scrutiny and result in a judgment based on a fair consideration of available evidence.

READINGS

BAIRD, A. C., *Discussion and Debate* (Boston, Ginn & Co., 1937), Chaps. 10-11.

CROCKER, Lionel, *Argumentation and Debate* (New York, American Book Co., 1944), Chaps. 10-11.

FRITZ, C. A., *The Method of Argument* (New York, Prentice-Hall, Inc., 1931), Chap. 11.

HOLM, James M., and KENT, Robert, *How to Debate Successfully* (Portland, Maine, J. W. Walch, 1946).

IRWIN, C. E., "An Intelligent Guide to Refutation," *Quarterly Journal of Speech,* Vol. 25 (April, 1939), pp. 248-53.

LAMBERTSON, F. W., "Plan and Counterplan in a Question of Policy," *Quarterly Journal of Speech,* Vol. 29 (February, 1948), pp. 48-52.

MUSGRAVE, G. M., "The Double-Summary Technique in Debate," *Quarterly Journal of Speech,* Vol. 32 (December, 1946), pp. 458-68.

NICHOLS, E. R., and BACCUS, J. H., *Modern Debating* (New York, W. W. Norton & Co., Inc., 1936), Chap. 15.

O'NEILL, J. M., and McBURNEY, J. H., *The Working Principles of Argument* (New York, The Macmillan Co., 1932), Chap. 16.

QUIMBY, Brooks, *So You Want to Debate* (Portland, Maine, J. W. Walch, 1948).

WALZ, W. C., "Some Problems of Rebuttal," *Quarterly Journal of Speech,* Vol. 20 (June, 1934), pp. 378-83.

EXERCISES

1. Make a four-minute speech comparing one of the above references with corresponding sections of this chapter.

2. Divide the class into pairs for rebuttal practice. One speaker makes a three-minute argument on some phase of the question used in class debates; the other, a two-minute rebuttal. The audience should identify the methods and comment on their effectiveness.

3. Make a written report on the refutation in an intercollegiate debate. If there is no opportunity to attend a debate, analyze one in the *University Debaters' Annual,* or similar publication.

4. Hand in the rebuttal cards used in one of your class debates.

5. Hand in a statement of the general plan for refutation prepared by your team for your final class debate.

6. From one of the great American debates, select passages that state and refute a single argument. One member of the class should explain the occasion of the debate and the issues involved; a second member should read the argument; a third, the refutation. Current materials for this exercise will be found in the *Congressional Record.*

7. Analyze the methods of refutation used in the following paragraphs. Could this refutation have been given with equal effectiveness by a student debater? Why, or why not?

a. "In the course of my former remarks, Mr. President, I took occasion to deprecate, as one of the greatest evils, *the consolidation of this government.* The gentleman takes alarm at the sound. 'Consolidation,' like the tariff, grates upon his ear. He tells us 'we have heard much of late about consolidation; that it is the rallying word for all who are endeavoring to weaken the Union by adding to the power of the States.' But consolidation (says the gentleman) was the very object for which the Union was formed; and, in support of that opinion, he read a passage from the address of the President of the Convention to Congress, which he assumes to be an authority on his side of the question. But, sir, the gentleman is mistaken. The object of the framers of the Constitution, as disclosed in that address, was not the consolidation of the government, but 'the consolidation of the Union.' It was not to draw power from the States in order to transfer it to a great national government, but, in the language of the Constitution itself, 'to form a more perfect Union,'—and by what means? By 'establishing justice, promoting domestic tranquility, and securing the blessings of liberty to ourselves and our posterity.' This is the true reading of the Constitution. But, according to the gentleman's reading, the object of the Constitution was to consolidate the government, and the means would seem to be the promotion of injustice, causing domestic discord, and depriving the States and the people of 'the blessings of liberty' forever." (From Hayne's speech in the Webster-Hayne debate)

b. "You charge that we stir up insurrections among your slaves. We deny it; and what is your proof? Harper's Ferry! John Brown! John Brown was no Republican; and you have failed to implicate a single Republican in his Harper's Ferry enterprise. If any member of our party is guilty in that matter, you know it or you do not know it. If you do know it, you are inexcusable for not designating the man and proving the fact. If you do not know it, you are inexcusable for asserting it, and especially for persisting in the assertion after you have tried and failed to make the proof.

You need not be told that persisting in a charge which one does not know to be true, is simply malicious slander." (From Lincoln's speech at Cooper Institute)

c. "I come to the testimony of the father. I find myself incapable of speaking of him or his testimony with severity. Unfortunate old man! Another Lear, in the conduct of his children; another Lear, I apprehend, in the effect of his distress upon his mind and understanding. He is brought here to testify, under circumstances that disarm severity, and call loudly for sympathy. Though it is impossible not to see that his story cannot be credited, yet I am unable to speak of him otherwise than in sorrow and grief. Unhappy father! he strives to remember, perhaps persuades himself that he does remember that on the evening of the murder he was himself at home at ten o'clock. He thinks, or seems to think, that his son came in at about five minutes past ten. He fancies that he remembers his conversation; he thinks he spoke of bolting the door; he thinks he asked the time of night; he seems to remember his then going to bed. Alas! these are but the swimming fancies of an agitated and distressed mind. Alas! they are but the dreams of hope, its uncertain lights, flickering on the thick darkness of parental distress. Alas! the miserable father knows nothing, in reality, of all these things." (From Webster's speech in the Knapp-White murder case. He is speaking of the father of the man who is on trial)

d. "Lawyers stand here by the day and read cases from the Dark Ages, where judges have said that if a man had a grain of sense left and a child if he was barely out of his cradle, could be hanged because he knew the difference between right and wrong. Death sentences for eighteen, seventeen, sixteen, and fourteen years have been cited. Brother Marshall has not half done his job. He should read his beloved Blackstone again....

"Why did not my friend, Mr. Marshall, who dug up from the relics of the buried past these precedents that would bring a blush of shame to the face of a savage, read this from Blackstone: 'Under fourteen, though an infant shall be judged to be incapable of guile *prima facie*, yet if it appeared to the court and the jury that he was capable of guile, and could discern between good and evil, he may be convicted and suffer death.'

"Thus ... one boy of ten, and another of nine years of age, who had killed his companion were sentenced to death; and he of ten actually hanged. Why? He knew the difference between right and wrong. He had learned that in Sunday School....

"My friend Marshall has read Blackstone by the page, as if it had something to do with a fairly enlightened age, as if it had something to do with the year 1924, as if it had something to do with Chicago, with its boys' courts, and its fairly tender protection of the young...." (From Clarence Darrow's plea in the Loeb-Leopold murder case)

CHAPTER 28

Evaluating Debate

THE VALUE OF debate as a method of deciding matters of public policy is not here in question. With all its shortcomings, debate is the foundation stone of democracy and the safeguard of individual liberties. This chapter considers the methods of evaluating specific debates.

I. BASES FOR EVALUATION

The first step in evaluating a debate is to determine its purpose. Classified on this basis, debates fall into three groups. In the first are legislative and judicial debates conducted by, or before, individuals who are legally empowered to decide the question. This group includes the informal pro and con remarks on motions that take place in the business meetings of organizations, as well as debates before juries and in legislative assemblies. The purpose is to secure a decision based on the evidence and arguments advanced by speakers on both sides.

The second group consists of debates on current problems held before public forums and similar organizations. Members of these audiences usually have no power to act on the issue. The purpose is to create an informed opinion that will result in an intelligent decision when the occasion arises.

Debates conducted primarily to train the participants constitute the third group. The debaters are members of school teams or of forensic societies. Sometimes, in practice sessions and tournaments, there is no audience. However, most schools schedule a number of public debates. These should serve the dual purpose of training the speakers and informing the listeners.

The process of evaluating a debate in terms of its purpose, consists of finding such answers as are available to the following questions.

461

A. Did the Debate Arouse Interest in the Problem?

Sometimes a public debate is held to focus attention on a problem, new to the public, rather than to secure immediate action. Bills are often introduced in legislative bodies for this purpose. The sponsor hopes, through committee hearings and assembly debate, if the measure gets that far, to create public opinion that will demand action at a later session. Important reforms may be discussed and debated for years before they are enacted into law.

The effectiveness of a debate in arousing public interest in the problem is difficult to measure. The size of the audience and the amount of newspaper space given to the meeting may be significant. Inquiries at libraries and bookstores will reveal any marked increase in calls for information about the subject. Discussion of the question in sermons, lectures, and editorials is another measure of the debate's effectiveness. The best evidence, though difficult to gather, is found in informal conversations or opinion polls. If people begin to talk about the question, the process of forming public opinion is under way.

B. Did It Provide the Basis for Intelligent Decision?

This question applies to debates that precede action on a bill or motion. A good debate should give the voter an understanding of the issues involved and of the strongest evidence available on both sides. He may not change his opinions; the debate may simply give him better reasons for retaining his original beliefs. Since individuals vary in ability and information, judgments on the value of a given debate may also vary. Those who know little about the problem may be helped while those who have made a special study of the measure may gain little. Parliamentary procedure makes possible the termination of debate as soon as two-thirds of those present decide that further discussion would be unprofitable.

C. Did It Change the Opinions of Listeners?

A vote at the end of a debate determines group action, but does not measure the full effectiveness of the speakers in changing opinions. The side winning the majority vote may have lost ground; the losers may have stated their case so effectively that the public will eventually adopt their proposal. The extent to which opinions are changed can only be discovered by attitude tests given before and at intervals

after the debate. The results of such studies are summarized later in this chapter.

In measuring the effects of a debate on listener attitudes, the nature of the question should be considered. If fundamental beliefs are not challenged, one debate may significantly change the opinions of 20 to 30 per cent of the audience. However, if listeners are asked to change practices that have prevailed for generations, or to abandon beliefs held since childhood, a single debate, no matter how skilled the speakers or how logical the argument, may seemingly have little immediate effect.

D. Was It Valuable Training for the Debaters?

There is convincing evidence, from observers and participants, that debate is, or can be, a valuable educational method. Speaking of the disputations that were an important feature of university training in the Middle Ages, Paulson says,[1]

> ... such intellectual tournaments, in which students were taught to defend a thesis against attack, did more to enable them to grasp a subject than the mute and solitary cramming for our modern examinations could possibly do. That method brought into play all the excitement of the contest, the triumphs of success and the disgrace of defeat, in order to emphasize the value of what had been learned, together with the importance of an alert wit and the readiness to use it.

The opinion of former debaters as to the value of their forensic experience is significant. Several years ago a questionnaire was sent to 200 debaters who had been out of college at least five years. Replies were received from 105. To the question, "What is your present belief concerning the value of your intercollegiate debating experience?" only three made replies that were even mildly unfavorable. The others regarded debating as a valuable part of their education. Thirteen said they had gained more from it than from any single course. Another question asked for a listing of the most important benefits derived from debating. Fifty listed the value of speaking when something (the judge's decision or audience approval) was at stake; thirty-eight said that they gained needed self-confidence; twenty-six, that they learned how "to go to the bottom of a question"; twenty-nine, that debating showed them how to analyze a current problem; fifty-one that they learned to "think on their feet";

[1] Quoted in the article on Disputations in the *Encyclopedia Americana*.

and twenty-two thought the greatest value of debating was that it taught them to be tolerant.

In 1947, Olson asked former University of Nebraska debaters to evaluate their experience. Replies were received from 163. To the question, "Does debating help you in your present occupation?", 155 said, "Yes"; 6 said, "No"; 2 were uncertain. To the question, "Would you advise any capable person, regardless of intended occupation, to debate?" 157 said, "Yes"; 2 said "No"; 4 expressed no opinion.[2] A number of investigations show that American college debaters are markedly above the average in scholarship, have more than their share of campus honors, and attain more than their quota of places in *Who's Who in America*. In 1947, about one ninth of the members of Delta Sigma Rho, national forensic honor society, who graduated before 1928, were included in *Who's Who*. The list includes 53 college or university presidents; 25 judges, including two members of the United States Supreme Court; 61 business executives; 43 members of governmental boards or commissions; 45 congressmen, governors, or U.S. senators; 46 ministers, including five bishops; and 32 writers or publishers. Slightly more than half of these former debaters are also members of Phi Beta Kappa.

Donald S. Bridgman studied the undergraduate records of 2,108 employees of the Bell Telephone Company. He found that good scholarship and substantial campus achievement in extra-curricular activities were most significantly related to success in the company. Among different extra-curricular activities, "the order of significance seems to be: first, forensic and editorial achievement; second, managerial; third, social; fourth, athletic; fifth, musical and dramatic." *Substantial* achievement in forensics meant membership on an important debate team or winning an important oratorical contest.[3]

II. EXPERIMENTAL STUDIES

Attempts to measure the effects of debates on the opinions of listeners by more precise methods than a "yes" or "no" vote on the motion began in the early 1920's with the use of the shift-of-opinion ballot. (For a description, see the chapter on "Evaluating Discussion.") Utterback reports that such a ballot was used at the Dartmouth-Co-

[2] Donald O. Olson, "Debating at the University of Nebraska," unpublished M.A. thesis, University of Wisconsin, 1947.

[3] Donald S. Bridgman, "Success in College and Business," *Personnel Journal*, Vol. 9 (June, 1930), pp. 1-19.

lumbia debate in 1924, and that "exactly one-third of the audience recorded at least a slight shift of opinion" on whether the United States should enter the World Court.[4] A total of 758 ballots were marked before and after the 1924 Oxford-Kansas debate on the prohibition question. Changes of opinion were recorded by 185 voters, about 25 per cent of the audience.[5] Also in 1924, a constitutional amendment that would abolish parochial schools was submitted to Michigan voters. Albion College students held a public debate on the advisability of adopting this amendment. Thirty per cent of the 298 voters shifted their opinion after hearing the debate.[6]

Woodward made the most extensive study of the effects of debating on listeners' attitudes. He analyzed the shifts of opinion recorded by 3,540 voters, members of 118 audiences who listened to debates on eight different questions. Many of the listeners were adults: members of luncheon clubs, lodges, and church groups. A summary of all ballots showed:

Before the Debate		After the Debate
1,303	In favor of the motion	1,652
1,162	Undecided	345
1,075	Opposed to the motion	1,543

Of the 1,303 who originally favored the motion, 51.9 per cent reported that their opinions were strengthened; 17.5 per cent, that their opinions were weakened; 30.2 per cent, that their opinions were unchanged. Almost identical results were reported by the 1,075 audience members who opposed the motion before the debate: opinions strengthened, 52.7 per cent; opinions weakened, 17.1 per cent; opinions unchanged, 30.2 per cent. The final ballots of the 1,162 who were undecided showed that 40.9 per cent changed to the affirmative; 43.3 per cent to the negative; while 15.8 per cent remained undecided. While about 70 per cent of those with initial beliefs registered a change of opinion, it is important to note that the majority of these changes were in the direction of strengthening the original belief.[7]

[4] W. E. Utterback, *Quarterly Journal of Speech*, Vol. 10 (June, 1924), pp. 315-16.

[5] H. A. Gilkinson, *Quarterly Journal of Speech*, Vol. 11 (February, 1925), pp. 100-01.

[6] H. L. Ewbank, *Quarterly Journal of Speech*, Vol. 11 (February, 1925), pp. 101-02.

[7] Howard S. Woodward, "Measurement and Analysis of Audience Opinion," *Quarterly Journal of Speech*, Vol. 14 (February, 1928), pp. 94-111.

Lund asked whether changing the order of presentation, so the negative argument is given first, had any effect on the final opinion of the listener or reader. Arguments of the same length and persuasive quality were prepared on both sides of three questions. Three groups received the affirmative arguments first; for three similar groups the order was reversed. Lund concludes that, "The consistency with which the first discussion was most effective in determining the final position of the subject confirms the presupposition of a law of primacy in persuasion.... In a debate, other things being equal, the affirmative ... should have the advantage." He adds, however, that, in "staged debates," the order of presentation is likely to be much less influential because of the more objective attitude taken by the audience toward the issue itself. In organizing his argument, "the debater should not follow the climactic order in presenting his argument, but should weaken sympathy with his opponent promptly by attacking the strongest argument first, thus lessening the force of his adversary's case as quickly as possible."[8]

The results of an experiment conducted by Knower are of interest here. He prepared two sets of speeches for and against the prohibition amendment, which had not then been repealed. One set of speeches, for and against, stressed evidence and logical argument; the other, persuasion and emotional appeals. The speeches were about 2,500 words in length and, aside from the difference noted, similar in content and quality. One group read the logical arguments for and against prohibition; the other, the persuasive arguments. Moreover, one half of each group read first the speech defending the original opinion, then the speech attacking it; for the other half, the order was reversed. Thurstone scales were used to measure changes in attitude. Knower found that "when two arguments are presented so that the subject reads what might be roughly referred to as a debate on the subject no significant *group* changes occur." There were *individual* changes of opinion, but they tended to cancel each other. Like Woodward, he found that "more subjects change in the direction of an intensification of the attitude previously held than in the opposite direction." His final conclusion, that "primacy in the order of reading influenced the amount and possibly the direction of

[8] F. H. Lund, "The Psychology of Belief," *Journal of Abnormal and Social Psychology*, Vol. 20 (July, 1925), pp. 174-96. Also see Harvey Cromwell, "The Relative Effect on Audience Attitude of the First versus the Second Argumentative Speech of a Series," *Speech Monographs*, Vol. 17 (June, 1950), pp. 105-22.

change in attitude," tends to confirm Lund's belief in a "law of primacy."[9]

In 1942, Sponberg added further evidence that the major argument should be presented first. He prepared two twenty-minute speeches on the question: "Should a young man, subject to military service, defer marriage until the war is over?" Each speech contained three arguments which had been ranked in order of importance by twenty judges. The most important was allotted eight minutes; the second, five; and the third, three minutes. This anti-climax order was followed in presenting the speech to one audience of 92 students; the reverse order, for another audience of equal size. Standard procedures were followed in testing both retention of information and shifts of opinion. Sponberg found that the eight minute argument was best retained and "significantly more effective" in changing opinions when presented first and that the "anti-climax order effected significantly greater retention of the entire speech."[10]

Millson studied the effectiveness of different styles of debating in changing opinions. He trained two debate teams, approximately equal in ability and speaking skill. The affirmative team varied its method of debating, using three different "modes": the conversational, the exhibitory, and the academic. The *conversational mode* he defined as the usual blend of argument and persuasion, delivered in the tone of direct, interested conversation. The *exhibitory mode* made greater use of appeals to the basic emotions and of rhetorical devices to secure vividness. The delivery inclined to the "oratorical." The *academic mode* relied on evidence and argument; the delivery was more uniform than in the conversational mode, and quite different in manner from the exhibitory. The negative team used the conversational mode in the twenty-three debates before non-academic audiences. The Woodward shift-of-opinion ballot was used. The exhibitory mode was most successful in securing favorable changes of opinion and in holding affirmative opinions existing before the debate. The conversational mode ranked second; the academic, third.[11]

---

[9] F. H. Knower, "A Study of the Effect of Printed Argument on Changes in Attitude," *Journal of Abnormal and Social Psychology*, Vol. 30 (January-March, 1936), pp. 522-32.

[10] Harold Sponberg, "The Relative Effectiveness of Climax and Anti-Climax Order in an Argumentative Speech," *Speech Monographs*, Vol. 13 (1946), pp. 35-44.

[11] William A. D. Millson, "Measuring Audience Reactions," *Quarterly Journal of Speech*, Vol. 18 (November, 1932), pp. 621-37.

Capel measured the attitudes of 213 debaters from thirty-two Wisconsin high schools on federal aid to education before and after the season's debates on this issue. Forty per cent had changed their attitudes significantly. Those at first mildly in favor of the position they supported in debate tended to believe more strongly in that side of the question. Those who were rather extreme in their views, tended to be less sure after the debates. The twenty-three students who debated both sides of the question, tended to shift towards a neutral position. Capel also tested the information and attitudes of 730 students in nine high schools, before and after hearing a debate. Forty per cent recorded significant changes of attitude. Contrary to the findings of previous experiments, these changes tended towards "lessening the strength of the initial attitude." He found no significant relationship between the amount of information and attitude changes resulting from listening to the debates. The attitude changes were in different directions and tended to counteract each other as far as simple "yes" and "no" votes on the question were concerned. Capel remarks that debate would not be a good method for the propagandist.[12]

Howell studied the effects of a season's high school debating on the student's ability to evaluate arguments, detect errors in reasoning, and draw valid conclusions from evidence. The scores of 218 members of debate squads in twenty-five Wisconsin high schools on the Watson-Glaser tests of critical thinking ability, were compared with scores made by a like number of non-debaters, matched as to scholarship, sex, and year in school. Both debaters and non-debaters showed gains on the post-tests. The debaters had higher scores to start with and slightly outgained the members of the control group. For some schools, the debaters' gains were significantly higher. The better debaters, as judged by the coaches, ranked higher in critical thinking ability. The boys consistently scored higher than the girls on these tests. Both had good grades: 50 per cent were reported as "A" students; 35 per cent had a "B" average.[13]

Brembeck, using the same battery of tests, measured the effect of a college course in argumentation on critical thinking ability. The scores made by 202 argumentation students in eleven colleges and

[12] Robert B. Capel, "The Effects of High-School Debating on the Attitudes of Debaters and Listeners," unpublished Ph. D. thesis, University of Wisconsin, 1939.
[13] William S. Howell, "The Effects of High School Debating on Critical Thinking Ability," *Speech Monographs*, Vol. 10 (1943), pp. 96-102.

universities were compared with those made by control groups in each institution. The argumentation students significantly outgained the control groups. In ten of the eleven schools, the students in argumentation classes had higher scores at the beginning of the semester. The 45 students with high school or college debating experience made significantly higher initial scores than other members of argumentation classes. The 100 men in the argumentation courses started off with higher scores than the 102 women, and made slightly larger gains.[14]

These experimental studies justify the following tentative conclusions:

1. Debaters may significantly change the opinions of from 20 to 40 per cent of the listeners. These opinion changes depend on such factors as the skill of the speakers and the intensity of the original beliefs.

2. Listening to a debate seems more likely to strengthen existing beliefs than to weaken them. In Capel's study, however, the reverse was true.

3. In a close debate on a well-balanced issue, individual shifts of opinion might tend to cancel each other. Thus there might be a number of individual attitude changes without reversing the majority vote of the audience.

4. In a good many cases, however, the shift of opinion is largely in one direction and changes the majority vote of the listeners.

5. The studies of Lund, Knower, and Sponberg suggest that the side of an argument presented first has an advantage. This does not always give the advantage to the affirmative; the audience may have already accepted the negative argument.

6. Millson's study suggests that student debating is sometimes too "academic" for public audiences.

7. Howell and Brembeck show that high school debating and college courses in argumentation improve critical thinking ability.

III. METHODS OF JUDGING

Judicial, legislative, and school debates are properly judged on different bases. Jury members supposedly have no specific information and no fixed opinion about the case. During the trial they listen to the evidence presented by both sides and to the arguments of opposing counsel. They render decisions on the facts of the case; the judge decides matters of law and the leniency or severity of punishment.

[14] Winston L. Brembeck, "The Effects of a Course in Argumentation on Critical Thinking Ability," *Speech Monographs*, Vol. 16 (No. 2, 1949), pp. 177-89.

The legislator, on the other hand, often enters the debate with information about the bill and opinions as to its value. He is free to get further information from any available source and to consult the wishes of his constituents. His vote is based on his answers to two sometimes conflicting questions: (1) Would the passage of this measure serve the public interest? (2) What do the folks back home think of it?

We are here mainly concerned with the judging of interschool debates. On this subject there has been much confused thinking, due largely to a failure to distinguish between these debates and those held in the actual settlement of some controversy. Conclusions concerning the judging of contest debates should be based on answers to three questions: (1) Why should there be any decision in interschool debates? (2) Who should give such decisions as are desired? (3) On what bases should school debates be judged?

A. Why Judge Debates?

Some understanding of the development of contest debating in the United States is necessary in answering this question. Debating societies occupied a preëminent place in almost every college, and in many other communities, until about 1880. Members took their turns at debating and their efforts were judged by the audience who voted, sometimes on what they thought about the question and sometimes on the merits of the debating. A senior or faculty member often served as critic, commenting on the work of each speaker. When, for various reasons, literary and debating societies began to decline in importance, intersociety and intercollegiate contests were arranged to stimulate lagging interest.

The early intercollegiate debates were judged by a board of three distinguished men who voted on the merits of the debating. Judges were chosen with the care that would be employed in selecting a jury for an important trial. In 1893, for example, the Wisconsin intersociety debate was postponed because the two teams could not agree on judges. The *Daily Cardinal* said, "Each side felt that the other was interested only in getting judges who were prejudiced on the question. . . . Finally it was agreed to leave the choice of the third judge to a faculty committee of three." After the Presidents of Northwestern University and the University of Chicago sent regrets, President Adams of Wisconsin was chosen. Judges for intercollegiate debates were selected after elaborate negotiations. The Wisconsin *Daily*

Cardinal for January 29, 1893, comments on the process of choosing judges for the Wisconsin-Illinois debate: "Choosing judges has always been a source of contention between intercollegiate debate teams, but the method proposed is expected to overcome these difficulties. Wisconsin submits three sets of names: six from Wisconsin, six from Illinois, and six from other states—and Illinois chooses one from each list."

This process was time-consuming and, in the opinion of many, placed too much emphasis on winning. To emphasize other values, some debates were held without judges. However, the Western Conference Debating League decided after a one-year trial of judgeless debates, in 1920-21, that much of the incentive for thorough preparation was lacking and began to use critic judges who, in addition to awarding a decision, analyzed the debate for the benefit of debaters and audience.

The use of a single critic judge was designed both to secure competent judges and to provide instruction in debating for speakers and listeners alike. It is widely used whenever decisions on the merits of the debating are desired. Early in the 1920's some schools had audience decisions, based on the shift-of-opinion ballot. Others asked audience members to vote on the merits of the debating. A more recent development is the legislative session in which the student legislators vote on the passage of the proposed legislation. The current practice is to have various types of decisions, as well as some non-decision debates, in the year's forensic program.

The reasons for decisions in school debates are summarized in these statements:

1. The only reason for debates in real life situations is the necessity for reaching a decision on a problem. School exercises should resemble life situations as nearly as possible. Moreover, training in winning and losing gracefully is a valuable educational discipline.

2. The decision usually stimulates the debaters to greater efforts, both in preparation and performance, than they would otherwise make. The desire to excel is a powerful motivating force that should not be discarded because it is sometimes unwisely used.

3. The decision is valuable because it gives the debater an evaluation of his efforts. If he loses, he should analyze his weaknesses and attempt to remedy them; if he wins, he should find out the reasons for his success so he can continue to use the same methods.

4. The decision is valuable if it gives members of the audience training in evaluating arguments. Every citizen, though he may never appear in a public debate, should be an intelligent listener. Listeners who

compare their own decisions with that of the official judge are taking part in a profitable educational enterprise.

B. Who Should Judge Debates?

We have seen that debates held in literary societies were often judged by members of the audience. Since they were interested in methods of debating, at least as much as in the topic, their judgment differed from that of the popular audience. When intersociety debates were held, it became necessary to devise a different method of judging. The answer was a board, usually consisting of three eminent citizens. This board had a twofold purpose: to give a verdict and to add dignity and importance to the occasion. Lawyers, statesmen, and ministers were chosen because of their experience in public speaking; court judges, because of their experience in evaluating evidence and argument. This practice was followed in early intercollegiate debates. For example, the Northwestern-Wisconsin debate of 1897 was judged by Governor Pingree of Michigan, Judge Brill of Minnesota, and Senator Beveridge of Indiana.

When the number of intercollegiate debates increased, it was naturally difficult to secure three distinguished judges for every event. At about the same time, faculty members began to take a more active part in training the debaters. They insisted that judges should know the objectives of intercollegiate debating and have experience in teaching argumentation. For a number of years, debates at most institutions were judged by three former debaters or debate coaches. This change to professional judges was deplored by William H. Davis who argued that "the one feature of debating which is indispensable to its success as a device for securing training in public speaking is the retention of able non-debaters as judges. Judged by them, debating will remain where it belongs—very close to actual life."[15]

The answer to the question, "Who should judge debates?" depends on the purpose of the event. If the objective is to train the participants in the methods of effective oral argument, the judging should be done by a critic, or teacher, qualified to give instruction in those matters. If the aim is to duplicate as nearly as possible the life situation where the speaker addresses his argument to a court or commission, the decision should be made by representatives of this group.

[15] William H. Davis, "Debating as Related to Non-Academic Life," *Quarterly Journal of Speech*, Vol. 1 (July, 1915), pp. 105-13.

If the purpose is to approximate the situation where the decision is made by the voting public, rather than by trained judges, the verdict should be given by members of the audience. Since one purpose of debating is to train participants to meet different situations, all three types of judging might well be used in a debate season.

C. On What Basis Should Decisions Be Given?

Judges in the first intercollegiate debates were instructed to "decide upon the merits of the debate, without regard to the merits of the question."[16] With the exception of occasions where such devices as the shift-of-opinion ballot are used, the same instructions are given today.

It has always been understood that these instructions represent the ideal rather than the attainable. No judge, whether he is listening to an intercollegiate debate or to an argument before the Supreme Court, can erase from his mind all that he knows and believes about the subject. The lawyer who represents a large corporation is careful to inquire whether prospective jurors are prejudiced against big business. The legislator hopes that his bill will be referred to a friendly committee. Moreover, there is a tendency to overrate the speaking ability of those with whom we agree, and to be severe in our criticisms of opposing speakers. Opposition papers reported that Lincoln's address at Gettysburg was even weaker than they had expected; only his loyal supporters praised it.

A primary qualification of the debate judge, however, is that he be relatively free from prejudice on the question and have some skill in distinguishing between the strength of an argument and the manner of its presentation. It is equally important that he be competent to instruct the speakers in effective debating and the audience in the art of intelligent listening.

When a simple ballot calling for an affirmative or negative vote is used, each judge makes his own definition of effective debating. While judges differ in the relative importance they assign to subject matter and delivery, and in their preference for different types of evidence and methods of analysis, they generally agree that decisions should be based on answers to these five questions:

1. Which team excelled in effective public speaking?
2. Which team made the better analysis of the question?

[16] R. C. Ringwalt, "Intercollegiate Debating," *Forum*, Vol. 22 (January, 1897), p. 635.

3. Which team was superior in supporting its case with good evidence and sound reasoning?
4. Which team was better at adapting its case to that of the opposition?
5. Which team made the better rebuttal speeches?

Before the debate begins, the judge should make sure that he understands the purpose of the contest. He should know whether the speakers are supposedly addressing a popular audience or a judge trained in listening and in following complicated lines of reasoning. He is usually expected to state the reasons for his decision; sometimes his statement to the audience is followed by a conference with the coaches and debaters.

CRITIC JUDGE'S BALLOT

Give each speaker a grade, from 1 (Poor) to 5 (Excellent), on each of the five elements of effective debating. Thus, the highest possible individual score would be 25; the lowest, 5.

	Affirmative		*Negative*	
	1st	2nd	1st	2nd
1. Analysis of question	( )	( )	( )	( )
2. Evidence and reasoning	( )	( )	( )	( )
3. Adapting to opposition	( )	( )	( )	( )
4. Rebuttal speeches	( )	( )	( )	( )
5. Effective speaking	( )	( )	( )	( )
Totals				

Affirmative score _____
Negative score _____

AUDIENCE BALLOT

Rank the speakers in the order of their excellence.

First: _____
Second: _____
Third: _____
Fourth: _____

I believe the _____ team, representing _____ college, did the better debating.

Unfortunately, the schedules at some debate tournaments do not allow time for a careful analysis of each debate. In such instances, the judge may be asked to use some adaptation of the critic judge's ballot, illustrated on the preceding page.

Decisions in school debates are valuable when they stimulate the speakers to make thorough preparation, provide training in winning and losing gracefully, and give suggestions for doing better next time. The audience decision, whether on the merits of the question or of the debating, records the effect of the speaking but not how, or why, the effect was produced. The critic judge provides such an analysis, but he does not always represent the judgment of the audience. Properly used, each method, and various combinations of methods, can contribute to the education of debaters and listeners.

READINGS

BRIGANCE, W. N., "The Debate as Training for Citizenship," *Educational Review*, Vol. 72 (November, 1926), pp. 222-5.

CROCKER, Lionel, *Argumentation and Debate* (New York, American Book Co., 1944), Chap. 12.

CROMWELL, Harvey, "The Relative Effect on Audience Attitude of the First versus the Second Argumentative Speech of a Series," *Speech Monographs*, Vol. 17 (June, 1950), pp. 105-22.

HARGIS, D. E., "A Note on Championship Debaters," *Quarterly Journal of Speech*, Vol. 34 (February, 1948), pp. 57-9.

HOLCOMB, Martin, "The Critic Judge System," *Quarterly Journal of Speech*, Vol. 19 (February, 1933), pp. 28-38.

JOHNSON, T. E., "How Should Debates Be Judged?" *Quarterly Journal of Speech*, Vol. 21 (June, 1935), pp. 396-9.

LAHMAN, C. P., *Debate Coaching* (New York, H. W. Wilson Co., 1936), Chap. 7.

LAASE, L. T., "An Evaluation of the Quality Rating System in Measuring Debate Achievement," *Quarterly Journal of Speech*, Vol. 28 (December, 1942), pp. 422-30.

NICHOLS, E. R., and BACCUS, J. H., *Modern Debating* (New York, W. W. Norton and Co., 1936), Chaps. 19-21.

PAGET, E. H., "The Audience Vote," *English Journal*, coll. edition, Vol. 17 (April, 1928), pp. 320-5.

PITT, C. A., "Debating Improves Social Adjustment," *Debater's Magazine*, Vol. 3 (Autumn, 1947), pp. 143-6.

WOODWARD, H. S., "Measurement and Analysis of Audience Opinion," *Quarterly Journal of Speech*, Vol. 14 (February, 1928), pp. 94-111.

EXERCISES

1. Make a four-minute speech based on one of the suggested readings. Give information not contained in this chapter and comment on differences of opinion.

2. Judge an intercollegiate debate according to the criteria given in this chapter and compare your decision with that of the official judge.

3. If you cannot attend an intercollegiate debate, use the transcript of a debate published in the *University Debater's Annual*, or similar publication.

4. Arrange to have the audience at an intercollegiate debate use different methods of judging and compare the results. For example, one third might vote on the merits of the question; one third on the merits of the debating; and one third might rank the speakers.

5. List the occasions where some form of debate is used in your community. What types of decision are given?

6. What criteria might be used in evaluating the Lincoln-Douglas and Webster-Hayne debates?

7. Analyze and comment on the reasoning involved in the following statements:

   a. Debates should be discontinued because they make the listeners less sure of their views on the question.

   b. Since judges often disagree, decisions do not mean anything and should be discontinued.

   c. Obviously, there is only one right side to a question. Therefore it should be the task of the leader to find the right side and present it to his group.

   d. Debating in political campaigns is bound to be ineffective, since only a few can understand the complicated economic and political issues. The only thing we can do is to let our leaders decide these questions for us.

   e. Since debates encourage sophistry, they should be replaced by discussions which encourage a search for truth.

8. Make a short speech on one of the following topics:

   a. Debate as a propaganda device

   b. The argument for nondecision debate

   c. "The judge was obviously prejudiced..."

   d. The first intercollegiate debates at our school

9. Study the records of former intercollegiate debaters at your school. Does the evidence indicate either that debate offers training for leadership or that potential leaders become debaters?

Selected Bibliographies

These bibliographies are by no means complete. We have included only materials that were available, and organizations that were active, when this book was written.

1. Transcripts of Discussions

American Forum of the Air (Ransdell, Inc., Washington 18, D.C.). Stenographic reports of the weekly series of discussions and dialogue-debates, heard over MBS. Single copies, 10 cents.

CBS Talks (Columbia Broadcasting System, Inc., 485 Madison Ave., New York 22, N. Y.). "A quarterly digest of addresses presented in the public interest." Sent on request.

Congressional Hearings (Superintendent of Documents, Government Printing Office, Washington 25, D. C.). Reports of testimony given in public hearings on pending legislation before Senate and House committees.

Discussion in Human Affairs, James H. McBurney and Kenneth G. Hance (New York, Harper & Bros., 1950). The appendix contains transcripts of two panels and a symposium, also the rules for the Delta Sigma Rho National Student Congress.

Discussion Methods, 2nd rev. ed., J. V., Garland and Charles F. Phillips, eds. (New York, H. W. Wilson Co., 1940). Brief descriptions and complete transcripts of informal group discussion, committee discussion, hearings, panel, symposium, etc.

Discussion Methods for Adult Groups, Thomas Fansler, ed. (American Association for Adult Education, 60 E. 42nd St., New York, N. Y., 1934). Case studies of the forum, the discussion group, and the panel. [Also see Fansler's *Teaching Adults by Discussion* (New York University, Service Bureau of Adult Education, 1938).]

Education on the Air, O. Joe Olson, ed. (Columbus, Ohio State University Press). Yearbook of the Institute for Education by Radio. Most issues contain transcripts of discussions in current radio series.

Journal of Social Issues, The Society for the Psychological Study of Social Issues (Association Press, 291 Broadway, New York 7, N. Y.).

Vol. 4 (Winter, 1948), contains stenographic reports of two informal group discussions. Single copies, $1.00.

Northwestern Reviewing Stand (Director of Radio, Northwestern University, Evanston, Ill.). Weekly stenographic reports of the series of discussions and debates, heard over MBS. Single copies, 10 cents.

Representative American Speeches, A. Craig Baird, ed. (New York, H. W. Wilson Co.). Annual publication containing stenographic transcripts of outstanding speeches and discussions of current public issues.

Town Meeting, Bulletin of America's Town Meeting of the Air (New York, Columbia University Press). Stenographic reports of the weekly series of symposiums and debates, heard over NBC. Single copies, 10 cents.

University of Chicago Round Table (Chicago, University of Chicago Press). Weekly stenographic reports of the series of panel discussions, heard over NBC. Single copies, 10 cents.

Vital Speeches of the Day (City News Publishing Co., 33 W. 42nd St., New York 18, N. Y.). Published semimonthly, each issue contains approximately ten full transcripts of current speeches or debates on public questions. Single copies, 25 cents.

2. Transcripts of Debates

Congressional Record (Superintendent of Documents, Government Printing Office, Washington 25, D. C.). Daily journal of legislative discussion and parliamentary debate in the Senate and the House.

Foundations of Democracy, Robert A. Taft and T. V. Smith (Chicago, University of Chicago Press, 1939). Transcripts of thirteen broadcast debates on political topics.

Intercollegiate Debates, Egbert Ray Nichols, ed. (formerly published annually by Noble and Noble Co., New York; now Redlands, Calif., Nichols Publishing House). Transcripts of various forms of intercollegiate debates, with occasional examples of college discussions, published annually.

University Debater's Annual, Ruth Ulman, ed. (New York, H. W. Wilson Co.). Annual collection of stenographic reports of various forms of intercollegiate debates, together with occasional examples of college discussions.

3. Serial Publications on Current Issues

American Education Press (400 South Front St., Columbus 15, Ohio). Publishes "Our Times," weekly survey of current affairs containing a guide for a Junior Town Meeting League discussion topic. Sent on request.

Armed Forces Talk, Office of the Secretary of Defense (Superintendent of Documents, Government Printing Office, Washington 25, D. C.). Weekly discussion guide on current national and international problems. Single copies, 5 cents.

Congressional Digest (1631 K St., N.W., Washington 6, D. C.). Published monthly, each issue giving pro-and-con treatment of a current public question, including the annual high school and college debate topics. Single copies, 75 cents.

Discussion guides: *American Mercury, Newsweek, Reader's Digest,* and *Time* are among the popular magazines which publish discussion guides on current topics. Service charges sent on request.

Foreign Policy Reports and *Headline Books* (Foreign Policy Association, 22 East 38th St., New York 18, N. Y.). Regular publications dealing with international affairs and American foreign relations. Single copies, 25 cents.

GI Roundtable (Superintendent of Documents, Government Printing Office, Washington 25, D. C.). Collection of pamphlets dealing with personal, national, and international problems, and including suggestions for use in various types of discussions. Single copies, 15 cents.

Let's Discuss It, Ohio State University Discussion Service (Ohio State University, Columbus 10, Ohio). Discussion guide and bibliographies on current public questions; published monthly, September through June. Sent on request.

NUEA Debate Handbook, Bower Aly, ed. (The Committee on Debate Materials and Interstate Coöperation of the National University Extension Association; distributed through University of Wisconsin Extension Division, Madison 5, Wis.). An annual analysis of the national high school debate topic, together with selected source materials.

Public Affairs Pamphlets (Public Affairs Committee, 50 Rockefeller Plaza, New York 20, N. Y.). Regular series of pamphlets on national and world affairs. Single copies, 15 cents.

Reference Shelf (New York, H. W. Wilson Co.). An annual series of handbooks, each dealing with a special problem in public affairs, and presenting pertinent materials on all points of view.

4. Sources of Audio-Visual Aids Materials

Catalogue of Selected 16 mm. Educational Motion Pictures (New York University Film Library, 71 Washington Square, New York 12, N. Y.). Lists films and recordings on current social and economic problems, available for rental. Sent on request.

Directory of U.S. Government Films (U.S. Film Service, Federal Security Agency, Washington 25, D. C.). Lists all available government films and filmstrips. Sent on request.

Educational Film Guide (New York, H. W. Wilson Co.). Monthly, except July and August, guide to current documentary and educational films; annual fall issue lists over 7,000 films.

FREC Radio Script and Transcription Exchange Catalogue (Federal Radio Education Committee, Office of Education, Federal Security Agency, Washington 25, D. C.). Lists available transcriptions and scripts, many available on loan without charge. Sent on request.

Filmstrip Guide (New York, H. W. Wilson Co.). Monthly, except July and August, guide to current filmstrips, slide films, etc. Also an annual cumulative edition.

Motion pictures, filmstrips, recordings, etc., available on rental: most state university extension divisions have a nominal rental service and publish free catalogues of available material, sent on request.

News Letter (Bureau of Educational Research, Ohio State University, Columbus 10, Ohio). Monthly annotated listing of current educational and documentary films, and other audio-visual aids, and recent publications in this field. Small service charge.

5. Current Materials on Discussion and Debate Methods

Adult Education Bulletin (Dept. of Adult Education, National Education Association, 1201 Sixteenth St., N.W., Washington 6, D. C.). Bimonthly publication containing frequent articles dealing with discussion techniques and activities. Single copies, 75 cents.

Classified Bibliography of Group Discussion, W. L. Brembeck and T. J. McLaughlin, eds. (Madison, Wis., privately published, 1948. Address Professor W. L. Brembeck, Dept. of Speech, University of Wisconsin). Books and journal articles on all phases of discussion.

Communication Workers of America (917 G. Place, N.W., Washington 1, D. C.). Occasional publications such as *Pointers on Discussion Leadership*. Prices on request.

Community Relations Service (386 Fourth Ave., New York 16, N. Y.). Distributes *It Pays to Talk It Over* handbook and discussion guides on current topics. Prices on request.

Coöperative League of America (343 South Dearborn St., Chicago 4, Ill.). Occasional publications such as *A Guide to Group Discussion*. Prices on request.

Freedom Pamphlets (Anti-Defamation League of B'nai B'rith, 212 Fifth Ave., New York 10, N. Y.) Series of publications treating current problems in human relations, such as *Group Dynamics and Social Action*, and *How Do You Talk About People?* Single copies, 25 cents.

Great Books Foundation (58 East South Water St., Chicago 1, Ill.). Publishes such pamphlets as *An Invitation to Thinking, Reading and*

Thinking, and *What it Takes to be a Great Books Leader.* Prices on request.

Group Discussion and Its Techniques (Superintendent of Documents, Government Printing Office, Washington 25, D. C.). Bibliographical review of current and standard materials for discussion leaders.

Human Relations (Tavistock Institute of Human Relations, London, and Research Center for Group Dynamics, University of Michigan, Ann Arbor, Mich.). Quarterly journal with frequent articles on discussion techniques and research. Single copies, $1.75.

Junior Town Meeting League (400 South Front St., Columbus 15, Ohio). "An international organization to foster discussion of current affairs by youth." Publishes such pamphlets as *Teaching Controversial Issues, Learning Through Group Discussion, Let's Have a Discussion, Make Youth Discussion Conscious, Discussion and Current Affairs.* Prices on request.

Journal of Social Issues, Society for the Psychological Study of Social Issues (Association Press, 291 Broadway, New York 7, N. Y.). Quarterly publication containing occasional articles on discussion methods and research. Single copies, $1.00.

League of Women Voters (726 Jackson Place, Washington 6, D. C.). Publishes frequent discussion outlines and pamphlets on conducting discussion. Prices on request.

Research Center for Group Dynamics (University of Michigan, Ann Arbor, Mich.). Occasional publications dealing with research in the group dynamics of discussion.

Speech Activities (Nichols Publishing House, Redlands, Calif.). Quarterly publication devoted to intercollegiate and high school forensics: articles on method, news of current activities, occasional transcripts of speeches, discussion and debates. Single copies, $1.00.

Speech association publications: *Quarterly Journal of Speech, Speech Monographs, Central States Speech Journal, Southern Speech Journal, Western Speech* (Address Executive Secretary, Speech Association of America, State University of Iowa, Iowa City, Iowa, for information). Quarterly or semi-annual professional journals containing articles on methods and research in various phases of speech, including discussion and debate.

Index

(1)